Joan Hoff Wilson

American Business
& Foreign Policy

1920-1933

Beacon Press Boston

to Dave,

for his loving patience

Copyright © 1971 by The University Press of Kentucky

First published as a Beacon Paperback in 1973
by arrangement with The University Press of Kentucky

Beacon Press books are published under the auspices
of the Unitarian Universalist Association

Published simultaneously in Canada by Saunders of Toronto, Ltd.

Printed in the United States of America

9   8   7   6   5   4   3   2   1

Library of Congress Cataloging in Publication Data

Wilson, Joan Hoff, 1937–
    American business & foreign policy, 1920–1933.
    Reprint of the ed. published by University Press of Kentucky,
Lexington.
    Bibliography: pp. 313–329.
    1. United States—Commercial policy.   2. United States—
Foreign relations—1923–1929.   3. United States—Foreign
relations—1929–1933.   I. Title.
HF1455.W49   1973   327.73   73–6628
ISBN 0–8070–5425–9

Contents

Acknowledgments

The research for this book was made possible through grants from the University of California at Berkeley, Sacramento State College, and the American Philosophical Society. The latter was of particular importance because it enabled me to duplicate a number of research notes lost in the fall of 1967.

In the early stages of my work on business and foreign policy I was aided by critical advice from Armin Rappaport, Lawrence W. Levine, and Thomas C. Blaisdell, Jr. I am especially indebted, however, to a longtime friend and teacher at the University of Montana, Jules Karlin, whose extensive comments about the style and content of the original manuscript went far beyond the boundaries of friendship and scholarship.

I would also like to extend my appreciation to the staff members at the American Jewish Archives in Cincinnati, the Roosevelt Library in Hyde Park, the Library of Congress, and the National Archives, and to those in the manuscript divisions at Stanford, Columbia, Princeton, and Yale universities. At the Herbert Hoover Presidential Library in West Branch, Iowa, I was professionally and personally assisted by Archivist Mrs. Fay Kelly (Martha) Smith in too many ways to enumerate or adequately thank, and I am deeply grateful to Senior Archivist Dwight M. Miller and to all of the library personnel at West Branch for facilitating my trips there.

Without the help of my husband Dave and two friends—Dee Scriven and Barbara Rosenthal—I probably would not have survived the last technical and tedious stages of the printing process. At least that time would have been spent much less humorously than it was had they not come to my rescue.

Introduction

The foundations of modern American diplomacy were laid during and immediately following World War I. They were based on
a combination of ideological considerations precipitated by the
actions of Imperialist Germany and by the Russian Revolution,
and the realization of unprecedented worldwide economic expansion by the United States. A number of the economic and
political foreign policies established or reinforced in this period
continued to influence the foreign affairs of the country beyond
World War I. There has been a tendency either to exaggerate or
to underestimate the role played by the business community in
the formulation of foreign policy between 1920 and 1933. This
study, therefore, examines the attitudes and actions of individual
businessmen, industries, and business or trade organizations to
determine the extent to which government officials were subjected
to pressure from various segments of the business community,
and the degree to which they responded.

I have used the term business community to refer only to entre-
preneurs who were involved in standard business or financial
enterprises, as opposed to farmers or professional people. The
term does not, however, describe a monolithic segment of the
population. On any given foreign policy issue the ideas and economic self-interest of business groups, and their influence on foreign policy, varied. For one thing, significant *occupational* differences created competition and misunderstanding between bankers,
export-import interests, manufacturers, and retailers. In addition,

sectional differences sometimes existed between businessmen due to geographical location, as well as between rural and urban enterprises in the same area of the country. There were also *political* differences between Republican and Democratic businessmen which, in foreign policy disputes, often revolved around partisan commitment to the concepts of nationalism or internationalism.

Finally, *organizational* and *dimensional* differences between large and medium-to-small firms affected not only their ideas about foreign policy but their effective means for influencing governmental decisions. For example, the structural organization of a company differs according to the size of the individual operation, and a noticeable managerial change occurs after more than 400 men are employed. Heads of firms with fewer employees, and especially one-man businesses, become bogged down in day-to-day management problems because of limited staffs. Such businessmen usually do not have the time to become informed or actively interested in foreign policy issues, not even those related to economic matters. Consequently, their impact on the formulation of foreign policy is only indirectly exercised through the public positions and lobbying activities of chambers of commerce or other local business or trade organizations with national affiliations to which these businessmen belong and passively consign the power to determine attitudes on foreign policy. Executives in companies with over 400 employees are in a better position, because of a greater division of labor, to keep abreast of, and to influence, foreign affairs. And, more often than small businessmen, they can anticipate how diplomatic actions will affect their economic interests.

With particular reference to the 1920–1933 period, it should be noted that two major organizational innovations took place in some of the biggest companies, such as General Motors, Sears Roebuck, Standard Oil of New Jersey, and Du Pont. First, a new wave of merger activity produced, in addition to horizontal and vertical structures, a few diversified firms, prototypes of today's conglomerates. Second, within the larger, vertically integrated corporations a more efficient, decentralized structure was introduced. These two trends were temporarily interrupted by the

Great Depression, only to be greatly accelerated by World War II. Such decentralized, multimarket corporations, with their numerous divisions and subsidiaries, created many more points of contact with the government than had previously existed. This does not mean that within such a modern firm there is perfect coordination of all its many levels in order to influence government officials in one direction alone. More often than not the opposite is true, that is, independent departmental actions contradict and neutralize one another on a given foreign policy issue, particularly an economic one such as the tariff. Nonetheless, one cannot deny the impact on American foreign policy of the diversity of business opinion and manifold influence resulting from structural decentralization and conglomerate mergers. Since World War I it has become exceedingly difficult to measure accurately the impact of their ubiquitous presence in the policy-making process.

The opinions of individual businessmen presented here, representing both large and small firms, have been derived from their public and private statements, including testimony before congressional committees, articles in business, financial, and industrial publications, the records of the Departments of State and Commerce, and manuscript collections. The positions of the specialized occupational segments of the business community can be found in many of these same sources as well as in the policy statements issued by national and sectional business or trade organizations and their journals. In the 1920s the exact opinions of the small and medium firms were more difficult to determine than those of larger ones because their owners were often less articulate and there were no public opinion polls or governmental bureaus purporting to represent the small businessman, as there are today. Yet before 1940 less than 1 percent of the nation's businesses consisted of more than 100 employees and the one-man operation was by far the most common economic unit. These small firms dominated the leadership and made up the rank and file of both the National Association of Manufacturers and the Chamber of Commerce of the United States before and after World War I. Similarly, the American Bankers Association tended to reflect the views of the average banker. While big business and financial interests began to challenge this traditional leadership during the war, not until the early 1930s did they consistently begin to replace it in these organizations. So for most of the period under discussion, the NAM, the national Chamber of Commerce, and to a lesser degree the ABA, have been used as sources for the opinions of the vast majority of ordinary businessmen and bankers.

Any study of business opinion requires that some attempt be made to show the relationship between public and private statements. Although it was not always possible to find private as well as public expressions for all the political or economic foreign policy issues considered, enough correlation was found to conclude that business leaders in the 1920s did not generally conceal their true convictions about foreign affairs, with the notable exception of the Allied debt issue. One of the major reasons why businessmen so often expressed themselves forthrightly in public was that they enjoyed a virtual monopoly on the imagination and rhetoric of the American people during the decade following World War I. Aside from some ideas emanating from literary circles or the ranks of organized crime, business philosophy and opinions went essentially unchallenged in the mass media before the Great Depression. Consequently, business leaders felt little necessity, at least until 1929, to temper their public statements on foreign policy to any significant degree.

This is not to say, however, that their political and economic actions were always consistent with their professed opinions. The public views of businessmen did not automatically result in immediate action; they were often simply very general reflections about life and world affairs. Many business ideas represented an almost instinctive commitment to an earlier era. They epitomized comfort and security in a rapidly changing postwar world. It was a world businessmen were helping to create, but one in which they were not yet completely comfortable or secure. Thus the discrepancies that did exist between business thought and action in foreign policy between 1920 and 1933 revealed the confused and often inadequate attempts on the part of businessmen to cope with altered postwar conditions that they did not fully understand, without entirely abnegating their traditional prewar values.

This book, in addition to describing the disagreements within the business community over foreign policy and the internal inconsistencies between business attitudes and activities, analyzes the ways in which business pressure was brought to bear on the government and the resulting impact on the formulation of policy. Delving into the labyrinth created by the interaction of government and business in American diplomacy proved extremely valuable for testing many of the standard assumptions about the role of the business community in foreign relations following World War I. Thus, the presumed desire of businessmen for a return to "normalcy" emerged in a new perspective, and it became clear that dissension prevailed within the business community over most foreign policy issues before 1929, with the exception of strong business opposition to recognition of the Soviet Union. This approach also reconfirmed the importance of Herbert Hoover, the "super businessman" of the period, not only in shaping American foreign policy, but in attempting to unite the business community behind his leadership. Finally, two generalizations about the 1920s and early 1930s—that the economic power of the business community was automatically translated into diplomatic power, and that economic and political foreign policies were coordinated with conspiratorial efficiency by government and business leaders— were both found wanting.

In 1929 Benjamin H. Williams described the potential power of the business community in relation to the ideal position it should assume in the formulation of foreign policy, by saying:

> The business groups are the most intelligently class conscious elements in American Society. From Boston to Los Angeles and from Seattle to Miami, chambers of commerce, luncheon clubs, boards of directors in their various meetings assembled, and trade journals give thought to the service which government can render in the promotion of industry, commerce and finance. Wealth and talent are at their command. They are inspired by an irrepressible enthusiasm and a dogmatic self-righteousness. Can anyone doubt but that as the decades of the twentieth century pass by, their influence in the molding of policies will continue to be powerfully exerted? It is right that in a system of representative government their voice should be heard. But such influences should be given weight only in so far as they are in line with the dictates of wise statesmanship,

taking into consideration the interests of the whole nation, today and tomorrow.

Unfortunately, no institutional means for tempering future business influence over American diplomacy, or for coordinating economic and political foreign policy to achieve the country's proclaimed humanitarian goals, had been developed on the eve of the Great Depression when this statement was written. Nor have they been since that time.

Three years after Williams wrote his book on economic foreign policy, a presidential commission reported to Hoover that the postwar diplomacy of the United States had alternated "between isolation and independence, between sharply marked economic nationalism and notable international initiative in cooperation, moving in a highly unstable and zigzag course." As far as it goes this is a fairly accurate contemporary description of American foreign policy between 1920 and 1933 with the key antithesis being independent activity versus international activity. Therefore I have chosen to refer to this "unstable" assortment of unilateral and collective diplomatic actions as *independent internationalism*. The term refers not to a foreign policy philosophy but to a pragmatic method for conducting foreign affairs, still followed today. Its implicit assumption is that the United States should cooperate on an international scale when it cannot, or does not want to, solve a particular diplomatic problem through unilateral action. Independent internationlism was not the term used by Republicans in the postwar years to describe their foreign policy, but it does allow the historian a shorthand method for referring to their "zigzag course."

The term independent internationalism also places in proper perspective the old debate about whether or not the diplomacy of the period was isolationist or internationalist. Clearly, internationalism did not prevail in all American diplomatic encounters after World War I, but it did become a basic consideration of leading businessmen and government officials, despite the extremely nationalistic stance of certain congressmen and business groups. At the same time, the more independent or unilateral attitudes embodied in the concepts national self-interest, military intervention, spheres of influence, and balance-of-power diplomacy were not eradicated from American foreign policy, although official statements over the years would lead one to think otherwise. What the term independent internationalism describes, therefore, is the method actually followed by the United States in its conduct of foreign affairs since 1920, devoid of such rationalizations and aphorisms as the Open Door, Pan Americanism, Stimson doctrine, or the Good Neighbor policy. Following a course of independent internationalism between 1920 and 1933, businessmen and government officials began to forge modern American diplomacy based on an amalgamation of ideological and economic considerations. That they failed to strike a balance between the two should not obscure the historical value of their attempt.

This study makes no attempt to discuss all the major foreign policy decisions of the postwar Republican administrations. It is only concerned with those issues and movements in which businessmen successfully or unsuccessfully tried to determine the course of events. I originally intended to include sections on relations with Soviet Russia and on the development of the role of ideology in policy making. Since limitations of space have prevented this, these aspects of American diplomacy in relation to the business community will be presented in a forthcoming work.[1]

Chapter One

General Business Views & Foreign Policy Trends, 1920

Almost as soon as the United States entered World War I, American businessmen began to speculate about the impact that conflict would have on the country. There had been, of course, some discussion in business journals about postwar issues, such as the problems of world peace and foreign trade, before April 6, 1917. But only after America's entrance into the war did the significance of the role the United States was destined to play in both the peace settlement and the economic reconstruction of Europe become obvious to most businessmen; they predicted that the nation would emerge from the war as the economic and moral leader of the world.

Such a grandiose view of America's world role had often been expressed during the last quarter of the nineteenth century by a variety of individuals and groups. It was the First World War, however, that transformed this ideal into reality.[1] Several internal conditions concomitant with the war effort confirmed in the minds of businessmen this belief in the economic and moral leadership of the United States. The first was the country's spectacular economic recovery following the 1913–1914 depression. Prosperity had returned as a direct result of the nation's ability to meet the demands placed upon its productive capacity by the Allied and neutralist powers.[2]

The second was the no less spectacular moral consciousness about foreign affairs which, under the wartime tutelage of Woodrow Wilson, reached new heights through exploitation of the crusading attitude and sense of dedication to high ideals that characterized the Progressive movement. This movement had always been strongly moral and nationalistic; the concern of Progressives about foreign policy was sporadic and usually subordinate to internal reform projects until Europe erupted in war. Then, like most Americans, they focused their attention ever increasingly on world affairs. Such a shift in emphasis did not initially represent any basic change in the philosophy or tenor of Progressivism, for nationalism and domestic reform were not necessarily antithetical concepts when viewed as part of the traditional "American mission" to serve as an example at home and abroad of social justice and democratic strength. So the Progressive movement, if not all of its membership, generally came to accommodate the morally righteous war that Wilson ultimately championed. Not only did the Progressive spirit permeate the American war effort, but Progressive tactics and language had become so pervasive by 1917 that they were used during and after the war to proselytize opposing foreign policies.[3]

Before the war businessmen had been intimately involved with certain Progressive economic reforms.[4] Some had also played prominent roles in peace societies and antiimperialist groups, while others had supported a number of the foreign, political, and military interventions under Presidents Roosevelt, Taft, and Wilson. As a matter of course, practically all businessmen shared with the liberal and conservative elements of society the prevailing ideas about America's unique moral mission in world affairs and the necessity of economic expansion abroad. Because of their association with the diverse domestic and diplomatic aspects of the Progressive era, businessmen were far from impervious to Progressive rhetoric by 1917. Consequently, when wartime prosperity and an intensely moral, Wilsonian approach to international relations occurred simultaneously between 1914 and 1918, clothed in Progressive terminology, the American business community succumbed to the idea that the enhanced moral and economic positions of the country were two sides of the same coin. More

than at any time in the past, businessmen were convinced that
the United States had become economically powerful because it
was essentially moral in its dealings with other countries. For
them the First World War fleetingly represented that illusive
amalgamation between the morality of democratic foreign policy
and economic expediency which Americans in general and the
business community in particular have for so long pursued and
so often confounded by equating democracy with capitalism.[5]

Confident in American righteousness, individual business
spokesmen and publications made innumerable simplistic statements in which the traditional American concepts of hard work
and thrift were combined with a sense of social service and patriotic responsibility and then morally associated with the country's
military and economic successes. By 1920 leaders of the business
community were firmly and publicly committed to these basic
premises of the ideology known as corporate liberalism. At the same
time they rhetorically equated their own self-interest and economic achievements with the notion not only that they were
serving their country through their endeavors, but that what they
did was a "glorious service to all humanity."[6] The idea of business
as a civilizing and uplifting force was certainly not new. But now
the war had reinforced the idea by producing examples of voluntary business leadership and personal sacrifice in government
service.

Thus the word "service" literally became synonymous with the
community effort of winning the war and continued as the single
most important slogan of the business community in the postwar
years down to the Great Depression. It should be noted, however,
that during and after the war businessmen themselves admitted
that only the "best upper class men in business are really genuine
in their belief [in service] and are consistent in its practice."
Obviously popular and governmental criticism of the rapid growth
of certain large corporations during the Progressive era, as well
as the close cooperation of these corporations with government
officials during the war, limited the development of such a sense
of social responsibility to primarily a business elite. Although
service became the byword, it was imperfectly practiced even by
this privileged group, let alone by the average businessman.[7] It

remained, nonetheless, a rhetorical indication of the way in which the business community generally rationalized its belief in the nation's economic and moral superiority by 1920.

Another indication of this belief can be found in ideas about what would constitute normal economic conditions following the armistice. If businessmen had expected to return to prewar conditions, it would have been somewhat difficult for them to justify logically the "new" moral and economic position achieved by the United States. They did not, however, anticipate any such return to an older era. Despite the fact that businessmen came to live under, and ostensibly approve of, the "normalcy" rhetoric of the Harding and Coolidge administrations, they were predicting by 1920 that the future economic development of the country would be atypical or antinormal. Even the demands for a return to the traditionally high Republican tariff were tempered by this realization of changing conditions.

A semantic difficulty should be noted here. Quite often individual businessmen and business editorials referred to a "new normal" for the postwar years, meaning that economic standards and living conditions would be different from the prewar normals. For example, banker Lewis E. Pierson referred to what he called a "new peace normality," while financier Paul M. Warburg said that "the normal of the past is not likely to be the normal of the future, which raises the question of what the normal ultimately will be." Looking back on the immediate postwar years, economist Wesley C. Mitchell confirmed in 1929 that "it was not 'business as usual' to which Americans returned . . . but business dominated by postwar conditions."[8] Thus, while business spokesmen often used terms such as normal, new normal basis, normality, and even normalcy, they used them optimistically to describe antinormal economic conditions in the sense that they were unprecedented according to prewar standards. Once this semantic ambiguity is recognized it becomes clear that American businessmen were neither predicting nor desiring a return to any former state of economic normalcy.[9] They did not, therefore, give to such terms the negative meaning traditionally attributed to them by historians studying Republican politics of the 1920s. Since this was the first decade in which the ideology of corporate liberalism prevailed, the same may well have been true of other groups.

Operating on a dual base of optimism and antinormal sentiment, businessmen came to believe that a different and better
world was emerging from the war experience. Gradually they
expanded their antinormal views to include not only postwar economic conditions, but to a lesser degree social, political, and
diplomatic expectations as well. Since most business organizations
are structured to anticipate economic changes, speculation within
the business community about postwar developments in these
other fields was not abundant. Nevertheless, with few exceptions,
by 1920 business spokesmen had committed themselves to the
notion that the war had brought about several positive changes
outside the realm of economics. These included, for example,
many vague statements about an improvement in human nature
and personal relationships resulting from the war effort.[10] More
specifically, Charles M. Schwab, president of Bethlehem Steel,
predicted that the democratic social order within the United States
had been strengthened because "all aristocracies except the one
of merit" were disappearing as a result of the "leveling process"
set in motion by the war. Or, as a delegate to the twenty-third
annual convention of the National Association of Manufacturers
(NAM) said: "We are all going to be more on a common level
. . . because the men who have risked their lives in defense of a
principle [democracy] are never going to allow that principle to
fall . . . in the future."[11]

These ideas about a "social renaissance" were closely related
to anticipated changes in labor-management relations. Concern
about this postwar development was expressed mostly by representatives of the Commerce Department, large corporations, and
important banking houses, such as Herbert Hoover, George W.
Perkins, Otto Kahn, Owen D. Young, Charles M. Schwab,
John D. Rockefeller, Jr., Henry Ford, Elbert H. Gary, Gerard
Swope, Edward A. Filene, and Alfred P. Sloan. Obviously these
men did not become advocates of trade unionism, but they did
pride themselves on their particular brand of conservative labor
leadership, known as welfare capitalism or industrial paternalism.
They generally perceived that the overt hostility toward unions, so
common on the part of large and small businessmen alike since
the 1890s, should be replaced with incentives and forms of cooperation.

Such prominent business leaders consciously attempted to draw laborers away from union radicalism by encouraging employee profit-sharing plans, lowering working hours, raising wages, sponsoring company unions with pension and welfare programs, providing savings and loan facilities, and utilizing technological innovations to improve working conditions and production efficiency. They also resorted to public relations tactics including not only massive advertising campaigns and well-publicized contributions to public health and welfare agencies, but also to educational programs designed to promote the "Americanization" of immigrant workers. Many of these ideas had been bandied about before the war but did not become commonplace in business thought until the 1920s, when they were linked to the concept of service by spokesmen for the most influential corporations. Accordingly Rockefeller asserted that the purpose of modern industry was "as much the advancement of social well-being as the production of wealth," and Ford urged the adoption of the principles of "social engineering" because "service always pays better than selfishness."[12]

By 1920 speculation about political changes more often than not centered on greater cooperation between government and business. Although the business community in general did not approve of the retention or extension of governmental control over industries introduced during the war, it did expect the government to lower taxes, to subsidize an American merchant marine and the development of air transportation, to protect and facilitate economic expansion abroad, and to provide "helpful and encouraging advice" on all economic matters. In particular, powerful corporate interests hoped for a new era in government-business relations in the postwar world. Ideally this would mean more institutionalized cooperation in the form of legislation promoting business combinations in foreign trade and encouraging trade associations. It also would mean fewer attempts by Washington officials to prohibit mergers and monopoly growth at home while an ever-increasing number of competent businessmen would begin to utilize the federal bureaucratic structure to regulate themselves with governmental approbation.[13]

This process whereby the government delegated growing

amounts of its power to business-dominated agencies had been greatly accelerated during the war with the creation of the War Industries Board and its major subdivisions, the commodity committees. Both were dominated by "dollar-a-year men" from the executive ranks of industry and finance who were in turn assisted by War Service Committees made up of private trade associations. Before and after the war such regulatory bodies came to rely upon special-interest groups for their expertise, personnel, and support; hence, private sectors ended up in control of the public boards and commissions which were originally established to regulate their activities. Thus, the distinction between public and private enterprises, in the area of military procurement and as far as civilian regulatory agencies were concerned, was becoming more apparent than real by 1920. Particular cases in point can be seen in the history of the Federal Trade and Tariff commissions, both of which were disowned by Progressives and embraced by business after 1925 because they had fallen into very permissive regulatory practices.[14] Business statements after World War I reflected recognition of this trend and the determination to promote what was considered a very desirable political change in government-business relations.

Just as the business community believed that the unity and cooperation demanded by the war were hastening the formation of new domestic relationships, so it also forecast altered relations in international affairs. With the signing of the armistice in November 1918, American businessmen were released from the patriotic necessity of disguising the fact that they were much more concerned with the economic than with the political aspects of foreign policy. For banking, investment, and import-export interests, the problem of restoring the economic health of the world loomed large; these businessmen believed that the war had removed the last remnants of economic nationalism and that economic interdependence had become the rule rather than the exception in international relations. Thus they reasoned that the most important practical and humanitarian responsibility of United States diplomacy was to take the lead in the economic reconstruction of war-torn Europe. Large manufacturing concerns, on the other hand, were more interested in protecting markets gained and technological advances made at the expense of European nations between 1914 and 1918.

These two positions were not mutually exclusive and were overshadowed by the agreement among all segments of the business community that economic expansion, in all of its various forms, should now take precedence over politics in foreign relations. This consensus was based on two conclusions that businessmen, with varying degrees of understanding, had reached after examining the impact of the war on the economy of the United States. First, vaguely sensing that the democratic nations of the world were moving in the direction of greater economic interdependency, most businessmen viewed enduring world peace as an economic rather than a political matter. Second, they recognized that the unusual prosperity created during the war had turned the United States into a creditor nation for the first time in its history. Naturally enough, in the ensuing decade, economists, politicians, and businessmen did not fully understand the complex ramifications of this dramatic change in American balance of payments and other economic dislocations arising after 1920.

In retrospect, however, it is relatively easy to see that certain prewar problems, accelerated during the years 1914–1918, "completely altered the equilibrium of international payments" in the postwar period. These economic maladjustments between nations were largely the result of overproduction in agriculture, the failure of the United States to adapt its commercial policies to its new creditor status (a condition the country probably would have attained by 1920 without the aid of wartime sales), and increased competition for dwindling foreign markets as manufacturing production increased, not only in the major industrial nations, but in the non-European areas of the world and in the new states created by the Treaty of Versailles. This latter trend is sometimes referred to as the "reversal of the process of international specialization" which was so characteristic of nineteenth-century colonialism. In other words, the war itself contributed only one new ingredient to the international economic problems that had been building up for most of the previous century: the payment of war debts and reparations.[15] What the First World War did was to accelerate existing balance-of-payment problems and to create the opportunity for the United States to replace British domination of international finance and commerce. By seizing such an opportunity, many business leaders reasoned, America would make the world safe not only for democracy but for Yankee capitalism as well.

This postwar attempt by American businessmen to create a new world community among industrialized nations[16] was based on the selective application of the principle of equal economic opportunity or the Open Door policy, as it was most commonly called. Its application was selective in that equal opportunity was most eagerly espoused in areas of the world where the United States faced serious economic competition after the war, such as the Far East and the Middle East, but was almost never encouraged in those areas where the opposite was true, for example, the Philippines, the Caribbean, and Central America. In principle the Open Door represented the antithesis of the concepts of balance of power and spheres of influence by calling for peaceful economic expansion as a substitute for political and military confrontations between rival powers. In actuality, equal opportunity in world trade and finance benefited the strongest competitor, and American businessmen were convinced of the postwar ability of the United States to compete successfully if granted the same opportunities as all other nations to buy, sell, and invest. But once having gained the upper hand, it was not unusual for American businessmen, with tacit governmental approval, to pursue a Closed Door policy when they could do so with impunity. This resulted in a form of American colonialism or economic imperialism based on the establishment of spheres of influence whenever this proved possible.

Thus, while the Open Door remained the official policy of Washington and an influential portion of the business community, the Closed Door remained its unofficial complement. The Open and Closed Door policies in tandem proved excellent vehicles for the practice of independent internationalism described above (see pp. xvi–xvii). They could be implemented with either collective or unilateral actions, depending on which was more advantageous for the corporate interests of the United States in a given area of the world. Subsequent chapters will discuss how both policies, amounting to a dual standard, were practiced with varying degrees of success between 1920 and 1933.

It was not, however, the Janus-faced application by the United States of the principle of equal economic opportunity that posed the most serious obstacle to the creation of an economically interdependent world under American tutelage. While the United States succeeded in asserting its commercial and financial leadership in the 1920s, it failed to build a world community, first, because conflicts between competing segments of the business community prevented the development of a single comprehensive plan for American expansion abroad; and second, because all the major industrial nations shared common economic assumptions which were in the process of becoming obsolete in the face of the massive maladjustments precipitated by the war and certain long-term trends which were not understood at the time.[17]

The most important of these postwar economic assumptions was the faith placed in the gold standard system and in the private, competitive market economy which it spawned. As international economic ills continued to grow, even after the middle of the 1920s, when the world generally had returned to fully convertible gold currencies, many nations unilaterally refused to act according to the traditional rules of the gold standard game. Although aware that the revived gold standard was malfunctioning, world leaders were unable to agree on effective cooperative action to remedy its defects, in part because they remained unaware of some of the underlying causes of the malfunctioning. The gold standard system had always demanded the sacrifice of a certain amount of economic freedom through the control of national volumes of credit by governments or central banking agencies (a condition automatically imposed in the nineteenth century by the supremacy of England in international finance). It also demanded the adjustment of domestic prices and income to correspond with each country's balance of payments.[18] But after World War I the gold exchange standard returned without the controlling influence once exerted by England. As a result, most nations chose to overvalue or undervalue their currencies and to manage their credit, if at all, primarily on the basis of national expediency rather than international considerations. This economic nation-alism stemmed from internal economic problems that all countries faced after the war, and from divisions within their respective business communities which often prevented an internationally-oriented policy's prevailing. Consequently, for example, the Fed-eral Reserve Board's actions to achieve domestic price stability sometimes contradicted its attempts to maintain the international gold standard or the two coincided only accidentally. This was because stable price levels required national planning based on managed-money programs independent of gold movements, while the gold standard was supposedly a self-correcting system based upon such movements.[19]

Since the widespread balance-of-payment problems through-out the 1920s reflected deficiencies in the domestic economies of most major nations even before the Great Depression, a world-wide economic equilibrium was impossible unless domestic efforts were made to direct private enterprise and unless drastic new solutions were undertaken at the international level. In retrospect, it can be seen that the trend, especially in the United States, was away from the types of governmental controls instituted during the war, and that the cooperative foreign actions attempted before 1925 often left the basic economic problems untouched. Between 1925 and 1929 an aura of prosperity, again especially in the United States, made international cooperation seem less urgent than in the immediate postwar years. Unfortunately, although this was the most propitious time for such cooperation, little of permanent value emerged from the international conferences held during these years. After 1929, of course, it was too late for effective collective action, as the unsuccessful establishment in 1930 of the Bank for International Settlements clearly indicated, for the depression stimulated even greater economic nationalism than had existed before.[20]

In some instances between 1920 and 1933, national leaders misunderstood or underestimated the seriousness of the economic problems they faced, such as the fact that basic reform of the world's political economy, not simply reconstruction of an earlier model, was required after the war. In other instances they were no more willing or politically capable than today's leaders of imposing upon their citizens the stringent economic and social restrictions necessary to facilitate the formation of a harmonious and mutually beneficial world community. Although professing a desire to establish such a community, the United States, as the only major postwar nation in a position to do so, opted for competition based on equal economic opportunity, a stance designed to produce American domination in foreign trade and finance, rather than true international cooperation, which would have required lowering its own economic expectations in the interest of world economic stability.[21]

Even so, United States economic diplomacy following World War I would not have exacerbated the international balance-of-payment problems as much as it did had there been a judicious coordination of domestic credit, tariff, war debt, and foreign loan policies. But disagreement among rival business interests and faulty economic theories prevented this. A case in point was the $10,621 million merchandise export balance which the country enjoyed between 1920 and 1929. This represented the greatest American export balance before World War II. Primarily financed by uncontrolled loans and investments, such an excessively favorable balance of trade contributed to a superficial prosperity at home while it obscured the basic economic disequilibrium that existed between major nations. For the economic health of the rest of the world, the United States could responsibly maintain such a merchandise export surplus only so long as it was not based on abnormally large gold imports (as was the case in the 1930s), and so long as the outflow of new capital for productive purposes exceeded foreign interest, amortization, and dividend payments of earlier capital exports. With the depression of 1929 this highly precarious cycle was broken when capital issues from the United States abruptly stopped. The wave of defaults which followed revealed numerous unproductive and high-risk loans and precipitated worldwide deflation.[22]

These and other weaknesses in the American effort to create a world community while reconstructing Europe were the result of a curious combination of ideas traditionally associated with the gold standard, such as the automatic adjustment of international payments through normal market forces, and the desirability of removing as much as possible controls over private enterprise and barriers to world trade, as well as new practices which emerged to cope with altered postwar conditions. Among these innovations were the appearance of managed money policies at the domestic level; international movements of so-called "hot money," that is, large short-term capital loans, especially to Germany; the approval of unproductive long-term capital issues which were not self-liquidating and which thus allowed millions of dollars to be "wasted" in the sense that they did not build up the capacity of the debtor nation to export or import; and the addition of the unconditional most-favored-nation principle to the high protective tariff views of the Republican party.[23]

Old and new ideas were combined after 1920, more out of confusion than by design, for only a handful of businessmen and government leaders began to perceive the enormous complexities and dangers inherent in the economic conditions of the postwar world. Two such perceptive individuals were New York financiers Frank A. Vanderlip and Paul M. Warburg. A third was Herbert Hoover.[24] All three were dimly aware that reform, in addition to reconstruction of economic systems, was necessary for world stability. Unfortunately even their mildest remedial recommendations, particularly those calling for a more equitable American trade balance, foreign loan supervision, and domestic monetary controls, were lost in a labyrinth of contrary advice based on the simplistic assumption that the country could retain its wartime economic advances only through uncontrolled expansion at home and abroad. This belief in turn reaffirmed in the minds of most businessmen and government officials the idea that domestic prosperity ultimately depended upon a foreign trade balance in which exports greatly exceeded imports. This was clearly the prevailing view by 1920, although the United States Chamber of Commerce, the National Foreign Trade Council (NFTC), and the vast majority of individual business spokesmen also maintained that economic interdependence and international cooperation were not incompatible with protected home markets and competition for foreign markets as long as the Open Door principle of "no favoritism" was observed.

Thus, representatives of all segments of the business com-

munity, with the exception of the National Association of Manufacturers and a few extreme protectionist groups,[25] talked simultaneously about competitive international trade and the postwar
cooperation necessitated by the economic interdependency of the
major industrialized nations. For example, not only well-known
individual bankers and businessmen, such as Vanderlip, Owen D.
Young, Benjamin Strong, Charles G. Dawes, Dwight Morrow,
Julius Rosenwald, Daniel Willard, Gerard P. Swope, and business-
oriented government officials such as William C. Redfield, Norman H. Davis, and Hoover, but also the collective leadership of
the national Chamber of Commerce and the NFTC, were essentially in agreement that one of the most encouraging developments following the war was the "growing recognition of the
interdependence of all civilized nations in matters of commerce
and industry."[26] These men were not, however, content with
making generalizations about the subject. Even before the armistice it was obvious to many of them, but especially to international bankers and financiers such as Thomas W. Lamont, Warburg, Strong, and Vanderlip, that for a near-bankrupt Europe to
buy from the United States and at the same time begin to produce
its own exports would require unprecedented financial aid, and
that the only postwar nation in a position to extend such aid
was the United States. So, in anticipation of the "reconstruction"
period to follow the cessation of fighting, a number of specific
plans were proposed to alleviate the obvious economic ills of
Europe and in the process promote an American-led international community of industrialized nations.

Most of the suggestions came from financial circles which
were in sharp disagreement with officials of the Treasury Department over whether or not government funds should continue
to be used in foreign finance. Influential bankers across the country favored such a continuation, while three successive secretaries of the treasury between 1918 and 1920, and most importantly Assistant Secretary Russell Leffingwell, did not. President
Wilson ultimately followed the policy of retrenchment recommended by the Treasury Department rather than the more comprehensive plans devised by leading financiers.[27]

This defeat of the use of federal aid in reconstructing Europe resulted in part from disagreement within the elite group of bankers who tried to influence government policy. By 1920 this segment of the business community had divided into two camps. One consisted of investment bankers and large investment houses in New York, plus their affiliates across the country, led by the House of Morgan and Chase National Bank. This group favored financial and commercial cooperation rather than competition with government and banking circles in England. It also preferred short-term (acceptance financing) credit as opposed to long-term investment programs in Europe in the years immediately following the war. The goal of this group, aside from the reconstruction of Europe, was to make New York City the financial center of the world through the gradual "Americanization" of the facilities of the British financial system. The theory behind this idea was that "the nation dominant in international long-term investment would make use of the world banking facilities of all nations." Therefore there was no need for America to duplicate the financial facilities England had already established throughout the world. The House of Morgan did not doubt that the United States would eventually dominate the field of long-term investments after the war, but in the winter of 1919–1920 the amount of capital available to international bankers was temporarily curtailed because approximately $4 billion in short-term credits owed to the United States were frozen as a result of a stagnant world trade situation, and because of heavy postwar domestic demands on private investment capital.[28]

Opposing the Morgan position was the nation's leading commercial institution, the National City Bank of New York, under the leadership of the Rockefeller family and Vanderlip. Backing this group were leading export manufacturers, such as United States Steel, General Electric, and other industries affiliated with the American International Corporation (AIC). This latter corporation was originally established in 1915 to loan money to the Allies and to encourage direct, long-term investment abroad during and after the war. It represented a means by which large industrial corporations in conjunction with the National City Bank of New York could take advantage of the war to invest in areas of the world long controlled by British, French, and German interests.

The AIC in essence represented a commercial banking and manufacturing faction that encouraged competition with English banking and export interests through the establishment of American branch banks, long-term credit, and permanent investment abroad. Manufacturers hoped that "construction of branch banks would somehow induce investment bankers in the United States to sell bonds" of foreign governments and in this manner finance "the installation of American technology" abroad. Individuals and corporations expressing interest in long-term investment abroad along the lines suggested by the AIC included: Eugene P. Thomas, president of United States Steel Products; the National Foreign Trade Council; James A. Farrell, president of the United States Steel Corporation; Edward J. Berwind, president of the Berwind-White Mining Company; Maurice A. Oudin, manager of the Foreign Department of General Electric; Secretary of Commerce William C. Redfield; Assistant Secretary of the Treasury Norman H. Davis; Hoover, as director general of relief in Europe; bankers Otto Kahn and Paul M. Warburg of Kuhn, Loeb and Company; and John Hays Hammond, retired engineer-turned-businessman.[29]

Like the House of Morgan, the National City Bank wanted New York to become the international financial center, but thought independent branch banks should be utilized to achieve that goal rather than waiting for the far-flung British banking facilities to Americanize. The ultimate goal of both factions was the same: "an independent American system" which would dominate world trade and finance in the wake of the war. In fact, Charles H. Sabin, representing the House of Morgan on the board of directors of the AIC, publicly expressed approval of long-term, direct investments. Obviously these two rival financial groups were not irrevocably split. Until 1922 they simply disagreed over the methods to be used to achieve a common goal.[30] This tactical disagreement among the nation's top financiers was serious enough, nonetheless, to weaken their cooperative efforts to keep the government in the business of foreign financing. It also presaged the later inability of bankers and manufacturers to cooperate on short-term tactics in the interest of a long-term strategy aimed at Americanizing the world's political economy.

The struggle between the House of Morgan and the National

City Bank was best illustrated in the implementation of the Edge Act passed by Congress in December 1919.[31] As an amendment to the Federal Reserve Act, the Edge legislation permitted bankers to combine, without fear of prosecution under the existing anti-trust laws, in order to provide private financing for American trade abroad. By the time of its passage the bill was supported by the two rival banking factions as well as by large manufacturers across the country. These influential segments of the business community had become reconciled to private financing of the reconstruction of Europe, for during 1919 all of their attempts to obtain government export guarantees and massive federal assistance for the financial and industrial rehabilitation of Europe failed.[32] Recognition of this failure was indicated as early as October 1919 at the Chamber of Commerce International Trade Conference, was confirmed with the passage of the Edge Act at the end of that year, and was reiterated at the Chicago Foreign Trade Financing Conference held under the auspices of the American Bankers Association (ABA) in December 1920, at which the NFTC, the United States Chamber of Commerce, the American Manufacturers Export Association, and the American Manufacturers Import and Export Association were all represented.

Before we turn to trends in political foreign policy as of 1920, certain facts should be noted with respect to the formulation of economic foreign policy. The circumstances leading to business support of the Edge Act and to the Treasury Department's insistence on the private financing of the reconstruction of Europe reflect patterns which were repeated later in the decade. First, although powerful elements within the business community had the ability to circumvent the antitrust laws and to establish a domestic corporate oligarchy, they evinced an inability both to dictate the government's economic foreign policy in the crucial years immediately following World War I, and, largely because of their conflicting self-interests, to cooperate at home or abroad to the degree necessary to achieve a lasting world community. At the same time officials in Washington indicated a refusal to accept the type of comprehensive responsibility for solving world economic problems urged by certain bankers. Instead, following the advice of the Treasury Department, the Wilson administration and its Republican successors tried in vain to return to the more traditional prewar federal practice of separating economic and political foreign policy whenever possible, in order to claim primary responsibility only for the latter.

Second, business and government leaders continued to assume, as they had before the war, that economic foreign policy, despite its obvious importance to the nation's welfare, was a relatively simple matter of guaranteeing unlimited economic opportunity via the Open or Closed Door and of providing occasional protection for American corporate interests. In other words, between 1920 and 1933, the use of force was looked upon as basically unnatural and detrimental to the American efforts directed at building a world industrial community. Later generations of policy makers, however, turned increasingly to economic and military sanctions as means for assuring continued foreign economic expansion. Thus, what was viewed as a natural and inevitable process in the 1920s was destined to become a dogmatic assertion often backed by actual sanctions or intimidation. Therefore the rationale behind postwar economic foreign policy, which looked askance at the use of force, placing its hope instead on American ability to compete peacefully in world economic affairs, was all but destroyed in the course of the 1930s and 1940s.

Third, business support of the Edge Act presaged the future inability of businessmen and government officials to coordinate economic and political foreign policy. Without such coordination the country's foreign economic policies have tended since 1920 to contradict or hinder its political and humanitarian goals abroad. As will be noted in following chapters, American foreign policy was uncoordinated at several levels following World War I. Then, as now, this resulted from conflicts between economic and political aims, contradictions between different programs within the realm of economic foreign policy, and the fact that domestic economic needs and political forces often worked to counter what was desirable from the standpoint of international economic cooperation.

Fourth, by 1920 little attempt had been made in either

government or business circles to delineate the ambiguous relationship that was rapidly developing between the foreign trade and investment activity conducted by private American citizens and the new position of economic and military power in which the United States found itself as a result of the war. This postwar inability or unwillingness to devise guidelines for the relationship between the public and private spheres of foreign policy led to the use of different criteria for diplomatic actions with little consideration for consistency or overall coherence. For example, between 1920 and 1933 unilateral or collective measures were enforced against Latin America, China, France, and Russia, whereas in disputes with Japan, England, and most European nations, military or economic force was not resorted to. At the same time no precise distinction was made as to the role the business community should play in developing political foreign policy nor about how much responsibility the government should assume for foreign economic activity undertaken without its knowledge or approval. The resulting confusion and ambivalence have encumbered the formation of a coordinated economic and political foreign policy during this entire century.

Finally, by looking back on postwar trends it can be seen that the ideological danger posed first by Imperialist Germany, then by Bolshevik Russia during the war, and still later by nationalist revolutions in China and portions of Latin America, literally forced Washington policy makers to formulate an ideological alternative based on the American brand of democracy and capitalism. And it has been on the assumption that this approach to foreign affairs would avoid the pitfalls of imperialism, fascism, and communism, that many leading government officials and businessmen have advocated the wholesale exportation of democracy and capitalism since World War I.[33] Simultaneously the powerful creditor status of the United States put it in a position to realize the most fantastic dreams of earlier economic expansionists. Therefore, in these two postwar conditions—hostile foreign ideologies and unprecedented economic opportunity—are found the dual foundations of modern American diplomacy.

Essential for the success of this kind of twentieth-century

diplomacy was the development of an integrated, orderly relationship between government and business in the conduct of
foreign affairs. By 1920, as noted earlier, such a process of in-
tegration and cooperation at the domestic level had been gradually
evolving for at least forty years. It was hastened by the Progressive movement, considerably accelerated by World War I, and informally institutionalized between 1920 and 1933.[34] In theory
this should have led to a coordinated economic and political
foreign policy for the United States. In practice it did not, largely because of differences within the business community which could not
be resolved. However, coordination was also hindered because in
the 1920s economic ideas associated with the concept of corporate
liberalism developed at a faster rate than political ideas associated
with ideological diplomacy. This meant that economic considerations often took unofficial precedence over political ones when
businessmen and government officials came together to formulate
foreign policy.

This is not to say that political foreign policy was ignored by
the postwar business community. On the contrary, it had long
been the concern of those businessmen engaged in foreign
trade, export manufacturing, and international finance. Moreover, there was indication of increased business interest outside
these specialized economic groups because of the ideological as
well as the economic considerations mentioned above. By 1920
those political foreign policy issues most often discussed within
the business community were the Treaty of Versailles and the
League of Nations, including the nationalist-internationalist dispute generated by the peace settlement, and the attitude of the
United States toward the new regime in Russia. As harbingers of
attitudes that would continue to be controversial in the next
decade the discussion was most important but was easily subject
to misinterpretation because of the general national uncertainty
following the armistice, which ended the fighting but did not
settle the conditions of peace. This postwar uncertainty in foreign
affairs was exacerbated in the United States by the unusual delay
in the treaty negotiations and the protracted fight over ratification, by the hysteria of the Red Scare, and by the depression that
set in during the summer months of 1920. So the political

foreign policy attitudes expressed at the beginning of the decade were often symptomatic of the uncertain times. As such they did not represent irrevocable positions and were subject to modification as the prosperity of the 1920s gradually stimulated a false sense of confidence within the business community.

On the question of the peace settlement, many spokesmen for financial, manufacturing, and general business interests expressed, in the broadest sense, a favorable interest in the Treaty of Versailles and in *some kind* of international peace-keeping agency.[35] Although two Pennsylvania millionaires, Henry Clay Frick and Andrew W. Mellon, headed the list of well-known business opponents of Wilson's League of Nations, business opposition was not the determining factor in the final defeat of the treaty and League. Conflicts involving presidential prerogative, opposing foreign policy philosophies, partisan politics, and personality transcended traditional sectional or economic differences of opinion within the business community and the country as a whole on this issue.[36]

Surprisingly enough, a segment of the business community nominally in favor of Wilson's peace package probably damaged its chances for ratification more than the few business irreconcilables led by Frick and Mellon. Composed largely of Republican bankers and financial publications on both coasts, this group was very critical of the economic aspects of the settlement, particularly those sections of the treaty concerning Allied rights and privileges in Germany and her former colonies. Serious doubt was also expressed about the ability of Article 10 of the League to preserve an Open Door for American expansion. To such international business figures as Hoover, Vanderlip, Kahn, Lamont, and Strong, in addition to financial publications such as the *Wall Street Journal, Magazine of Wall Street, Pacific Banker,* and *Bankers Magazine,*[37] the economic stringency of the settlement would "sacrifice" United States initiative and capital to inter-Allied control.[38]

Thus when American leaders at Versailles failed to incorporate the idea of equality of economic opportunity into the peace treaty and to prevent severe Allied discrimination against Germany's future economic status, the basic postwar expectations of this segment of the business community were threatened. The "anti-Open Door" features of the treaty did not satisfy even the businessmen who were members of the United States delegation, including such staunch Democrats as Bernard Baruch and Norman H. Davis. These two men later defended the economic aspects of the settlement, apparently out of the belief that the United States was in a position to insist on equality of treatment in the long run because it controlled most of the available capital in the world. Like Wilson, they also insisted that the League of Nations provided the means "for eliminating the other objectionable features of the Treaty."[39]

Prominent Republican businessmen, however, lacked this faith in either the ability of the capital resources of the country or the League of Nations with Article 10 to bring about world acceptance of the Open Door policy espoused by the United States. Apparently Hoover was the only Republican business figure to alienate Wilson by informing the president of his objections to the treaty's economic provisions while the Paris negotiations were in progress,[40] but others quickly followed suit once the terms of the proposed settlement were made public. Kahn and Vanderlip were particularly vitriolic in their public denunciations, referring to the settlement as "ill-omened" and "conceived in hatred and malice." Like Hoover, however, these two bankers remained convinced of the efficacy of a world organization and privately expressed regret at the failure of the League and treaty to pass the Senate for the last time in March 1920.[41]

It is difficult to determine the influence of statements that vacillated between outright rejection of the treaty on economic grounds and private acceptance of certain political principles upon which it and the League were based. In most instances, the qualified approval of the treaty and League, with reservations, by men such as Hoover, Kahn, and Vanderlip was not as widely publicized as their most intemperate public pronouncements against the settlement. The mass media could not, of course, be expected to report these private sentiments, but it also ignored both the various public business communiqués to Republican and Democratic Senators in favor of the League in some form, and the last-minute efforts of eastern financial interests to exert pressure on Senate leaders to bring about a compromise on the League issue.[42]

Therefore the financial community's criticism of the League, circulated by the media, contributed indirectly not only to the rejection of the peace settlement but also to the rise of postwar nationalism. Neither of these developments was desired by the international business figures who were the leading critics of the economic features of the peace treaty. Saddened by the final defeat of the Treaty of Versailles, Norman H. Davis wrote a friendly but firm letter to the English economist John Maynard Keynes, a leading opponent of the treaty, pointing out the undesirable impact such criticism had had on American foreign policy attitudes in the immediate postwar years. Another Democratic businessman, Bernard Baruch, concurred with this judgment.[43] But it is doubtful that Hoover or leading Republican bankers ever fully comprehended the wider implications of their attacks on the treaty and League.

The vast majority of American businessmen did not participate in this complicated economic debate over the peace settlement. Instead, they allowed the various national organizations with which they were affiliated to speak for them. The publications of these interest groups indicate that the average businessman, like so many Americans by 1920, had initially approved of the treaty provisions for ending the war and the concept of an international organization to preserve peace, for the vaguest of humanitarian reasons. With the exception of rabid Wilsonians such as Norman H. Davis, Vance McCormick, Newton D. Baker, George Foster Peabody, Henry Morgenthau, Sr., and southern Democratic businessmen, however, approval of the treaty and League within the business community was not based on any emotional or rational commitment to the president's foreign policy ideals.[44] If the rank and file of businessmen, who were predominantly Republican,[45] thought about the peace settlement at all, it appears to have been in terms of partisanship and general self-interest. Consciously or unconsciously, they wanted to "Republicanize" the treaty and maximize any economic or other advantages it contained for America, irrespective of the worldwide implications of the document.

The most common business argument in favor of ratification coupled the idea of self-interest with a frank admission that the treaty was far from perfect in its present form. The arguments based on self-interest were varied. They ranged from immediate concern for the foreign economic interests of the United States to the political threats that might arise if the country was unrepresented at League sessions in the future. Some businessmen reasoned that arms reduction, which was considered a postwar economic necessity, might require American membership in the world body. Others thought that ratification would do much to thwart the spread of communism in Europe, and to end the general economic and political confusion at home and abroad.[46] Perhaps the most utopian of the self-interest arguments appeared in the three publications representing national organizations made up largely of small or medium-sized business representatives— the *Nation's Business, American Industries,* and the *Journal of American Bankers Association* (ABA *Journal*). It consisted of the desire to turn the League into an "enormous fiscal corporation" because peace among nations in the postwar era "must be established on industrial, and not on political relations."[47]

The one Republican spokesman who embraced all of these arguments of self-interest in his private and public statements was Herbert Hoover. An early and consistent critic of the peace settlement, at the end of the debate over ratification he was nonetheless urging Wilson to accept all of the Republican reservations so that the United States could become a member of the League. Hoover believed more deeply than most Republican critics of Wilsonianism that Americans could no longer enjoy the "pretense of an insularity that we do not possess." The League with the United States as a member could "minimize war," according to Hoover. But, most importantly, he pointed out economic difficulties which would accrue if we did not participate, saying "the solution of domestic problems, such as the size of our armament, reduction in taxation, and the prevention of agricultural and industrial depression and consequent unemployment, is dependent upon stability abroad and upon our access to the world's markets which today are endangered by discrimination against us through our inability to exercise our veto under the Treaty." Hoover never denied that these "issues of self-interest" constituted less noble reasons for supporting ratification than the ones commonly used by the Wilsonians. Nevertheless, he and many other Republican businessmen relied on such economic arguments to distinguish their position from that of the extremists (including the Bolsheviki) who "advocated against any League at all," and that of the president's staunchest Democratic supporters.[48]

Qualified business approval of the treaty and League, whether based on partisan or economic expectations, was not enduring. By 1923 leading Republican business figures such as Hoover, Vanderlip, Kahn, Henry Ford, Charles G. Dawes, and John McHugh, president of the Mechanic and Metals National Bank of New York, were disillusioned with the ineffectiveness of the League and other glaring inadequacies of the peace settlement, most of which they had predicted. While Hoover and certain Democrats, namely, George Foster Peabody, Baruch, Davis, and Newton D. Baker, continued to press for cooperation with the League, most Republican businessmen did not advocate membership in that body after 1925. Even among Democratic businessmen enthusiasm for the League waned during the course of the decade.[49]

Instead, Republican and Democratic businessmen, like the administrations of the 1920s, increasingly based their hopes for peace and prosperity on a variety of limited and piecemeal solutions rather than on any coordinated comprehensive program. These solutions included disarmament proposals, adherence to the World Court, the Dawes and Young plans for reparation payments, and trade expansion through the Open and Closed Door policies. By the end of the decade the League was not an important concern of businessmen except for a few determined Democrats who were still chafing over the role that partisan politics had played in keeping America out of the world organization.[50]

In addition to spawning arguments of self-interest and partisan suspicions, the debate over ratification renewed a much broader and more basic foreign policy controversy concerning the general philosophy of American foreign policy as embodied in the terms internationalism and nationalism. This was not the first time such a theoretical dispute had arisen. It had been particularly apparent in the debates over the various arbitration treaties before World War I, and no single political party can be said to have monopolized one position or the other. The same held true for the immediate postwar years, although Woodrow Wilson did temporarily cast the Democrats in the role of internationalists over the League issue.[51] The controversy over the League was simply the first of a series of postwar confrontations between nationalists and internationalists which divided Progressives and conservatives alike over the means necessary to secure America's newly acquired economic and political status in the world. Traditional isolationism had become, of course, a virtual impossibility; thus, few in government circles and even fewer in business advocated complete disengagement or withdrawal from foreign affairs in the 1920s.[52]

Not only were nationalist and internationalist positions seldom found in unadulterated forms, but neither was intrinsically more idealistic, moralistic, or realistic than the other except perhaps on a purely rhetorical level. However, given the widespread use of Progressive terminology by both sides following World War I, even this distinction is dubious. Moreover, to describe the melange of unilateral and collective actions which emerged in this period as isolationistic, nationalistic, internationalistic, moralistic, idealistic, or realistic is to obscure the underlying diplomatic method which in fact gave, and continues to give, a modicum of coherence to an otherwise confusing foreign policy. This diplomatic method is independent internationalism as defined above, and it should not be confused with such foreign policy principles as the Open and Closed Doors, Pax Americana, Dollar Diplomacy, the Good Neighbor, and so forth.

Generally speaking, the business community had not aligned itself solidly with either the nationalist or the internationalist camp by 1920 because neither extreme seemed to serve the immediate economic needs and interests of the United States. This is not to deny that nationalists and internationalists alike were committed to some form of economic expansion. But the latter, under the influence of Wilson, appeared to associate world leadership with unlimited political and economic cooperation (including, critics said, free trade)—a concept which broke too sharply with traditional American policies to be accepted, other than at a rhetorical level, by most businessmen. At the same time, nationalists such as Theodore Roosevelt and Henry Cabot Lodge favored more of the same; that is, economic expansion at the expense of foreign competitors and backed by a high tariff, the United States Navy, and balance-of-power arrangements with other major nations. So they continued to place the political power and prestige of the nation above strictly economic considerations. This philosophy no longer satisfied the business community, which was now openly proclaiming the ascendency of economic over political foreign policy. Finally, a smaller group of extreme nationalists led by Senators William E. Borah and Hiram Johnson questioned the wisdom of exporting surpluses and democracy in the same package, as much from fear of foreign entanglements as from suspicion that the methods of both the Wilsonian internationalists and the Roosevelt-Lodge nationalists would lead to economic and/or political imperialism. Thus, the Borah-Johnson nationalists became irreconcilable opponents of the League because they saw it as an instrument of aggression as well as a threat to American sovereignty. They also were far too critical of the methods and motivations of the large corporate interests in the country to be acceptable to influential businessmen during the immediate postwar years.[53]

Many businessmen seemed to gravitate intuitively toward a middle ground between these extremes on the League issue, and once again Hoover best represented their position. On February 23, 1920, in an address delivered at Johns Hopkins University, he said:

> The war has brought us many new relationships which we cannot escape. Our old relations will be expanded, or at least, better organized by the League; they are expanded by conditions in the Treaty as distinguished from the League, by our vitally enlarged economic and social interest abroad, by the calls of humanity in the alleviation of misery. *We have two extreme views among our people upon the policies we should adopt in all these matters. One contends that the ideal is isolation—leave Europe to herself; the other contends for at least moral domination as a mission of international justice. Many of us want neither extreme.* Assuming that

some day it will be ratified in some form, the nature of our policies under the League has yet to be developed. We hope for its immediate energies in the reduction of armament, the development of engines of reconciliation, of arbitration and codes and a court of international justice. We hope for its influence in the destruction of the economic barriers set up before and since the war, which stifle the recuperation and the free entry of our commerce over the world. Some of us hope that the League will not interpose in international differences except at the last stage necessary to mitigate the growth of conflict. Some of us have no liking for mandates of any European state, for we would thus plunge ourselves territorially into Europe itself. Most of us have no ambitions to moral or other domination.[54]

Hoover's middle position appears to have been based on the notion that limited moral and political involvement with the world, accompanied by controlled economic expansion, was desirable and could be distinguished from the less desirable extremes of overly righteous internationalism, blatant power politics, or excessive preoccupation with the dangers inherent in League membership. By 1920 this middle position was not clearly enough developed or articulated by the business community as a whole, or by its most influential members, to affect appreciably the political or economic foreign policy of the United States. It did, however, reflect business impatience with the Wilsonian, Roosevelt-Lodge, and Borah-Johnson factions, none of which seemed to confront the economic realities of the postwar world. In terms of the lingering struggle for membership in the League of Nations after 1920, this position remained both ineffectual and short-lived. Businessmen drifted into the nationalist or internationalist camps as the original fury over the peace settlement subsided. In doing so they unwittingly undermined the American dream of creating a world community among major industrial nations after the First World War by failing to unite behind a cooperative foreign policy program.

As will be seen, financial interests, import-export groups, and large manufacturers with foreign markets tended to become more internationally oriented in regard to diplomatic affairs between 1920 and 1933, while the average businessman became more consciously a nationalist than he had been before the war.

This was because sectional, occupational, and dimensional self-interest were more apparent to individual businessmen on subsequent foreign policy issues than had been the case with the League. Certain political and economic foreign policy questions, for example, placed businessmen in the Midwest, South, and West against those in the East, manufacturers and general retailers against bankers and export-importers, and moderately prosperous businessmen against the magnates. These divisions usually occurred when leaders of Hoover's caliber and ability could not convince business nationalists and internationalists of the mutual advantages of a middle position of cooperative action on economic foreign policy. More often than not, Hoover and others with semicomprehensive plans for reconstructing Europe and solving the world's economic problems through American leadership, failed to unite the business community except when an ideological threat, such as that posed by nationalist revolutions, helped to bring about temporary reconciliations between these opposing elements.

In summary, then, the dominant business creed that had emerged by 1920 contained a basic assumption about the economic and moral leadership of the United States. This assumption was based in part on optimistic expectations of a prosperous and essentially antinormal postwar world—a world in which businessmen envisaged general improvements in the human condition and significant changes in socioeconomic, political, and diplomatic relationships. Although their economic views, in particular, were usually not adequate to cope with altered postwar conditions, tremendous potential existed for the creation of an American-led world industrial community and for the coordination, under business-oriented politicians like Hoover, of the political and economic foreign policies of the United States. That neither potential was realized between 1920 and 1933 should not obscure the historical importance of the policies pursued. Most of them were the result of the climax in the Progressive movement reached under Wilson and of the impact of the world war. These two phenomena triggered speculation about and reevaluation of business ideas, bringing into clear focus for the first time many of the trends inherent in the actions and attitudes of businessmen and other groups in American society since at least 1900. The long-term influence of the Progressive movement in shaping some of these ideas cannot be underestimated, but it was World War I which made them realities for most businessmen and government leaders. This combination of war and reform thus set the stage for the 1920s to become the first modern decade of the twentieth century in domestic as well as foreign policy—a fact often overlooked because of the devastating impact of the Great Depression on these postwar policies.

Chapter Two

Disarmament & the Peace Movement, 1920–1933

Disarmament was a favorite, if futile, preoccupation of the American people for approximately fifteen years following World War I. Between 1918 and 1933 the United States government, with widespread public approval, participated in four disarmament conferences. Only two of these—the Washington Conference on the Limitation of Armament, 1921–1922, and the London Naval Conference of 1930—resulted in signed agreements between the participating nations. It is all too easy to dismiss these treaties for lack of enforcement provisions and the entire postwar disarmament movement for being predicated on the familiar but nonetheless fallacious assumption that there is a direct correlation between the accumulation of weapons and the likelihood of war.[1] Every peace movement no doubt contains too many people who mistake militarism, a symptom of political fears and economic rivalries, for the basic cause of war. This was certainly true in the 1920s. Saying this, however, does not negate the fact that for a time after World War I, disarmament agreements "founded upon a respect for treaty obligations and a belief in the good faith of contracting parties" was judged by many Americans as one of the necessary and practical steps for preserving peace.[2]

Of the four disarmament meetings to be discussed, the Washington Conference stands out as the most successful in the sense that it produced what probably amounts to the most comprehensive set of political and arms limitation agreements the United States has ever signed. The 1921–1922 session came at a unique time in the diplomatic history of this century: a time when the major military powers were not yet preoccupied with ideological considerations and so could negotiate with some modicum of mutual trust which avoided the problem of "international control and inspection"; and a time when their economies were not yet dependent upon defense production so that the question of actual arms reduction, in addition to future limitation, could be considered.[3] In other words, the Washington Conference occurred when modern diplomacy based on a combination of ideological and economic considerations was just beginning to take form; when a relative balance of economic and military power still existed among the leading nations; and when technology had not yet produced weapons which defied quantitative controls. Thus, limited disarmament in the early 1920s instilled more legitimate hope and was more popular among the masses than it has been since. Finally, since the American military-industrial complex was in a nascent state, the relationship of the business community to the disarmament movement presents an interesting contrast to what it has become today.

The most striking aspect of that relationship was the absence of organized business leadership before the Washington Conference met in November 1921. Not until September 27 did the board of trustees of the San Francisco Chamber of Commerce pass a resolution formally approving the arms meeting. When this belated resolution was submitted to other business organizations the response was quite favorable, especially in the western states of Washington, Oregon, Nevada, Arizona, and New Mexico. Also, business groups in Detroit, Minneapolis, Akron, Hartford, Paterson, N.J., Pasadena, Sacramento, Salt Lake City, Spokane, and Portland indicated support for the conference immediately before and during the time the delegates were negotiating in November. In addition, the conference was endorsed by the Associated Industries of Massachusetts and the National Association of Credit Men.[4] But such organized business *endorsement* of the Conference for the Limitation of Armaments should not be confused with organized business *pressure* in bringing about that conference. National business groups did not directly petition the executive or congressional branches of the government in favor of a disarmament conference between December 1920 and July 1921, when the women's and church groups in alliance with Senator William E. Borah were most eagerly trying to influence official action.[5] Also, a collection of the private appointments of Charles Evans Hughes for the years 1921–1923 does not contain any indication that representatives of national business organizations conferred with him about disarmament before either the preliminary or the formal invitations were issued in July and August, respectively.[6]

The same passivity was evident in business publications. Few carried articles supporting the idea of an arms limitation conference before the issuance of the preliminary invitations. After the major powers had indicated they would attend, the idea was endorsed by all the leading business journals, but even this support did not emerge in full force until September. Four major business publications which did comment on disarmament before the administration announced its plans for a conference were *Bradstreet's,* the *Bankers Magazine,* the *Wall Street Journal,* and the *Nation's Business.* Of these four, the first two initially expressed reservations about the feasibility of disarmament in the near future. In two February editorials, *Bradstreet's* questioned the validity of disarmament in view of contemporary world unrest, and then pointed out Harding's personal opposition to the idea of calling a special arms conference.[7]

The *Bankers Magazine,* on the other hand, emphasized that there was no inevitable causal relationship between armaments and war, saying:

> Quite properly . . . the enthusiasts for immediate disarmament are attaching altogether too much importance to navies and armies as provocatives of war. . . . The seemingly ineradicable propensity of mankind [for conquest], racial hatred, religious prejudices, national vanity, territorial greed, personal ambition, and trade rivalries —these are the causes of war about which no dispute exists. . . . Why then, should we give up that in which our security rests [that is, armaments] until these real and known causes of war are stamped

out or at least diminished until their dangerous responsibilities are reduced to a tolerable minimum?

This bankers' monthly went on to maintain that "a disarmament of the mind and heart of man" would have to precede any de facto reduction of armaments. As late as October 1921, it was stating that the time for disarmament was not yet ripe.[8] Despite these initial reservations, both of these publications later supported the results of the Washington Conference. But their early editorial comments did not lend support to the disarmament movement in the spring and summer of 1921.

The other financial publication to discuss disarmament before July was the *Wall Street Journal*. In the early months of 1921 the *Journal* did not specifically support the groups most actively engaged in petitioning Congress and the president, and was, moreover, editorially opposed to all of Senator Borah's postwar projects. While taking a strongly partisan stand against the call of the outgoing Democratic administration for increased naval building, the newspaper supported disarmament (under Republican leadership) consistently from December 1920 until the Washington negotiations ended in February 1922. This is somewhat surprising in view of the nationalistic position assumed by the *Wall Street Journal* on several other diplomatic issues of the decade, and probably resulted more from hostility to the disarmament endeavors of the League of Nations and from considerations of economy, than from any theoretical commitment to multilateral disarmament. Also, in the early 1920s the *Wall Street Journal* was not overly concerned with preparedness because it was convinced that England would never support the Japanese against the United States and that Russia would not be a powerful force in the immediate future. By 1927–1928 the growing military strength of both Japan and Russia led this publication to urge preparedness and to question the desirability of disarmament in terms of national security.[9]

A fourth major business publication to take up the issue of disarmament was the organ of the United States Chamber of Commerce. In May 1921, the *Nation's Business* carried an article entitled "Uncle Sam and Your Pocket Book," which graphically demonstrated that of the $53.46 that each man, woman, and child theoretically paid in annual taxes, $50.00 went for "war, past, present and to come."[10] While the article underscored the idea of economy, it did not advocate disarmament as such, nor a disarmament conference. As with the three other publications cited above, it can be concluded that while the *Nation's Business* chose this highly indirect way of making people aware of the economy which could be effected in the area of military spending, it did not lend significant support to the organized disarmament movement before the fall of 1921.

Individual businessmen were not as reluctant to speak out as were the national business organizations and publications. Prominent business spokesmen publicly supported the disarmament movement as soon as it began to coalesce around the Borah resolution at the end of December 1920. Much of the early personal support can be found in the *New York World,* which for two weeks beginning on December 26 carried numerous letters and telegrams in support of the Borah resolution and the principle of disarmament. Among the business leaders quoted by the *World* as expressing favorable opinions were: Bernard Baruch; Herbert Hoover; Otto Kahn; Oscar Straus; Cyrus H. McCormick; W. H. Hayward, president of the Baltimore Chamber of Commerce; Paul Warburg; Elbert H. Gary; James Bowron, president of the Gulf States Steel Company; George Foster Peabody; W. H. Crawford, manager of the Portland, Oregon, Chamber of Commerce; and W. D. Alexander, president of the National Screw and Tack Company. While all these men favored the principle of disarmament most of them did not specifically endorse an American-sponsored disarmament conference, and Straus, McCormick, Hayward, and Peabody explicitly stated that they favored disarmament under the auspices of the League of Nations.[11] Other prominent individual businessmen who spoke in favor of disarmament either before or after the Washington Conference began included: Edward N. Hurley, chairman of the United States Shipping Board; Fred I. Kent, vice-president of the Bankers Trust Company, N.Y., and chairman of the Commercial and Maritime Commission of the *ABA;* Charles M. Schwab; Thomas W. Lamont; J. P. Goodrich; Paul Warburg; Frank A. Vanderlip; T. Coleman du Pont; Pierre S. du Pont; John Hays Hammond;

George E. Roberts, vice-president of the National City Bank, N.Y.; and E. A. Filene, president of William Filene Sons and Company, Boston.[12]

None of these men testified before the House hearings held in January and February 1921, nor had they conferred with Secretary of State Hughes about disarmament before July. Aside from Hoover, none was in a key position to influence government action. And although Hoover was personally in favor of both land and naval disarmament, the Washington Conference was one of the few events of the decade about which the Department of Commerce did not keep the business community well informed. As late as September 1921, a representative of the American Bankers Association, unaware of the administration's plans to appoint an advisory group of prominent individuals, inquired about whether financial advisers would be needed for the sessions. Aside from a few letters after the conference began, there was almost no correspondence between Hoover and businessmen on the subject even though the Commerce department prepared the statistical data on economic conditions abroad for the highly publicized Advisory Board to the American delegation.[13]

The business community, therefore, did not in any sense lead the drive for arms limitation in the critical months before the Republican administration decided to call the Washington Conference. Businessmen ultimately proved receptive to both the principle of disarmament and the results of the conference primarily for economic reasons, but they played no significant role in bringing about the meeting. This generalization can be made also with respect to the three other major disarmament conferences held in the next twelve years.

In addition to this absence of leadership, it is worth noting that the business community did not divide along functional or sectional lines over the issue of disarmament in the early 1920s. These divisions did appear later during the disarmament conferences of 1927, 1930, and 1932–1934, but at the time of the 1921–1922 meeting most business groups were caught up in the worldwide reaction against wars and weaponry.[14] For example, financial, banking, export-import, manufacturing, and general business journals, organizations, and representatives all endorsed the opening of the conference and the treaties which resulted four months later. Following a characteristic practice on diplomatic issues, however, there was a noticeable absence of editorial comment in the United States Chamber of Commerce publication, the *Nation's Business*.[15] In contrast, the usually taciturn *Iron Age* and *American Industries* were quite vocal in favoring disarmament because they wanted to counter the suspicion that industry in general, and particularly companies associated with munitions and steel production, opposed the idea of arms limitation. In this effort *Iron Age* advantageously employed the prodisarmament statements of Charles M. Schwab and Elbert H. Gary.

Speaking at the twentieth general meeting of the American Iron and Steel Institute in November 1921, Schwab acknowledged that the Bethlehem works would lose money if a disarmament agreement was reached, but said "such a thing as financial loss can be of no consideration when compared to the inestimable boon to mankind which would be involved in the realization of that magnificent plan [Hughes's November 12 proposal to the Washington Conference]. What red-blooded American would not, indeed, make any sacrifice if the burden of armament could be lifted from the shoulders of humanity. . . . But . . . if the statesmen now assembled in Washington . . . should find it possible to bring about disarmament and permanent peace, gladly would I see the war-making machinery of the Bethlehem Steel Corporation sunk to the bottom of the ocean." Gary echoed his colleague at the same meeting and displayed his usual optimism by predicting that peace brought about through limitation of armaments "will mark an epoch of the greatest business prosperity, as well as the largest measure of happiness that the world has ever witnessed."[16]

Editorially, *Iron Age* pointed out that the steel in the thirty American vessels which Hughes proposed to scrap represented a scant 1.6 percent of the total 1920 steel output. Other pertinent statistics were used in an apparent effort to bolster the self-confidence of the steel industry as well as to appease hostile public opinion. It was emphasized that the steel industry had been built "on the pursuits of peace," and that the "prosperity of peace" was much more profitable in the long run than the "budgets of war." Despite these pronouncements, steel prices dropped on the stock market following the opening of the conference, thus revealing the ephemeral nature of the steel industry's prodisarmament arguments. By 1926 the steel spokesmen were expressing either indifference or hostility to the disarmament movement. Like other segments of business, steel producers had been temporarily repelled by the war, but were even less committed to drastic arms reduction than other businessmen. Sensing this, contemporary peace enthusiasts placed little stock in the altruistic statements issued by the industry in the immediate postwar years.[17]

The major attempt of the National Association of Manufacturers to clarify its position came in the November 1921 issue of *American Industries,* which was entirely devoted to the relationship of arms reduction to industry. This issue carried a total of 40 articles and statements by financiers, industrial leaders, statesmen, and editors. In the December issue four more opinions were printed, making a total of forty-four, only one of which could be considered unconditionally opposed to arms limitation within the limits of national security, and it was not from a businessman. *American Industries* concluded that the symposium had shown that all of the contributors agreed "that anything that insures the material limitation of armaments will free industry for the greatest era of prosperity and advance the world has ever known." A typical statement was made by W. O. Washburn of the American Hoist and Derrick Company, who wrote: "Forgetting all about humanity, which was done with remarkable success by all parties to the late war—forgetting all about humanity, war is bad business and bad for business. President Harding's Disarmament Congress is a practical attempt to relieve the world from the burden of taxation and apprehension which the modern war entails. In my opinion, it should have the active co-operation of every far-seeking business man."[18]

The predominant emphasis in the NAM symposium and in practically all of the business statements on disarmament was on the economic aspects of the problem. This preoccupation was one of the ways in which business opinion could be distinguished from that of the sectarian and humanitarian elements leading the disarmament movement in the United States. Both used peace and economy as the two major reasons for immediate arms limitation, but the churches, the women's organizations, and the civic groups naturally stressed the abstract goal of peace over economic expediency.[19] Altruism did not motivate the business world on this issue, nor did it often appear in the business rhetoric of the period. Businessmen looked upon disarmament almost exclusively as a business proposition from which they and the world stood to gain.

In particular, the business spokesmen anticipated a tax reduction from any multilateral agreement on arms limitation. It associated such a reduction with immediate economic recovery and future economic expansion. They maintained that anything which would curtail government spending, such as a cutback in military expenditures, was a prerequisite for relieving the heavy postwar tax burden. The *Coast Banker* predicted in August 1921 that if the Washington Conference resulted in a reduction of army and navy expenditures, "millions now being poured into the federal treasury will be available for industrial and commercial pursuits, and we shall have immediate revival."[20] Or as *American Industries* stated: "Every reduction in governmental expenditures . . . lessens the taxes imposed and adds a corresponding sum to the amounts available for business extension and improvement. . . . American industry will welcome practicable limitation of armaments as one step in the reduction of business-stifling taxes. All such reductions stimulate business enterprise, encourage production, decrease unemployment, and increase sales. The benefits of increased prosperity reach every corner of our land and bring confusion to the agitator and preacher of discord."[21]

At the same time arms reduction was considered important to businessmen for foreign as well as domestic economic reasons. Unsound currencies, unbalanced budgets, and the general European economic instability after the war were attributed in part to the maintenance of excessive military machines. A popular argument of the early 1920s stated that between 75 and 90 percent of the national budgets of the United States and other countries was used to pay off the expenses of past, present, and future wars. In this sense Germany was sometimes singled out as being fortunate, since the peace treaty prevented her from wasting resources and capital on armaments.[22] To some business internationalists, such as Frank A. Vanderlip, reduced military expenditures were a "prerequisite to stabilizing [foreign] currency." More generally, Bernard Baruch viewed the burgeoning arms race among nations as "a crime against humanity and civilization," which was postponing the constructive work of postwar reconstruction. Hoover was convinced that the money spent on naval armament alone following the armistice "would have contributed materially to the entire economic rehabilitation of the world." Even business nationalists, such as John Hays Hammond, spoke of the "economic waste involved in 'armed peace,' " and of the "insensate waste of the capital so greatly needed to rehabilitate industry . . . [and] indispensable to the welfare of civilization." By the fall of 1921 business nationalists and internationalists agreed that the postwar arms race was "essentially uneconomic" in terms of both American and European self-interest.[23]

In summary, the business world generally came to praise the Five Power Treaty for limiting battleship construction in the name of economy and specifically in the name of tax reduction, business recovery, and stabilization of economies at home and abroad. World peace was, of course, desired as well, but in the disarmament rhetoric of the business community it more often than not appeared as an incidental bonus or by-product of these economic goals. Businessmen were as tired of war as any other segment of the American population; however, they characteristically justified their position in terms of material expediency and their basic belief that international relations were "primarily commercial and economic relations."[24] Such a belief implied that peace was the result of economic prosperity and stability. Thus, the slowness with which organized business enthusiasm was generated for disarmament rested in the final analysis on whether or not the rank and file of businessmen were convinced that the purpose and accomplishments of the Washington Conference would be financially beneficial.[25] Since naval expenditures did somewhat cushion the postwar slump in 1920,[26] it was not until the summer and fall of 1921 that the economic benefits of disarmament became as clear to business and industrial associations as they had been earlier to a few farsighted business spokesmen. So for most businessmen it was the tempting prospects of tax reduction and business recovery from a depression which belatedly brought them into the peace and disarmament camp.

It is interesting to note that when H. G. Wells criticized Americans for supporting disarmament for mercenary reasons, the *Wall Street Journal* felt compelled to answer the charge. The exact reasons why people supported disarmament were irrelevant, according to a *Journal* editorial, as long as reduction was achieved "and carried out in good faith." With this and similar statements the *Journal* unconsciously laid bare the major fallacy in the business world's support of disarmament.[27] Since business support was almost exclusively economic it waxed and waned in direct relation to economic conditions in the United States. This meant that in the long run businessmen generally lost their enthusiasm for disarmament as the postwar depression vanished in the prosperous 1920s. Consequently, their primary reason for supporting disarmament in 1921 made them only temporary, foul-weather friends of the movement.

While the business community commented about disarmament mainly in economic terms, there was one economic aspect of the Washington Conference discussions which was less well articulated and understood by the average businessman than all others. It was summed up in the catch-phrase Open Door doctrine. Originally, at the end of the nineteenth century, this term had embraced two distinct principles based on the myth of the China market: commitment to the territorial and political integrity of China, and commitment to equal economic opportunity in that country. But by the end of World War I it was most commonly and most vaguely associated with commercial relations in the Far East.

A typical postwar inquiry to *Nation's Business* about commerce and the Far Eastern question to be discussed at the Washington Conference, read as follows: "Why is it that the discussion of economic issues in the Far East must precede disarmament? I'm just a plain business man, and if limitation of armament will reduce taxes I'm for it strong. But what has the 'Open Door' got to do with it? I'm free to own I don't know what the 'Open Door' is . . . . Can you tell me briefly what it is and what it has got to do with disarmament?"[28] And the typical answer was that the Open Door doctrine represented the desire on the part of America "to provide equality of commercial opportunity for all nations in China." Sometimes reference was also made to the enormous market potential of the Oriental nations, and to the spheres of influence of European countries, which were "contrary to sound business practice" and which contributed to "international friction and war." Thus the standard definition of the Open Door as carried in most postwar business journals argued in essence that disarmament would preserve the territorial integrity of China by weakening foreign spheres of influence in the Far East. This, in turn, would permit unlimited expansion of American trade in that region.[29]

In reality, by 1920 the Open Door policy of the United States was both narrower and broader than this standard business definition would indicate. It was narrower in the sense that it was often used to disguise American commercial designs in China and Manchuria and to defend, somewhat speciously, Russian sovereignty in Siberia. Since neither of these goals could be accomplished except at the expense of Japanese expansion in the areas concerned, international control of the Chinese Eastern Railway and Japanese withdrawal from Siberia and Shantung were the specific economic objectives of the United States at the Washington Conference. By 1921 the concept of the Open Door also encompassed very broad aims; defined by Wilson in the third of his Fourteen Points as "the removal, so far as possible, of all economic barriers and the establishment of an equality of trade conditions among nations." This very general American interpretation of the Open Door doctrine had been opposed by the Allied powers following the war because they realized that the United States was in a better position than they to compete for world trade. The Entente nations had hoped to control postwar commerce at the expense of all other countries, including the United States, by instituting a system of trade preferences among themselves.[30]

Given the powerful economic position of the United States after the war, any universal application of the Open Door doctrine would have logically led to American domination of world trade and finance. Naturally this goal of equal economic opportunity was supported by both Democrats and Republicans with general business approval in the early 1920s, yet none of these complex aspects of the Open Door policy was clearly presented in any of the major business journals when they discussed the Washington Conference. Although the term Open Door was frequently mentioned, it was almost never related to American-Japanese commercial rivalry in the Far East, to the danger posed by Japanese occupation of portions of China and Manchuria to American interests, or to the importance of the control of the Chinese Eastern Railway. Superficial treatment of the Open Door doctrine as it specifically related to postwar conditions in the Far East was especially evident in the publications that served the small or average businessman, such as *Nation's Business* and *American Industries.*

Such inadequate business coverage occurred in part because the economic details of the Far Eastern question were not publicized by the administration in the same flamboyant manner as were the disarmament features. Also, because these issues were so highly controversial, they tended to be discussed unofficially rather than at the scheduled meetings of the delegates. For example, a total of fifteen minutes was devoted officially to the subject of the Japanese occupation of Siberia. Through private negotiations, however, Hughes was able to secure from Japan a vague pledge to withdraw at an early date. While the control of the Chinese Eastern Railway was one of the most (unofficially) discussed topics at the conference, the official committee recommendation lamely suggested that the problem "be dealt with through proper diplomatic channels." Finally, the discussions which led to the separate Shantung Treaty signed by China and Japan never appeared on the public agenda of the conference. Ostensibly this treaty restored to China control of Shantung, but it proved to be of dubious practical value since the final terms allowed the Japanese to retain control of the important Tsinan-Tsingtao Railway for fifteen years.[31]

In retrospect it can be seen that the Washington Conference

accomplished little in the long run by way of strengthening the economic and political position of China or reducing the power of Japan in the Far East, despite the disarmament arrangements of the Five Power Treaty, the substitution of a Four Power mutual security treaty for the abrogated Anglo-Japanese Alliance, or the much heralded Nine Power Treaty which embodied an Open Door and effectively annulled the Lansing-Ishii Agreement of 1917. Regardless of these long-term deficiencies, the conference was judged a success by contemporary standards, largely because many limited goals were achieved. It did, for example, relieve the immediate and dangerous tension created by the postwar naval race; it improved political relations between the United States and England through the elimination of the Anglo-Japanese Alliance; it did allow China a little more time in which to put her house in order; and it did temporarily reinforce mutual trust and stabilize the existing balance of power between the major nations by making compliance with the treaties voluntarily rest on good faith and national honor rather than on inspection plans based on burgeoning ideological suspicions.[32]

Moreover, the conference accurately reflected the independent internationalism of the new administration, for it implicitly demonstrated to the world that the United States was willing to cooperate with other nations on arms limitation as long as it was done outside the auspices of the League of Nations and as long as the standard American diplomatic dicta about disarmament prevailed. It also reflected what Republicans believed to be a practical, as opposed to Wilsonian, approach to establishing the political harmony necessary for a world economic community. Unfortunately the Republicans placed too much emphasis on a single, spectacular solution. The Washington Conference was an impressive beginning to what appeared to be a reassertion of American diplomatic leadership after the failure to ratify the Treaty of Versailles.[33] But the effort was not sufficiently sustained or coordinated with other international problems for the United States to contribute positively to the economic and political reconstruction of the postwar world.

Thus, this first major diplomatic effort of the Republicans was a short-run success but a long-term failure which ended in widening the gap between the country's stated foreign policy goal of opening the door to a sovereign China, and the means it was willing to use to attain its objective. Secretary Hughes and others such as Hoover and Thomas Lamont hoped to rely on private economic cooperation between Japan and the United States in the peaceful, economic development of China. (See Chapter 7 below.) Except for very limited objectives the use of force was out of the question. Accordingly Hughes told the American delegation to the Washington Conference, "This country would never go to war over any aggression on the part of Japan in China . . . the most that could be done would be to stay Japan's hand."[34] In general American leaders in the 1920s shared this aversion to using force; the world community they wanted to create was to be based on the economic, not the military, superiority of the United States.

As it turned out, the most long-lasting achievement of the conference, at least from Secretary Hughes's point of view, was the incorporation of the Open Door doctrine in a multilateral treaty. By transforming what had been an expedient unilateral proclamation on the part of the United States at the turn of the century into what he thought was a binding international obligation, Hughes theoretically solved all of the economic and political foreign policy problems facing this country in the Far East. The combination of the Nine, Five, and Four Power agreements appeared to satisfy Japan's long-run aspirations while protecting China's territorial integrity and keeping the door open for American expansion. In practice, however, a codified Open Door doctrine created more difficulties in that part of the world than it remedied because the doctrine was violated more often than honored by most of the Nine Power signatories, including the United States. This was particularly true after 1929, yet successive secretaries of state continued to insist on the treaty's viability.

The potential significance of this codification of the Open Door doctrine, and the magnitude of the economic issues considered behind the scenes at the Washington Conference were recognized by only a handful of government officials, financiers, and international businessmen. The insights of this small group were not shared with the general public or the average businessman. But even these "insiders" could not possibly anticipate that more ideologically-oriented generations of the future would condemn these political and arms limitation agreements for not containing enforcement or inspection provisions. Such provisions were considered unnecessary or undesirable by leading American officials throughout the 1920s, especially after Soviet Russia came out in favor of them in the middle of the decade.[35] In view, therefore, of the ignorance of most businessmen about the economic and political realities which prompted the calling of the Washington Conference, it is not surprising to find most of them, along with the general public, approving of its results in terms of what they perceived to be their own immediate self-interests, that is, peace and economy, and in the name of the illusive Open Door.

Significant partisan opposition to the results of the Washington Conference came from a small, hard-core group of Wilsonian businessmen and politicians, headed by Norman H. Davis. Their criticism focused on the Four Power Treaty, which called upon the United States, Britain, France, and Japan to respect each other's rights and territorial possessions in the Pacific and to consult with one another in the event of "aggressive action" in that area. The Davis group considered this treaty a violation of the "entire spirit of the League of Nations" because it did not provide for "equality of rights and respect for the territorial and political integrity of all nations" interested in the Far East. Most Wilsonian internationalists, such as Davis, Newton D. Baker, George Foster Peabody, Bernard Baruch, and Henry Morgenthau, Sr., questioned whether lasting disarmament was possible until aggression was brought under control by the League and Article 10. They had supported the League "in order to do away with alliances and balances of power." Since the Four Power Treaty appeared to them to be an exclusive alliance, it not only contradicted the Open Door by creating a "sphere of special privilege," but also was the "direct antithesis of [international] cooperation."[36]

Davis personally carried his criticism of the treaty to the point of blaming it for precipitating the 1922 Rappallo Agreement between Germany and Russia. This had occurred, he explained, because the United States had tied itself to Japan and was indirectly encouraging the exploitation of Siberia by the Japanese, while

European nations were trying "to crush Germany and slice off portions of Russia." Under these circumstances the two nations naturally united. Although these Democratic internationalists gave qualified approval to the Nine and Five Power treaties, they generally opposed the entire conference as a "sporadic special effort" and a "partial and half-hearted step" on the part of the United States. In other words, the Washington Conference represented a piecemeal rather than comprehensive solution for preserving peace, to both these devotees of the League in the 1920s and a later generation of critics.

It is misleading to equate Democratic opposition to the Four Power Treaty with opposition from such extreme Republican nationalists as Hiram Johnson and William E. Borah, although they were political allies on this question. Democratic opposition did not represent a retreat from Wilsonian internationalism, which was based on the desire to create the machinery for securing peace in the Far East collectively for all nations, rather than for a privileged few who might exercise unilateral or bilateral force to protect their interests at the expense of others. In short, the Wilsonians viewed the Four Power Treaty as a poor substitute for the League of Nations. When the Senate approved the treaty there was little consolation for these Democratic internationalists even though twenty-three of the twenty-seven negative votes were cast by members of their party. The most positive view they could take was to hope that its passage would lead to greater international involvement and ultimately membership in the League.[37]

Generally speaking, approval of the three major treaties of the Washington Conference could be interpreted as a rejection of traditional isolationism in favor of economic internationalism based on a formal recognition of the Open Door, or as commonsense nationalism based on the demand for naval parity with England.[38] In any case, the nineteenth-century concepts of isolationism were found wanting as Republicans sought to satisfy both the internationalists and nationalists with an independent internationalist policy which would allow the United States to participate in world affairs and to protect her interests without joining the League of Nations or entering into bilateral alliances. The only significant division within the business community occurred over the Four Power Treaty, and it reflected a partisan struggle which separated Democratic business internationalists from their Republican counterparts. Business internationalists did not normally oppose one another over issues of political foreign policy in the 1920s, except on proposals which the Wilsonians deemed inadequate substitutes for the League, such as the Four Power Treaty and later the World Court and the Kellogg-Briand Pact.

While Republican politicians spearheaded the disarmament movement during the decade, they also heavily supported army and navy appropriation bills. This apparent contradiction was in line with the tradition that defense appropriation is supported more strongly by the party in power than by the one that is not. For example, the percentage of Democrats voting in favor of military bills after 1933 was greater than the percentage of Republicans, while the reverse was true for the years 1920–1933. Also, it should be remembered that support for disarmament in the 1920s, especially from businessmen, did not represent much outright pacifism. Organized business groups, like the two political parties, never pretended to support total or even partial disarmament at the expense of national security.[39] In fact, businessmen displayed a greater eagerness and efficiency when organizing against any drastic reductions in military personnel and materiel than they had originally shown for the Washington Conference.

As early as April 11, 1922, less than a month after the Senate ratified the work of the conference, the Chamber of Commerce of the United States began to study the naval requirements of the country. As a result of this inquiry, the board of directors of that organization submitted a report to President Harding, members of his cabinet, and the House of Representatives, recommending that naval personnel not be cut below the figure of 86,000 suggested by Harding and the Naval Affairs Committee of the House. In addition, the executive board of the chamber sent letters to chamber groups throughout the country asking them to consider the report and to inform their congressmen of their opinions. In May the tenth annual National Chamber of Commerce convention passed a resolution stating that the organization was against any reduction in the army and navy "below the strength

conservatively requisite for the preservation of national safety."
The resolution concluded with the now familiar words "adequate
military preparedness upon the part of the United States is the
best continuing guaranty of permanent peace."[40]

At the same time the influential Chicago Association of Commerce was organizing Illinois business groups against what it
considered the failure of Congress to appropriate adequate funds
for the navy. Joining in this campaign were the Illinois Chamber
of Commerce, the Illinois Manufacturing Association, and various
smaller business groups from the Chicago area. In support of the
Chicago movement, 100 chambers of commerce in the Mississippi Valley wrote letters to Congress protesting the proposed cut
in naval appropriations.[41] Although the editor of the *Army and
Navy Journal* exaggerated when he said that this action demonstrated that "the entire Middle West" was behind the Chicago
protest, the action did, nonetheless, represent considerable activity
on the part of business groups in an area traditionally considered
either apathetic or antipathetic to navy appropriations. What is
truly significant in this case is that congressmen from the Great
Lakes states and the Great Plains areas remained indifferent to
this and later preparedness agitation by business groups, and
consistently registered the least support for army and navy appropriations of any geographical section of the country between
1921 and 1933.[42] During this same period these congressmen
strongly supported all disarmament treaties. It would appear that
if Republicans and Democrats from the Middle West thought
they were representing public opinion in their home states by
voting against military appropriations during the "business
dominated twenties," they were ignoring business sentiment. This
is a good example of political leaders discriminating among the
various "publics" which form over foreign policy issues.

When the president of the National Association of Manufacturers also spoke out in favor of adequate preparedness in the
spring of 1922 he was expressing his organization's attitude as
well as his own. Writing in the May issue of *American Industries,*
John E. Edgerton stated that in the appropriations controversy
he favored the "judgment of naval experts rather than that of
legislators of limited experience." On his instigation thousands of

telegrams were sent to Congress from NAM groups all over the country. In fact, so consistently did the NAM oppose a cut in naval funds in 1922 that Admiral R. E. Coontz personally praised the organization for its support. It was a common practice both before and after 1922 for navy men speaking before the NAM to point out incidents taking place in remote areas of the world in which the United States navy had come to the aid of American trade activities. And of course NAM members were well aware that they could count on navy support in Congress for bills subsidizing the merchant marine.[43] Businessmen as individuals and in groups also supported the first and second Navy Day celebrations in 1922 and 1923, as well as subsequent ones in the decade.[44] This constitutes additional evidence that the business community was much more active and assumed more leadership in the preparedness campaigns following the Washington Conference than in the disarmament movement prior to the fall of 1921.

Such postconference activity did not mean that businessmen had been hypocritical in their earlier support of disarmament. But their support did prove ephemeral for various reasons. First, it was clear from their belated entrance into the disarmament movement and their preparedness activity following ratification of the Washington treaties that drastic and altruistic disarmament was never a goal of American businessmen. Aside from a few internationalists, their position had been reticent and conservative from the very beginning. Second, with the return of prosperity after the 1920–1921 depression, the immediate economic advantage of disarmament became a less important consideration. In fact, the tax reductions so desired by businessmen were ultimately obtained in the 1920s through Secretary Mellon's revenue bills, and were essentially unrelated to arms reduction.[45] Third, most of the controversial but unpublicized economic problems behind the Washington Conference were settled by the middle of the decade through independent negotiations among Japan, China, and Russia. The results were an indirect repudiation of the American attempt to institute an economic settlement in the Far East along the lines of the Open Door policy.[46] This, in turn, confirmed doubts among international financiers and businessmen about the efficacy of arms conferences in settling serious political and economic differences among countries. Fourth, the idea of the navy as a necessary peacetime protector of the largely expanded trade interests of the United States had become more entrenched within the business community by the end of the decade.[17] And finally, the 1929 depression was so severe that it did not conjure the same reactions from the business community as had the milder one at the beginning of the decade. Instead of making disarmament appear to be a major economy measure as well as an opportunity for worldwide political and economic cooperation, the Great Depression triggered international recriminations, suspicions, and economic withdrawal among businessmen. All this fostered nationalism and cautious preparedness rather than greater cooperative efforts toward disarmament.

This diminishing business support for disarmament and the general peace movement can be briefly traced by considering the business community's reactions to the disjointed government efforts represented by the Geneva Disarmament Conference of 1927, the Kellogg-Briand Peace Pact of 1928, the London Naval Conference of 1930, and the Geneva Disarmament Conference of 1932–1934. With respect to the 1927 gathering it can be stated that businessmen were not overly concerned with its failure, and in some instances had even presaged such an outcome. If anything, the deadlock at Geneva in 1927 confirmed their growing disillusionment with and indifference to the idea of peace through naval ratios.[48] Business organizations representing the small manufacturers and medium-sized businessmen in particular tended to ignore the embarrassing results of the 1927 conference. As noted above, this lack of diplomatic comment was characteristic of the various local and state trade organizations and general business groups. More vocal segments of the business community, such as the export manufacturers, considered the failure at Geneva insignificant since the likelihood of war with Japan was "remotely improbable" and with England was literally "impossible." Another argument of this economic faction was that land disarmament was "the real discouragement of war" since there was something in the "nature of navies which make more for peace than war."[49] (That "something" more often than not was the belief that the American navy served to protect commercial interests abroad.) Like government officials, these businessmen thought the greatest responsibility for arms limitation did not lie with the United States, but with the large land-army nations of Europe.

Financial and banking concerns, on the other hand, were less indifferent to the 1927 debacle, and at the same time were more knowledgeable about and more critical of the circumstances surrounding the conference. That it had been reduced to a three-power parley because of the refusal of France and Italy to accept President Coolidge's invitation did not augur well for success, according to *Bradstreet's* and the *Wall Street Journal*. Other representatives of the financial world criticized the lack of preparation for the conference by the State Department, and the predominance of naval officials among the various delegations. Most noteworthy, however, was the fact that some bankers and financiers had begun to question whether arms limitation offered the best means for insuring peace. Some reasoned that the stabilizing influence of the major nations would "decline with the abatement of their military and naval equipment," and that therefore further disarmament might not be desirable since it could "invite depredation by the enemies of civilization." Others were of the opinion that political, economic, and possibly even moral problems had to be worked out before arms limitation would be effective. This led a few Republican financiers to fall back on the Wilsonian idea of using the League facilities to obtain more political security for nations before proceeding with any more disarmament plans.[50]

To complicate matters there was sectional disagreement within banking and financial circles over the 1927 Geneva Conference. Publications in the Midwest were much more pessimistic and critical about the failure of the negotiations than eastern and southern banking journals, which reflected a more sanguine international point of view. Business statements from the Far West were more cynical about the whole idea of disarmament and strongly in favor of preparedness by 1927. In the blunt words of the *Coast Banker,* the prosperity of the United States precluded disarmament because "we owe a duty to ourselves and the world to safeguard our prosperity [from even] partial disarmament."[51]

This sentiment spread across the country during the Sino-Soviet conflict over the Chinese Eastern Railway in 1929 after Secretary of State Henry L. Stimson had futilely tried to bring the Kellogg-Briand Pact and the moral force of public opinion to bear in that controversy.

So by 1930 the business community was extolling the virtues of preparedness and denigrating arms limitation and the activities of pacifists more than at any time since the war. Preparedness propaganda appeared stronger in the statements and publications representing the moderately prosperous businessmen scattered throughout the country than in those of spokesmen for large firms, but this fact is somewhat misleading because it was the owners of the big industries who possessed the greatest knowledge about the government's military planning. For example, the number of articles and statements about national defense and the relationship between the navy and industry in peacetime rose steadily in nationalist business publications in the last half of the decade. In part, this was due to a concentrated effort by naval officers who spoke to numerous business groups about the importance of industrial preparedness (the ability of private industry to convert to wartime production), and the necessity for a strong navy to protect American commerce. This latter idea was so entrenched in military circles that even the advocates of air power were forced to accept it by the end of the decade.[52]

The War Department placed particular emphasis on industrial preparedness in the 1920s because it opposed the stockpiling of military weapons and supplies on the grounds that they would become obsolete before they were needed. Unlike other major nations the United States did not maintain arsenals in time of peace and so government officials deemed the conversion of private industry an absolute necessity in time of crisis. In 1927 it was estimated that it "would require an initial expenditure in excess of two billion dollars" to construct federal arsenals "to meet probable war requirements . . . under the War Department General Mobilization Plan." Such a "colossal expenditure" was considered unnecessary in this economy-minded period and so industrial preparedness was promoted instead. As a result the United States opposed all attempts at international meetings to place controls or limits on private production of munitions.[53]

A less publicized, but no less important, reason for growing business support of military and industrial preparedness was the quiet continuation of cooperation between businessmen and the War Department after the armistice. The relationship between the War Industries Board and army and navy personnel was far from perfect at the end of the war, but a working compromise had been reached in the area of military procurement that had not existed before. Then with passage of the National Defense Act of 1920 this wartime tie was institutionalized for peacetime purposes in the figure of a civilian businessman who, as an assistant secretary, would be in charge of the War Department's supply bureaus and military procurement. While this organizational change in itself did not immediately stimulate business interest in preparedness, it did provide the means throughout the decade for continued recruitment of business advisers to aid in updating the War Department's supply and procurement procedures. Literally thousands of individual businessmen were granted reserve officer commissions by the army and were given the opportunity through the Army Industrial College or the War Department's Business Council to realize their dream of greater cooperation with the government (discussed in chapter 1 above). Industrial preparedness, became, therefore, a common term within business circles by the end of the decade, although aside from Bernard Baruch, few prominent business figures publicized their role in military planning. Therefore it was not surprising to find General MacArthur, rather than an industrialist, lecturing the House Subcommittee on Appropriations in 1932 about how importantly the superior productive capacity of American manufacturers figured in the defense plans of the United States. The modern military-industrial complex was emerging, no doubt, but in a relatively unpublicized and unobtrusive manner despite several congressional investigations into the problem in the early 1930s.[54]

Following the 1927 Geneva Disarmament Conference, public indications of the changing business attitudes toward disarmament and the related peace movement were best reflected in the debates over the Kellogg-Briand Pact and the World Court. While all segments of the business community approved the pact, only the policy statements of the NAM and the United States Chamber of Commerce were entirely uncritical. Again, spokesmen for the financial and export manufacturing interests showed more sophistication in evaluating the attempt to renounce war than did other business groups. They made it quite clear that they approved of the Pact of Paris outlawing war only because it could "do no harm," not because they anticipated any concrete results from it. Neither the uncritical business nationalists nor the more skeptical business internationalists were leaders in the peace movement which led to the adoption of the pact. Furthermore, because of their heightened interest in preparedness, business nationalists in general did not see any contradiction in their endorsement of both the Kellogg-Briand Pact and the 1928 naval bill for increasing the number of American cruisers. At the same time, business internationalists publicly held the vague hope that the pact might stimulate world sentiment in favor of peace and disarmament,[55] while privately many of them continued to assist the War Department in its planning.

In contrast to its reaction to outlawing war, the business community was less divided and more actively involved in the promotion of the World Court idea throughout the decade. This represented a carryover from the prewar days when world court proposals and international arbitration, rather than disarmament, had been very popular among members of peace societies. Republican businessmen and lawyers had dominated these societies and many individual Republican business leaders continued to advocate a judicial approach to world peace after the war.[56] Business groups such as the United States Chamber of Commerce and the American Manufacturers Export Association consistently supported adherence to the World Court in the 1920s, and businessmen generally were convinced of the advantages of settling international disputes through a judicial body which would function "independently of governmental agencies." They also harbored the vague hope that somehow the World Court would be able to facilitate debt agreements between nations and create the "good feeling necessary for international trade."[57]

The establishment of the International Court of Business Arbitration by the International Chamber of Commerce at the end of 1922 further encouraged business support of the World Court until the Senate finally ratified the court protocol with five reservations on January 27, 1926. After members of the World Court refused to accept the fifth reservation, relating to advisory opinions, businessmen endorsed the new court protocol, which was drafted largely under the leadership of Elihu Root in 1929. Only the *Wall Street Journal* categorically opposed adherence before 1926, and even this nationalist publication acquiesced to Senate approval by saying that the reservations had made the court protocol innocuous enough to be acceptable.[58]

All three Republican presidents in the decade and their secretaries of state recommended adherence to the court. In particular, Kellogg and Stimson worked closely with Root to revise the statute of the court so that no advisory opinions could be rendered if the United States objected. Hoover, less enthusiastic about the World Court than his secretary of state, delayed presenting the "Root formula" to the Senate until after the 1930 Hawley-Smoot Tariff and the London disarmament treaty were approved by Congress. Despite what appeared to be a strong American consensus in favor of the court, and Hoover's assurance that adherence did not "constitute any entanglement in the diplomacy of other nations," the Senate took no action on this matter between 1930 and 1933.[59]

In defiance of the executive branch of the government, public opinion, the business community, and the prewar commitment of prominent Republicans to the idea of a World Court, William Borah led the Senate opposition in 1926 and again in the early 1930s. Two major arguments were employed by the anticourt group. One was that the court represented simply another scheme on the part of international bankers; the other denounced adherence as a "back door to the League." Aside from the *Wall Street Journal,* Republican business publications did not subscribe to either of these arguments.[60] The recalcitrance of some senators on this issue raises the question of how influential popular sentiment is in matters of foreign policy. There was no national organization supporting the anticourt senators, while there were numerous groups, including the United States Chamber of Commerce, which notified the Senate Foreign Relations Committee and the secretary of state of their approval. Quantitative studies have indicated that organized opinion groups have a better chance of influencing foreign policy when the issue involved has a low crisis level; that is, when the problem does not generate a critical situation demanding an immediate decision by the president.[61] The World Court was a noncrisis issue that proves the exception to this generalization because, despite organized and widespread public approval, adherence was never obtained.

The average Democratic businessman was much less enthusiastic about the World Court at the beginning of the decade than his Republican counterpart. By 1930, however, business nationalists of both parties were endorsing membership in the court. Nevertheless, Democratic internationalists voiced considerable partisan criticism of both the Kellogg-Briand Pact and the World Court because these two proposals seemed to be inadequate Republican substitutes for the League of Nations. As with the Four Power Treaty, the criticism was almost exclusively contained in the private opinions of a small, dedicated group of Wilsonians under the leadership of Norman H. Davis. By the last half of the decade, these Democratic businessmen and politicians had become more temperate in their public remarks than they had been in 1922 because support for their position had begun to wane among the rank and file of the party.[62]

For example, Norman Davis and other Democratic internationalists had agreed in 1923 that if the United States was unwilling to enter the League of Nations, it would be hypocritical to consider joining the World Court. But by 1930 they were urging adherence and had accepted the revised court protocol. They still maintained that membership would not produce the millennium predicted by some Republicans, but did admit by the end of the decade that it might have a "good psychological effect outside the country," and might even indirectly aid the cause of disarmament. Democratic internationalists continued throughout the decade to support arms limitation, but never gave up their conviction that genuine disarmament and peace would not come until political problems between nations were alleviated through international agreements involving the use of sanctions against aggressive nations. Consequently, they privately considered the Kellogg-Briand Pact a "mere gesture without courage," but they publicly supported it. Newton D. Baker probably best summed up the attitude of this group toward the pact when he said, "I am inclined to think we ought to join hands to get Kellogg's multilateral treaty approved by the Senate and to make at least that much progress assured, rather than endanger this step, little as it is."[63]

While a greater percentage of Democrats than of Republicans voted for both the World Court in 1926 and the Kellogg-Briand Pact in 1928, hard-core Wilsonians were far from completely pleased with these moderate, Republican-sponsored forms of internationalism.[64] To a lesser degree, the same was true of Republican internationalists within the business community. As a result, business internationalists, with few exceptions, found themselves increasingly outside of the peace and disarmament movement after 1922, insofar as its adherents professed to be pacifists or enthusiastically or uncritically endorsed the uncoordinated programs exemplified by disarmament ratios, the World Court, or the Pact of Paris. Even the less discerning business nationalists found it more difficult as the decade progressed to justify these means for preserving world peace on economic grounds, and so they followed rather than led mass opinion on these issues. Therefore, although in the prewar period businessmen had often dominated the various peace societies, in the 1920s they did not.

Before considering business reaction to the two disarmament conferences of the early 1930s, we must review Hoover's position. By the time he became president, his ideas on disarmament were clearly defined. Although he was extremely optimistic about the prospects for continued peace in 1929, he recognized that the Five Power Treaty of the Washington Conference had not stopped competitive building in auxiliary naval categories below the capital ship level. As a result he noted that there was naval "disparity not parity" between England and the United States. He further believed by the end of the decade that disarmament was necessary not only for economic reasons but also because it would bolster the Kellogg-Briand Pact. Yet he emphatically opposed using military or economic sanctions to enforce the pact. It would be, he said, "contrary to the policy and best judgment of the United States to build peace on military sanctions." And he deplored the hatred, demoralization, and starvation which had resulted from the use of economic sanctions during World War I. His opposition to economic sanctions to implement the pact was so firm that it survived contrary advice not only from Secretary Stimson, but also from the International and United States chambers of commerce and individual businessmen.[65]

Instead of considering military and economic sanctions, Hoover philosophized about the role of "public opinion of the neutral world" in maintaining peace and enforcing disarmament agreements. He realized, however, that the use of public opinion was limited to those issues which could be clearly presented in concrete terms. For example, it could easily be demonstrated to people that economic sanctions producing widespread starvation were wrong, whereas legalistic matters of foreign policy, such as freedom of the seas or debt payments, could not so easily be dramatized in black and white images. On the assumption that people everywhere could be rallied against the evils of armed aggression, he remained determined "to seek for methods to summon public opinion of the world in support of those nations which rely upon the pacific settlement of controversies."[66] As president, Hoover demonstrated more concern for the attitudes and role of the public on the disarmament question than he did on other controversial foreign policy issues, such as the tariff, debt policy, and the Manchurian crisis. Although he enjoyed personal popularity as secretary of commerce and as president before the depression, Hoover never pandered to popular sentiment. As an "engineer-businessman" turned politician, he usually talked about public opinion more than he based his decisions or actions upon it. In preparing for the 1930 London Naval Conference, however, he paid particular attention to newspaper surveys and national polls, and generally gave unprecedented consideration to public reactions when formulating disarmament policy. This was because the disarmament and peace movement had developed over the decade into a strongly organized, popular force, and because Hoover personally believed that moral sanctions based on public opinion constituted the best way to preserve peace abroad and domestic prosperity at home.[67]

The 1930 London conference was the last disarmament meeting of the period to receive widespread attention from the business community. Perfunctory and almost docile approval was expressed for the agreement determining cruiser ratios, even though it was usually acknowledged that few could understand its technicalities and that naval experts from all the nations involved disagreed over its military significance.[68] In part the docility was induced by the 1929 investigation of William B. Shearer's activities at the 1927 Geneva conference. Exposure of his pressure tactics on behalf of the shipbuilding industry, followed by Hoover's denunciation of such interference with international negotiations, led to a "discrete silence" even on the part of the Navy League lobby while the London conference was in progress. Former Secretary of State Frank B. Kellogg vehemently protested to Stimson in 1929 about the rumor arising from the investigation which implied that the Geneva conference had failed because of Shearer's actions. But Stimson and Hoover took advantage of the rumor to prevent any similar lobbying at the 1930 conference, and refused to acknowledge publicly Kellogg's explanation of the insignificance of the Shearer affair. While the Hearst papers, the American Legion, the Daughters of the American Revolution, the *Army and Navy Journal,* and the Council for the Prevention of War actively opposed ratification of the treaty, the business community quietly acquiesced to the administration's campaign in favor of passage.[69]

Despite general business approval of the London Treaty, Hoover had to call a special session of the Senate in July 1930 to obtain its ratification. Much of the criticism of the cruiser ratios from the Naval Board focused on the rather minor point of whether the United States should have been granted twenty-one instead of eighteen 10,000-ton cruisers with eight-inch guns in order to reach parity with England. Hoover pointed out that this involved less than 3 percent of the entire fleet, and that even the naval experts could not agree "on the relative merits" of the 30,000 tons of ships armed with eight-inch guns which the treaty did not accord the United States, and the 38,000 tons of ships with six-inch guns which it did. The most difficult feature of the treaty which Hoover had to try to explain to the Senate and the general public, however, was why the ratios agreed upon required the United States to increase rather than decrease its overall cruiser tonnage. To many in the antiwar movement this disarmament agreement encouraged preparedness, not peace. The reason was obvious, according to Hoover. The United States had "lagged behind" England and Japan in building cruisers since 1922 and must now catch up in the interests of national defense. At the same time he emphasized reductions in other naval categories.[70]

The business community was not disturbed by this apparent contradiction of a disarmament treaty requiring an arms build-up. The depression had prompted many businessmen to support the London Treaty in the name of economy, the main argument they had used in support of disarmament in 1921 and 1922. But it should be remembered that the rank and file of businessmen were also favorably disposed toward preparedness by the end of the decade. And as the depression worsened, the "huge sums" which the government was going to have to spend on cruisers to establish parity with England were eagerly anticipated as a stimulus to business. At the same time, the more internationally oriented segments of the business community began to link the disarmament proposals with the inter-allied debt question in a last desperate effort to strike a bargain with European countries. This was a particularly popular idea among large American banking interests, but was not taken up by the American government until the end of 1932. And since European countries had all along favored linking the war debts with reparation payments, nothing ever came of the disarmament-debt approach. Although they supported the treaty, business internationalists nevertheless continued to argue, as they had in 1927, that "other forms of rivalry between nations," such as shipping, tariffs, and financial and trade relations, "were more dangerous to world peace than naval armament."[71] The depression initially strengthened their commitment to this position, but economic nationalism ultimately triumphed in the early 1930s.

By the time of the 1932 Disarmament Conference at Geneva, Hoover was firmly committed to the limitation of land forces for economic reasons. The time had come, he told the United States ambassador to Germany in the spring of 1931, to convince the peoples of the world that the arms race in Europe was "at least one of the malevolent forces . . . producing and keeping up this depression." It is to his credit, however, that even in the midst of the depression he was able to perceive that land and sea disarmament was not the whole answer to world peace. In a memorandum to Stimson he said, "I recognize that armament is both a cause and effect of political instability and that while there are many points of political friction that need cure, yet they cannot be cured by any political agreements that the world is prepared to accept. But one of the contributions to the cure is the dissolution of fear which haunts the world as a result of its massed armaments."[72] As it turned out, it was economic rather than political instability which caused the 1932 Geneva Disarmament Conference to falter and finally collapse.

This economic complication was dramatized in the preliminary stages of planning for the conference when it became apparent that an economic conference at Lausanne would take place concurrently, and later when the 1933 London Economic Conference necessitated the temporary adjournment of the Geneva meeting. Thus, a series of overlapping events beginning with Hoover's debt moratorium on June 20, 1930, and the outbreak of war in Manchuria between China and Japan in September of that year, climaxed in 1932 with the proclamation of the Stimson Doctrine in January, the convening of the Geneva Disarmament Conference in February and of the Lausanne Economic Conference in June, and finally the November presidential election.

The complex relationship between the Geneva and Lausanne conferences was revealed in a series of transatlantic telephone conversations between Hoover and members of the American delegation to the disarmament conference. Hoover was aware that the European nations might use the Lausanne meeting, regardless of the actions of the Geneva group, to bring pressure to bear once again upon the American government for cancellation of the war debts. He was particularly concerned that this would, in turn, create resentment in the United States and threaten any agreements reached at the disarmament conference. Hoover made it clear in his talks with the delegation that if Britain sided with France at Lausanne and thereby endangered the negotiations at Geneva, the United States would be forced to play a more demanding role as the world's leading creditor.[73]

At the same time the president recognized the urgent need for "something big and definite" to be accomplished at Geneva. He wanted the conference to reach a quick settlement, not only to avoid pressure from Lausanne, but also because of the domestic political situation. If an agreement was negotiated before the Democratic National Convention, he was convinced it would prevent disarmament from becoming a political issue in the forthcoming election. And so to stop the conference from "dawdling" and force it to "come to realities," he proposed in June a one-third reduction of all "armies in excess of the level required to preserve internal order . . . [and] abolition of certain 'aggressive' arms." While Germany, Italy, and Russia accepted the idea, England and France procrastinated. As the Democratic convention approached, Hoover asked the Democratic members of the delegation, Norman H. Davis and Senator Claude Swanson, to use their influence to get a plank into the party platform approving of his one-third plan. Neither the Democrats nor the Geneva conference accepted this suggestion.[74]

At this point, however, Hoover was probably overestimating possible public reaction to both conferences. As early as April 1932, he had been informed of the "relative apathy among the American people" toward disarmament, and there is little evidence that the situation had changed by the summer months. The domestic impact of the depression, rather than the debt and disarmament questions, had become the major concern of most people. This was also true of most businessmen. Their interest in the protracted Geneva gathering between 1932 and 1934 was completely overshadowed by private economic problems and the first New Deal legislation. The strongest reaction Hoover received on the question of armaments came from aircraft and munitions manufacturers when he proposed discretionary arms embargo legislation to Congress at the end of 1932. These specialized industries, supported by the commerce department, argued that such action would not restrict foreign hostilities because any curtailment of arms shipments from the United States could readily be replaced by European competitors, and in the process American unemployment, already acute, would rise, especially in a number of cities in New England, New York, Ohio, and Illinois. Spokesmen for this segment of the business community consistently opposed all arms embargo legislation in the 1930s. Before 1933, however, most nationalist business publications prudently ignored this issue and simply reiterated earlier positions on disarmament, and most of them did not bother to comment on the demise of the conference in the spring of 1934. By that time business internationalists had lost all hope that a bargain involving inter-Allied debts and disarmament could be worked out. Their earlier suspicions about the inability of disarmament to insure peace and economic stability seemed totally confirmed.[75]

In summary, there was probably more sustained business activity and leadership demonstrated for preparedness than for disarmament after 1922. Never leaders in the peace and disarmament movement, businessmen had been initially stimulated to support it by vague sentiments about peace and internationalism, which accompanied the transitory antiwar outburst in the early 1920s, or by postwar ideas about economizing. Consequently in the absence of a comprehensive government plan for world disarmament following the Washington Conference and in the presence of strong government endorsement of industrial preparedness and a strong navy for commercial protection, it is no wonder that business interest in disarmament diminished as the prosperity of the 1920s and cooperation with the War Department increased. This marginal interest finally disappeared altogether after 1933 as a result of the political and economic nationalism stimulated by the depression and the rise of military dictatorships.

Chapter Three

American Commercial Policy, 1920–1933

Since foreign trade was considered essential to continued domestic prosperity,[1] the major international economic problems which concerned the American business community in the 1920s were tariff policy and foreign loans and investments, along with the related issues of intergovernmental debts and German reparation payments. These topics were intimately connected with the expansion of American markets abroad, and prominent businessmen considered all of them when they formulated plans for the reconstruction of Europe. Debate within the business community began on two of these issues, the tariff and foreign loans, immediately after the signing of the armistice, and opinions were clearly defined by the end of 1919. While the Edge Act of that year temporarily settled the loan question by endorsing the principle of privately financed foreign trade, action on permanent tariff revision was postponed while the Senate considered the Versailles Treaty, farm-relief legislation, tax revision, and the soldier's bonus.

As a consequence of this delay the tariff theories held by business groups in 1920 were subjected to reconsideration and modification in light of the increasing fear of foreign competition, the continued demand for high duties to protect the "war baby" industries, the financial clauses incorporated in the peace treaty, the intensified struggle between nationalists and internationalists over economic foreign policy, the return to power of the Republican party, and depressed prices following the war, especially for agricultural products. One result of all this was the national-istic reversion to excessive tariff rates in the decade following the war. But during the same period the United States government officially adopted an unconditional most-favored-nation position and opposed quantitative restrictions (import quotas) for pro-tective purposes. Both these internationalist practices continued to influence American commercial policy long after the high Republican duties of the 1920s were abandoned.

The congressional debates and hearings over the Fordney-McCumber bill reflected almost all of the various aspects of this postwar reevaluation of tariff policy. In its final form the 1922 tariff represented a compromise between the two major divisions within the business community. On the one hand, business nationalists were pleased with the return to high duty provisions, insisting that tariff protection was strictly a domestic concern independent of foreign conditions or attitudes. Business inter-nationalists, on the other hand, cognizant of the impact tariff duties had not only on the American economy but on world trade balances as well, favored moderate rates, at least until Europe returned to the gold standard, in order to prevent flooding the domestic market with cheap goods from countries having de-preciated currencies. Most importantly, they thought that moder-ate rates would encourage the acceptance abroad of uncon-ditional most-favored-nation clauses in commercial treaties and thereby aid American trade expansion all over the world.[2] Thus, business internationalists supported the so-called flexible pro-visions of the 1922 tariff because they hoped the president would use them to lower rates and to encourage greater equality of treatment abroad, that is, an Open Door, for the United States. To understand how these nationalist and internationalist views were woven into the Fordney-McCumber Act it is necessary to analyze tariff opinion within business and government circles at the end of the war.

Representatives of both parties and the business community agreed by 1920 that the expansion of United States trade which had resulted from the war should be maintained in the face of revived competition from the Allied and Central powers. In the most general sense this meant that even the Democratic administration no longer viewed the tariff as a means for revenue only. Rather, as Wilson told the Illinois Manufacturers' Association, the tariff was related to "the large world of international business," and duties should be flexible and scientifically devised for "facilitating and helping business and employing to the utmost the resources of the country in a vast development of business and enterprise." This position was reaffirmed by various spokesmen for government and business who addressed the annual conventions of the National Foreign Trade Council (NFTC) on the topic of postwar trade between 1916 and 1920.[3] While all agreed future tariffs should be scientifically designed to promote trade abroad in addition to providing some protection for home markets, there was no consensus on exactly how this should be accomplished.

By the beginning of the 1920s the term "scientific tariff" technically meant a tariff "removed from politics." This usually referred to taking the rate-making process out of the hands of Congress and placing it in the keeping of a nonpartisan, independent investigatory agency. Unfortunately for the Progressive members of Congress, who were the strongest advocates of such tariff reform before the war, even their low-duty tariff of 1914 did not prove to be above political and economic machinations.[4] And tariff legislation continued to be subjected to logrolling and lobbying long after the Progressives created a permanent tariff commission in 1916. So every time a general, scientific tariff revision was proposed in the decade following World War I, there was much uneasiness and speculation within the business community and complaints about disturbed business conditions because no single, scientific means for determining duties could be agreed upon.[5]

To complicate matters, business and government officials disagreed over two types of scientific tariffs. The one favored by protectionists was the "special bargaining" or negotiable tariff based on bilateral commercial concessions like those found in the reciprocity treaties of the nineteenth and early twentieth centuries. According to a 1919 report by the Federal Tariff Commission, these early reciprocity agreements were characterized by each party's making "special concessions to the other with the intention that the transaction shall be looked upon as a particular bargain and with the understanding that its benefits are not to be extended automatically . . . and freely to other states." With minor variations this type of restricted reciprocity remained a standard feature of American tariff policy from 1778 until the outbreak of World War I. It was rooted in intense economic nationalism and the desire to obtain maximum advantages for the United States. Every concession or special arrangement granted under reciprocity treaties became "in effect a penalty upon the commerce" of all other countries, unless, of course, the concession was "generalized" through the unconditional application of the most-favored-nation principle.[6] Since the United States prior to 1922 rarely employed the unconditional form of this principle, the Federal Tariff Commission concluded that businessmen and politicians, while theoretically favoring the idea of obtaining equality of treatment, had in fact "contended for equality of opportunity to bargain [that is, negotiate], but not for identity of treatment; for the removal and prevention of discriminations, *but not for the same terms to all States at all times* and in relation to all trade." In addition, the concessions offered by the United States in these early reciprocity treaties were exclusively for noncompetitive articles. While American tariff policy before 1922 was considered negotiable, the effects of such negotiation were negligible.[7] For the most part, therefore, the end product of the country's reciprocity arrangements was inequality rather than equality of treatment because of the conditional application of most-favored-nation clauses and the use of the "concessional method," which in essence penalized all nations with whom bilateral treaties had not been negotiated.

The other kind of scientific tariff was dimly foreshadowed in the protectionist tariff of 1909, but began to come into vogue among internationalists during World War I. It embodied the concept of nonnegotiable flexibility determined by prescribed formulas rather than that of bargaining for special concessions.[8] By 1920 this type of tariff found support among those who favored trade expansion based on equality of treatment for American exports as well as among those who were simply interested in strict equalization of the costs of production at home and abroad. Supporters thought these basically conflicting goals could be achieved by empowering the president to lower or raise duties within limits prescribed by Congress, or to take other administrative action, in order to offset all foreign discriminations against American goods, ships, or citizens and to equalize foreign and domestic costs. Although this method appeared more aggressive or combative in principle than the more traditional concessional method, the Federal Tariff Commission noted that "it should be borne in mind that when additional duties are put into effect solely for the purpose of securing equality of treatment, and are therefore subject to termination as soon as such treatment has been attained, they can hardly give reasonable ground for complaint."[9]

While the flexible tariff was technically compatible with either protectionist or free-trade assumptions,[10] extremely high duties could not be considered strictly in keeping with the flexibility theory, since the idea of equality of treatment was based on the belief in ever-expanding markets abroad. This belief, in turn, stemmed from confidence that the United States could "hold its own or perhaps excel others in all markets where goods are not discriminated against—that is to say, where they are accorded most-favored-nation treatment." It followed that consistent and intelligent adherence to a scientific, flexible tariff demanded a belief in moderate or low tariff duties, because commitment to such a tariff policy obligated "the nation proclaiming it to refrain from discriminatory practices in regard to its own markets."[11] Since the Democrats were traditionally associated with lower tariff duties than the Republicans, it was natural that the Federal Tariff Commission and other proponents of moderate rates and flexible provisions for promoting an Open Door commercial policy appeared to have more influence with the Wilson administration by the end of the war than did the protectionists. Such a tariff was the perfect economic complement to the political internationalism embodied in the League of Nations and provided a possible means for bringing other nations into line with the new economic position in which the United States found itself after the war.[12]

Tacit as it was, this fragile tariff understanding between the executive branch of government and the financial and big business interests, represented primarily by the NFTC, carried over from the Democratic administration of Woodrow Wilson to the Republican administration of Warren G. Harding. In his first annual message to Congress, Harding called for tariff "flexibility and elasticity," saying that adjustable rates were necessary "to meet unusual and changing conditions which cannot [now] be anticipated." In this message and in a later letter to Senator McCumber he stressed the antinormal commercial conditions of the postwar years and recommended that the powers of the Tariff Commission be enlarged.[13] Business internationalists agreed with the president's proposals, as far as they went, but, as a group, they wanted more assurance that flexibility would mean the downward revision of rates that proved higher than necessary and that endangered foreign acceptance of the most-favored-nation principle. Also they were less committed to the "equality of cost" concept than was Harding.[14]

Having survived the controversy over the economic provisions of the Versailles Treaty and the election of 1920, the government-business understanding on tariff policy received a serious setback during the 1920–1921 depression, and gradually succumbed in the course of the decade to a coalition of protectionist elements within the nationalist wing of the business community, Congress, and the executive branch. Defeat of the internationalist point of view on the tariff came by degrees. Beginning with the postwar depression and the passage of the Emergency Tariff Act in 1921, this defeat was hastened by the contradictions of the Fordney-McCumber tariff, by the failure of President Coolidge to push for lower rates under its flexible provisions, and by the inability of the State Department to obtain foreign agreement to unconditional most-favored-nation treaties. Final defeat came during the depression of 1929, when President Hoover publicly sided with business nationalists in favor of continued high duties.

The first postwar depression of the early 1920s set in motion this process of disintegration. One of the direct results of that period of deflation was the Emergency Tariff Act of May 1921. Wilson, resisting rising protectionist pressure, had vetoed a similar bill in March. In doing so he was falsely accused of being a "free trader" by proponents of the measure because he employed an argument with which the financial and import-export elements of the business community were in complete agreement. His argument was based on the ideas that to sell abroad the United States had to buy, and that high duties at home were injurious to American markets in foreign lands and prevented payment of the war debts owed to the United States.[15] Harding, taking office shortly after Wilson's veto, proved less impervious to the demands of midwestern farmers and traditional Republican protectionists than the Democratic president had been, much to the irritation of the influential segment of the business world represented on the National Foreign Trade Council.

This temporary defection of the executive from the ranks of the moderate tariff advocates resulted in the unscientific, inflexible Emergency Tariff Act. It was a depression-born tariff with high duties covering certain agricultural products "to meet present emergencies." Farmers, however, were not the main beneficiaries of the act, although Republican protectionist propaganda by 1921 had finally convinced them that they would be.[16] In practice, Title II, which contained anti-dumping provisions, and Title IV, which placed a temporary embargo on foreign dyes and chemicals, benefited the small American manufacturer more than the produce and livestock duties of Title I aided the American farmer.

The extreme protectionist position of the domestic manufacturer and his stake in the Emergency Tariff were clearly demonstrated at Senate hearings in the debate over the currency conversion section of the bill. Originally, House Bill No. 2435 contained an exchange equalization provision which would have authorized the secretary of the treasury to reevaluate foreign goods entering the United States when he became convinced that the currency of the country producing the goods had depreciated 66⅔ percent from the normal rate of exchange. This provision was strongly endorsed by young "war baby" companies that had organized during the war to replace products formerly imported from the Central Powers. A typical representative of these companies was the Doll and Stuffed Toy Manufacturers' Association of New York. The provision was just as strongly opposed by import-export associations, such as the newly formed

National Council of American Importers and Traders.[17] The latter argued that by arbitrarily setting a limit on the amount of depreciation which could take place, Congress would in effect be placing additional duties on all products of Italian or Central European origin. Since it was unlikely that the exchanges of any other countries would fall below the limit of 66⅔ percent, enforcement of such a provision would undermine America's aim "to grant equal opportunities to all countries." For example, it was estimated that the increase in duties would range from approximately 1.4 times normal on all Italian products to 61 times normal on Polish imports.[18] To men such as Thomas J. Doherty and Arthur Dunn, who represented importers and exporters across the country, both the exchange equalization provision of Title IV and some of the high agricultural duties of Title I amounted to placing embargoes on certain foreign products and would adversely affect American markets abroad.[19] This argument was used also by financial publications and bankers who opposed the Emergency Tariff bill as well as by large American firms that utilized imported goods, such as Colgate and Company, Metcalf Brothers and Company, W. R. Grace and Company, and the Federal Sugar Refining Company.[20] Obviously such companies opposed the Emergency Tariff bill as much out of self-interest as out of their commitment to internationalism in economic foreign policy.

On the other side of the issue, H. D. Bowie, testifying on behalf of the Doll and Stuffed Toy Manufacturers' Association of New York, emphatically insisted that "If there ever was a time when there was an emergency, if there ever was a time when something ought to be done it is now. . . . The question is to keep out German goods, at least to the extent where we can fairly compete with them. . . . We need something . . . some emergency measure that will drive the American buyers back to the American manufacturer."[21] Of the twenty-one men who testified at the April hearings conducted by the Senate Finance Committee, fifteen were in basic agreement with the case presented by Bowie. This same attitude was reflected in *Iron Age,* the magazine representing "independent" iron and steel firms. Such companies were more strongly in favor of a protected home market than United States Steel, the undisputed leader of the industry.

Ultimately, the high agricultural duties of the Emergency Tariff remained in the final draft of the bill, while the exchange equalization provision (along with another protectionist feature—American valuation) was eliminated by the Senate as requested by the Tariff Commission. The *American Economist* explained that House protectionists yielded to the Senate on these points in the spring of 1921 because the "emergency bill mattered little." In other words, House protectionists fully expected to obtain their original goals in the permanent Fordney-McCumber legislation, in part because they were counting on collecting a political debt from the farm representatives whose areas were supposedly the beneficiaries of the emergency bill. Before 1921, congressmen from agricultural constituencies had traditionally exercised a moderating influence on those in favor of high duties for manufactured goods. Now the farm representatives were also caught up in the logrolling process so characteristic of congressional tariff making. Thus, according to the *American Economist,* the amended Emergency Tariff Act did not represent the influence of the testimony of importers and exporters, or the advice of the Tariff Commission, so much as it represented a tactical retreat on the part of House and Senate protectionists.[22]

With Harding's blessing, Republican congressmen overwhelmingly approved a measure which had nothing in common with the international or Open Door approach to world trade based on flexible provisions. In the Senate, 97.7 percent of all Republicans voted for the measure, while House Republicans turned in a vote of 98.4 percent. An unusually large number of Democrats, yielding to agricultural pressure, followed suit, despite the opposition Wilson had expressed for a similar bill before he left office. A little over 19 percent of the Democratic senators and 11 percent of their colleagues in the House voted approval. Both of these percentages were higher than the Democratic vote for either the 1922 or the 1930 tariff.[23]

The Emergency Tariff of 1921 constituted a setback in the realm of tariff cooperation between the executive branch of government and the large financial and trading elements of the business community. Calling the upward trend of the emergency duties an "inexcusable blunder," A. Barton Hepburn of the Chase National Bank pointed out that the Republican platform of 1920 had re-

frained "from any definite commitment of the party on an early increase in tariff rates."[24] The act can only be interpreted as an almost
hysterical reaction on the part of Congress, farmers, medium-sized
domestic manufacturers, and government representatives in the
wake of war and depression.

The battered tariff understanding between the executive branch
and big business had much more practical and productive sig-
'nificance with respect to the major tariff revision which took place
in 1922. Nonetheless, the financial, import-export, and large
manufacturing concerns of the country still had to share the
Fordney-McCumber legislation with Republican protectionists.
The result was high tariff duties and flexible provisions which
authorized the president to raise or lower tariff duties up to 50
percent ad valorem in order to equalize the difference between
domestic and foreign costs of production (Section 315), and to
exclude entirely or to impose penalty duties up to 50 percent ad
valorem on any product to offset discrimination or unfair competition on the part of foreign nations or their citizens (Sections
316–317). Clearly the Fordney-McCumber tariff was a contradiction in theory and practice. Section 315 was never effectively
employed in the 1920s to counter the effect of the import
schedules and of almost a dozen differential duty clauses placed
in the original legislation. Since the same contradictory combination of high rates and flexible provisions was included in the
Hawley-Smoot tariff of 1930, the following analytical generalizations apply to both acts.

As a part of the country's economic foreign policy, the
American tariff normally represents a noncrisis issue. Such economic issues can be more readily influenced by pressure groups
outside of the government than those foreign policy problems
which have a high crisis level. Of all the foreign policy pressure
groups, those who concentrate on specific economic matters, such
as the tariff or foreign investments, have a better chance for
success than those groups who champion broad political problems,
such as war and peace. Although it is extremely difficult for any
organization of citizens to influence foreign policy, the less important the issue and the lower its saliency, the greater the chances
for group influence.[25]

The most effective lobbyists on the tariff in the 1920s represented small and medium-sized companies, and they dominated the tariff hearings held before the House Ways and Means Committee and the Senate Finance Committee. Of all those testifying at the 1921–1922 and 1929–1930 Senate tariff hearings, only two were major business figures.[26] At these hearings the small or medium-sized domestic manufacturers and agricultural producers constituted the "greatest devotees of the tariff," while import-export organizations, supported by large manufacturing companies which used imported material in their operations or had subsidiaries or markets abroad, were either conspicuously absent or formed the opposition.[27]

This dimensional and functional division over tariff policy was more sharply defined after the war than before because of several major changes in the postwar economic position of the United States. These changes were recognized first by the internationally-oriented groups within the business community, and led them to conclude that the traditionally high American tariff and conditional application of the most-favored-nation principle were obsolete. First, the United States was no longer a debtor nation. Second, half of the country's exports now consisted of manufactured goods. Both these facts encouraged European nations to begin to discriminate against American exports, especially if they considered the tariff rates of the United States too high. However, in the absence of an international gold standard, some protection was necessary in the immediate postwar years. Hence business internationalists decided that moderate duties accompanied by flexible provisions and an unconditional adherence to the most-favored-nation principle constituted a better way to stabilize prices, to prevent future discrimination, and to promote trade in the name of the Open Door, than the high duties and restricted reciprocity approach of the past. Thus, the division within the business community over tariff policy was greater after the war because the drastically altered balances of payments between nations were not equally appreciated by all businessmen. With only slight exaggeration, therefore, Senator David I. Walsh of Massachusetts said that the testimony on the 1922 tariff revealed "for the first time in American history [that] the representatives of great big business are here asking for the lowering of rates and the representatives of small business . . . are asking for excessively high rates."[28]

One indirect result of this division over tariff policy was the literal paralysis of the general business associations during the struggle in Congress over rate schedules. Neither the Chamber of Commerce nor the NAM sent representatives to testify at the 1921–1922 hearings, and in 1929 their representatives limited their remarks to the administrative rather than the rate provisions of the proposed bill. In contrast, specialized trade associations, whose status had been improved during the war by the War Service Committees, operated with highest efficiency during the tariff hearings in the 1920s. The major cotton manufacturers' associations, for example, formed a special Consolidated Committee to prepare briefs and duty schedules. In 1922, members of this committee not only testified before congressional hearings on behalf of all textile producers in the country, but also met privately with congressmen. Cotton manufacturers were generally quite pleased with the Fordney-McCumber tariff and continued to secure high duties for their industry throughout the decade.[29]

The division within the business community over tariff policy also resulted in an uneven contest. On paper the two sets of opponents appeared somewhat evenly matched. In practice they were not. The odds were all on the side of the medium-sized domestic manufacturers and the producers of raw materials. Noting this fact, the *American Economist* smugly commented that "there is apparently a feeling among many of the [Senate] Committee members that when importers complain . . . the proposed measure must be of real value to American industry, and the importers do not often obtain many of the changes that they ask."[30] A more likely reason why the import-export groups had so little influence at these tariff hearings stemmed from their position within the business community and from the peculiar difficulty they had in explaining their stand on the American protective system.

For example, the importers' organizations often represented limited geographical areas, such as the Foreign Commerce Association of the Pacific Coast, or the National Council of American Importers and Traders. The latter organization was established hastily in the spring of 1921 to oppose the Emergency Tariff. At that time the director of the new group, Thomas J. Doherty, testified before the Senate Finance Committee that the National Council represented 275 members, most of whom were located in the New York area. Under questioning from Senator Boies Penrose, Doherty insisted that "the potential members run into thousands," and that even though the organization had only been in existence a month, it had members in Chicago, New Orleans, Minneapolis, Indianapolis, and St. Louis. Eight years later the composition of the organization had not substantially changed, for out of 493 members only 39 were listed as having headquarters outside of New York City.[31] Such geographical concentration obviously limited the national influence and appeal of importers, as House and Senate committee members were well aware.

In addition, importers lacked "nearly all the means to power possessed by manufacturers" because they seldom represented any great investment of capital and could not point to a large number of domestic industries that depended on them.[32] Finally, the fact that importers were looked upon as outsiders limited their influence at congressional hearings. They were outsiders in the sense that they were not as well informed about the process of tariff making or about the briefs and proposals presented at the hearings as were the professional lobbyists representing various independent domestic manufacturers and trade associations. Importers commonly complained during the hearings held before both the Fordney-McCumber and Hawley-Smoot tariffs were passed that they were insufficiently informed about opposing briefs or proposed rate increases. According to Thomas J. Doherty, his group had little time to prepare for the hearing in April 1921. In fact, when testifying on Friday, April 22, he complained that "it was not until Monday that I had assurance that we would be able to be heard."[33] Such statements did not appear in the testimony of the "insiders," that is, the professional lobbyists for high rates who had not only years of experience with tariff-making procedures but also direct information and aid from congressmen identified with certain economic interests in their states.

At the same time, importers and all others who testified in opposition to high rates were automatically considered "outside" the normal protectionist consensus of the country in the 1920s—a consensus fostered first by postwar nationalism and later by the 1929 depression. The importer, in particular, was commonly thought of as the "agent of foreign interests" and a "potential malefactor," or was described as making extremely high profits by being the "man whose chief interest is in bringing the products of cheap foreign labor to the American market."[34] More often than not the importer was questioned by hostile and antagonistic congressmen. The tariff hearings convey the distinct impression that while importers were permitted to testify they were not really listened to by most committee members.

This tacit dismissal of the testimony of importers and company representatives in opposition to higher rates left these men in a particularly pathetic position at congressional hearings. Although they criticized portions of the proposed tariff bills they also felt compelled to reiterate their basic belief in the protective system. On August 2, 1921, Doherty was asked by Senator James E. Watson of Indiana if he was a free trader. When he denied this, he was asked if he was a protectionist, and his answer was: "I am. I am a straight-out Republican, and expect to continue to be one and I am a protectionist. But I do not believe in any more prohibition than we have now."[35] According to a telegram presented at the same hearing by Thomas H. Eddy, representing Marshall Field and Company, a group of Chicago bankers and merchants tried to make it clear that they believed "in a fair measure of protection to American industries," but they opposed the American valuation provision of the Fordney bill because it was "designed solely in the interest of the domestic producer who fixe[s] the amount of duties his competitor is obliged to pay."[36] Or as Ward Thoron, treasurer of the Merrimack Manufacturing Company, said in opposition to the proposed dye embargo: "we feel they [the dye manufacturers] ought to be protected. Our quarrel is not over the question of protecting them . . . but to the way in which they want to be protected."[37] These professions of faith in the protective system, true as they were, did not ingratiate importers or manufacturers whose enterprises depended upon foreign raw materials with congressmen. Such statements seemed instead to compromise their opposition to the particular rates and provisions which had prompted them to testify in the first place.

The disadvantageous position of importers and other proponents[38] of low or moderate tariff rates was aggravated by the apathy of most businessmen toward tariff revision as long as their particular interests were not adversely affected by the high duties being proposed. The tariff internationalists were also victims of certain congressional procedures. Tariff hearings were not sufficiently publicized, information about duties was not equally available to all those testifying, and the protectionist lobbyists who dominated the hearings were usually favored by individual congressmen on the investigating committees. There is little doubt that the rate-making process of the 1920s reflected no credit upon the legislative system.[39] Nonetheless it provides an excellent example of the intricate relationship between congressmen, the executive branch, and special interest groups. It also represents nationalist influence over economic foreign policy at its worst.

Although congressional hearings provide one of the best sources for distinguishing the functional and dimensional split within the business world over tariff legislation, they do not adequately reflect the opinions of those international bankers and export firms or large exporting manufacturing companies that did not testify. From the proceedings of the National Foreign Trade Council, financial publications, and private statements, it is clear that these economic groups tried to hold a middle course on the tariff in the interest of international cooperation. They were for neither free trade nor high protection, but for keeping American as well as foreign markets of other major nations free and unhampered by economic barriers. For the most part they had supported a high tariff policy before the Underwood tariff of 1914, and this was particularly true of American bankers. But their greater understanding of the changed postwar political economy of the world finally undermined the prewar alliance between this segment of the business community and the purely domestic, high-tariff manufacturing concerns.[40]

So in the twelve years following the war, international bankers allied with importing and exporting concerns in opposition to the high duties of the 1922 and 1930 Republican tariffs. In 1922 this segment of the business community tried to counter extreme protectionism by supporting the flexible provisions of the Fordney-McCumber Act, and after 1930 advocated reciprocal agreements to offset the rates contained in the Hawley-Smoot tariff. This group defended both flexibility and the "new reciprocity" for the same economic reasons they opposed high tariff duties; that is, that tariff barriers at home did not accord with America's postwar creditor position, would not facilitate the repayment of debts owed the United States, and did not encourage the expansion of foreign markets.

Well before the introduction of the 1922 tariff bill these business interests, along with the NFTC, the Tariff Commission, and the executive branch, united behind the concept of flexibility. Yet the original House Bill No. 7456 did not contain flexible provisions and did not endorse the unconditional most-favored-nation principle. Instead, the Fordney bill of June 21, 1921, contained sections 301–303 based on the old reciprocity or special bargaining theory.[41] The same day that Fordney introduced his bill, the State and Commerce departments acted to replace the offensive sections with the flexible provisions recommended by the Tariff Commission and endorsed by the NFTC and the United States Chamber of Commerce.[42]

In a 1919 report entitled *Reciprocity and Commercial Treaties,* and later in its 1920 *Annual Report,* the Tariff Commission had suggested that equality of treatment, that is, the Open Door principle, be adopted as a goal of American tariff policy. This was to be achieved by employing a penalty method (in the form of additional duties) whenever most-favored-nation treatment was not accorded the United States. Officials of the commission and the Departments of State and Commerce all concurred on this point and also agreed that the protective principle of cost equalization should be used, when possible, to lower rather than raise tariff rates, especially when duties proved to be excessive. This internationalist coalition made up of the two departments, the Tariff Commission, and the NFTC united behind a detailed criticism of the House bill, written by Commissioner Culbertson on July 16, 1921. And with tacit White House approval they proceeded to oppose Sections 301–303 of the proposed Fordney bill.[43]

Since most of the contact between congressmen and these internationalists was unofficial, the records do not indicate precisely why or when the Senate Finance Committee decided to follow Culbertson's recommendations. Possibly agreement came on November 28, 1921, at a meeting between President Harding, Hoover, Senator Smoot, and all the members of the Tariff Commission. In any event it occurred sometime between July 16, 1921, and April 24, 1922, when Smoot introduced flexible provisions as amendments to the original Fordney bill. These provisions were substituted for the special concession clauses of the House bill and became Sections 315–317 in the final draft of the Fordney-McCumber tariff. From the beginning it had been clear that the internationalist coalition intended Section 315 to be used to lower duties and Sections 316–317 to be used to insure equality of treatment for American traders.[44]

There is no indication, however, in the Senate tariff hearings or in the *Congressional Record* that the Senate Finance Committee understood the "actual potentialities and purpose," especially of Section 317 as interpreted by the State and Commerce departments, the Tariff Commission, and the NFTC. As noted earlier, President Harding in his first annual message had said nothing about using flexibility to promote the Open Door through the adoption of the unconditional most-favored-nation principle. There was a corresponding lack of comment in major business journals on this point. In fact, because Section 317 received so little attention from Congress, the business community, and the public at large while the Fordney bill was being drafted, it can only be assumed that a small group of government officials in the executive branch, and those businessmen represented primarily by the NFTC were ultimately responsible not only for the drafting and adoption of Section 317, but also for its decidedly internationalist interpretation. There is no evidence from the tariff hearings or floor debate that the senators themselves, with the possible exception of Smoot, intended either Section 315 or Section 317, but especially the latter, to be used to further internationalist ends. On the contrary, there is evidence in the sparse

Senate debate that the intention of Congress on Section 317 was just the opposite.[45] At the same time no confusion exists over the origins or intent of the high duties of the Fordney-McCumber tariff. Clearly these were the product of pressure from small and medium-sized domestic manufacturing concerns strongly backed by individual members of both houses of Congress. The same generalization holds true for the high duties of the Hawley-Smoot tariff of 1930.

An identical nationalist-internationalist split within government and business circles can be observed in a much more publicized aspect of the 1922 tariff controversy. This was the issue of American valuation. American valuation meant the computation of ad valorem duties for imported goods based on the current wholesale price of competitive products produced in the United States, as opposed to the wholesale price in the producing country. The American valuation method had never been employed for any significant length of time before World War I. High protectionists had supported it from time to time, especially in 1909, 1913, and 1920–1922, as a means of preventing undervaluation, of securing more revenue by imposing the same duties on all similar items regardless of origin, and of avoiding fluctuations in rates due to depreciation or recovery of foreign currency.[46] Included among the proponents of American valuation in the early 1920s were numerous congressmen, the NAM, and the various state and local manufacturing associations represented at the 1921 National Conference of State Manufacturers' Associations, the independent iron and steel producers, the American Valuation Association, and the National Association of Woolen Manufacturers.[47]

The United States Chamber of Commerce was unable to produce a "decisive majority" for or against the plan, indicating its nationalist-internationalist division. In fact, a few members resigned as a result of the attempt made to "secure American business opinion upon tariff principles." Although the twelve members of the national Committee on Tariff Principles opposed American valuation 11 to 1, a national referendum on the issue indicated that the rank and file of chamber members were almost evenly divided (985 opposed, 843 in favor).[48] The proportional discrepancy between the alignment within the committee and the referendum vote clearly demonstrated that on this issue the internationalist rhetoric and position of the chamber's national leadership did not reflect the serious division within the organization. It is also an indication of why the national positions assumed by the United States Chamber of Commerce on questions relating to economic foreign policy between 1920 and 1933 were often ambiguous or misleading.

A less enervating division existed within the ranks of the National Association of Manufacturers. Sixty-nine large member firms went on record in opposition to American valuation and demanded a public accounting of the number of ballots that had actually been cast on the issue at a special tariff convention held in January 1922.[49] Unlike the national Chamber of Commerce, however, the NAM came out strongly in favor of American valuation.

Prominent among the opponents of American valuation were financial journals, the American Bankers Association, the American Manufacturers Export Association, and export-import interests in general, the National Wholesale Dry Goods Association, and the National Retail Dry Goods Association, which included some of the largest department stores in the country. They argued that to abandon the traditional foreign basis of valuation would unnecessarily increase tariff duties, would literally allow American manufacturers to control tariff rates through their ability to determine domestic selling prices by production control, and would be impractical and costly to implement since all of the customs information and court decisions for over 100 years had been based on the practice of foreign valuation.[50]

At the Senate hearings held in July and August of 1921, proponents outnumbered opponents of American valuation four to one. With the exception of the Tariff Commission, the division within government and business circles remained the same as it had been with respect to high duties and the flexible provisions. When individual members of the Federal Tariff Commission testified, all of them made it clear that "the commission has not acted as a commission in preparing any statement on which we are all agreed" on the issue of American valuation. Of the five commissioners who appeared, three favored the new method, one expressed no opinion, and one pointed out that American valuation at best represented only a "temporary solution to the exchange problem" and in all probability would not cure the commercial instability which prevailed in the early postwar years.[51]

Following the pattern established above, the original House bill represented the nationalist position by calling for a complete conversion to the American valuation plan. But Section 402 of the House bill was "regretfully" abandoned by the Senate Finance Committee under the influence of Senator Smoot, and the more traditional practice of foreign valuation or "equality-of-cost" prevailed in the final draft as Section 315(b). The change seems to have been precipitated by pressure brought to bear upon the Senate by the same internationalist elements within the government and the business community which also supported the flexible provisions of the Fordney-McCumber Act.[52] But the internationalists were not completely successful on the issue of valuation, for under the terms of the 1922 tariff American selling prices could be used to determine ad valorem rates "whenever the President, upon investigation of the differences in the cost of production of articles provided for in . . . this Act . . . shall find it thereby shown that the duties prescribed . . . do not equalize said difference."[53]

To strong opponents of American valuation the power granted to the president under Section 315(b) constituted a sellout. A scathing Senate minority report stated that this section would allow a president under the influence of protectionists to rehabilitate the American valuation principle. As it turned out, between 1922 and 1929 only two dutiable articles were transferred to the American selling price. A large number of coal tar products, however, were subject to American valuation throughout the 1920s under the terms of the 1922 tariff.[54] In the 1929–1930 tariff revision the question of American valuation was given less publicity and consideration; nonetheless, a provision similar to Section 315(b) was present in the Hawley-Smoot Act.[55]

Neither the internationalists nor nationalists were completely satisfied with the 1922 tariff, for indeed its excessive duties and the intent of the sponsors of the flexible provisions contradicted one another. Furthermore, this tariff never became an integrated part of any comprehensive plan for asserting American leadership while solving Europe's postwar economic problems. It was simply one of several stopgap, piecemeal measures which contained a mixture of unilateral and collective features so characteristic of the independent internationalism of the period. Banking interests were particularly critical of the new tariff, as were large companies engaged in importing or in establishing markets abroad. The opinions of both groups were amply represented by the NFTC during the course of the decade. In addition prominent academicians, nongovernmental economists, and individual businessmen such as Wesley Clair Mitchell, Harry T. Collins, John D. Black, Donald M. Marvin, William Starr Myers, Harold U. Faulkner, William S. Culbertson, Thomas Lamont, Paul Warburg, Bernard Baruch, Otto Kahn, Frank Vanderlip, Benjamin Strong, Henry Ford, Julius Rosenwald, Norman H. Davis, and Edward A. Filene—all indicated personal dissatisfaction with the Fordney-McCumber Tariff. Their arguments against it ranged from the shortsightedness of the rate schedule in terms of the spirit of international cooperation, to the detrimental effects it would have on United States trade and the repayment of Allied debts.[56]

In contrast, from the ranks of federal officials, small and medium-sized manufacturers, and other nonfinancial segments of the business community and farm representatives, came a different set of criticisms. These nationalist views appeared in the numerous publications of regional trade and tariff associations, in articles carried by chambers of commerce and NAM journals, and in *Cotton, Iron Age,* the *American Economist,* and the *Protectionist.* Supporting the high duties of the 1922 tariff, this business group was generally critical of the powers given the president and Tariff Commission, against using the flexible provisions for lowering duties, disappointed over the fate of American valuation, and suspicious of "altruistic internationalists" and bankers whom they accused of being free traders.[57]

As was to be expected, however, once the Fordney-McCumber Tariff went into effect there was a certain amount of grudging acquiescence to it on the part of both sets of antagonists, with the nationalists being less reluctant in their support than the internationalists.[58] Among the nationalists, only representatives of the "independent" iron and steel companies remained sharply critical of the 1922 rates until they were revised in 1930.[59] John A. Topping, president of the Republic Iron and Steel Company, typified the point of view of these companies in an interview printed a month after the act went into effect. Predicting a rise in production costs, higher prices for steel, and a decline in the export steel trade because of the import tax levied on certain raw materials, he was forced to look for relief through the application of the flexible provisions which his industry had opposed during the hearings.[60]

In retrospect Topping's willingness to resort to these administrative provisions appears somewhat prophetic. By the end of the decade business internationalists had essentially abandoned flexibility as a means for promoting world trade and equal opportunity, while nationalists were by then firmly committed to the concept in the name of protectionism. Nationalists had also come to believe that sporadic congressional tariff revision, with its unsettling effects on business, could be avoided in the future through a properly functioning flexible tariff. That is, by 1930 flexibility was receiving more support from the president and protectionist groups than from the Federal Trade Commission or the NFTC— two of the original proponents of Sections 315–317 in the early 1920s.[61] In fact, during 1928 importers unsuccessfully sought to have Section 315 with its cost equalization clause declared unconstitutional. There was little doubt in their minds that the application of this section had left something to be desired. Of the thirty-eight duty changes proclaimed by Presidents Harding and Coolidge under Section 315 upon the advice of the Tariff Commission, only five decisions lowered the ad valorem duties and these were on insignificant items.[62] Upward flexibility was not what business internationalists had anticipated when they originally supported the flexible provisions of the Fordney-McCumber Tariff. In addition, they had no way of knowing that administrative measures like these and others were well on their way to constituting an "invisible tariff" which would become the bulwark of a future generation of protectionists.[63]

Part of this misuse or disuse of the flexible provisions resulted from the composition of the Tariff Commission. According to the last of the original Wilsonian commissioners, Edward P. Costigan, who resigned in protest in 1928, the impartiality of the commission had been destroyed by Republican appointees in the 1920s.[64] For example, Harding's three appointees, Commissioners Thomas O. Marvin, William Burgess, and Henry H. Glassie, were all strong protectionists and were associated with the Home Market Club of Boston, the domestic pottery industry, and the sugar interests of Louisiana, respectively. Costigan was also critical of Harding's and Coolidge's tight control over the activities of the commission and the latter's refusal to act on recommendations calling for lower duties on sugar, linseed oil, and halibut. In addition, according to Costigan, the commission had failed to inform American farmers of the very limited benefits they were receiving from many agricultural duties. Costigan resigned after becoming convinced that not even the two-year Senate investigation of the commission was going to bring about the necessary reforms to insure that the flexible provisions would be scientifically applied in the interest of lowering rates.[65] His attitude, nevertheless, continued to influence most internationalists within business and government, as well as those Progressives who by 1929 no longer supported flexibility.

In connection with this switch within business and government circles on the question of flexibility, it is necessary to consider Herbert Hoover's position on both of the Republican tariffs of the decade. His tariff views are significant not only because of the influential national offices he occupied, but also because he was one of the internationally prominent business figures of the period who simultaneously supported what appeared to be contradictory positions; namely, high protective duties and expansion of American trade through an Open Door based on the unconditional most-favored-nation principle.[66] As secretary of commerce he had been part of the internationalist coalition that drafted Sections 315 and 317 of the Fordney-McCumber Tariff. Accordingly, Hoover had backed Costigan's efforts to increase the investigatory powers of the Tariff Commission and never indicated any dissatisfaction with the State Department's attempts to negotiate treaties assuring equality of treatment for American merchants. Yet he also defended with dogged consistency the duty schedule of the 1922 tariff. Judging from the praise heaped upon Hoover before 1929, most businessmen agreed that his methods for promoting commerce, regardless of any inherent contradiction in his tariff views, had been eminently successful at home and abroad.[67] It was only as a depression president that he began to face serious criticism on this score.

According to Hoover's way of thinking, however, there was no actual or apparent contradiction in his commercial policy. He viewed the tariff as simply one aspect of his multifaceted domestic and foreign program for transforming "the whole super-organization of our economic life." Within his proposed system, based on voluntary, private planning and cooperation to insure equality of opportunity at home and abroad, tariff protection was absolutely necessary for maintaining an expanding domestic market. By this Hoover meant not only a domestic market for American manufacturers and farmers, but a domestic market for foreign goods. He and most officials in the Commerce Department firmly believed that the volume of imports to the United States depended upon the internal prosperity of the country more than the height of its customs duties. At the same time they looked upon the protective system as one of the means for maintaining the high American standard of living. All nations, Hoover told a critic of his tariff policy in 1930, proceed on the "basis that domestic prosperity will result [from import duties] and that the protective principle is in itself the largest encouragement to foreign trade through the creation of buying of their own citizens."[68] With equal conviction he asserted again and again between 1921 and 1933 that the American tariff did not "strangle the buying power of foreign nations" by diminishing their exports to the United States, did not hamper European recovery or economic development in Latin America, and did not contribute to the downward course of trade after the depression deepened in the early 1930s.[69]

Most of these contentions were based on data gathered by the Commerce Department before and after 1929. While the interpretation given these statistics, especially those which exaggerated the importance of the increase in American imports during the 1920s, can be questioned in retrospect, at the time they represented the best work of some of the country's most able statisticians and economists.[70] For example, figures were cited which showed that of the total exports from twenty-nine major countries, the United States had accounted for 10.5 percent in 1913 and 17.7 percent in 1925. Using the same years and countries it was shown that the percentage of their total imports coming from the United States only increased from 15.9 percent to 20.4 percent. Myopically it was then concluded: 1) that American duties were not too high, and 2) that because the proportion of United States imports slightly exceeded its exports with these countries, their postwar recovery had been materially aided. Ignored were the broader questions of whether or not the United States was "importing as much as the surplus on her balance of payments on current account required," and the degree to which increased American exports were responsible for the overall decline in the exports of western European nations following the war.[71]

While relying on figures which favorably compared United States imports with exports and which minimized the importance of tariff levels, Hoover also defended import duties by pointing out that the American trade balance did not consist of the movement of commodities alone. There were "invisible exports" from the United States, he said, making it possible for European nations to buy American products and pay off their war debts without resorting to direct shipments of goods. Greatly overestimating the monetary value of these hidden items, Hoover described them in terms of the money newly arrived immigrants sent back to their native lands, the dollars American tourists spent abroad, the freight and insurance charges paid to European companies, and interest payments on foreign investments in the United States. With the exception of the money spent by tourists each year, these categories of expenditures constituted a more significant portion of the American trade balance *before* World War I than after. This did not prevent Hoover from periodically predicting, on the basis of Commerce Department studies, that these invisible exports could create an unfavorable overall balance of trade for the United States.[72]

Finally, Hoover's support for Republican protectionism survived even the 1929 depression for the following reasons. First, he was convinced that world prosperity had been undermined and deflation triggered largely by "internal economic and social currents" abroad, rather than by the economic foreign policy of the United States. And like so many of his contemporaries, Hoover dismissed the possibility that the causes of the American depression, which in turn drastically affected the already unstable economic equilibrium of the world, were domestic economic deficiencies. He therefore placed the entire blame for the depression on the unsound fiscal policies of some European nations, and on the economic defects of the Treaty of Versailles.[73] Second, believing in the business cycle theories of economist Wesley Clair Mitchell, he did not think the economy could manage itself, especially in time of crisis; however, he did not consider the Hawley-Smoot Tariff a depression issue. His intention in calling for a tariff revision in the spring of 1929 was to obtain higher rates exclusively for agricultural products—not to ward off any impending economic disaster. The tariff had been a prominent issue in the 1928 campaign and was regarded by many as "the touchstone for the foreign policy of the Hoover administration."[74] In terms of simple political expediency it was wise to try to deal with it quickly in his first year in office. Congress, however, had other ideas.

Hoover defended the general upward tariff revision which emerged a year and a half later, not out of blind faith in either protectionism or the democratic nature of the rate-making process, but because he was convinced on the basis of available statistical evidence that it could do no harm to world trade even in time of depression, and because he thought he could make the improved flexible provisions work where other presidents had failed. He also had a basic political reason for supporting the high duties: party unity. This reason loomed larger in his considerations after he became president and faced the problem of placating nationalists and internationalists, not simply within the business community, but in the country generally. His critics to the contrary, Hoover's defense of nationalist duties throughout the decade did not in his own mind contradict his internationalist dreams of controlled economic expansion within the parameters which always guided him: namely, Department of Commerce statistics and his comprehension of the domestic and foreign aspects of American prosperity. The added ingredient of national politics did not change these.

This is not to say that there were no contradictions in Hoover's economic foreign policy. The most glaring one was his refusal to admit that high American duties were in fact "artificial restraints" of trade and often "deprived foreign producers of a 'fair price' for their goods," as did the international cartels he so vehemently attacked, such as the English rubber monopoly.[75] As secretary of commerce, his tariff views and his crusade against foreign monopolies generally received widespread support within government and business circles. But by the time Hoover became president, this concensus had failed to break down European trade barriers in the name of the Open Door.[76] Moreover, the internal economic contradictions in the American tariff policy had been made abundantly clear over the decade by the actions of nationalists in Congress when they obstructed the State Department in its negotiation of most-favored-nation treaties, and by the logical insistence of England and France that their preferential tariff systems were no more discriminatory than the double-edged quality of a swinging door.

So within the business community Hoover found greater disharmony over the tariff in 1930 than had existed in 1922. Naturally the high rate schedule satisfied most nationalists, but the president faced overt hostility among many internationalists when he called for improved flexible provisions. Flexibility had not only failed to bring about a significant reduction in duties, as this group had desired, but had also demonstrated the economic and administrative impossibility of equalizing the differences between foreign and domestic costs of production. Disillusionment among leading businessmen and economists had been building for some time on these questions, but became increasingly apparent after the 1927 World Economic Conference sponsored by the League of Nations. Although the principle of equality of treatment and the unconditional most-favored-nation clause were approved by all members of the Committee on Commerce, and the delegates overwhelmingly endorsed a resolution "demanding that the building of tariff walls cease," the State Department continued to make little headway with its Open Door commercial treaties. Part of the trouble stemmed from the fact that some League members wanted to make sure such bilateral treaties would not hamper any future multilateral economic agreements, that is, regional preferential conventions.[77] Most of the State Department's difficulties lay elsewhere, however.

Between 1923, when the Harding administration officially sanctioned the negotiation of commercial treaties with most-favored-nation clauses to promote the Open Door doctrine, and March 1929, State Department officials were able to negotiate only eight such treaties. At the latter date three of them had not yet gone into effect and only one of the remaining five was with a major power. Approximately a dozen executive agreements with such clauses had been concluded, but none of them involved major nations, either. By 1933 the picture had not substantially changed with the addition of four more treaties and five more executive agreements. Together these treaties and agreements were with countries which accounted at best for only 20 percent of American exports. Even if one includes various conditional pledges which still existed between the United States and other countries, almost 50 percent of all American exports went to countries with which no most-favored-nation commitments of any kind had been concluded.[78]

This less than inspiring record (as far as business internationalists were concerned) was partially the result of the suspicion on the part of foreign nations that the Open Door principle was simply a device for spreading "universal severity and universal ill treatment" by asking them to lower their tariff barriers while the United States maintained its. By refusing to discuss American duties at international conferences, State Department representatives never convincingly answered this charge. Instead, they argued after 1925 that since most foreign currencies had been stabilized on a gold basis, "tariff levels were less important relatively than the rationalization of tariffs." At best this meant that existing tariff barriers "would be less harmful" if all nations would adopt the more efficient, modern methods of collecting customs charges practiced by the United States. The State Department was further compromised in its foreign negotiations to obtain equality of treatment by the discriminatory reservations which the Senate frequently attached to Open Door commercial treaties. Despite foreign protests, the State Department was also unable to get Congress to remove the deferential clauses from the 1922 and 1930 tariffs even though these clauses were inconsistent with the most-favored-nation treaty obligations of the United States. Thus it was clear to business internationalists by the end of the decade that European nations, especially France, continued to move in the opposite direction from the United States on tariff policy; that is, toward individual reciprocal arrangements rather than the Open Door. The acting secretary of state, Joseph P. Cotton, admitted as much in 1930 when he told the unofficial United States representative to the Geneva conference on tariffs that the meeting was of great importance to the United States because it was hoped it would become "the first step in a possible reorientation of European trade and tariff policy."[79]

Just as disillusionment among business internationalists was mounting in the late 1920s, a temporary victory for American tariff policy occurred. This was the successful negotiation and ratification of the International Convention on the Abolition of Import and Export Prohibitions and Restrictions in 1927 and 1928. This Prohibitions Convention formalized the postwar commitment of the United States to abolish quantitative restrictions as a means to protect domestic industries, and thus made opposition to import quotas a formal part of the commercial policy of the United States until after World War II. Even though Secretary of State Frank B. Kellogg called for the "prompt operation of the Convention" because of its importance to American commerce, it did not receive much publicity within the business community for it was an issue upon which nationalists and internationalists agreed: the former because they viewed such administrative restrictions as unnecessary with the return of high duty protection after 1920; the latter because such quotas were deemed an improper form of commerce control since they did not permit price adjustments based on volume trading to take place and because they contradicted the unconditional most-favored-nation principle. Aside from codifying what had become a natural practice of the United States since World War I, this convention failed in the long run to promote the Open Door abroad because only eight nations ratified it without debilitating reservations. By the end of June 1934, all eight (including the United States) had withdrawn from the agreement.[80] It was not until the Democrats returned to power under depression conditions and abandoned the high, nonnegotiable tariff of the Republicans, that the strength of American opposition to quantitative restrictions was truly tested.

With such a history of failure in American efforts to obtain world acceptance of an Open Door commercial policy, it is easy to see why business internationalists were moving away from tariff flexibility to achieve this goal by the end of the decade,[81] and why business nationalists were moving to endorse it as never before.[82] Faced with the possibility that flexibility would remain under the influence of congressional and business nationalists, despite Hoover's insistence that this would not be the case if his improved flexible provisions were adopted, bankers and big business interests now viewed the Hawley-Smoot bill as unpalatable. They were no longer willing, as they had been in 1922, to accept high duties in return for promises of downward revision through flexibility and a "scientific and wholly just administration of the law" through a stronger Tariff Commission. Consequently internationalists were much more outspoken in their criticism of the 1930 tariff than they had been of the Fordney-McCumber legislation.[83]

Included among the opponents of the tariff by 1930 were James D. Mooney, vice-president of General Motors; Norman H. Davis; General Atterbury, president of the Pennsylvania Railroad Company; Elmer H. Youngman, editor of the *Bankers Magazine;* Owen D. Young; Thomas W. Lamont; Albert H. Wiggin, chairman of the Chase National Bank; Charles E. Mitchell, chairman of the National City Bank of New York; Henry Morgenthau, Sr.; Oswald Garrison Villard, editor of the *Nation;* Chester H. Rowell, editor of the *Fresno Republican;* Henry Ford; Charles Sabin; Newton D. Baker; and Edward Riley, vice-president of the General Motors Export Corporation.[84] In all, Hoover received over 400 direct, personal communiqués in opposition to the Hawley-Smoot tariff. This did not include the hundreds of letters, both for and against the bill, which were sent to the Federal Tariff Commission or to Congressman Willis C. Hawley and Senator Reed Smoot.[85]

At Hoover's request his correspondence secretary, Lawrence Richey, compiled a folder of the "more important protests against the [1930] tariff." Richey selected thirty-six. Among the more notable were those from Ivy Lee, the public relations agent for Standard Oil; the well-known economist, Irving Fisher; and Democratic internationalist, Norman H. Davis. Lee pointed out to Hoover that he made it his business "to study the trend of public sentiment in the United States," and warned the president that "there has seldom been in this country such a rising tide of protest as has been aroused by the tariff bill." He pointed to opposition from Republican manufacturers and predicted a further drop in American export trade if the bill was passed. Fisher argued against the bill on economic grounds, pointing out that big business within the Republican party did not support it. He also told Hoover that his reputation "for not being a politician" would be enhanced if he vetoed it, and that if he did not, the tariff "would make us more than we already are the most hated nation" in the world. Davis also stressed opposition among leading Republican industrialists, bankers, and railroad executives. He talked about the "crazy greed" of the proponents of the bill, and forecast that if it was passed, the reaction to it would "sound the death knell of high protection." As a low-tariff Democrat, Davis noted that he would welcome this result if it were not for the immediate economic effects the tariff would have on the country.[86]

In addition to the opposition of the American Bankers Association and of business internationalists of both parties, a 1930 poll of newspaper editors in New England and eight other industrial states showed that 103 out of 111 believed international relations would be harmed by the Hawley-Smoot Tariff; 80 out of 125 agreed that it would have "injurious" economic results; and 64 out of 100 thought that "manufacturing conditions did not warrant passage." Across the country, 38.9 percent of all Republican newspapers expressed "some opposition to the prevailing high tariff policies" of their party. Also, over a thousand economists and a "whole group of college professors," plus 24 foreign nations, registered formal protests against the bill and recommended that Hoover veto it. But he did not. Walter Lippmann commented at the time that the president's approval of the bill represented a typical example of his "aversion from [*sic*] the processes of popular government."[87]

Hoover was not swayed by this impressive public outcry because he chose, for a combination of political and economic reasons, to listen not to the critics but to the proponents of the bill; namely, the business nationalists, who were heavily represented in Congress, and the lobbyists for the medium-sized manufacturers in the country. These groups were cooperating with one another and remained firmly in favor of the excessive Hawley-Smoot rates, and, most importantly, remained in control of the tariff-making process. In contrast, those opposed to the bill were less well represented in Congress, less well organized, and consequently less able to influence Congress or the president. Their opposition was essentially ineffective because, despite the prominence of some of the individuals involved, they lacked effective political organization to oppose both Congress and the executive branch of government. By the end of the decade, therefore, the nationalists were taking advantage of the president's commitment to flexible provisions because upward flexibility since 1922 had served their purposes well. There had been some criticism even among those nationalists about the slowness with which rate changes were effected in the 1920s, but such criticism had never become widespread. Likewise, Hoover relied on nationalist support for lack of any other to defeat his political opponents in Congress and to strengthen what he considered to be the essential internationalist features of the legislation.[88] It made little difference that the president and the protectionists were supporting flexibility for basically different reasons; their alliance was a very successful one from a political point of view.

Because Hoover had not lost his faith in flexibility, he believed that the 1922 provisions could be improved if the powers of the president and the Tariff Commission were enlarged. In particular, he felt that the commission had degenerated into merely a "statistical agency," and so he tried to make it a genuinely nonpartisan, rate-making body. This would, he said, put an end to the "orgy of logrolling in Congress" and remedy "serious inequities and inequalities." In this sense his ideas on flexibility clashed with those of the protectionists, who had benefited from the defects of 1922 flexible provisions and wanted to keep them with only minor changes. Thus Hoover personally had to spearhead the drive to obtain stronger power for the commission. In addition, he was much more concerned with the power of the president to change rates than were most of his supporters.[89] He did share with the tariff nationalists, however, the obsolete idea of basing rate changes upon the difference between costs of production at home and abroad as embodied in Section 315. This was an unworkable formula, but Hoover and protectionist groups tenaciously supported it well into the 1930s.[90]

As in 1922, the congressional vote in favor of the tariff in 1930 was predominantly Republican. But it is interesting to note that a greater percentage of Democrats voted for the Hawley-Smoot bill than had voted for the Fordney-McCumber one. Senate Democratic support for high tariff protection rose from 8.3 percent in 1922 to 15.3 percent in 1930. At the same time the Senate Republican support for tariff nationalism declined slightly from 89.6 percent to 75.9 percent. A similar rise in Democratic votes and decline in Republican votes took place in the House of Representatives.[91] By the end of the decade it was clear that war-generated protectionist views were firmly established within the ranks of the traditionally low-tariff Democrats. Strong opposition for different reasons came from business internationalists and Progressives within the Republican party and probably accounted for the loss of a few votes on that side of the ledger. Ultimately, however, nationalism prevailed in 1930 as the understanding between the executive branch of government and big business completely disappeared and flexibility came to be championed by protectionists within both parties. The Great Depression, as James A. Farrell noted in 1933, precipitated nationalist economic policies all over the world.[92]

Although Hoover never claimed the Hawley-Smoot bill was perfect, he defended his signing of it on June 17, 1930, by denying that rates had been raised and by pointing out that the provisions of the bill fulfilled "the repeated demands of statesmen and industrial and agricultural leaders over the past twenty-five years." He also predicted there would be no serious reaction abroad. In this he was proved wrong, just as business internationalists and the State Department had feared.[93] Thirty years later Hoover wrote to John F. Kennedy favorably comparing the Hawley-Smoot Tariff with the proposed 1962 Reciprocal Trade Act. Ironically, he and his nationalist supporters had opposed the reciprocal trade ideas of the Democrats when they were originally introduced.[94] Time had not only dimmed the former president's memory of the bitter conflict between nationalists and internationalists over the 1930 tariff, but had also obscured his position in that conflict—a position based in large measure on his nationalist concern for preserving the American standard of living.

As the depression wore on, the internationalist segment of the business community turned to a new kind of tariff reciprocity in order to achieve equality of treatment and a reduction in duties. During the early New Deal period, and largely under the leadership of Cordell Hull, a trade agreements amendment was attached to the Hawley-Smoot Tariff. This Reciprocal Trade Agreements Act of June 1934 was described as a product of neither nationalism nor retaliation but as a "means of tariff reduction instead of, as hitherto . . . an excuse for tariff raising."[95] Under New Deal reciprocity, Franklin Roosevelt was authorized to enter into trade agreements with foreign countries without being hamstrung by the necessity to equalize the differences in the cost of production between American and foreign goods, as earlier presidents had been. In exchange for reductions in the American tariff schedule Roosevelt could bargain for lower foreign tariffs, "increases of foreign import quotas, and other benefits on a wide range of American agricultural and industrial products." Such bilateral treaties would then be "generalized"; that is, applied unconditionally to all third countries through most-favored-nation treaties. None of these reductions in duties had to be approved by Congress.[96] These features liberated the power of the president and distinguished the reciprocal trade policy of the New Deal period from the traditional nineteenth-century version of reciprocity. So the American tariff became negotiable and reciprocal once again, but for the first time the intent of the legislation was downward and the negotiations included major commodities.

New Deal reciprocity should not, however, be confused with free trade. Even the 1934 act with its unconditional most-favored-nation provision was aimed at "expanding foreign markets for the products of the United States," not at increasing imports. There was never any question of abandoning the Open Door doctrine or the goal of unlimited economic expansion. What the Democrats did in essence was to complete, not initiate, the basic features of the commercial policy of the United States, which the Republicans had begun to formalize in the 1920s and which prevailed until after World War II. They did this by retaining the two principles contained in the earlier unconditional most-favored-nation treaties and the Prohibitions Convention, while discarding a third principle—the high nonnegotiable duties of the Republican tariffs of 1922 and 1930. In doing so, the Democrats removed the theoretical inconsistency between most-favored-nation treatment and high tariff walls which had plagued Republican commercial policy. Rallying behind Secretary of State Cordell Hull, the New Deal internationalists found, nonetheless, that in practice they still had to share tariff policy with the nationalists led by George N. Peek. The latter were insisting that the import quotas and higher duties authorized by the National Industrial Recovery Act and by amendments to the Agricultural Adjustment Act be honored. Consequently some import quotas were formally imposed on agricultural products and informally imposed on Japanese cotton textiles during the depression years.[97]

In general, however, the United States has reconfirmed its post-World War I commitment to the Open Door through most-favored-nation clauses and to removal of quantitative restrictions at various economic conventions since 1933. But American support for the latter has been seriously undermined since 1948 when the government insisted on "escape clauses" in all of its trade agreements. Such clauses allow the imposition of import quotas or raised duties on items which threaten domestic industries.[98] Thus as the world position of the United States has changed since 1920 from that of a nation with no balance-of-payments problem—confident of its ability to compete with foreign producers—to the opposite, some technical aspects of the American tariff have changed accordingly. A double standard or contradictory commercial policy nonetheless continues to prevail as it did in the 1920s, with the United States still espousing an Open Door for other nations, while only selectively following such a course itself. And the goal of such a dual policy remains the same: American domination of world trade.

Chapter Four

Hoover & Foreign Loan
Supervision, 1920–1933

The nationalist-internationalist split which occurred within the business community over tariff policy was also evident with respect to other economic foreign policy issues, such as loans and investments and the related problems of intergovernmental debts and German reparation payments. The average domestic businessman, however, was much less concerned with these questions than he was with the tariff controversies of the decade.

Sometimes this lack of interest was due to a sense of inadequacy, but more often it represented apathy. In at least one case, a steel manufacturer on the Pacific Coast refused to consider the suggestion of the American Manufacturers Export Association for an "international conference of businessmen to make suggestions and recommendations to their various governments concerning the inter-Allied debt." He objected to the proposal because he believed that the secretaries of state and of the treasury were better qualified to decide debt policy than "the average American businessman," who did not possess the necessary economic and diplomatic knowledge.[1] On the other hand, most businessmen were simply indifferent to basic international economic issues. According to a 1926 NAM committee report, "the great majority" of its members did not give any "serious attention to foreign trade possibilities or the influence of that trade on their own industrial activities."[2] Consequently, nationalist economic opinion, while it tended to be consistent in the 1920s, was less frequently articulated by the organizations and publications representing the small or medium-sized enterprises across the country than was internationalist opinion.

The sharpest controversies over all economic foreign policy issues, with the exception of the tariff, were found within the ranks of that segment of the business community whose affairs were worldwide. It was not uncommon for business internationalists who had been united in opposition to high tariff duties and in favor of an Open Door commercial policy, to disagree over loan, investment, debt, and reparation policies. More than any other single fact, this internecine conflict proved disastrous for their dreams of establishing a world economic community. With respect to loans and investments it has already been pointed out that banking and financial internationalists had divided into two camps by 1920. As the postwar depression of 1920–1921 subsided, however, so did the disagreement between the House of Morgan, backed by the investment bankers across the country, and the commercial banking and export manufacturing interests headed by the National City Bank and Frank A. Vanderlip. Their reconciliation was to be expected on this issue since both groups hoped to make New York the international financial center of the world. They simply had been temporarily unable to agree upon how such a common goal was to be achieved in the economically unstable years immediately following the armistice.

International trade was generally sluggish through 1921. This was due to the uncertainty of exchange markets with so many nations having gone off the gold standard, to frozen credits, and to a temporary shortage of investment capital following the war. One result was a decline in number of the foreign branches of American banks which had been established between 1913 and 1920 under facilities provided for by the Federal Reserve System.[3] The total number of such banks (excluding the foreign affiliates of private investment banks) dropped from 181 at the end of 1920 to 120 in 1924. The greatest loss in this period came in Latin America, where 37 percent of the foreign branches had been established. The number of branches declined from seventy-two and three agencies to forty-five and one agency. Where there had been thirty-two American banks represented in eight Latin American countries in 1920, there were only twenty-six banks in seven countries by 1924.[4]

This decrease in branch banks temporarily undermined the attempt on the part of National City and its affiliates to make New York the center for the exchange of short-term dollar acceptances. There was, however, no corresponding drop in the expansion of capital investment abroad because manufacturing corporations had begun to invest in Europe and other parts of the world by establishing their own foreign subsidiaries. This method of direct investment and independent financing further decreased the need for foreign bank branches and freed at least the giant companies from their traditional reliance upon American bankers. By 1924 large American companies constituted a strong third partner in the international financial system of the United States, along with the National City and Morgan interests.[5] As of 1929, American manufacturers had invested $1,821,000,000 in approximately 4,000 foreign branch plants. This was greater than any other single kind of direct investment up to that time, out of a total direct foreign investment of $7,553,000,000.[6]

With the return of prosperity after the postwar depression, an increasing capital surplus enabled the United States through the "dual method of the long-term loan and the foreign branch-factory and subsidiary" to turn New York into the undisputed international financial center of the world (even though Britain still dominated in the area of short-term acceptances). Confirmation of the financial leadership of the United States came in 1924 when an American businessman engineered the Dawes Plan for Germany, and American bankers organized by J. P. Morgan floated $110 million of the $200 million Dawes Plan loan. Another indication of this country's leading financial position can be seen in the figures for net portfolio investments. In 1924 these totaled $4,564,900,000, with the greater part of them having been made between 1922 and 1924. By 1929 the net portfolio investments amounted to $7,839,000,000. When total portfolio and direct investments are combined, the resulting figures show the value of the entire foreign investment of the United States increasing from $6,955,600,000 in 1919 to $17,009,600,000 in 1929.[7] Naturally these massive amounts precipitated a debate within government and business circles over financial control.

Before World War I there had been no systematic attempt on the part of Washington officials to supervise or aid business activities abroad, although a few erratic actions were taken in various parts of the world beginning in the late nineteenth century because the government wanted to see trade and investment increase, particularly in the Far East. For example, under William McKinley and Theodore Roosevelt, the State Department had promoted the American China Development Company, and under William Howard Taft, American bankers had been encouraged to participate in loans negotiated by the China Consortium. In fact, Taft's secretary of state, Philander C. Knox, proclaimed the right of the State Department to influence and direct foreign investment in China and elsewhere.[8] In 1913 Woodrow Wilson dramatically forced American bankers to withdraw from the consortium because certain provisions of a proposed loan impinged upon the "administrative independence" of China. His action clearly indicated that government supervision of loans could be negative as well as positive, although at the time Wilson thought he was freeing American economic interests from the restraints of the consortium. Wilson reversed his position in 1918 out of fear of Japan's growing economic power in China, and urged American bankers to reenter the consortium. This time the American Banking Group agreed to obtain governmental approval of all loans to China in order to insure that the four powers involved (England, France, Japan, and the United States) honored Chinese sovereignty and preserved the Open Door. In return for their participation in the Consortium, American bankers were assured that the government would make public its approval of Chinese loans in the future and because of the risks involved would "aid in every proper way . . . to insure the execution of equitable contracts made in good faith by its citizens in foreign lands."[9] In this manner a mild form of loan control became associated with government-guaranteed equality of treatment, that is, the Open Door in China.

Other sporadic attempts to supervise economic foreign policy outside of the Far East included Secretary of State William Jennings Bryan's ban on loans to belligerent governments in 1914, which was abandoned the following year, and periodic government interference with economic activities in Latin America, which had become standard policy since the 1890s. For example, in 1917 the United States informed Ecuador that it would not approve any more loans to that country until the claims of an American railroad company were met. At one stage in the protracted postwar dispute with Mexico over subsoil rights, American bankers promised the State Department that they would refrain from making any financial arrangements with Mexico which would "afford her real assistance in the reconstruction of her affairs" until the United States' terms for recognition were met.[10] Bolshevik Russia constituted another area of the world where economic restrictions were imposed by the State Department. In both Russia and Mexico the attempts to control political and economic relations were in reaction to revolutions in those countries and were based on political ideology as much as on the economic assumption that nations must honor international obligations and contracts before they could be accorded recognition and enjoy normal economic intercourse.[11]

By 1920, therefore, the pattern had been established whereby bankers voluntarily accepted periodic loan control by the government in three important underdeveloped areas of the world: China, Russia, and portions of Latin America. They did so either to secure a federal guarantee of an Open Door for their activities, or because nationalist revolutions had created such critical political and economic conditions as to warrant their temporary cooperation with government restrictions. Before and immediately following the First World War, however, the United States government had not established any hard and firm guidelines which had, in turn, been acknowledged by bankers for portfolio or direct investments. And when certain Washington officials made an attempt to do just this in the early 1920s, strong banker resistance to the principle of financial supervision quickly surfaced.

The central figure in the postwar attempt to develop systematic control over the foreign loan policy of the United States was Herbert Hoover. Shortly after the war he had urged American bankers to organize an independent corporation and to practice "economic statesmanship" by setting up their own standards for lending abroad which would prevent "fraud, waste, and loss." Hoover hoped that the financial community would take the initiative not only in providing the necessary private credits for

Europe's recovery, but also in guaranteeing the quality of such loans. When his advice had not been acted upon by the time he became secretary of commerce, he began to work to obtain effective government supervision of loans.[12] His failure to obtain this is one of the most important facts in the development of modern American economic foreign policy.

The first meeting of the Harding administration to develop a postwar loan policy was held on May 25, 1921. In attendance were the president, Charles Evans Hughes, Andrew Mellon, Hoover, and banking representatives Thomas W. Lamont and Milton E. Ailes. At this conference it was decided that the government should be informed of future loans so that "it might express itself regarding them." The only formal business confirmation of the agreement was contained in a letter written to Harding on June 6, 1921, by J. P. Morgan. It maintained that the State Department would be kept "fully informed of any and all negotiations for loans to foreign governments," and that the House of Morgan had contacted "all people who have anything to do with issuing foreign loans."[13] In spite of the Morgan letter, the tenuousness of the entire arrangement was apparent from the fact that no official announcement of any agreement was made until March 1922.

Between the May 1921 meeting and the March 1922 statement, Hoover worked to obtain "definite and firm standards" for judging each loan, and became increasingly alarmed as the months passed and the number of foreign loans increased without the government reaching any clarification on standards. He was particularly worried in December 1921 over loans which were used for military purposes in Europe. The bankers themselves complained that they were unsure what kind of information the government wanted from them and how much time it needed to consider a loan. Finally in February 1922, Hoover thought the loan situation critical enough to insist on another meeting with the president, cabinet members, and banking representatives.[14] The result this time was the so-called "ruling of 1922." Issued as a press release by the State Department on March 3, the statement was critical of banking and investment circles for not "sufficiently" understanding that they were to keep the department informed about the "flotation of foreign bond issues in the American market." It was admitted that the government could not require bankers to comply with this request, and that the government would not, in any case, "pass upon the merits of foreign loans as business propositions, nor assume any responsibility whatever in connection with loan transactions." This ruling applied only to loans which were to be publicly offered to foreign governments or foreign corporations. It did not cover privately held loans and appeared to be aimed primarily at controlling loans to those countries that had borrowed from the United States during the war.[15]

Such limited government supervision fell far short of the loan control Hoover wanted by the spring of 1922. His ideas were highly developed by that time and were shared by Grosvenor M. Jones, chief of the newly created Finance and Investment Division of the Bureau of Foreign and Domestic Commerce (BFDC). Both men agreed that the government had a clear responsibility in the matter and should not avoid the issue by assuming a noncommittal attitude. The responsibility was threefold. First, there was the responsibility to the American investor who had "been induced to believe that foreign loans are necessary to put the world on its feet," and "who will in the last analysis look to the Government to protect his interests in foreign loans whether they have been approved by the Government or not." Second, there was the responsibility to the banker "who should have the benefit of such advice and guidance [as] the Government may be able to give." And third, there was the responsibility to the foreign nations who might be tempted into "unwise borrowings and unsound fiscal policies" if the credit facilities of the United States were used too freely.[16]

It was Hoover's opinion, therefore, that loans should be judged in terms of "their security, their reproductive character, and the methods of promotion." In addition to judging loans on their economic merits, he contended that to be "reproductive" they should be earmarked for projects which would improve living standards, increase consumer consumption, and contribute to social stability. He thought that loans which were used for military expenditures, for balancing spendthrift budgets, or for bolstering inflated currencies represented a waste of American surplus capital and "generally would be disastrous" because such loans would not increase domestic productivity or aid in the "economic rehabilitation of the world." To insure these standards, three different departments had to cooperate in considering the loans, according to the Hoover plan. The Commerce Department would advise upon the fiscal soundness of the country involved and the reproductive character of the proposed loans; the Department of the Treasury would consider whether or not the nation had satisfactorily funded its war debts to the United States, and the Department of State would rule upon the financial transactions in terms of national interest and political desirability from a diplomatic point of view. Recognizing that some of these suggested standards required that the government assume a paternalistic attitude toward foreign governments, Grosvenor Jones recommended in a memorandum to Hoover that the decisions of the government not be made public.[17]

Probably the most controversial aspect of Hoover's loan control policy concerned whether or not foreign governments should be required to spend a portion of the proceeds from American loans for American products. Rumors about such restrictive clauses had been circulating within the business community since 1921, and the secretary of commerce had contributed to them in a February 22, 1922, statement made in Chicago. Apparently, however, Hoover did not support purchasing clauses as such. What he wanted was to secure for American manufacturers equal opportunity in bidding for contracts. After having failed to do this privately in connection with a National City Bank loan to the State of Queensland in Australia in February 1922,[18] he tried to bring the financial community over to his point of view through public pressure and through the increased public services of the BFDC under the direction of Julius Klein. With publicity and friendly federal persuasion, Hoover, Klein, and Grosvenor Jones hoped to create voluntary cooperation between the manufacturing and financial segments of the business community along the lines established by the British government. Although leaders of the American Bankers Association promised to help Commerce officials obtain certain legislation in return for economic information, they never agreed to place purchasing or equal bidding clauses in foreign loan contracts.[19] The BFDC ultimately did prove to be an invaluable source of aid for businessmen in general, but it was not able to bring about even the moderate kind of voluntary cooperation between bankers and manufacturers that Hoover desired on foreign loans because of the conflicting views of these two interest groups.

Thus, when powerful manufacturing concerns launched a campaign in March 1922 to convince all government officials that "at least twenty percent of the proceeds of all foreign loans" should be spent in the United States, this was far beyond what Hoover and Jones felt to be equitable. As Jones pointed out: "It is unfair to loan a man money and tell him that he must spend it in your shop regardless of conditions as to price, quality, delivery, etc. It is a galling condition to impose. It would lend color to the talk that is going around . . . that the United States seeks to impose its financial domination upon the world. It would call forth the clamor that accompanied the agitation against 'dollar diplomacy' when Mr. Knox was Secretary of State." Hoover agreed that the most he could ask for would be reproductive loans with provisions granting American producers "equal opportunity in bidding for contracts and supplying materials under such loans." In addition Hoover expressed the hope that any installation originally built with American materials would "necessitate continuous subsequent purchase of spare parts" from the United States.[20] Despite these qualifications, the Department of Commerce expediently allied itself with the manufacturers in their drive for purchasing clauses, in the hope that general loan control would be achieved in the process.

The leadership of the manufacturers' movement was impressive. It consisted of the National Foreign Trade Council under the guidance of the NFTC secretary, O. K. Davis, and council member Maurice A. Oudin, vice-president of General Electric. Members of the council represented such important firms as United States Steel, Standard Oil, Westinghouse, United States Rubber, and International Harvester. The idea of purchasing clauses was naturally very popular among the large export manufacturers in the country. Local boards of trade and chambers of commerce, however, representing the less specialized and non-exporting, smaller business firms tended to ignore or reject the official NFTC position.[21] So essentially the battle lines were drawn within the ranks of big business—prominent bankers on one side and powerful manufacturers on the other.

The controversy reached a high point in the spring and summer of 1922. During this period both Benjamin Strong, governor of the Federal Reserve Bank of New York, and Thomas W. Lamont of the House of Morgan sharply criticized not only the restrictive clauses in loan agreements, but any federal control over foreign capital issues. Strong's protest was made directly to the State Department on April 14 after he learned that Hoover might try to discourage "foreign loans whose proceeds were not to be spent in the first instance for American products." His memorandum to Secretary Hughes attacked the assumption of Hoover and the large manufacturers that the restrictive clauses would increase American exports and thus guarantee future American prosperity (in addition to relieving the immediate problem of domestic unemployment left in the wake of the depression). On the contrary, Strong argued that "restriction of the character now being discussed will result in a reduction of our export trade just to the extent that the restriction attempts to require borrowers to buy goods in this market at higher prices than they can be obtained elsewhere and so defeats the negotiation of such loans: Prices control where trade goes." Less convincingly, Strong also denied the contention of Hoover and the manufacturers that the British government imposed similar restrictions. Such purchasing clauses, he argued, were simply the "result of better cooperation after many years of experience between that department of the British business organization which supplies credit and another department which manufactures and exports goods."[22] This, of course, was exactly the type of informal control that the Department of Commerce wanted to exert.

In terms of the future direction of American economic foreign policy, the most important part of Strong's memorandum was devoted to a general criticism of loan supervision by the government. He opposed any restrictions "for the purpose of influencing foreign governments in their domestic policies." That is, Hoover's standards for "reproductive" loans should not be employed because they "might well mean that all foreign governments with unbalanced budgets and which are spending money for unproductive purposes will be unable to borrow in this market, and in consequence the American export trade will be cut down by the exact amount of all such loans as are thereby prevented from being placed here." He also did not think it advisable for the government to consider the economic merits of loans. In a June letter to Hughes he asked, "if our government undertakes to pass upon the goodness of a loan, even in a minute degree, does it not inaugurate a system of responsibility to which there may be no termination except by the assumption of full responsibility?"[23]

While Strong denied the government the right to pass on the economic soundness of individual loans, he did not maintain that the government should shun all political responsibility in the event loan contracts were not honored abroad. Obviously, like most bankers and businessmen of the 1920s, he wanted government protection without government control. Most important, however, was the implicit assumption in Strong's remarks concerning the soundness of foreign loans. One is led to believe from them that if Washington denied the right to determine the "economic merit" of capital issues, bankers would automatically perform this function. As will be seen, increasingly after 1925 they did not.

After assuring Strong that his position would receive serious consideration, Hughes forwarded his memorandum to Hoover and the secretary of commerce replied on April 29. Hoover began by stating that he agreed with the Federal Reserve Board governor that foreign loans were vital to the world and the commerce of the United States. But he categorically denied that any standards should be established by the government, saying, "It appears to me that the Federal Government has certain unavoidable governmental and moral responsibilities toward these operations, and that our bankers have certain internal responsibilities to our commerce." He then reviewed his position on loan control in great detail, explicitly pointing out that he favored only very moderate purchasing clause guarantees. Earlier than most government officials, Hoover understood the predicament facing the government if indeed it found itself politically but not economically responsible for foreign loans, as Strong had implied. So he argued:

> In the political category it may be stated that credits from our citizens to foreign governments or municipalities have a different complexion from either internal credit operations or even of credits to private persons abroad, *in that there is no method by which failure in payment of such loans can be prosecuted, except by the diplomatic intervention of our government.* There rests upon the Federal Government, whether desired or not, an implication that it will assist our citizens in relation to such transactions. To impose such lines of conduct on defaulting governmental creditors as will recover to our citizens their due is a path which has led to infinite complexities in international relations. It is perfectly possible to carry an argument against foreign loans to an extreme, but even a moderate view should certainly go to the extent of creating some concern in the Federal Government *that the security and form of these loans should, at the outset, involve the fair hope that the Federal Government will not be required to enter upon intervention.*[24]

Hoover saw more clearly than other members of the cabinet that the political and economic responsibilities of the United States to its citizens could not be artificially separated for the convenience of businessmen or politicians who preferred to close their eyes to the complex relationship between the two. His loan control policy represented an attempt to coordinate economic and political foreign policy in a way that has only been gradually and very imperfectly accomplished since World War II. His failure to convince Strong and other international bankers of the validity of his position meant, in essence, that America's economic empire expanded after 1920 with little political direction except where ideological considerations perverted common sense, as was the case with Soviet Russia. Otherwise vague notions about the Open Door, in terms of equality of economic opportunity, about Pan Americanism, in terms of United States hegemony in Latin America, and about the sanctity of contracts, were substituted for responsible federal controls based on coordinated political and economic considerations. Moreover, there was a tendency to apply these abstractions indiscriminately, rather than to consider the individual merits of each situation. The result of Hoover's failure has been that the productivity of foreign investments, which he valued so highly was only given lip-service by the State Department in the 1920s and is no longer an important criterion in the country's foreign aid program.[25]

By the end of the summer of 1922 it was evident that the Department of Commerce in temporary alliance with the NFTC movement had not succeeded in bringing about effective government supervision of foreign loans, but Hoover continued to try to secure moderate voluntary cooperation from bankers and manufacturers. Although these two rival groups haggled for the rest of the decade over purchasing clauses and over theories about international trade, the fundamental issue of responsibility and productivity which Hoover had originally championed was never seriously considered by either side. Bankers steadfastly resisted cooperation with manufacturers on restrictive purchasing clauses. And with the exception of selected loans to China, Mexico, Russia, Germany (before the 1924 Dawes Plan), and France (until 1928), bankers also circumvented federal control over their lending power.[26] By the middle of the decade some bankers were ignoring Hoover's war on foreign monopolies by attempting to loan money to such cartels as the Brazilian Coffee Valorization and European Potash, while others were contemplating indirect loans to Russia.[27] After 1925 criticism of loan control increased in business publications, until the *Bankers Magazine* was saying in 1932 that it was "difficult to see why the practice of scrutinizing foreign loans should be maintained after the necessity for it has disappeared." Arguing that there was some justification for the policy immediately following the war, the editor concluded that in light of the Dawes and Young plans, "its continuance now is of doubtful propriety."[28]

Throughout the decade international bankers and manufacturers buttressed their opposing positions with economic theories and statistics. But in the short-run, for all of their earlier talk about postwar cooperation, their arguments usually degenerated into a debate over quick profits.[29] Obviously bankers would gain more if they negotiated as many unrestricted loans as possible, while manufacturers preferred fewer loans with the guarantee that American products would be purchased. Without a substantial degree of cooperation between these segments of the business community, as Hoover understood only too well, the United States could not nurse the world's economy back to health or develop permanent prosperity at home. Ironically on this issue Hoover found himself thwarted by business internationalists—his normal allies in the financial reconstruction of Europe—because they were less concerned with preserving American capital for productive development of domestic and foreign resources.[30]

In contrast, business nationalists generally tended to praise what they dimly perceived to be the official loan control policy of the government in the 1920s, and to criticize the activity of international bankers, especially after 1929 when numerous countries defaulted on American loans. During the depression, *Iron Age* carried this position to its logical extreme by criticizing loans which had been made to Germany, and concluding that economic isolationism would not have become a derogatory term immediately following the war had it not been for the actions of importers, international bankers, and theoretical economists. While this is an extreme example, nevertheless, functional antagonism, that is, nonfinancial interests versus financial interests, was a basic cause of the division within the business community over loan and investment policies. A 1927 nationalist writing in the *Nation's Business* denounced international bankers because he believed their loan policy was directed toward forcing a lowering of the tariff. His argument was that Europeans would insist on paying off these debts in goods, and ultimately the tariff would be lowered to accommodate them. The financier James Speyer confirmed the existence of nationalist hostility toward the banking community over loan policy when he wrote to Norman Davis in 1932 that he doubted whether "interested people in Europe and bankers there and the League of Nations officials generally realize the attacks to which 'International Bankers' have been subjected in this country" because of their participation in certain League of Nations loans.[31]

Just as the business community divided over loan policy, so did government groups. It is now apparent that the Department of Commerce under Hoover fought a losing and increasingly lonely battle within the Republican administrations between 1921 and 1929. Opposition to Hoover's program came from Presidents Harding and Coolidge, from Secretary of the Treasury Andrew W. Mellon, and from individual members of Congress and the Federal Reserve Board. Principally, however, it was opposed by the State Department under Secretaries Hughes and Frank B Kellogg.[32] Their opposition does not seem to have stemmed from pressure generated by bankers' criticism of Hoover's loan supervision program. Rather, it arose out of a jurisdictional dispute between the Departments of State and Commerce and a personal disagreement between Hoover and Hughes over standards for conducting an economic foreign policy designed to secure American leadership in the postwar world.

Hoover had entered the cabinet with the understanding that he would have a "voice on all important economic policies of the administration." In his determination to expand the functions of the Department of Commerce, he ran headlong into the traditional supremacy that State Department officials exercised over American foreign policy. Immediately following Harding's inauguration the two departments began to clash over control of commercial personnel abroad. In particular, Hoover wanted agents from his department to assume certain duties normally performed by consular officers. The State Department countered Hoover's aggressiveness by backing the Rogers bill of 1921, which would have specifically given the secretary of state control over the foreign activities of all government officials, by lending support to those congressmen who criticized the work of the Commerce Department as a "wasteful duplication" of consular and diplomatic officials, and by endorsing the book *The Foreign Service of the United States*. Written by Consul General Tracy H. Lay, this work consisted of a strong defense of the State Department's foreign personnel as compared to those of the Commerce Department. Nevertheless, Hoover succeeded in expanding both the domestic and the overseas operations of his department, and most American businessmen were convinced by the end of the decade that the Commerce Department was better equipped than the

State Department to service their interests at home and abroad.[33]

Hoover was not so successful in this jurisdictional controversy when it touched upon the issue of loan control. While the original Rogers bill never passed Congress, it did reflect the concern of such men as Representative John Jacob Rogers, former Under-Secretary of State Frank L. Polk, and Secretary Hughes. The unified control of foreign affairs by the State Department, they felt, might be undermined by Hoover's insistence that those foreign policy matters which were largely economic (for example, loans) fell exclusively under the purview of the Commerce Department. Although Hughes agreed in principle with Hoover's contention that modern diplomacy was becoming more and more a combined problem of economics and politics, in practice he clung to the more traditional idea of separating, whenever possible, private economic activity from the public political functions of the State Department. But at the same time he jealously guarded his department's traditional monopoly over foreign policy by telling Hoover that capital exported abroad by American bankers was not "foreign to the work of the State Department," and by refusing to relinquish his authority over loan control. He tried, however, to placate Hoover with the ambiguous promise that he would not withhold any material which was "pertinent to the work of the Department of Commerce." Thus, by the end of 1921 an uneasy truce had been reached between the two departments for exchanging information on loans, but Hughes retained final jurisdiction over all proposed loans.[34]

No such truce was ever reached over loan standards. When Hughes said the State Department should respond to the "imperative demands of American business," he did not think this entitled the government to channel private investment abroad through direct economic control. Neither did his successor, Frank B. Kellogg. So both men preferred not to comment on the "economic feasibility" or "validity" of private loans. They were primarily concerned with establishing only very general political controls over economic relations between the United States and other nations. By this they meant that they opposed loans to unrecognized governments or to ideologically hostile countries, or those intended exclusively for military expenditures or any activity that ran "counter to the clearly defined policies of this Government." But Hughes and Kellogg steadfastly refused to make economic judgments on the foreign financial transactions of American citizens. At the same time they were less chary of resorting to force to protect American interests abroad than Hoover. Of course, Hoover approved of the same set of political controls, but in addition he wanted the government to make sure that loans were economically sound, that they would be used for productive purposes, and that the recipient country was not already "over-borrowed," so as to avoid possible future default and/or intervention on economic grounds.[35]

For example, in 1924 Hoover became disturbed about the numerous loans being made to Germany. He feared that service on some of these private loans to German states and municipalities might ultimately interfere with Germany's ability to meet its reparation payments under the Dawes Plan. Once again, he and Grosvenor Jones agreed that the government had a responsibility to individual investors and should not inadvertently place itself in the position of being responsible for loans which might default. The State Department did not act upon Hoover's warnings until the fall of 1925. At that time it began to point out to bankers privately that they should inform prospective American investors about the possibility of a conflict between payments on private loans and those on the Dawes Plan. Most of the major banking firms replied that Owen D. Young had assured them they did not have to worry about this kind of problem, and the government did not push the matter any further for two years. Then in September 1927, the State Department publicly announced it was going to consider carefully all future loans to German states and cities, and would place an embargo on those which threatened the Dawes Plan annuities. Despite confirmation of Germany's extravagant fiscal policies from S. Parker Gilbert, a Morgan partner and agent general for reparations payments, and despite Hoover's proddings, no loan to Germany was ever publicly opposed by the State Department on these grounds even when it was privately admitted that a particular transaction was undesirable.[36]

Inevitably, therefore, there were disputes between the Departments of State and Commerce over economic foreign policy, but in the long run they agreed more than they disagreed over specific loans.[37] Loans which violated the Open Door by creating foreign monopolies were refused, such as those to Brazil for coffee valorization and to European potash cartels. A ban was placed on a loan to a Czechoslovakian brewery because the "administration could not consistently approve a loan for the manufacture of a beverage abroad considered illegal at home." There also was general agreement that war debts had to be funded before the United States would permit private loans to the Allied countries. Russia and France were the major nations to suffer from this ruling, although Belgium and Italy were also temporarily affected by it in the 1920s.[38] By and large, however, most of the loans submitted to the government before 1929 were approved by both departments. The point is that even when State and Commerce officials agreed to oppose or approve certain loans, they sometimes did so for basically different reasons because of jurisdictional jealousy and because they were not always using the same set of standards to determine what the government's responsibilities were in promoting a world economic community.

Hoover's loan control program was a victim of this interdepartmental strife and of opposition from segments of the business community. Although he continued to speak out about the need for tighter restrictions on loans and to issue private warnings about the wild borrowing by Latin American nations, outside his own department his exhortations received scant support after 1922. His position on restrictive clauses, which had never been strong enough from the standpoint of the large manufacturers, was always too strong for international financiers. Writing to Secretary Kellogg in 1926 about purchasing clauses he reiterated that the government had "no authority to impose any such conditions upon foreign loan issues in the United States," while continuing to recommend that the State Department require future loan agreements to guarantee Americans "equal opportunity with other nationals in bidding upon supplies and construction." His consistency on these points throughout the decade accomplished little in the way of loan supervision or business unity. It did, however, allow Hoover's former Commerce associates to argue during the Senate investigation of foreign loans in 1931 and 1932 that their department had been more cautious in approving public flotations than the State Department. This does not alter the fact that the warnings and negative reports issued by Commerce officials went largely unheeded.[39]

Although the State Department proved a major stumbling block to Hoover's loan control program, members of the Senate can be added to the list of government officials who helped to undermine his moderate plans for supervision. In 1925 and again in 1927 a subcommittee of the Senate Foreign Relations Committee conducted hearings on the role the government was playing in guaranteeing foreign economic investments. The hearings were the result of Senate resolutions requesting the president to ask the Departments of State, Commerce, and the Treasury, and the Federal Reserve Board to refrain from 1) directly or indirectly "engaging the responsibility of the Government of the United States . . . to supervise the fulfillment of financial arrangements between citizens of the United States and Sovereign Foreign Governments," and from 2) "in any means whatsoever giving official recognition to any arrangements which may commit the Government of the United States to any form of military intervention in order to compel the observation of alleged obligations."[40]

Precipitated by American military intervention in the Dominican Republic, Haiti, and most recently Nicaragua, the testimony at these hearings revealed that the conflict between the government and bankers and the disagreement within the business community over loan supervision were not generally known at the time. It was usually assumed by the critics of United States policy, who dominated the sessions and who based their opinions on events in Latin America, that cooperation between government and business internationalists was uniform and equally effective in other parts of the world, when in fact it was not. Consequently the testimony did not convey to the public the complexity of the postwar relationship between government and business. In addition it was misleading with respect to the financial soundness of foreign loans made prior to 1926.[41]

Despite these shortcomings (and in part because of them) the Senate hearings of 1925 and 1927 stimulated more public criticism of placing the military power of the United States behind foreign economic transactions, and of the practice of assuming internal financial functions in parts of Central America and the Caribbean.[42] To the degree that these activities were misconstrued to be part of Hoover's desire to see all loans "approved," the hearings increased the pressure upon, and in some cases further encouraged, government officials outside of the Commerce Department to soft-pedal loan control.

The irony of such a reaction lay in the fact that Hoover had issued more warnings against loans to Latin America than for any other part of the world, and that he was on record in opposition to the use of armed intervention or any other means of coercion, including the threat of nonrecognition, against foreign governments with whom the United States carried on economic relations, with the exception of Russia. This is not to say that Hoover avoided any opportunity to paternalistically advise foreign nations about their economic affairs. He also eagerly encouraged American business abroad in a variety of ways, from attempting to establish tax exemptions on certain kinds of European investments to legalizing import pools. Nevertheless, he did on occasion discourage economic activity if he thought the venture was economically unsound, and he was not willing to back with armed force the foreign business his department encouraged and promoted. Indeed, this had been a fundamental point of disagreement between Hoover on the one hand and Hughes and the international bankers on the other from the beginning of the decade. The latter felt it was the duty of the government to protect all American loans and investments abroad, while Hoover wanted to insure the economic soundness of such transactions to minimize the possibility of the United States being called upon to intervene.[43]

In retrospect it can be seen that a policy of government control of capital issues was not achieved between 1920 and 1929 because of dissension and misunderstanding within government and business circles. This coincided with a period of unprecedented American prosperity and the desire among business internationalists to assume responsibility for the economic reconstruction of

Europe. Thus, the warnings issued after 1925, not only by Hoover but also by a few financiers such as Lamont and Vanderlip and the more cautious banking houses of J. P. Morgan and Kuhn, Loeb, and Company, against easy credit policies, "indiscriminate lending," speculation, and the violent competition among American bankers abroad, were ignored or dismissed for smacking of economic isolation. These warnings for the most part were too few, too general, and too late. Riding a high tide of confidence born of prosperity and a "long defaultless period," most bankers who should have known better, and investors who apparently did not, unconsciously lowered their economic standards as they raised their economic aspirations between 1925 and 1929.[44]

It is difficult to determine the exact results of the very mild form of loan control which was practiced by the government in the 1920s. Obviously the refusal of the State Department to make economic judgments did not always work to the advantage of the American investor. As one manufacturing journal pointed out, "Offerings of obviously doubtful worth have been approved as readily as thoroughly sound ones when the 'interests' of the Government itself did not require disapproval." But a similar criticism could have been made of Hoover for discouraging sound loans, for example, to foreign cartels. Even before the depression began, some businessmen suspected that "the interest of the investor is the last thing considered" by the government in approving loans. This condemnation does not appear as relevant today as it did in the early 1930s, when defaults became common; it cannot be proven that such government discouragement or encouragement as did exist resulted in either "more sound or unsound loans" in the period between World War I and the Great Depression.[45] If bond issues were denied access to the United States market, they usually were sold abroad, anyway. Often portions of these loans would then be bought by American bankers and privately redistributed in this country. Loan and investment control by the government was negligible, to say the least, particularly if it is remembered that only public flotations in the United States came under scrutiny. No attempt was made to officially regulate private bank credits or bond issues which were floated abroad.[46]

Hence, the massive portfolio and direct investments made in

the 1920s were essentially unsupervised by the government. They were accompanied by operations of the Federal Reserve Banks in restoring gold standards and in promoting currency stabilization abroad. These private investments and Federal Reserve credits would have contributed substantially to the general economic rehabilitation of the postwar world had they been part of a truly cooperative economic foreign policy which was not contradicted by the tariff, trade, and intergovernmental debt policies of the United States. The most comprehensive cooperative action for controlling international finance did not come until 1929 with the proposal by the Young Committee to establish the Bank for International Settlements. Originally designed not only to facilitate the transfer of German reparation payments but also to coordinate national monetary policies through the central banking systems of the major nations, its powers were emasculated before it came into existence.

Therefore, in the absence of effective national and international controls, public and private loans in effect obscured the economic instability created by American insistence on debt collection and high tariffs by allowing foreign nations to meet their debt payments and to purchase unprecedented amounts of goods from the United States. Had this country adopted a less traditional attitude toward the Allied war debts and German reparation payments, there would have been no need for either the abnormal amount of short- and long-term foreign loans or the excessive expansion of American exports which occurred after the war. Only strong loan control in conjunction with lower tariffs, increased imports on the part of the United States, and cancellation of the outstanding intergovernmental debts would have changed the world financial situation before 1929. While it is doubtful if these policies would have prevented the depression, in all probability they would have made it less severe.[47]

Chapter Five

Allied War Debts & German Reparations, 1920–1933

Low tariff duties, increased imports through most-favored-nation agreements, and federal control of long-term capital issues all proved unacceptable to certain business and political interests between 1920 and 1933. This meant that the postwar dream of reconstructing Europe behind a cooperative, American-led effort depended, in the last analysis, upon how the United States dealt with the related problems of inter-Allied debts and German reparation payments. Together these two issues represented the most important variables with respect to the economic stability of the western world prior to 1929. Theoretically the war debts were a powerful lever that the United States could use 1) to help break down preferential trading systems abroad in order to substitute its Open Door policy; 2) to obtain a reasonable reparations program for Germany; and 3) to bargain for changes in the terms of the Treaty of Versailles, especially those concerning mandated territory and other economic privileges which the Allies had reserved for themselves. In the course of the 1920s, however, the United States did not use the Allied debt question to its best diplomatic advantage.

Ignoring for the moment the contemporary moral arguments for and against payment, it is now clear that all debts, whether incurred during the war, resulting from the terms of the peace settlement in the form of reparations, or resulting from repudiation and nationalization as in the case of the Russian debts, could be satisfactorily settled only if they were considered a common problem to be worked out at international conferences. Unfortunately for the economic health of the postwar world, the United States insisted on handling these debts strictly on a commercial basis, and never officially recognized the connection between any of them. Operating on the assumption that international obligations had to be honored, the government chose to isolate and deal with each as a separate economic issue.

From the time of the Paris Peace Conference and regardless of the party in power, the United States consistently adhered to two major principles in the 1920s and early 1930s. The first was that the war debts of the Allies should not be cancelled nor even discussed at international meetings; the second was that German reparation payments should not be linked or simultaneously discussed with the war debt question. The former position was justified on the ground that the loans to the Allies represented purely business transactions and as such were "solely matters of domestic policy . . . and . . . not subject to international agreement." Each foreign country was expected to make arrangements to fund its debt payments by negotiating individually with Washington. The second position was adopted out of the fear that European governments would make their debt settlements contingent on Germany's payment of reparations, and thus in the long run force the United States to be responsible for the collection of the reparations. American officials suspected that once such a situation was achieved, European nations would automatically reserve for themselves the right to suspend debt payments or at least drastically reduce them if Germany defaulted on her payments to them.[1]

The business community was deeply divided on these two principles. While the general public and business nationalists passively backed the official position, business internationalists disagreed and vacillated among themselves over both. Consequently, the controversy over debt and reparation policy centered within the internationalist segment of the business community, as had also been true of the loan policy controversy. But in this instance the focal point of disagreement can be narrowed even further because it occurred almost exclusively among bankers. The debate over debts and reparations was limited to a single profession because of the purely financial nature of the issues involved, and because of the highly technical and complicated economic arrangements which emerged over the course of the decade. The division among bankers over debt cancellation was more evident in the immediate postwar years than during the depression. Those who publicly advocated complete or partial cancellation made their strongest appearance between 1918 and 1923. The movement assumed worldwide significance in 1920, when a memorandum circulated in the United States and abroad calling for a conference of businessmen from all parts of the world to discuss postwar economic problems. One of the recommendations in the European version of this memorandum called for consideration of cancellation of the inter-Allied debts. Forty-four prominent Americans, including representatives of the United States Chamber of Commerce and the major banking houses across the country, signed the document. Nonetheless, largely because of the fear of debt cancellation, Washington refused to endorse the memorandum or the resulting conference held in Brussels during October 1920.[2]

Although some members of the Wilson administration, including Secretary of the Treasury William Gibbs McAdoo and his assistant secretary, Norman H. Davis, advocated plans for scaling down the Allied debt payments, the Democrats left office in 1921 after setting a precedent against debt cancellation which their Republican successors never publicly repudiated. The attempts by the Harding, Coolidge, and Hoover administrations to collect the war debts, however, were less greedy than is usually contended. Much of the "Shylock" interpretation of the American position comes from the less than forthright way in which the issue was presented to the American people by government and business spokesmen. For example, in 1922 during the height of the cancellation controversy, Herbert Hoover, as a member of the World War Foreign Debt Commission, initially supported writing off the prearmistice debts in order to strengthen "our moral position" and enhance the "probabilities of payment." When told by his colleagues on the commission that Congress would never accept such a proposal he then recommended that the United States forgo collecting interest payments and spread the repayment of the principal over an undetermined number of years based on each debtor's capacity to pay. Again the plan was considered unacceptable to other members of the commission, who insisted that Congress would never approve a debt-funding agreement which did not at least "preserve the appearance of repayment of both principal and interest." Congress had made this clear when it responded to the request of Secretary of the Treasury Andrew Mellon for authority to refund foreign debts, by creating the five-man commission with the following instructions: interest rates were to be no less than 4.5 percent; repayment of the principal of all war debts was required in twenty-five years; and under no circumstances was cancellation to be considered. Subsequently under the influence of Hoover and other moderate members of the War Debt Commission, such as Secretaries Hughes and Mellon, it was decided not to follow these instructions. They were so harsh, it was argued, that if enforced they would "gradually strengthen the forces of repudiation and cancellation." As the practical-minded Mellon later noted, "If we insist on too difficult terms, we [will] receive nothing."[3] Little attempt was made, however, to clarify publicly what the policy of the commission, as opposed to that of Congress, actually was toward the repayment of Allied debts.

Beginning in 1923, debt-funding agreements were negotiated by the commission which 1) made the funded principal slightly less than the total debt prior to funding, by recalculating the accrued interest at 4.25 percent rather than the original 5 percent; 2) extended the payments on the new funded principal over sixty years; and 3) fixed interest rates to be paid over the whole period of payments on the funded principal ranging from .3 percent to 3.3 percent. The average interest rate for the fifteen nations that agreed to refund their war debts in the 1920s was 2.1 percent. While these debt-funding agreements gave the "appearance of repayment," they in fact reduced the combined outstanding indebtedness of the Allied nations by approximately 43 percent. This was a form of partial cancellation which was accepted in practice, but not in name, by Congress and other government officials who were convinced that popular opinion would not tolerate the admission of cancellation.[4]

It was not so much a question of the United States attempting to collect every last dollar as of government officials adopting a policy of partial cancellation in the name of refunding. This encouraged European nations to hold out for even better terms, for they were seldom presented with a quid pro quo offer by Washington officials. It also misled the public into thinking that these were normal debts capable of being paid off in a normal business fashion. Even the few concessions which the Allies made with respect to German reparation payments and mandate privileges in the Middle East did not in the long run contribute significantly to a world economic community because they were not comprehensive enough to stabilize economic conditions in Germany or to bring about anything but sporadic and grudging cooperation in other parts of the world. Too little generosity surreptitiously extended was possibly worse than none at all. What the situation required was more quid pro quo bargaining aimed at integrating the debt question into a comprehensive and coordinated economic and political settlement for Europe. About the only politicians who publicly identified with refunding agreements as examples of outright cancellation were some strongly nationalistic Progressives, but their most ungenerous viewpoint did not prevail, as Congress gave its approval to all of the new debt settlements in the course of the decade.

Hoover, in contrast, always referred to these reductions as "concessions," never as cancellations, because there had been no "cancellation of the capital sum of any debt." Throughout the decade he privately remained willing to sacrifice interest payments for short periods of time as long as the funding agreements were not based "on deferment of the payment of the principal," for that would "steadily undermine the whole probability of repayment." Publicly, however, he encouraged the anticancellation forces in the country, and refused to admit there was any legal or economic connection between German reparations and Allied war debts. His irritation over the reluctance of the debtor nations to comply with what he considered very generous debt-funding agreements made him a leading critic, while secretary of commerce, of those "Americans who loved Europe more and America less . . . [and like] our international bankers agitated for cancellation night and day." In 1929 he did verbally offer to exchange most of the remaining English war debt for Bermuda, British Honduras, and the island of Trinidad, but Prime Minister Ramsay MacDonald refused to consider his proposal.[5] After the depression began, Hoover's principled opposition to cancellation became more rigid in the face of French and British propaganda calling for. repudiation of all intergovernmental debts, but as will be noted below, his responsibilities as president finally forced him to modify his position.

Frank A. Vanderlip was probably the best known international banker whose ideas on Allied indebtedness were like those of Hoover. Immediately after the war he had quietly and privately favored partial cancellation. By 1922 he had abandoned this idea and was proposing that the justness of the debts should be fully acknowledged as long as the United States played the "role of a very lenient creditor." Unlike Hoover and the government, however, Vanderlip believed that public opinion could be reeducated so that the burden of payments on European nations could be reduced to a bare minimum. He also went beyond Hoover's view of the debt situation when he suggested that after generous terms had been negotiated, all payments which were made on the debts should be immediately reinvested by the United States "in [European] reproductive enterprises so as to contribute toward industrial reconstruction [t]here and to improve production." Vanderlip had demonstrated since the war a special interest in the financial and political rehabilitation of Eastern Europe and so he maintained that a good portion of the money repaid to this country should be invested in the newly established Eastern European nations.[6] Despite his interest in the well-being of Europe, at no time after 1922 did he advocate cancellation of the war debts.

Looking back on the increasing rigidity of the debt position of Vanderlip and Hoover, it is possible to see a parallel development within American banking circles on the same question. As a group, bankers exhibited immediate postwar magnanimity and then either gradually developed stubborn resistance to the idea of cancellation or became cynically resigned to the fact that the debts would never be paid, regardless of United States policy. At the same time, like government officials, they assumed there was overwhelming public disapproval of any form of cancellation. The general attitude of American bankers was best represented by the American Bankers Association. State banking groups usually did not express themselves on the issue, and regional banking associations often assumed a sectional bias which was not representative of national banking opinion. The 1922 ABA convention can be considered the climax of the public procancellation movement among the country's leading bankers between 1918 and 1923. At that meeting cancellation was favored in varying degrees by such business internationalists as Fred I. Kent; Thomas W. Lamont; Sir Reginald McKenna, chairman of the London Joint City and Midland Bank; John McHugh, president of the Mechanics and Metals National Bank, New York; Thomas B. McAdams, current ABA president and vice-president of the Merchants National Bank, Richmond, Virginia; and all the members of the Commerce and Marine Commission of the association.[7]

None of these men, however, were in favor of complete cancellation, and none favored even partial cancellation except in return for "balancing budgets, and curtailment of inflation, the reduction of armaments, and the elimination of governmental waste" on the part of America's European debtors.[8] Partial cancellation at this time usually meant up to 50 percent of the estimated $11.5 billion which Europe owed the United States by 1922. One of the strongest advocates of cancellation, Fred I. Kent, suggested the figure of 70 percent at the convention, but this figure was higher than most procancellation bankers were willing to commit themselves to publicly.[9] By 1923 the basic difference between Hoover and these bankers was that they were willing to consider reducing the capital amount of indebtedness and he was not. As president Hoover continued to be suspicious of most international bankers on the debt question because of the attitudes some of them expressed at this 1922 ABA convention.

Additional financial figures who can be considered in the procancellation camp in the first half of the decade were Charles E. Mitchell, president of National City Bank, New York; Paul M. Warburg of Kuhn, Loeb, and Company and formerly a member of the Federal Reserve Board; Newton D. Baker; Otto Kahn; C. T. Jaffray, president of the First National Bank of Minneapolis; Benjamin M. Anderson, Jr., economist for Chase National Bank, New York; Frederick W. Gehle of the Mechanics and Metals Bank, New York; Bernard Baruch; and J. P. Morgan.[10] Still others who could not bring themselves to call for cancellation did the next best thing by proposing a moratorium on debt payments. Included in this group was Benjamin Strong who, in a private letter, suggested postponement of both interest and principal payments until it could be determined "whether it [the debt] could be paid or to what extent it could be paid." Alvin W. Krech, president of the Equitable Trust Company of New York, was somewhat more specific when he proposed a "holiday of ten years for our Continental Allies, during which time the debt would be considered non-existent." George E. Roberts, vice-president of the National City Bank, New York, was of the opinion that "under the circumstances there seems nothing to do but postpone collections until such time as conditions become more normal toward the reception of payment changes." Some suggestions about reducing debt payments included tempting ideas for increasing the economic power of the United States at the same time. Accordingly, George G. Allen, president of the Garland Steamship Corporation, favored cancellation of the interest on the war debts as long as payments on the principal were used by the United States to buy foreign securities. James A. Farrell, president of United States Steel, promoted an idea popular among large manufacturers whereby the entire foreign indebtedness to the country would be exchanged for investment and ownership "in foreign property of a more or less public service nature." One of the most interesting of these transfer schemes came from a business-oriented government official, Julean Arnold, the commercial attaché at Shanghai. He recommended that in lieu of paying their obligations, Britain, France, and Belgium should be required to turn over their railway and commercial concessions in China.[11]

Except for the proposals of a handful of internationalists who were openly for cancellation, most of these plans proposed in the early 1920s did not contain the term cancellation, but all of them implied that the inter-Allied debts could never be paid in full. The same implication was present in the statements of those banking interests and financial publications that supported the government's program of "debt adjustment" through funding agreements.[12] Their major reason for discussing the subject so circumspectly was the belief that it was very unpopular with the American public. Although bankers were urged in 1922 by the ABA president to brave criticism and to take positions "upon both public and private questions without fear . . . and with no apologies," few did so on the war debt question. Instead, those internationalists in favor of cancellation or substantial debt readjustment invariably couched their ideas in language designed to make them publicly palatable. They always referred diffidently to popular opposition and accommodated it in the hope that it would ultimately change.[13] Nationalists, of course, who opposed cancellation, used the prevalent belief in the power of public opinion and the official position of the United States government as a bulwark against any form of debt repudiation.[14] In actuality the role played by the public in determining this particular phase of American economic foreign policy was probably considerably less than was admitted at the time.

One of the best examples of the deference shown by banking internationalists to what they thought was public opinion occurred when the *ABA Journal* denied in its December 1922 issue that there had been strong procancellation sentiment at its November convention. This denial marked the beginning of the organization's public retreat from cancellationist views. By 1929 the ABA was firmly committed to the government's position that Europe could fulfill her financial obligations if debts were adjusted to each nation's "capacity to pay." This meant that the ABA supported not only the American funding agreements but also the Dawes and Young plans, which purported to establish reparation payments for Germany on the same principle. By 1933, however, the depression had forced the ABA to admit that even the adjusted debts were "unpayable," as many of the original cancellationists had maintained over a decade earlier. This pessimism about the repayment of war debts, which had always lurked in the minds of some international bankers—Paul M.

Warburg, J. P. Morgan, Otto Kahn, Norman Davis and Owen D. Young—now became the dominant sentiment of the financial interests of the country.[15]

Yet fewer bankers' voices were heard advocating some form of cancellation in the early 1930s than had been the case a decade earlier. Since the economic crisis seemed to discredit everything the American banking profession had done and stood for in the postwar period, its members became even more rigidly defensive about the sanctity of economic obligations, and thus debt repudiation was more distasteful to bankers than ever before. They also became less internationally oriented about tariff policy and further loans to foreign creditors. Given this development within the banking community, it was possible by 1933 to find among the opponents of cancellation some business organizations, publications, and individuals who had earlier been in favor of some form of cancellation or who had taken internationalist positions on other questions involving political or economic foreign policy.[16]

Contrary to the trend within procancellationist circles, the ranks of those business elements opposed to cancellation steadily increased between 1923 and 1933. This was due in large measure to the almost blind faith the vast majority of businessmen placed in the fifteen debt-funding agreements Washington negotiated during the decade, and in the Dawes and Young plans of 1924 and 1929 which purportedly solved the difficulties involved in German reparation payments.[17] These same businessmen also tended to look upon increased world trade as a panacea for most postwar economic problems. If international trade could only be increased enough, argued groups like the International Chamber of Commerce and the NFTC, then the remaining portions of all intergovernmental debts would stand a better chance of being paid.[18] Nonetheless, it should not be forgotten that a knowledgeable minority of anticancellationists remained as pessimistic about the possibilities of repayment, despite the funding agreements, as did those who favored cancellation. Norman Davis, for example, privately admitted in 1926 that "the debts, of course, are not going to be paid, and we are not going to collect much except ill-will." Yet he worked diligently for both the Hoover and Roosevelt administrations trying to collect some portion of what was owed the United States by the former Allied powers.[19]

Probably the most pessimistic anticancellationist publication of the period represented the opinions of southern cotton manufacturers. Noting as early as 1923 that everybody in Washington went around saying that the debts must be paid, *Cotton* insisted that in private few really thought they would be. In 1925 the journal's editor wrote, "While all agree that the debts ought to be paid, few who have given the subject close scrutiny have any notion that any large portion of them ever will be collected." In 1926 *Cotton* viewed the debt settlements negotiated by the United States as "representing little more than postponements," and predicted that all of them would have to be renegotiated in the near future. The editor clearly saw that the Allies would be making their payments to the United States with money borrowed from this country. He was convinced that they had agreed to funding arrangements "not out of eagerness to pay, [but] rather as a necessary preliminary to more borrowing." Yet he could not bring himself to support the logical conclusion to be drawn from his analysis of the debt situation, that is, cancellation.[20] This stubborn clinging to a principle which was beyond practical realization was characteristic of many opponents of cancellation by the end of the decade. Accordingly, the *ABA Journal* concluded that almost any solution would be more acceptable than "lazy and reckless" cancellation (including the transfer to the United States of former German colonies taken over as mandates by the Allies), and that anything "would be better than allowing a great international swindle to be written into history."[21]

Although the most significant disagreement over how to handle the war debts occurred among international bankers, there is evidence that sectional and partisan divisions also existed. Generally speaking, large metropolitan bankers and big business concerns, especially those in the East, were more likely to favor cancellation or drastic debt reduction than were midwestern, western, or southern bankers and businessmen.[22] Such sectionalism was noticeably present during a debate held at the twentieth annual convention of the American Institute of Bankers at Portland in July 1922. The institute's debate league had held elimination rounds throughout the year on the question: "Resolved, that the United States should enter into an agreement for the mutual cancellation of the inter-Allied debt." In the final competition at the convention, a New York team took the affirmative position and a Seattle team, the negative. The *Coast Banker* later reported that the decision had been unanimously in favor of the negative presentation, and that it was a popular one because the sympathy of the largely western audience of bankers was "with the opponents of cancellation as a matter of principle."[23] As Ralph Easley of the National Civic Foundation noted in 1926, it was easy to get certain prominent eastern businessmen on the Committee of One Hundred to oppose full payment of the war debts, but support from the West and Midwest was needed to get Congress moving in a new direction on the question. And these sections of the United States were "opposed to any policy that looks to this countries [*sic*] giving up any money."[24]

Another type of sectionalism, which sometimes assumed partisan overtones, concerned the suspicion held by strong nationalist Republicans, such as Hiram Johnson, William Borah, George W. Norris, Robert LaFollette, James Couzens, Robert E. Howell of Nebraska, and Arthur R. Robinson of Indiana, that debt accommodation represented a conspiracy on the part of intellectuals, J. P. Morgan, and other eastern, international bankers. Democrats, particularly southern Democrats, also singled out the Morgan interests and Wall Street people as the "sinister influences" behind debt reduction or cancellation. This opposition of western Republicans and southern Democrats to major eastern bankers was based in part on the argument that debt reduction would place an added economic burden on the American taxpayer, especially the debt-ridden and drought-stricken farmer and the neglected veteran. They also maintained that private loans to most of the countries signing debt-funding agreements were in danger, and therefore it was necessary from the standpoint of a "ruthless and selfish minority" in the East to have the public debts reduced in these countries.[25]

Partisanship over the issue of war debts was not limited to this traditional sectional hostility toward the East. It had even stronger roots in President Wilson's opposition to cancellation at the Paris Peace Conference. Consequently, the Democratic party started out in the postwar era officially committed to repayment. This was reflected in its voting record in Congress on the Debt Funding Act, on the major debt-funding agreements, and on Hoover's moratorium. Between 1921 and 1931, Democrats gave less support to these measures involving partial cancellation and temporary postponement of payment than did the Republicans. For example, 52.8 percent of Senate Democrats voted for such legislation compared to 87.3 percent of Senate Republicans. The respective percentages for the House are 46.5 and 93.4.[26] But it should be noted that these figures are at variance with Democratic and Republican editorial opinion across the country for the same ten-year period. Samples from *Literary Digest* indicated that of the total circulation of all newspapers advocating the passage of the funding agreements, 45.7 percent (or ten newspapers) were controlled or owned by Democrats, while only 21.7 percent (or eight newspapers) could be considered Republican. Of the total circulation of newspapers opposed to debt adjustments, 47.8 percent (or fourteen newspapers) were Republican and only 29.6 percent (or six newspapers), Democratic.[27]

So it may be questioned how truly representative of Democrats and Republicans at large were the votes in Congress on debt accommodation between 1921 and 1933. In terms of business opinion, the Congressional voting pattern was probably less representative of the average Republican businessman than of his Democratic counterpart. According to one contemporary observer, "no Republican business man, however opposed to the Administration's policy on the matter, wanted to take a stand because it would be resented in Washington. On the Democratic side, most of them felt the same as the Republicans. They wanted the money for the poor Liberty Bond taxpayer."[28] While the typical Democrat probably remained passively loyal to Wilson's original position on the war debts, a number of leading Wilsonians, including Norman Davis, James T. Shotwell, Ray Stannard Baker, and Owen D. Young, moved in the direction of greater debt accommodation during the 1920s. A tiny minority, headed by Newton D. Baker, became outright cancellationists. The more moderate internationalist business group led by Davis and Young tried to rationalize their increasing leniency on the question of war debts by maintaining that Wilson had modified his attitude on them before his death because he was becoming "disturbed about our policy of selfish nationalism that was so blind to our duties and our interests."[29] Thus, by the time Hoover became president the issue of intergovernmental debts was not only a complicated world economic problem, but had created domestic divisions as well. Hoover personally remained opposed to cancellation, but the depression forced him and others to reconsider the entire question.

By the spring of 1931 the financial situation in Germany was deteriorating at an alarming rate.[30] Hoover's personal record of the events leading to the proclamation of his moratorium on all intergovernmental debts indicates that he conferred with the United States ambassador to Germany, Frederic M. Sackett, on May 6. Sackett described the political instability and the general economic plight of the German people and predicted a collapse of the German financial structure and revolution in the fall unless reparation payments under the Young Plan were suspended. Hoover agreed to study the situation, but told the ambassador that "it was difficult to see what could be done as we were not a party to reparations." He also referred to a favorite theory of his, namely, that increasing armament was "one of the fundamental [economic] difficulties of all Europe," but admitted that "this did not so much directly concern Germany." On May 7 he asked Assistant Secretary of Commerce Julius Klein to provide him with figures showing the relationship between war debts, reparations, military expenditures, and import-export figures for Europe and the United States. He also requested similar information from the State Department, and inquired about the attitude of the German delegates to the International Chamber of Commerce concerning conditions in their country. He was told "they took the gloomiest view."[31]

On May 11 Hoover informed Secretaries Stimson and Mellon about his conversation with Sackett. The president suggested to them that since both the funding agreements with the United States and German reparation payments were "predicated upon capacity to pay in normal times," possibly the depression had now made such payment impossible. He still insisted, however, that "there was no relationship between reparations and the debts due the American government," but within weeks his actions were to belie these words. The two secretaries apparently made no concrete replies to this suggestion, but Hoover was aware that they differed with each other and with himself on the war debt question. Mellon was as firm an anticancellationist as Stimson was a cancellationist, and Hoover's position was somewhere in the middle by the spring of 1931. Moreover, his relationship with Stimson and Mellon was beginning to show signs of strain for other reasons.[32]

A few days after this meeting, when the Creditanstalt, the "most important banking institution" in Austria, failed,[33] Hoover became convinced that Sackett had been right and that a total collapse in Central Europe was imminent. Meeting with Stimson again on May 19, Hoover read to him a portion of a speech he was to deliver early in June at Indianapolis, which would prepare the American people to accept further reduction of the debt payments.[34] The speech denied the idea of outright cancellation or permanent revision. Stimson approved of the draft, and then Hoover proceeded on May 20, 21, and 22 to confer with the chairman of the Federal Reserve Board about European economic disintegration. Eugene Meyer assured him that the financial system of the United States could stand the shock, and that the "Federal Reserve could at any moment expand [its] credit facilities." In the last days of May the Federal Reserve Bank of New York did take the lead in making temporary loans to sustain the Austrian National Bank. These were followed by similar Federal Reserve loans to the central banks of Hungary and Germany in June and July, and finally to the Bank of England in August. Nevertheless, the economic situation in Austria and Germany continued to deteriorate at an even more rapid pace than Sackett had predicted.[35]

On June 5 Hoover called a meeting of Secretaries Stimson and Mellon and Under-Secretary of the Treasury Ogden L. Mills. He proposed a one-year moratorium on the war debts in return for reciprocal action by the Allies with respect to reparation payments. Stimson immediately agreed to the proposal, Mellon "stated his unqualified disapproval," and Mills opposed it on technical grounds, saying that the executive did not have the authority to issue such a moratorium on that portion of payments

which represented interest, and that "it would be impossible to
secure without a special session of Congress because it would
break down the debt structure." Hoover reiterated his idea in the
face of this three-to-one opposition, but agreed that further inquiry should be made into the financial situation at home and
abroad.[36] Later the same day, Thomas W. Lamont of the House
of Morgan contacted Hoover by telephone, suggesting that the
United States defer payments on the principal of the Allied debts
(which amounted to less than $80 million out of total annual
payments of $250 million).[37] Lamont implied that his recom-
mendation was altruistically motivated because "his firm had no
money in Germany" while other American banking institutions
did. Hoover rejected the suggestion, arguing that the amount
involved was too small to provide a "basis for discussion [and]
for amelioration of the German situation." He specifically noted
in his diary that he did not convey to Lamont anything about his
moratorium plan. The next day he asked Senator Dwight W.
Morrow, a former partner in the Morgan firm, to talk to New
York bankers about the German situation, warning him against
mentioning the moratorium.[38]

Hoover decided to introduce his moratorium plan at a full
cabinet meeting on June 8. The following day Senator Morrow
and Under-Secretary Mills met with the president and ambigu-
ously informed him that action should be taken "at some point."
Morrow and Hoover believed that the "New York bankers were
panicky over the situation in Germany and Austria." So they
thought they would allow things to develop a little longer in
order to insure acceptance of Hoover's moratorium at home and
abroad. They agreed to send George L. Harrison, governor of the
Federal Reserve Bank of New York, to Europe to investigate
current conditions. But the trip never took place because there
was a run on the Central European banks beginning the week of
June 14, and this kept Harrison in New York "to take care of
possible crisis there." Between June 9 and June 15, Stimson and
Mills consulted with Owen D. Young, Harrison, and other bankers, including S. Parker Gilbert, the former agent general for
reparation payments under the Dawes Plan and a member of the
House of Morgan. In the meantime Hoover called Eugene Meyer

and asked him to contact Bernard Baruch about the crisis in
Central Europe. Both Meyer and Baruch favored waiting "until
the situation developed lest we fail to get support," but it was
the opinion of Stimson, Mills, and the bankers they contacted
that the time had come to present the moratorium proposal.[39]

It was at this point that Hoover hesitated. He felt that the
situation "had reoriented itself" after the German minister of
finance made some irresponsible public statements which precipitated the run on German banks. He explained to Stimson and
Mills "that instead of being able to predicate action on the general
movements for world recovery we were faced with a bankers'
panic and action by the Germans which greatly embarrassed all
preliminary negotiations; that I could not act without approval
of the leaders of both political parties with any hope of securing
cooperation by Congress; that I must have time in which to
develop this." And so he "declined their repeated telephone
urgings to take action" and said he would keep in touch with the
situation and begin to contact congressional leaders on his trip
West. After his return he would decide when to act.[40]

During his tour through several mid-western states between
June 15 and June 20, Hoover and Mills consulted with congressional leaders about the moratorium. By June 20 they had obtained pledges of support from nine Republican senators (including Borah, Morrow, Arthur Capper, and Arthur H.
Vandenberg) and twelve Democratic senators (including Cordell
Hull, Carter Glass, Thomas Walsh, Robert Wagner, and Claude
A. Swanson), in addition to fourteen Republican and four Democratic members of the House of Representatives.[41] After Democratic Senator William H. King apparently leaked information
to the press about the project, Hoover, fearing that garbled
accounts might be released which would "cause great conflict in
Europe," made his proposed moratorium public on June 20. At
the time of the announcement Mellon, Mills, and the Treasury
Department in general had accepted the idea.[42] Although the
moratorium proposal had originated with Hoover, when it was
made public it represented agreement between the president, the
Treasury and State departments, individual members of Congress,
and important eastern bankers and financiers.

Although the moratorium fell far short of solving Europe's financial difficulties, all the major creditors of the United States, with the exception of France, gave their approval. In part, the French resented not having been consulted by the American government in advance about the moratorium. The declaration was also particularly embarrassing to them because of all the Allies they had remained the most committed to the postwar slogan *le Boche payera tout.* They argued their case, therefore, on technical points related to reparations payments, one of which was that the so-called unconditional portion of the Young annuities should not be included in the moratorium. This amounted to 660 million marks a year, and it had been stipulated in the Young Plan that the unconditional payment was not subject to postponement of any kind. In the two weeks that it took to overcome this and other French objections, Hoover became irritated with all of his major advisers.[43]

In a series of Washington meetings and transatlantic telephone conversations,[44] the president, Secretaries Stimson and Mellon (both in Europe ostensibly on vacations), Under-Secretaries Mills and William R. Castle, Jr., and Ambassadors Sackett in Berlin and Walter E. Edge in Paris revealed a number of petty as well as important differences of opinion. At first Hoover appeared disgruntled with Stimson for taking a vacation at this time, with Edge and Mellon for seeming to side with the French, and with Castle and Mills for not agreeing completely with him on every point. The role of mediator between Hoover and his advisers during this tense two-week period fell to Dwight Morrow. Over the objections of both Mellon and Mills, on July 6 Hoover finally forced French acceptance of the moratorium, with reservations, by threatening to leave France out of the plan altogether. Even so, the moratorium came too late to prevent a general banking panic in Germany and soon enormous sums of short-term credits were frozen—the very thing that Hoover had hoped his moratorium would prevent.[45]

Hoover tried to solve the short-term credit problem by having Castle suggest to the British that they call a "stabilization" or "stand-still" conference in London to prevent further withdrawal of foreign funds from Germany, and hopefully to arrange new short-term credits for the country. The transatlantic conversations which transpired before and during this conference indicate not only significant points of disagreement between Hoover and Stimson, who along with Secretary Mellon attended the conference, but also the independent action taken by the House of Morgan, which almost wrecked the president's plan for a conference to stabilize German short-term credits. Hoover's prime concern in the days before the conference met was that the French would attempt to turn the German credit problem into a political question involving intergovernmental financing. Hoover naturally viewed it as a "banker-made" crisis whose solution was a matter of supplying private credit, rather than the climax of international economic disequilibrium which had been building up since the war. His immediate fears were realized when, at an intermediate meeting in Paris, the French delegates proposed an international loan of $500 million for Germany. They did this knowing full well that American bankers would not participate in any such long-term loan; their government had been so informed by the House of Morgan.[46]

This indiscreet action by Morgan placed the Hoover administration in an embarrassing position. Hoover did not want to be made personally responsible for killing the French loan proposal. He wanted the British to share the blame since the Bank of England was no more eager than Federal Reserve officials to participate in another long-term loan for Germany. The Morgan telegram to the French government seemed a deliberate attempt to prevent German stabilization and to strengthen the bargaining power of the French. Hoover and Stimson bitterly resented the interference by the House of Morgan and both complained to representatives of the firm about the unauthorized telegram. The more volatile Stimson literally ordered them to "quit this damn nonsense" because it could "spoil" the entire conference. But the damage had already been done by the time the reprimands were delivered, and the French went to the seven-power conference at London on July 20 with a slight advantage.[47]

To counteract the enhanced French position, Stimson pressed Hoover for a constructive plan that he could present at the conference. In the course of their conversations about this, Hoover received the impression that Stimson and Mellon basically favored a loan to Germany because they insisted that the situation in Germany was much more serious than his Washington staff was telling him. Although Stimson repeatedly denied that he was asking Hoover "to put up any more money," he did accuse two of the president's close financial advisers and officials of the Federal Reserve System, Eugene Meyer and George Harrison, of receiving "their advice from Morgan." Hoover denied this accusation and the end result of their misunderstanding was that Stimson demonstrated considerably less enthusiasm for Hoover's stabilization plan than the president desired.[48] At the same time, the secretary of state also appeared more sensitive to the national pride of both Germany and France than Hoover thought necessary.[49]

Hoover's anger at the French, however, was greater than that toward either the House of Morgan or his secretary of state. He was confident that most American bankers would back his stabilization proposal and possibly even make more short-term advances to Germany if other nations did likewise. In truth, from the standpoint of self-interest they could not do otherwise. Over half of all German short-term obligations were in the United States: approximately $800 million out of a total of $1.4 billion.[50] Much of it was in the form of bank acceptances, both sixty- and ninety-day paper, which lacked collateral. The share held by New York banks alone of these largely "kited" bills was $420 million. France, on the other hand, was carrying less than 5 percent of the whole load of German credits and had started to reduce this amount as rapidly as possible, much to Hoover's consternation, after he announced his moratorium on June 20. American bankers held firm, however, and it soon became apparent that it would be possible to stabilize German credits without the participation of the French.[51]

Thus, despite the preconference maneuvering of the French and the House of Morgan, the London conference met July 20–22, and the seven nations attending accepted the general principle of stabilization by recommending that the short-term creditors of Germany stop withdrawing their funds. The details of stabilization were subsequently worked out in August and went into effect in September. Although Hoover obtained essentially what he wanted from the London meeting, in the course of the three days of negotiations his relations with Secretaries Mellon and Stimson continued to deteriorate. Neither Stimson nor Mellon had wanted to release the details of Hoover's "standstill" proposal until after it had been presented to the conference. Hoover interpreted this as a lack of confidence in and/or enthusiasm for his plan, and finally, with Mills's and Castle's support in Washington, he issued it over the protests of his secretaries of state and the treasury. This caused some diplomatic embarrassment for Stimson. The secretary of state had been trying to convince the French, who since the moratorium were overly sensitive to "being dictated to by Washington," that stabilization of German credits was an Anglo-American idea. Consequently, he had been denying press reports emanating from his own department (over Castle's signature) which described it as "Mr. Hoover's plan." Hoover wrote in his diary on July 22 that the "publication of the plan clarified the air and brought the conference in London down to realities. Stimson, however," he concluded, "has thrown a cloud over the whole business by an interview with the press in which he accredited [Ramsay] MacDonald with having initiated the plan." This jealous desire to be given full credit for originating policy was a harbinger of Hoover's later attempt to prove that he alone was the author of the Stimson Doctrine which resulted from the Manchurian crisis.[52]

The development of the moratorium and stabilization proposals is important, therefore, as an indication of the tension within Hoover's official family and his reliance on certain eastern financial advisers. It is also significant because it represented his belated recognition in practice, if not in theory, of the relationship between the war debts and reparations. He continued, nevertheless, to deny this relationship in public, never realizing apparently that this position on the part of the United States had retarded the development of international monetary equilibrium for over a decade. Unfortunately for his reputation as a "super-businessman" with an impeccable understanding of the world's political economy, Hoover's moratorium and stabilization programs did not restore international confidence in the face of the deepening depression. At best they temporarily delayed the inevitable; that is, repudiation of both the inter-Allied debt and the reparation payments which took place at Lausanne in the summer of 1932. The role that reparations played in the events leading to this meeting and to the London Economic Conference of 1933 completes the final phase of Hoover's economic foreign policy as president.

Hoover had been one of the most vocal critics of the reparations section of the Versailles Peace Treaty. As secretary of commerce he continued to think of the reparations arrangement as "entirely unworkable." At the same time he recognized the reparations question as one which greatly affected the commercial policies of the United States, and so he told Secretary Hughes in 1921 that he wanted to have access to all cables and other information concerning these German payments to the Allies. Hughes did not readily accede to Hoover's assertion that the "reparations problem is essentially a commercial problem," and even implied in one letter that the Commerce Department could not be trusted with such information. Hoover persisted, arguing that it was "utterly impossible to separate a consideration of the political phases from the commercial phases" of the reparations payments. Hughes never conceded this point, but the same tenuous accommodation was reached on the exchange of reparations information as had been on foreign loans. While the Departments of Commerce and State publicly adhered in the 1920s to the position that war debts and reparations were entirely separate issues, Hoover privately acknowledged at the beginning of 1923 that European "continental stability cannot be secured unless there is a settlement of interlocked debts, reparations and disarmament." But it was not until 1931 that he was forced to formulate and try to implement such a coordinated settlement.[53]

Until that time his actions with respect to reparations had been relegated, as were those of Secretaries Hughes, Kellogg, Stimson, and Mellon, to supporting the Dawes and Young plans. Officially the United States government did not participate in the 1924 and 1929 meetings which produced these payment schedules, but, in fact, government officials appointed the American experts to both special commissions. The government also used its influence to get J. P. Morgan and Company to sponsor the American share of the loan necessary to put the Dawes Plan into operation. And in 1930 the Young Plan loan, in which the Morgan firm, the First National Bank of New York, and the First National Bank of Chicago were the principal sponsors, also had the moral, if not the legal, endorsement of the United States government.[54]

The government's oblique approach to the reparations question was determined by Senate opposition to American participation in the reparations commission established by the Versailles Treaty, and by the prevailing assumption of American officials that the Europeans would like nothing better than to have the United States become legally entangled in their political intrigues to obtain compensation from the Germans. The Dawes and Young plans were in essence the government's unofficial alternatives to the periodic threat of German default on reparation payments. As such, they constituted tacit recognition that the success of the funding agreements signed with the United States depended upon the payment of reparations to the Allies, although this was never admitted or explained to the public. Consequently, the extent to which American economic interests were being promoted abroad by the government, and the degree to which economic foreign policy was being placed in the hands of private individuals rather than public officials was obscured even further than it had been with respect to international loans and investments.[55]

Senator Joseph P. Robinson, a Democratic internationalist who often supported Republican internationalists such as Hughes and Hoover, perceived the danger in such administrative abdication of public responsibility on this all-important issue. As early as the beginning of 1923 he criticized Hughes's proposal for an informal meeting of private experts to determine reparation payments by saying, "The responsibility of conducting foreign affairs must not be left to bankers, merchants and bond brokers in their private capacities. It must primarily devolve upon the chief Executive. The issue [*sic*] to be met are Governmental. Therefore, the power that should grapple with them is not private responsibility, but public authority." On this point Robinson was supported by Norman Davis, who despite his praise for the "admirable work" of the Dawes Commission, questioned the back door approach to economic diplomacy which it represented. As might be expected, this Wilsonian said it would have been unnecessary to appoint such an unofficial group had the United States been represented on the League of Nation's Reparation Commission. More importantly, however, he deplored leaving

> to private citizens, acting on invitations from foreign governments, the task of helping to bring order out of world chaos. This sort of participation [in world affairs] is inadequate, undignified and cowardly. The problems of the day are too great, too vital to our security and prosperity, to be left to this haphazard treatment. They should be dealt with, [and] they could be better dealt with, by officials and delegates of the United States Government, chosen and trained for the work, empowered to speak for America in measured and responsible terms.[56]

Needless to say, such warnings from Democratic internationalists about confounding public and private responsibility in foreign affairs went unheeded. Moreover, even as government and business sources issued optimistic predictions about the effectiveness of the Dawes Plan, and later of the Young Plan, Germany's economic and political situation grew steadily worse. As with the question of the Allied debts, it was not so much a question of the United States taking an ungenerous view of the situation, as of not doing enough to bring about a candid and consciously coordinated economic and political settlement in Europe based on changed postwar conditions.[57]

Approval of the Dawes and Young plans by business internationalists provides a good example of the well-intentioned but inadequate handling of economic foreign policy. Uniting as they had been unable to do over the question of Allied debts, these businessmen argued that both plans scaled down the reparation payments to Germany's postwar capacity to pay. Thomas Lamont went so far as to call the international loan accompanying the Young Plan "the final liquidation of the War so far as the settlement of great economic questions is concerned." There was also a consensus among business internationalists that the two commissions represented a "new practical idealism" in the conduct of foreign affairs whereby the "old diplomatic method of international dealing" between politicians had been replaced with unofficial conferences conducted by businessmen acting as private citizens. The business community and public in general accepted these positive generalizations about the Dawes and Young settlements without any real understanding of the technicalities involved. One such technicality was the fact that, despite the predominance of economic expertise in the negotiations, both were political adjustments of the reparations question based on large loans to Germany which were not self-liquidating. This meant that in the long run they exacerbated the balance-of-payments problem for the lending countries, especially England, as well as for Germany.[58]

This blind support from within the business community undermined any practical consideration of alternative solutions and prevented most legitimate criticism of the plans from enlightening public opinion on the entire question of reparations and their relation to the war debts. The American Association Favoring Reconsideration of the War Debts did devote considerable effort to a critique of the operation of the Dawes Plan in 1927, but aside from Newton D. Baker, George W. Wickersham, and Henry B. Joy, former president of the Packard Motor Company, few prominent politicians or business figures aided the efforts of this organization. Consequently, by 1930 the commitment of the government and business community to the collection of both reparations and war debts was complete, and continued despite the sporadic recommendations of a few economists, academicians, and business internationalists to the contrary.[59]

After Hoover issued his moratorium American financial leaders and politicians worked frantically to prevent permanent cancellation of all intergovernmental debts. Privately there was no longer any attempt made to insist that debts and reparations were not linked. It was also privately acknowledged by business and government leaders that drastic reductions in both types of payments were inevitable. But the decade-long refusal of American officials to take a candid position on the debts resulting from the war and to mold intelligent congressional and public opinion on the subject placed Hoover in a difficult position which was further complicated by the impending presidential election.[60]

The president and his political and business advisers employed two standard tactics in the face of the growing threat of debt cancellation. The first consisted of the unsuccessful attempt to have European nations concentrate on the relationship between reparations and land armaments at international conferences. In defense of this position, business internationalists had long argued that disarmament provided the best means for reducing the national expenditures of the debt-ridden Allied nations and hence their dependence on large reparation payments.[61] This tactic failed at the Geneva and Lausanne conferences in the early 1930s. The other course simultaneously pursued by the Hoover administration had been initiated earlier by Secretary Hughes—the use of private financial experts to supplement normal diplomatic communication about economic problems. In this case Thomas W. Lamont was the unofficial liaison who tried before the opening of the Lausanne Conference in June 1932 to present an economic alternative to complete cancellation, and at the same time to impress foreign leaders with the delicate position of the Republicans in an election year. Hoover and other party leaders were convinced that the United States could not negotiate new debt settlements with the Allies nor extend the moratorium before the nation went to the polls in November. To do so would allow the Democrats to hang a "cancellation tag" on the Republican party.[62]

So Lamont suggested to European officials that at Lausanne they agree to delay reparation annuities for three to five years with payment to be resumed after that time according to the degree of economic recovery in Germany. Lamont defended his proposal by saying that the "American business community as a whole," especially the "banking fraternity," was in accord with the administration's position on intergovernmental debts, and that like most Americans, businessmen were opposed to total cancellation. It was Lamont's guarded opinion that if the Allied nations at the Lausanne Conference were willing to commit themselves to a final and moderate settlement with Germany, American public opinion might become more lenient on the war debt question in 1933 after the election dust had finally settled. Specifically he said, my guess would be at the end of that period the world and public opinion in general would have undergone such a change that . . . there might be on both sides of the water . . . a unanimous sentiment for sweeping away the whole quagmire of Reparations and inter-Governmental debts. This, of course, is projecting ourselves a long distance into the future. But it may be well to keep all this in mind because, while at Lausanne I believed in the principle of no complete cancellation, I do not disguise from myself the fact that German Reparation payments have probably come to about their end.

This prophecy was never fulfilled because, as Lamont and his associates in the House of Morgan had so long feared, the English backed the Germans at Lausanne in demanding virtual cancellation of the reparations, contingent upon a similar eradication of existing war debts.[63]

Faced with the reality of Allied repudiation, Lamont then urged the Hoover administration to postpone the war debt payments which were due on December 15, 1932. He argued that this action would provide the needed additional time for another readjustment of the debts and would also avoid further alienating the Allies and thereby endangering the negotiations at the Geneva Disarmament Conference. In a telephone conversation with Stimson, Lamont said Owen D. Young had intimated to him that Roosevelt would not actively oppose such a postponement of Allied payments. Despite Lamont's advice, Hoover refused to recommend to Congress any postponement. He did offer the debtor nations the option of meeting the December 15 deadline by making their payments in their native currencies with the balance to be paid at a later date in dollars. At this point Lamont's role in the last months of the Hoover administration became one of trying to explain his government's unpopular position abroad to his foreign "associates in the business world" in the hope that they could convince their respective political leaders to accept Hoover's offer. Lamont was convinced that both Hoover and Roosevelt were committed to reviewing the entire debt question in favor of the Allies, and that payment of the December installment in native currencies opened the door to de facto postponement for the time being. His efforts were temporarily successful, for with the exception of France, the major Allied nations met their December payments.[64] These were, however, the last payments to be made by the principal Allied debtors of the United States.

Hoover's last and most original attempts to salvage the debt and reparations debacle came after his defeat for reelection. During the winter months of 1932–1933 he tried to obtain the cooperation of president-elect Roosevelt in reviving the Debt Funding Commission. A year earlier the Democratic Congress had refused to approve such action, and so Hoover thought Roosevelt's endorsement was necessary if the commission was to be recreated. More significantly, Hoover also wanted Roosevelt to help him appoint a nonpartisan delegation to the forthcoming London Economic Conference, and to agree to coordinate all future discussions with European nations about disarmament, debts, and other economic and monetary problems. To achieve coordination, the president proposed the creation of an "interlocking directorate" selected by himself and Roosevelt from the delegates to the Geneva Disarmament and London Economic conferences. With these suggestions Hoover implicitly acknowledged the reciprocal relation between the major economic problems confronting the world, and hinted that a comprehensive settlement was now the only solution. In particular, spokesmen for the administration began to indicate that for the first time since the war the United States was officially ready to bargain with foreign nations on specific issues, for example, further reduction of the war debts in return for restoration of the gold standard, the stabilization of world currency exchanges, reduction of quotas on imports, or general disarmament.[65]

Obviously Hoover's emphasis on the importance of the London Conference and on coordinated economic discussions represented his belief that the causes of the depression were foreign, not domestic, and therefore international financial measures were necessary for recovery. In vain he sought Roosevelt's concurrence on this theoretical point. But at the same time, Hoover was also trying to obtain Roosevelt's consent to diplomatic methods that would insure a continuation of the moderately internationalist position on debts and reparations which had evolved in the last years of his administration. He was convinced that no significant comprehensive negotiations could be conducted before March 4 unless the president-elect made it abundantly clear to Congress and Europe that there would be no basic change in economic foreign policy after the inauguration. Such a commitment from Roosevelt would have dispelled most of the suspicions Hoover and others held about his economic internationalism.

Privately, for example, Roosevelt had strongly condemned the moratorium because he mistakenly thought it had been too hastily devised at the insistence of New York bankers, and that even if it proved effective for Europe it would not alleviate unemployment in the United States. Many business-oriented Democrats, who had supported Republican efforts to devise debt and reparation payments according to the capacity of the debtor to pay, worried that the new president still adhered to the rigid 1919 party policy laid down by Wilson, and that he would "shut the door to such moratoriums and adjustments as may . . . appear to be essential to a restoration of the economic fabric of this nation." Newton D. Baker in particular feared that William Randolph Hearst might exercise undue influence over Roosevelt.[66] As it turned out, these fears were warranted, but a political scientist from Columbia University named Raymond Moley proved an even greater obstacle to the practice of economic internationalism in the early years of the New Deal than Hearst or other well-known Democratic nationalists.

Under the tutelage of such men as Moley and William C. Bullitt, Roosevelt groped toward an economic foreign policy of his own. He began by refusing to endorse any of the diplomatic machinery Hoover proposed. A long-time friend of Roosevelt, Louis B. Wehle, has noted that the president's characteristically intuitive nature was a hindrance to him when it came to deciding economic, fiscal, and monetary policies because he was incapable of "sustained effort or attention." And it appears that Moley played the major role at the first meetings and communications between Hoover and Roosevelt in November and December 1932 and January 1933, insisting that Hoover had all the authority he needed to initiate debt discussions through normal State Department channels, and that these should be kept separate from the discussions of other economic and political problems. Moley and other members of Roosevelt's original Brain Trust simply were not convinced of the urgency of reaching new debt adjustments before the meeting at London. In fact, they would have preferred to see both the war debt negotiations and the conference postponed indefinitely. Therefore, in the winter of 1932–1933, the rhetoric of the president-elect and his representatives seemed more dogmatic on the questions of repayment and the separation of debts and reparations than that of the incumbent. Ultimately Hoover's idea of using preconference settlements as levers to obtain better terms on other matters at London, and his proposal for coordinating disarmament and all economic negotiations (although agreed to in theory by Roosevelt on February 3, 1933) were in practice rejected by the incoming administration. Roosevelt did agree with his predecessor on several points; namely, that each debtor nation must negotiate independently with the United States, that there should be no immediate cancellation of the war debts, and that these debts should not be discussed at the London Conference.[67]

On foreign policy matters the Brain Trusters did not embrace international cooperation in economic foreign policy during the first year of the New Deal because they feared that such measures as currency stabilization based on the conventional gold standard, and drastic reduction of intergovernmental debts would conflict with their plans for coping with the depression through independent federal planning at home. Roosevelt's decision in the spring of 1933 to abandon the gold standard, and his subsequent rejection of the innocuous stabilization agreement of the London Economic Conference in favor of unilateral devaluation of the dollar, confirmed Hoover's worst fears about the economic nationalism of the New Dealers. Some of these actions also dismayed many of the older Democratic business internationalists, such as Norman Davis, Newton D. Baker, and Bernard Baruch. In general, Wall Street bankers, with the notable exceptions of J. P. Morgan and Frank A. Vanderlip, opposed Roosevelt's economic policies in 1933, but their advice was not heeded as the new administration faced the dilemma which had plagued all major nations since World War I: whether to take the collective actions demanded by the rules of the international gold standard game or the unilateral ones dictated by the need for domestic stabilization. While the Republicans in the preceding decade had straddled this contradiction, the Democrats in the early 1930s clearly opted for the nationalist course. Outside of the large eastern banking centers, however, the New Deal's inflationary measures were welcomed not only by the recently formed Committee for the Nation (a business group led by James H. Rand, Jr.), but also by the traditionally nationalist organizations representing the small businessmen and farmers of the South and West, who were also strong opponents of cancellation.[68]

Thus, the controversy over Allied debts and German reparations ended in cancellation contrary to the expressed desire of Democratic and Republican administrations since 1918. Neither Wilson's idealism nor Hoover's business sense nor Roosevelt's intuitiveness produced a practical alternative to cancellation in the intervening years. The differences between the policies of the three administrations were largely ones of method rather than principle. There was no New Deal for intergovernmental debts, just greater indifference to their political and economic significance. The same moral opposition to cancellation prevailed as had at the beginning of the 1920s.[69]

The history of the American struggle against repudiation, unlike that of the loan control issue, has been replete with references to public opinion by businessmen and politicians who stated that their anticancellationist views were dictated by the will of the people. While historians have generally reiterated this assertion its truth is highly doubtful for a number of reasons. First, the issue was too technical and complex for most businessmen, let alone the man in the street, to understand. Even after the depression had brought intergovernmental debts into dramatic focus, Thomas W. Lamont confessed to the prime minister of England that "it is hard for the average American to know what it is all about."[70] No doubt the typical citizen of the 1920s, realizing that he was responsible for the personal debts he incurred, expected this axiom to apply to economic obligations between nations, just as today there is the widespread assumption that since individuals must attempt to balance their monthly and yearly incomes, so should the national government. Both positions are essentially moral ones which simplistically equate the financial actions of private individuals with those of nation states. In neither situation can it be documented that this kind of public opinion influences government policy because the sentiments expressed remained then, as now, poorly articulated and unorganized. Second, the ease with which the downward scaling of debts was accepted without mass outcries against cancellation each time a funding agreement was negotiated either confirms this basic lack of understanding or implies a potential malleability or outright indifference of the public on this issue.

Third, a survey of articles in *Reader's Guide to Periodical Literature* indicated that popular interest in the reparations question peaked between 1922 and 1924, and between 1925 and 1928 in the case of Allied debts. By 1932 the number of articles appearing in the mass circulation magazines on these two related issues had declined by two-thirds from their peak periods. It can be assumed that in this era before public opinion polls and television, the people at large were no more informed or aroused about the possibility of cancellation than were the publications they read.[71] This same survey indicated that the depression did stimulate widespread interest in domestic economic conditions and to a lesser degree in foreign commerce and investments, but not in intergovernmental debts. Moreover, the favorable reception given Hoover's 1931 moratorium negates the existence of any wall of popular hostility to actions which were justified in terms of economic recovery. Government officials used the shibboleth of economic recovery effectively in 1933 to insure acceptance of Russian recognition, and it is conceivable that it could have been used to obtain approval of some form of cancellation, at least after 1929, as Americans became increasingly predisposed to grasp at any plan that promised to alleviate the depression. Reluctance to try to obtain popular approval of cancellation had characterized the national leadership up to the depression, but by the early 1930s there appears to have been less rational justification for it in terms of mass opinion than there was immediately following the war. As Thomas Lamont noted in 1932, the people were leading Congress in support of the moratorium and were ready to go along with practically anything Hoover did to end the European economic crisis.[72]

Fourth, once the threat of cancellation became imminent in the early 1930s there is no evidence that Hoover, Stimson, or the Brain Trusters devised their specific counter-proposals by tapping grass-roots opinion.[73] As noted in previous chapters, government policy in crises is seldom determined by pressure group influence on public officials. In this instance there was no well-defined economic interest group which had a solution to the problem.

Fifth, in Congress the hard-core nationalist opposition to cancellation, although vociferous, had not been powerful enough to prevent the passage of the debt-funding agreements which reduced Allied indebtedness by over 40 percent in the course of the decade, or to defeat Hoover's moratorium. Until 1934 and the passage of the Johnson Act, these nationalists exercised more influence over the political than over the economic aspects of American foreign policy.[74] Moreover, between 1921 and 1933 there was a conspicuous absence of constituent material in the *Congressional Record* on the topic of war debts. Most of what did appear came not from the general public but from special economic groups whose prosperity was dependent upon trade with some of the debtor nations. Copper and automotive interests, for example, communicated to various Congressmen that they favored the Italian debt settlement because Italy was a good customer.[75]

In the last analysis it appears that government officials and prominent businessmen created and nurtured, rather than followed, anticancellation opinion for over a decade. If politicians thought they heard strong opposition to debt repudiation it was because they were tuned in to nationalist business opinion and vice versa. It is evident that business internationalists made a less-than-heroic effort to insist publicly on the logic of cancellation even though privately they remained very pessimistic about the possibility of repayment. When Owen D. Young told Hoover that he regretted the "very existence" of the war debts he was not expressing an atypical position among leading financiers.[76] Yet he and his colleagues eschewed nearly all responsibility for molding that opinion. They assumed, as did the business nation-alists, that Americans were vitally interested in the problem of intergovernmental debts before the depression, and would react violently to any candid proposal for cancellation. In this case both opponents and proponents of cancellation were captives of the traditional attempt of American leaders to justify their action or inaction in foreign affairs on the basis of public opinion.[77] In retrospect it appears likely that they were confounding public thought with their own ideas or with those of a particular interest group.

Chapter Six

Manifestations of the
Closed Door, 1920–1933

Whether the United States pursued an Open or Closed Door policy (through a combination of collective and unilateral actions referred to here as independent internationalism) depended upon the power of other nations in various parts of the world. In the remaining chapters, therefore, I shall discuss the practice of independent internationalism as it was used in attempts to open or close regions of Latin America and the Far East. Between 1920 and 1933 these two areas often received similar diplomatic treatment from the United States, except that a Closed Door policy was reserved for Latin America and an Open Door policy for the Far East.

In both areas, for example, government and business coopera-tion usually overshadowed disagreement, at least until the de-pression of 1929. This cooperation resulted largely from the unsettled political and economic conditions in such developing countries as China and the republics of Central and South America. It was to the advantage of businessmen, especially exporters, international bankers, and companies with foreign con-cessions or franchises, to support government policy in return for aid in negotiating financial and commercial contracts and for protection of property and investments. Such aid and protection were viewed by the business community in the 1920s as implicit rights, and by the government as official or unofficial duties, depending upon the circumstances.[1] In both Latin America and the Far East the practice of independent internationalism was characterized by the indiscriminate application of political doctrines and economic principles which often placed the United States in opposition to revolutionary activity. This in turn widened the gap between the stated humanitarian goals and reforms of Washington in these areas and the means the government was prepared to use to achieve them. Finally, in neither area did American officials resort to cooperation with the League of Nations until the early 1930s.

During the period under discussion, businessmen also linked the Far East and Latin America in a variety of ways. Acknowledging that World War I had placed the United States in a unique position to begin to capitalize on trading and investment opportunities in developing areas of the world, the business community was very optimistic about future economic relations in both the Orient and the Southern Hemisphere. Even the unfavorable balance of trade which the United States experienced with the countries of South America and the Far East (in contrast to the favorable balance with Europe and Canada) was not interpreted negatively. Commercial organizations used the unfavorable trade balance to exhort American businessmen to sell more to Latin Americans and thereby bring exports more in line with imports, while bankers viewed it as an added guarantee against default on the service and repayment of loans. Of course most businessmen and government officials took a dim view of revolution and confiscation of property. Such actions were especially disturbing to bankers and this was reflected in their reluctance to extend economic support to such countries as Mexico and China during periods of extreme upheaval. Nothing, however, could dispel completely the idea within government and banking circles that American investment and commerce would ultimately contribute to the overall stability of these poorer, struggling nations.[2]

In contrast to most international financiers, American exporters seldom allowed the rapidly changing political scene in Latin America and the Far East to dampen their perennial optimism about trade relations. It was pointed out at the 1921 convention of the National Foreign Trade Council that trade with Mexico had increased despite the revolution which had raged there for

over a decade. Whereas Mexicans had purchased products from
the United States worth $63.8 million in 1910, by 1920 the
figure had risen to $195 million. To exporters these statistics
indicated that the Mexican revolution was primarily political,
not mercantile. Although Mexican purchases fell off somewhat
during the height of the subsoil controversy of 1921–1922, the
NFTC could still point proudly to the increasing amount of trade
Americans had conducted with Mexico prior to the recognition
of the Obregón government. Likewise, delegates to the 1923
NFTC convention were advised to ignore the endemic political
instability of the Far East in their quest for new markets. Indeed,
trade with China survived the Nationalist Revolution of 1925–
1928, and was far more affected by the depression in 1931–1932
than by the Manchurian crisis.[3] The difference of opinion between banking and commercial interests over the potential economic opportunity in the Far East and Latin America remained
one of degree rather than kind. So the two areas continued
throughout the decade to be viewed by most businessmen as at
least potentially ripe for American development.

There was also general agreement within the business community during the 1920s that the United States had no imperialist designs in these areas of the world. With particular reference
to Latin America it was argued that since foreign investments
and trade represented voluntary actions, the "economic and
financial penetration . . . by American interests . . . could not
be otherwise for reasons of propinquity and mutual convenience."
As long as the United States did not intervene with force to collect
specific debts but simply to protect property and lives, the country
was guiltless of the charge of economic or political imperialism.
When armed interventions did occur in Latin America, according
to the prevailing business interpretation, they could not be "attributed directly to investments by Americans," because they
were based on much broader grounds, such as the Monroe Doctrine, which provided for the "security of the United States against
conspiring European governments." Political and military interventions were said to be in the best interest of all Latin American
republics because they served as a "deterrent against new revolutions." As will be seen below, after 1925 business attitudes

toward intervention became more tempered with respect to both Latin America and the Far East, except for the minority of Sinophiles within the business community who urged the United States government in the late 1920s to protect at least the economic, if not the humanitarian, objectives of the Open Door in China.[4] But the general assumptions about the benevolence and inevitability of American economic expansion remained unchanged.

The end result of such reasoning was the unplanned, but not unintentional, consummation of a financial empire in the Caribbean and portions of Central and South America after World War I and the unsuccessful attempt to achieve the same thing in the Far East. Since the Second World War the American economic empire has spread to the Far East, Europe, and elsewhere, for it has been aptly noted that "financial control is the American adaptation of imperialism." As the result of unchecked private activity, more intense perhaps than could have been achieved through centralized, governmental planning, American economic expansion has achieved an imperialist posture which must now be continually promoted and guarded by the government. What emerged as a natural and undirected pattern in the 1920s, occasionally encouraged and protected by administrations which avoided institutionalized commitments, persists today in a more methodical fashion. Hence, the following prediction about South America, made in 1930 by William S. Culbertson, the American ambassador to Chile, can now be seen to have capsulized the stereotypic philosophy behind the economic expansion of the United States throughout the world.

> In spite of competition or even propaganda, American business will more than take care of itself. Our efficiency in production and distribution will excell [sic]. Furthermore, American capital will be the controlling factor in public and private finance in these [South American] countries simply because the greatest reservoirs of savings are to-day in the United States. Opposition and criticism may divert or slow down these tendencies but they cannot defeat the final result, namely, that American civilization, material and cultural, is bound to impress itself upon, and I believe, benefit these peoples. If anti-American critics wish to describe this as our "imperialism" let them make the most of it. It is the natural result of our

expanding life which, having achieved commendable results at home, is seeking new opportunities over-seas. We do not need to assert to the British or others that our position in Latin America rests on a political basis. It is unnecessary to rest our case (for which we find many good precedents in the politics of European countries) on a right to a trade sphere of influence in South America. We can successfully rest it solely on the fact, of which I see every day evidence, that the expanding forces of our economic life will give us first place in South America whether we consciously promote trade and finance or whether we indifferently leave them to take their upward course.[5]

Between 1920 and 1933 it was possible for Culbertson and leaders in government and business to believe that economic expansion could be maintained simply through the encouragement of individual initiative abroad, disarmament agreements, antiwar pacts, and a minimum of unilateral political or military intervention. It was even thought that a properly functioning, worldwide Open Door policy might become an effective substitute for the League of Nations by providing a peaceful means for nations to compete in developing areas. But the depression killed the unconsciousness and innocence of American foreign policy at the height of its success. Since that time the endless pursuit of economic expansion via an Open or Closed Door (depending upon which was more advantageous for the United States) can no longer be explained away as a spontaneous, unplanned phenomenon proving the superiority of capitalist free enterprise over all other economic systems. Instead, it has been accompanied by an increasingly complex series of economic incentives and agreements between government and business, plus political and military commitments between the United States and other nations. Contrary to Culbertson's prediction, neither government officials nor businessmen any longer believe in the luxury of "indifferently" allowing commerce and investment "to take their upward course." The assumption that business can take care of itself in foreign ventures is no longer considered practical, especially as more and more foreign countries begin to question the "material and cultural" benefits accruing to foreign nations from American economic expansion.

Operating unwittingly in the doomed innocence and optimism

of the first half of the 1920s, Secretaries Hughes and Hoover subscribed completely to the philosophy which later inspired the prediction of the American ambassador. Accordingly, they mapped out a foreign policy for Latin America which met with the approval of most businessmen. Convinced that American capitalism required foreign economic expansion, Hughes and Hoover insisted that all underdeveloped countries honor the "sanctity of contracts" and demonstrate the willingness as well as the "ability to perform international obligations." Both men denied, however, that it was a policy of the United States to collect "ordinary contract debts" by force. On the contrary, they defended a limited interpretation of the Monroe Doctrine, excluding the Roosevelt Corollary, but not ruling out the application of economic pressure and of justifiable unilateral intervention in order to protect "legally vested American rights." Much to the bewilderment and frustration of many Latin Americans they simultaneously embraced Pan Americanism, which stressed hemispheric cooperation based on the principles of equality and independence for all American nations. Such cooperation was, in their estimation, facilitated by advances in science and technology, especially in the field of communications, and could only lead to greater progress and prosperity for the people of North and South America. Thus, while proclaiming the equality of American countries, and maintaining that the United States had no imperialist designs or desire to interfere with the internal policies of individual countries, Hughes and Hoover asserted it was nonetheless their duty to encourage constitutional government, to discourage "unwarranted uprisings," to protect "the legitimate freedom of commerce," to prevent confiscation or repudiation of lawful American investments, and to promote political and legal institutions such as existed in the United States.[6]

The differences of opinion which did exist between the two men over Latin American policy contributed to the jurisdictional competition between their respective departments. In general Hughes was less critical of past interventions in the Caribbean and Central America and less suspicious about some Latin American loans than was Hoover, while Hoover was less critical of commercial arrangements than Hughes. If anything, Hughes outdid

Hoover in his public praise for American "economic penetration" of the Southern Hemisphere, which he once described as "the highest expression, from the material standpoint, of international confidence and good will." It was the secretary of state, rather than the secretary of commerce, who uncritically publicized the economic potentiality of Latin America when he said it was in this area of the world that the United States had "its greatest opportunity to exhibit wise practicality without departure from the liberal ideals upon which its prestige and moral influence must ultimately depend." Hoover, as noted in chapter 4, privately questioned certain Latin American loans and in 1925 even encouraged the NFTC to undertake a critical review of trade relations with South America.[7]

Hughes's approach to Latin American foreign policy was also more legalistic than Hoover's. For example, the secretary of state devoted considerable time and effort to promoting the establishment of legal bodies for the obligatory arbitration of "justiciable" disputes between American states. The climax of his efforts in this direction came after he left office in December 1929 with the signing of the Pan American Treaty of Arbitration at Washington. Pan Americanism, according to Hughes, consisted of this kind of legally binding arbitration, "this sympathy with the great purposes of peaceful settlement, this mutual confidence in effective collaboration." Long before the 1929 treaty had been signed, Hughes succeeded in substituting Pan American arbitration and cooperation as an alternative to any action the League of Nations might have taken in disputes between Latin American republics, such as the Panama-Costa Rica claims over the Coto district and the Tacna-Arica controversy between Peru and Chile. He also saw to it that League observers were excluded from the 1923 Pan American Conference and this ban carried over to the 1928 conference, as well. In addition he opposed the Geneva Protocol of 1924, in large measure because it would have allowed the League to intervene in disputes between the United States and Latin republics.[8]

And so upon Hughes's initiative and with Hoover's tacit approval, the American door closed out even mediation by the League of Nations for the decade of the 1920s. It was not until the end of his term in office that President Hoover and his secretary of state allowed the League of Nations to enter into a controversy between two Latin nations. This occurred at the beginning of 1933 in the struggle between Peru and Colombia over the river port of Leticia. After Hoover and Stimson had failed to obtain a settlement by invoking the Kellogg-Briand Pact, they and their successors agreed to an investigation of the affair by a League commission—the first to enter Latin America.[9]

Finally, Hughes made certain semantic distinctions which Hoover simply ignored. In particular, Hughes was critical of the indiscriminate use of the term intervention by critics of the American government. He argued that the United States had never intervened with military force or set up customs receiverships or other forms of financial supervision with the intention of permanently "interfering in the internal political affairs or administration" of the countries involved. Therefore, he concluded, such actions were not in any sense imperialist but simply "non-belligerent interpositions." Despite the presence of the marines in the Dominican Republic, Haiti, and Nicaragua when he was appointed secretary of state, the policy of the United States remained, Hughes insisted, one of nonintervention because "we limit our interposition to a pressing exigency well established; . . . we are not seeking control of peoples of other lands or to interfere with the governments they desire; . . . [and] our purposes are reasonable and can readily be justified to the governments that accept the principles of international law and perform their admitted international obligations." When the United States had interfered financially or militarily in countries in the past on the basis of treaty rights, as it had in the case of Cuba or the Canal Zone, Hughes was even more certain that this should not be described as intervention. After leaving office Hughes finally admitted that he had been unable to get the Latin Americans to accept his definition of "non-belligerent interposition," but this did not prevent him from delivering at the Havana Conference of 1928 one of the strongest defenses on record of the legal right of the United States to act unilaterally in Latin America.[10] What he never admitted was that most Americans did not accept the term "non-belligerent interposition" either. And Hoover was one of them.

The secretary of commerce initially did not theorize about the political foreign policy of the United States in Latin America. After obtaining control of the Inter-American High Commission from Treasury Secretary Andrew Mellon at the end of 1921, Hoover steadily established his hegemony over Latin American economic affairs, except in the areas of oil and cable development and bank loans. In these three areas the State Department retained basic control.[11] Peripherally he was also interested in improving cultural exchanges, but he seems to have shared with other government and business leaders the common view of Latin America as a convenient laboratory for testing old and new economic and political theories.[12]

Gradually, however, Hoover began to sense the growing resentment in Latin America against what were deemed to be spurious legalistic arguments, political interference, financial imperialism, and unwarranted unilateral use of force on the part of the United States. There was also growing dissatisfaction within the United States about the government's Latin American policies as evidenced by the Senate hearings of 1925 and 1927 discussed in chapter 4 above. Realizing by the end of the decade that such resentment at home and abroad might harm future economic relations between the United States and Latin America, government officials such as Hoover, Kellogg, and Stimson, and, to an even greater degree, business internationalists Thomas W. Lamont and Dwight Morrow, began to register dissatisfaction with the policy of dollar diplomacy based on arbitrary intervention. As early as 1923 Morrow had advised President Coolidge to establish a "consistent policy" in Latin America by ending the "dual control exercised by the War Department and the State Department." In 1928 Lamont, speaking for Morrow and other investment bankers, denounced the use of force in collecting debts as "unrighteous, unworkable, and obsolete."[13]

The practical, business side of Hoover's nature prompted him to become publicly more critical of the policy of military intervention as it had been practiced since 1900 than Hughes had ever been. He had expressed serious reservations about intervention beginning in 1922, and later he came to view the American experience in Haiti and Nicaragua as a too expensive, ineffective, and negative means of protecting lives and property and advancing the cause of democracy and capitalism. The Kellogg-Briand Pact further compromised the presence of American marines in Haiti and Nicaragua. So beginning with his tour of Latin America as president-elect in 1928, Hoover began to refer to the United States as a "good neighbor" of the southern republics, while emphasizing more and more the reciprocal cultural and economic interests of the two regions. By substituting cooperation, friendship, confidence, and participation in technological advancements for the traditional policy of arrogance and intervention, he thought the "material and spiritual progress" of North and South America would be assured. After assuming office he found support for his good neighbor philosophy within the State Department in the persons of Henry Stimson and William R. Castle, Jr. Unfortunately his good intentions in the area of political foreign policy were hampered by his economic policy; he was never able to live down his reputation for supporting high tariffs and loan standards which appeared antipathetic to the economic interests of certain Latin American countries. Scarcely six months after his goodwill tour the International Pan American Committee, made up largely of big business leaders, confidentially reported there was "more widespread anti-United States comment" in all of Latin America than "at any other time since the Panama affair of 1903 and President Roosevelt's coup d'état." The committee attributed this increased hostility to the proposed tariff legislation of the new Hoover administration.[14]

Although the government did not change its high tariff policy or make any significant attempts to collaborate with individual Latin American nations on economic matters, Hoover and his secretary of state did begin to act like better, if not good, neighbors in political affairs. They directed the marines, for example, to protect only those Americans in coastal areas after new violence broke out in Nicaragua in the spring of 1931. This refusal to deploy troops into the interior for the protection of lives and property represented a new departure in relations with Central America. Hoover and Stimson also refused to interfere with the growing tyranny of the Machado regime in Cuba in the early

1930s, when the power still existed to do so under the Platt Amendment and when the United States ambassador to Cuba was recommending nonmilitary steps for the government to take. It was during the Hoover administration that arrangements were made for the removal of the marines from Haiti and Nicaragua, although it must be admitted this was not done with any great haste. In fact, in Cuba, Haiti, and Nicaragua the administration was accused of procrastinating because American bankers and sugar companies did not desire any action against Machado and because business interests in the other two countries apparently did not want the remaining marines and American military advisers evacuated with undue dispatch. Consequently, despite the refusal to intervene in revolutionary situations or to use nonrecognition as a means of undermining revolutionary governments (except in Central America, where the United States continued to honor a 1923 nonrecognition treaty), and despite the apparent acceptance of the J. Reuben Clark memorandum, which separated the Roosevelt Corollary from the Monroe Doctrine, the good neighbor "mutuality" that Hoover wanted to force between the United States and Latin America was far from perfected when he left office. He did improve the quality of diplomatic representation in Latin America through the appointment of career officers to top positions, and his administration marks the beginning of a conscious attempt on the part of the United States to create a good neighbor attitude. In the long run, however, Hoover's rhetoric remained more impressive than his actions in Latin American relations. It was left for the administration of Franklin Delano Roosevelt to give more concrete substance to what later became known as the Good Neighbor policy.[15]

While political guidelines for Latin America gradually changed during the 1920s, trade and investment figures developed their own independent patterns. By 1930 the United States still had troops in Haiti and Nicaragua and some form of American financial supervision existed in El Salvador, Bolivia, the Dominican Republic, Haiti, Nicaragua, Cuba, and Panama.[16] In that same year exports to Latin America, including the Caribbean and Central America as well as South America, totaled approximately 18 percent of all United States exports, or $680 million, while imports from Latin America were slightly over a quarter of the total imports of this country, or $781 million. Direct and portfolio investments in Latin America were a little less than one-third of all American investments abroad, that is, between $5 and $5.5 billion. By the end of the decade the area constituting the twenty republics of Latin America ranked first, followed by Europe and then Canada, as the major outlet for United States capital. Before the war this money had gone primarily into Mexico and Cuba in the form of direct investments in properties owned or controlled by American nationals, but by 1930 there were more direct investments scattered throughout Latin America than in Canada and Europe combined. In addition, portfolio investments made in the South American countries of Brazil, Argentina, Colombia, and Chile increased following World War I. Interest rates for all Latin American loans were on the average higher than those going to Europe or Canada. Because of the political instability of many southern republics, 7 or 8 percent was charged rather than the normal 5. A pattern or trend can also be seen in the relative distribution of investments by industries. Before 1925 most American capital in Latin America had gone into mineral and agricultural production, mainly oil and sugar. Then there was a shift into public utilities, manufacturing, and processing of agricultural products for export. Petroleum investments continued to grow during the entire decade, extending from Mexico into Colombia and Venezuela.[17]

This large capital outlay triggered a debate over the relationship of loans to trade. Commerce Department officials were not as convinced as American bankers that these Latin American investments significantly increased exports; often they did not contribute to the productive capacity of the borrowing countries and almost never did they specify that American goods were to be purchased. (Hoover's futile attempt to correct this situation is discussed in chapter 4 above.) As a result, the Commerce Department complained it was "difficult to establish a direct and specific connection between the increase in such loans and the increase in American exports to the borrowing countries." There was, according to Commerce officials, a closer relationship between direct investments and demands for the manufactured products of the United States than was the case with portfolio loans. Even with direct in-

vestments, however, allowance had to be made for "large expenditures for land, concessions, native labor, and supplies, as well as
for engineering and technical services." Statistics confirmed that
the increase in investments far exceeded the increase in exports.
Between 1913 and 1930, for example, portfolio and direct
investments increased over 300 percent while exports to Latin
America increased only 87 percent. The result was that the balance
of trade remained unfavorable for the United States, but the overall
balance of payments did not. Obviously there was some correlation between investments and trade, but it was not in the direct
proportion international bankers wanted the American public,
manufacturers, and government officials to believe. The unfavorable trade balance provided unofficial collateral for loans, which
bankers were reluctant to admit or to forfeit by including trade
clauses in their contracts.[18]

The figures for trade and investment by 1930 indicate that the
change in emphasis from the Monroe Doctrine to Pan Americanism to the Good Neighbor idea did not in any way hamper the
economic expansion of the United States in Latin America. Neither
did the full development of the Good Neighbor policy by the New
Dealers. Although the purpose of this policy, according to
Roosevelt, was to establish a "kind of hemisphere partnership"
by eliminating the threat of military and financial aggression by
the United States, it resulted primarily in a shift of political tactics.
By officially renouncing armed interventions and nonmilitary interference in financial and political affairs at Pan American
conferences in 1933 and 1936, the Democrats did not swerve
from the path leading to economic domination of Latin America.
It was simply a question, as Hoover had recognized, of goodwill
being better for trade than "arbitrary intervention." This did not
mean that the United States was going to stop trying to influence
Latin American governments through the "customary methods of
diplomacy." Neither did it mean that government officials and
businessmen had ceased to look upon Latin America as the
most accessible ideological proving ground for the exportation of
capitalism and democracy. In other words, the Good Neighbor
policy signified business as usual with less muscle and more
public relations.[19]

The depression complicated the economic task of the New

Dealers by ending loans to Latin America until 1939. By 1935, 85 percent of all Latin American dollar bonds had defaulted, compared with 52 percent for Europe and 3 percent for Canada. Despite these defaults and the absence of the public flotation of new issues, trade between the United States and Latin America, which also declined because of the depression, gradually recovered after 1933 with the aid of reciprocal trade agreements and assistance to American exporters from the Export-Import Bank. By the middle of the decade the United States was sending to Latin America over half of its cotton and steel-mill exports, one-third of its leather, rubber, silk, paper, electrical, and industrial exports, and one-fifth of its automobile exports. The pattern of portfolio investments, however, remained frozen until World War II.[20]

The United States did not become a good neighbor in the early 1930s just to improve trade relations injured by an economic crisis. Washington officials expected the Latin American republics to reciprocate by doing the things traditionally desired by this country. That is, in return for the Good Neighbor policy, Latin Americans were to establish stable governments, honor political as well as economic obligations, and extend equitable treatment to American citizens and their property according to the standards of due process which existed in the United States. There was opposition from Mexico and other countries to the unilateral assertion by the United States of its right to define what was equitable. In the course of the decade Washington modified its position to the degree that it accepted the right of expropriation as a negotiable issue, and unofficially began to regard the property rights of corporations or private individuals as a secondary concern to what Under-Secretary of State Sumner Welles called the "national policy." This meant that national security took precedence over business interests if the two were in conflict. It should be remembered that neither the 1933 nor the 1936 nonintervention pledge, nor the abrogation of the Platt Amendment in 1934, was related to the issue of national security. So it was possible for Roosevelt to assert in 1938 that the United States would intervene in Mexico if this country's security was threatened there by European aggression. As a result of World War II, national security as a justification for intervention in Latin America began to transcend all the self-denying components which had gone into the Good Neighbor policy.[21] Since the advent of the Cold War, national security has been broadly redefined in ideological terms involving both political and economic considerations. Latin America represents, therefore, an area of the world in which the United States has had its greatest success in establishing a sphere of influence by applying the Closed Door policy to control or eliminate foreign competition. Although portions of the foundation for this success had been laid before World War I, it was largely constructed during the 1920s.

Outside of Central America and the Caribbean, which have been extensively documented, one of the best examples of the Closed Door at work can be found in American relations with Brazil between 1920 and 1933. Although Britain had dominated trade and investment in Brazil until 1913, by 1930 the United States had become the leading buyer and seller for the country, and was beginning to encroach upon English preeminence in the field of investments. Whereas the United States had purchased 32 percent of all Brazilian exports and accounted for 15 percent of all Brazilian imports in 1913, these percentages rose to over 45 percent, or $215,992,000, in the case of exports by 1928, and over 26 percent, or $117,511,000, for imports. Few Brazilian loans had been floated on the American market before World War I, but twenty years later almost a quarter of the foreign debt of Brazil, or $557,001,000, was held in the United States. Most requests for loans to South America received government approval in the 1920s with the exception of Brazilian coffee loans which, according to the Commerce Department, were for the purpose of establishing a monopoly "unfair to American consumers."[22]

The first time the Commerce Department went on public record in opposition to the valorization of coffee by the Brazilian government was in 1922. This Brazilian practice of building warehouses in the interior of the state of São Paulo, buying coffee on the open market, and storing it to maintain or raise the world price, dated from 1907. Valorization operations continued sporadically until by 1925 coffee was sold by planters at fourteen cents a pound, then held at São Paulo until twenty-two to thirty cents a pound was received. The resulting rise in retail coffee prices in the United States was approximately 100 percent. Consequently the Commerce Department began to oppose all loans to Brazil which it suspected would be used to "artificially force up the price of coffee to the American consumer." While Hoover was able to gain the support of the State Department in his attack on the coffee monopoly, his policy was resisted by two different groups within the business community.[23]

Banking firms, of course, such as Dillon, Read and Company, and Speyer and Company, made it clear their prime concern was that the United States should "not lose the financial leadership and prestige that goes with it" because of restriction on loans to Brazil. They also pointed out to no avail that valorization loans would come from other foreign countries if the United States closed its door on them. Grosvenor Jones, chief of the Finance and Investment Division of the BFDC, criticized such companies for "looking at the matter purely from a banker's standpoint" rather than considering the "effect such additional borrowing would have on the price of coffee." Hoover agreed, adding: "If European financiers were willing to enter into a gamble to hold the price of coffee at a point which curtailed consumption and stimulated production to a point where today we have a world surplus, that was a matter for their own responsibility . . . but that if they did, it was better that it be done by some outsider than done by American bankers against the interest of the American public." Hoover denied the United States had any responsibility to prevent bankruptcy in São Paulo. He viewed the state's plight as the "result of their own folly," and sanguinely noted that the bankruptcy of São Paulo might be one of the best lessons for the world, since it would clearly demonstrate that the "American people cannot be perpetually held up in these ways." As in his battle against the British rubber monopoly, Hoover was indifferent to the possibility of foreign bankruptcy because "such monopolistic control of commodities is illegal in this country, and our citizens cannot be asked to submit to it from other countries," regardless of the consequences. No bankruptcy developed, however, after the State Department refused to approve the loan. As Dillon, Read and Company had predicted, the money was obtained from London sources, and a portion of the 1925 loan was sold indirectly in the United States, anyway. Thus, Hoover was not as successful in combating the coffee monopoly as he had been with the rubber monopoly. But he did bring the issue and himself to the attention of the public, there was a temporary stabilization of coffee prices in the last half of the decade, and a vigorous first attempt had been made to force Brazilian compliance with American demands by closing the door on a certain type of loan.[24]

In addition to arousing the opposition of a few international bankers, Hoover's position on valorization also antagonized another element within the business community—the individual coffee roasters and importers. These businessmen, like the financiers, were unable to weaken the opposition of the secretary of commerce to coffee valorization loans. The National Coffee Roasters Association could not even obtain the secretary's permission to use his name in an innocuous public statement to the effect that the United States was not basically opposed to assisting the São Paulo coffee planters. Representatives of the association also unsuccessfully tried to impress Hoover with the possibility of "extensive bankruptcy" in São Paulo. Unlike the bankers, they said that such a bankruptcy would "have a serious reflex [*sic*] on American trade and even create a great deal of ill feeling toward America in that province." Their prime concern was, of course, for the businessmen their organization represented who were dependent upon São Paulo for their supply of coffee.[25]

In order to neutralize the criticism from this group, which was symptomatic of a division existing within the coffee industry between importers, roasters, jobbers, and distributors, Hoover in 1926 promoted the formation of the National Coffee Council. The council never developed the united front Hoover knew was essential if a buying pool or buyers' boycott was to bring effective pressure upon the Brazilian coffee producers. The coffee distributors and retailers, for example, were much more disposed to go along with the Commerce Department's loan policy, its ideas on cooperative buying and, if necessary, boycotting, and its plans for developing new sources of supply in Colombia, Hawaii, Puerto Rico, Cuba, and the Philippines; they did not fear the possibility of the development of coffee substitutes as much as did the importers and roasters. Commercial attachés in Rio de Janeiro worked diligently for the council despite the fact that the industry as a whole was not in complete agreement with the department's objectives. While privately admitting that his basic objective was to thwart "all attempts of the São Paulo coffee speculators to borrow money in the United States," Hoover did not want the details of the government's Closed Door intentions disclosed. As he told Senator James Couzens, "We do not wish by means of misinterpretation in the matter of Brazil, to create the feeling that we are not fundamentally cooperating with the Brazilian people in advancing their interests."[26]

Misrepresentation resulted, nonetheless, and as president-elect, Hoover felt particularly obliged to include Brazil in his tour of Central and South America to improve his image there. In December 1928 he spoke to a Brazilian audience about the "economic mutuality," confidence, and friendship existing between the two countries. Clearly his crusade against the coffee monopoly had come to an end. From the beginning it had been seriously hampered by the opposition within the business community. Once the depression set in, coffee prices were so reduced that the valorization scheme collapsed of its own accord. Hoover was thus freed to act along less controversial Closed Door lines, namely, the pursuit of greater American control over Brazilian trade and investments. So in 1930 the government approved a loan to São Paulo, after being assured by bankers that it would not be used for valorization purposes. A year later a wheat-for-coffee exchange was negotiated by the Federal Farm Board to mitigate the effects of the depression on American wheat farmers. When Brazil logically followed this transaction by imposing an embargo on flour importations for eighteen months, Hoover answered the complaints of domestic flour millers and bankers (who tended to oppose all barter proposals) by noting that "the trade made by the Farm Board saved the Brazilian Government from collapse." (As secretary of commerce he had not shown such concern for the state of São Paulo when the coffee monopoly was a reality.) At the same time the State Department worked behind the scenes to mollify the flour millers by making sure all the contracts for flour shipments made before the embargo announcement were honored. By 1932 the government was no longer opposing any loans to Brazilian coffee growers.[27] Thus, the depression initially encouraged a modification of the Closed Door policy toward Brazil's coffee industry. In the long run, however, the depression strained relations between the United States and Brazil and other Latin American countries as revolutions and defaults accumulated after 1929, and paved the way for a stronger application of other Closed Door policies of an economic nature in the 1930s.

In contrast, during the first years of the depression the political foreign policy of the United States toward Brazil and South American nations in general became more lenient. Initially, in accordance with a 1922 joint resolution, arms embargoes were automatically imposed against the rebels when a revolution broke out. This traditional response embarrassed Secretary Stimson on occasion, as in the case of the 1930 revolution in Brazil, where the rebel forces won. While the arms embargo policy of the Hoover administration was never officially changed, it was used less and less frequently as the number of revolutions increased. Concurrently Hoover and Stimson began to grant de facto recognition to whichever side established control as long as the new regime displayed an intention to hold "free elections" and to honor international obligations. There were approximately sixty revolutions in Latin America between 1929 and 1933, of which a little over twenty were successful. In only seven of these did the United States actually withhold recognition pending free elections. Even if they had been predisposed to do so, Stimson and Hoover would not have had the time to pass moral and political judgment on all of the revolutionary situations which arose, as Wilson had done. They also did not find it practical under the circumstances to apply, as Hughes and Kellogg had done, the 1923 treaty between Guatemala, Honduras, Costa Rica, El Salvador, and Nicaragua, to all of Latin America. This treaty stated that governments created by coups d'état or revolution would not be recognized. Although the United States had not signed the treaty, it strictly adhered to its principles by refusing to recognize revolutionary governments in the 1920s. The Hoover administration abandoned this policy for South American countries in

1930, and in 1934, when the Central American treaty was nullified by the original signatories, the Hoover-Stimson policy of granting de facto recognition was taken up by Roosevelt and Hull and applied to all of Latin America.[28]

The question of supplying arms to Latin America remained a problem for the Hoover administration despite the change in recognition policy. First, it became increasingly onerous, if not impossible, for the United States to try to control the use of the weapons. For example, in July 1932 twenty-eight planes were sold to Brazil when a new revolution broke out. The official justification was that the "transaction seemed advantageous to American Commerce, not only in furnishing our factories with orders but in avoiding the diversion of these orders to foreign competitors." By September, however, Francis White, assistant secretary of state for Latin American affairs, began to fear that Brazil would use these planes as indiscriminately against civilians as the Peruvian government recently had used its planes in putting down rebellion. As a result, the State Department recommended that it would be wise "to keep the government out of any such transactions" in the future. Second, the problem of supplying arms to Latin America became even more complicated in the early 1930s when South American nations began to engage in wars with one another for the first time since the nineteenth century. After unsuccessfully trying to apply both the Kellogg-Briand Pact and the Stimson Doctrine of nonrecognition in disputes between Paraguay and Bolivia over Chaco, and between Peru and Colombia over Leticia, Stimson obtained Hoover's approval (over the objections of all other cabinet members) to ask Congress for an arms embargo to be invoked at the president's discretion against belligerent nations on the condition that other major arms-producing countries agreed to cooperate. Under strong pressure from the munitions and aviation industries, Congress failed to act and the Hoover administration left office without ridding itself of the obsolete anti-rebel policy established in 1922.[29]

Nonetheless, the record of Hoover and Stimson in political foreign policy was more successful overall than their record in economic foreign policy, possibly because the former was more flexible. They changed the recognition policy of the United States toward South America, withdrew the marines from Nicaragua, and tried to revise the policy governing arms sales. They failed, however, to give any more substance to the policy of requiring free elections than their predecessors. It was clear that when Americans actually supervised such elections, as they had in a number of Latin American republics since 1900, the policy, like that of military occupation, proved more expensive and time-consuming than it was worth. Admitting this, Hoover and Stimson still remained committed in theory to the principle of free elections, but it is to their credit that they did not permit this principle to become an end in itself as has been the tendency since World War II.[30] They were less successful in the realm of economic foreign policy because the depression defied traditional economic principles. For example, Hoover and Stimson continued to insist that Latin American nations honor their contractual obligations at the very time when default became the rule rather than the exception in international relations. With few modifications the Closed Door remained the policy of the United States in the Southern Hemisphere. Once again, economic relations with Brazil will serve as the representative example.

Upon hearing of Hoover's moratorium on intergovernmental debts in June 1931, several Latin American republics expressed the hope that it would be extended to include them. Both the State and the Commerce Department were against such action, but the rumors about a moratorium for Latin America persisted throughout 1931 and 1932 even after Hoover officially denied them by pointing out that only government loans made during the war qualified. During the same period rumors also arose concerning the likelihood of unilateral moratoriums by individual Latin states. The first speculation about a two-year Brazilian moratorium reached the State Department in May 1931. Apparently this step was being recommended by Sir Otto Niemeyer, who was conducting a study of Brazilian finances for a group of London bankers. Hoover was aware that such a moratorium would be "a terrific blow" to American investors. There was also the possibility it would "drive another nail in the coffin" of the Republican party. During the summer of 1931 the State Department repeatedly denied any knowledge of whether or not Argentina,

Chile, Uruguay, or Brazil would default, and Hoover refused to see most of the businessmen who wrote him requesting appointments to discuss their solutions to the Latin American economic crisis. He did, however, take enough note of the recommendation of General Palmer E. Pierce, chairman of the board of Standard Oil of New Jersey and a representative of the National Foreign Trade Council, to arrange for the general to see Treasury Secretary Andrew W. Mellon. The average businessman's suggestions were courteously answered but essentially ignored by the executive branch while it was formulating an economic foreign policy for Latin America during the depression.[31]

When speculation first arose about Latin American defaults, Secretary of State Stimson sent confidential cables to all American embassies in Latin countries instructing them to "unofficially communicate" disapproval by the United States of any unilateral or collective moratorium plans. The embassies were also told to exercise their "influence in an informal manner" over the presidents of their respective countries to thwart any such plans. A sequence of defaulting began, nevertheless. Bolivia was the first to declare a suspension of foreign payments in December 1930, followed by Peru in March 1931, then Chile in July, and finally Brazil in September. While financial companies turned to the State Department for aid, the complaints of individual bondholders were mainly directed toward Congress and resulted in a Senate investigation. By the end of 1933 all Latin American countries, with the exceptions of Argentina and Haiti, had instituted unilateral moratoriums on their foreign debts.[32]

The first business reaction to the Brazilian default was communicated to the government by the financial firm of White and Weld. This company feared that the current negotiations in London were aimed at readjusting the federal loans of Brazil and would work to the disadvantage of Americans who had invested heavily in state and municipal bonds. In a protracted debate with the State Department between 1931 and 1933, White, Weld and Company and similar firms were unable to obtain official backing for the position of the private investors they represented. This was because the State and Commerce departments seriously questioned whether "all holders of the several types of Brazilian foreign bonds" would receive fair and equal treatment if the claims of only these few firms were considered. Washington officials also insisted that they could not undertake to act as mediators between the state and municipal bondholders and Brazil. Finally, it was pointed out to White and Weld that they were using the wrong method by approaching the government of the United States. They were advised to bring their case directly to Brazilian authorities on their own.[33] To say the least, this advice from the government must have sounded strange to the banking and investment firms, since the State Department had freely extended its good offices so that most of these municipal and state bond issues could be negotiated in the first place.

While individual companies were vying with one another to obtain government intervention in Brazil on behalf of their bond-holders, a few bankrupt private citizens also approached the government with desperate pleas for aid. Walter Lafferty, for example, wrote to William R. Castle in 1931 saying he had been ruined by the depression and requesting an appointment as a special agent for the State Department to travel to Brazil in order to determine what the best course of action would be. Lafferty warned the department not to leave the matter in the hands of the sponsor banks, explaining, "They have deserted us. The banks coldly say our bonds no longer have any collateral value whatever, and we are being closed out even if we owe 10% on them. It is cruel and awful. Some of my São Paulo State 8's, 1950, for which I paid 103 in 1928, worth 81 April this year, sold yesterday on stock exchange at forced sale for 12 and ⅜! Can Washington remain passive and leave it to the banks?" Several weeks later Castle answered Lafferty, regretting his difficulties but denying that the government could aid him in any way, since the bond issues represented private transactions. The more abusive letters from private investors which talked about the "lousy and crooked foreign loans" went unanswered.[34] Senators investigating the sale of bonds exhibited more concern for the plight of the average person, but were powerless to help him recoup his losses.

Ultimately the Brazilian and other Latin American debt situations were partially resolved in a manner which appeared to place the State Department on the side of the large commercial interests rather than the bondholders and financiers. At the beginning of 1933 George L. Harrison of the Federal Reserve Bank of New York wrote to Harvey H. Bundy, the assistant secretary of state, about a meeting he had had with representatives of International General Electric and Electric Bond and Share Company about the Brazilian moratorium. These firms had large investments all over the continent; those of Electric Bond and Share totaled over $89 million in South America alone. Like the financiers, they feared Brazil and other Latin American states were trying to obtain assistance from London in the form of credit from the House of Rothschild. If this occurred the inroads made by Americans since the war in Brazil and other southern nations would be lost to the British. This they said was intolerable because "if there is one part of the world which American business has come to look upon as its own territory, it is South America." Consequently they proposed that the Federal Reserve Bank of New York help American businessmen and investors in Latin America by granting the credit and loans which private bankers were now withholding. Harrison did not approve of this use of the Federal Reserve System and neither did the State Department.[35]

The financial stalemate with Brazil remained unchanged until the spring of 1933, when approximately $30 million in American commercial credit was frozen by the Brazilian government. This prompted several American companies, such as Standard Oil of New Jersey, Westinghouse Electric International Company, Atlantic Refining Company, Caloric Company, Electric Bond and Share Company, and the Texas Company, to enter into a financial agreement with the Bank of Brazil to free this currency. The transaction was endorsed by Fred I. Kent of the New York Reserve Board, the National Foreign Trade Council, and the Council of Inter-American Relations. It was opposed by representatives of the bondholders because "it was unfair to give manufacturers and exporters the exclusive benefit of the liberation of exchanges." Although Under-Secretary of State William Phillips privately approved of the action, he told Roosevelt it made him feel "uneasy." As Phillips saw it, by not taking a stand one way or the other with respect to the complaints of the bondholders, the government was in essence favoring "one group of American creditors as against another." That is, by refusing to delay a settlement which could only benefit the commercial interests in order to bargain for a resumption of the service on defaulted bonds, the government through inactivity cast its lot on the side of the manufacturers and exporters. The standard reply of the State Department to bondholders who complained of this injustice was that "our historical policy has been one of noninterference in transactions between private citizens and foreign governments."[36]

The same position was taken in other South American countries. In the case of at least two, Colombia and Argentina, the government actually brought great pressure to bear on American bankers to renew loans in order to protect American commercial interests. More often than not, however, private commercial firms had to provide the necessary financing themselves. Defaults were handled slightly differently in the Caribbean and Central America, where the financial control by the American government and bankers was considerably greater due to treaty or other contractual agreements. With Washington officials openly involved in arranging renewals, bankers were not as reluctant to continue to carry old loans as they were in South America. It is indicative of the change in Latin American policy under Hoover and Roosevelt that no military interventions resulted from the numerous revolutions, defaults, frozen exchanges, embargoes, and threatened confiscations precipitated by the depression.[37]

Generally speaking the position of the Democrats on defaults remained very much like that of the Republicans they replaced. The major difference was that the Roosevelt administration more readily admitted that "demands for current necessities [commercial credit] must take priority over payments of old debts." By the same token it was unequivocally asserted that "frozen deposits in foreign countries clearly deserve priority over payments on bonds" since the former represented the working capital of American corporations. This was the position assumed by the Federal Reserve Board, the National Foreign Trade Council, and General Pierce during both administrations. At the same time the Democrats did try to placate irate bondholders with the Securities Act and with the creation of the Foreign Bondholders Protective Council. The idea for a private bond-holders' council had originated under Hoover in the summer of 1932, but was not finally organized by the government until after he left office in 1933. The delay resulted in part from the insistence of both Stimson and Hull that the council should be made up of influential bankers who were not identified with investment houses which had handled Latin American issues. Presumably this prerequisite would guarantee that the council would act as the disinterested representative of all American bondholders. Over the protests of Senator Hiram Johnson, Hull, Roosevelt, the Departments of Commerce and the Treasury, the OEA and the Federal Trade Commission continued the Republican policy of opposing the establishment of such a council as an official federal agency. But both administrations promised full cooperation "within proper limits" to a nongovernmental council representing all bondholders.[38]

So despite denials to the contrary, the Foreign Bondholders Protective Council ended up the "product of Government initiative," in essence a quasi-official group which added to the confusion of public and private responsibility on the issue of foreign loans. Even with this strong, albeit indirect, backing by the government, the council was unable to obtain much compensation for Americans with Brazilian bonds. The British debt plan, devised by Otto Niemeyer and finally accepted by Brazil, contained only a few minor modifications for the relief of Americans who held municipal and state bonds.

The favoritism shown by the Hoover and Roosevelt administrations for the large commercial interests operating in Latin America was not due simply to the strong suspicions both presidents happened to harbor about eastern financiers, and the reluctance of the State Department to admit it had fostered some questionable loans. It was due largely to the belief that the southern market was the key to the recovery of the entire export trade of the United States. For the duration of the depression the New Dealers tried to devise new tactics to stimulate exports. In particular, trade agreements reached at the Montevideo Conference at the end of 1933 and the creation of the Export-Import

Bank in 1934, whose loans required the purchase of American goods, marked a turning point in the official promotion of Yankee domination of trade with Latin America. Thus, the Export-Import Bank made loans to American exporters from its inception, and began providing credits to Latin American governments after war broke out in Europe in 1939. Also, the new commercial inroads made by Japan and Germany in the early 1930s were effectively exposed as examples of "economic aggression." This allowed the United States to justify a further closing to other nations of Latin America's commercial door. The trade agreements made with Cuba and Brazil in 1934 and 1935, for example, were intended among other things to end Japanese and German trade with these two countries. So the Closed Door policy toward Brazil and all of Latin America not only survived the depression, despite the withdrawal of credit by American bankers in 1930, but also emerged more strongly than ever in the course of the 1930s under the guise of the Good Neighbor policy.[39]

As an experiment in exporting capitalism and democracy, the economic and political foreign policy of the United States toward Latin America was of dubious success in the 1920s and 1930s from the standpoint of the developing countries. Businessmen themselves complained on occasion about the unbalanced, one-crop economies of most of the southern republics, few of which achieved a viable democratic system. The triumph of the Closed Door should not, therefore, be considered synonymous with a prosperous, democratic Latin America, despite the fact that it has been enormously profitable for American businessmen.

Chapter Seven

Manifestations of the Open Door, 1920–1933

After the end of World War I, the United States pursued the Open Door policy in a greater variety of geographical locations than it did the Closed Door because of the greater economic and political competition that existed outside the Western Hemisphere. This was especially true in the Far East, the Middle East, the East Indies, and Russia. In the case of the Far East the Open Door was invoked in response to general economic and political considerations, some of which dated back to at least 1900, but all of which finally fell victim to the Manchurian crisis of 1930–1932.

In the other areas mentioned above, however, Washington officials went out of their way to apply the Open Door concept to aid the development of a single and relatively new industry. This was the petroleum industry, whose rapid postwar expansion created two general problems for the American government. One involved mediating domestic disputes between the large, vertically integrated oil companies and the small independent producers over such issues as tariff and transportation rates, conservation and leasing practices, and the stabilization of prices for crude oil.[1] The other concerned enforcement of the Open Door to prevent foreign governments from discriminating against American firms attempting to acquire and operate petroleum property abroad. Both problems reached crisis proportions following World War I because of an exaggerated fear of an oil shortage between 1919 and 1924, and then a lingering suspicion among many government officials and businessmen for the rest of the decade that the oil reserves in the United States and Mexico were rapidly being depleted. Although neither condition materialized, both critics of and apologists for the industry contended that everything, from modern civilization and world peace to national security and the new standard of living represented by the automobile, depended upon the efficient as well as sufficient extraction of oil from domestic and foreign sources.[2]

For twelve years as secretary of commerce and president, Hoover periodically tried to solve the domestic and foreign problems created by the oil industry. His closest adviser on oil matters was a personal friend and fellow engineer from California, Mark L. Requa.[3] Neither man wanted the government to control the industry, but they agreed it needed official aid to a greater degree than ever before "to perform its service to the public," especially in the area of conservation. Accordingly Requa confided to oilman J. Howard Pew in 1925, "It is up to industry . . . to see that cooperation on the part of government is intelligent, wise and helpful; a condition that has unfortunately been lacking in the past. In other words, 'the paramount business of the American citizen is the business of government.' . . . I do not believe in undue or unnecessary government interference or tinkering. This latter is what the [oil] industry must face if it elects to follow the 'laissez faire' doctrine." Hoping that the industry would voluntarily cooperate, Hoover and Requa recommended domestic conservation measures utilizing improved technology, only to find that oilmen seldom followed their scientific advice for reducing national petroleum production. The result was rampant competition and overproduction at home and abroad by the end of the decade. The *ABA Journal* explained this apparent industrial insanity by noting the obvious: "Whenever oil is discovered, the owner or lessee of the land naturally is anxious to recover it before it is drained away by wells on neighboring land."[4]

The philosophy behind the Commerce Department's oil policy remained constant throughout the decade. It consisted of an understanding between government officials, engineers, military personnel, and conservationists in regard to those resources considered essential to the national interest. This coalition had been formed in the Progressive era, reached maturity in the 1920s, and has remained essentially stable since that time. It was based on a relatively simple thesis which emphasized the necessity of standardizing costs and of employing new methods to discover, develop, and *conserve* oil and other strategic raw materials within the United States, while *exploiting* those same resources abroad behind the banner of the Open Door. National defense and security constituted, therefore, the major rationale behind the conservation of the domestic oil fields. The preservation of "naval and military petroleum supplies" within the United States was, according to Hoover, the primary reason behind President Coolidge's appointment of the Federal Oil Conservation Board in 1924. Even though the board was created on the heels of the Teapot Dome scandal, its recommendations had little effect on the wasteful practices within the industry, and the leasing of federal reserves to private, competitive operators continued unabated until Hoover became president and instituted a policy of "complete conservation of government oil." Through his administration's strict leasing policy and other measures relating to production, the interests of conservation and efficiency were both served.[5]

When it came to foreign oil fields, Hoover's policies definitely favored the large oil companies and were not always internally consistent. For example, he supported the Open Door development of foreign oil fields which ostensibly endorsed the principle of competition, but did not object when a development was monopolized by one or two large firms as long as one was American. Hoover and Requa also staunchly supported the American Petroleum Institute in its efforts to establish an oil corporation under the Webb-Pomerene Act for the cooperative acquisition of foreign oil despite the danger that oil from such a corporation would harm the independent domestic producers by further lowering the price of crude oil. And of course the Commerce Department was caught up in the basically anomalous nature of the government's postwar oil philosophy, which espoused conservation at home and exploitation abroad. All of these inconsistencies were either justified or obscured by the overriding consideration that oil was absolutely necessary to the national interest of the United States. Naturally, therefore, Hoover assured

Representative John E. Raker that his department was aiding "independent oil producers to secure foreign holdings of oil lands in South America and elsewhere with a view to enabling them to continue to supply oil to the United States in event of exhaustion of their oil holdings here." Requa went one step further in supporting the systematic exploitation of foreign oil by recommending a "policy of petroleum . . . that would become so fixed a feature of our diplomacy that it could not be changed at the whim of some party or person temporarily in power."[6] Thus, the procurement of new oil fields became a foreign policy goal which created political as well as economic problems for the government whenever American oilmen encountered opposition abroad.

The Wilson administration had been the first to face this dilemma and between 1918 and 1920 had begun to come to the aid of the oilmen. Recognition was sometimes withheld from governments, such as those of Mexico and Russia, which threatened oil property ownership. In addition, Wilson had insisted at the Paris Peace Conference that the Open Door be honored in all of the former colonies and territories of the defeated powers which were designated as League mandates. The Wilsonians also endorsed direct legislative retaliation in the form of the General Leasing Law of 1920, which prohibited foreign nationals and companies of countries discriminating against American oil firms from leasing fields in the public domain. Finally, before leaving office the Wilsonians specifically expanded the Open Door doctrine to include the oil-rich areas of the world. According to Secretary of State Bainbridge Colby, the United States had been generously allowing foreign nations to draw upon its oil resources. Although the United States produced 60 percent of the total output of crude oil, only 8 percent of the world's petroleum resources were in continental America. So Secretary Colby told the British foreign minister that American demands for oil exceeded the domestic supplies and therefore the United States government wanted its citizens to have the "opportunity to explore and develop the petroleum resources of the world wherever found."[7]

Once the Republicans came to office, Hoover and Hughes elaborated upon the basic policy inherited from the Democrats.

In theory the two secretaries promoted a policy of impartiality toward all American companies competing in foreign oil fields, and most emphatically insisted upon a complete Open Door for all nations and all companies. Their policy even included the United States as fair ground for foreign nationals as long as their respective governments reciprocated, although restrictions were placed upon oil prospecting by aliens in the Philippines, Costa Rica, and Haiti. Furthermore, by the time Secretary of State Frank B. Kellogg reviewed the Open Door policy as it applied to the government's oil diplomacy in 1928, it had come to stand for not only "equality of treatment with all other foreign nationals in oil territory, but also for treatment equivalent to that accorded to the nationals in the country in question."[8] Clearly the Open Door received its broadest application since 1900 under the Republican administrations of the 1920s, as the government aided American businessmen in obtaining a share of the world's oil fields.

The most contested areas in the postwar scramble for petroleum resources by the major industrial nations were located in Mesopotamia (which became Iraq in 1921), Persia (now Iran), Russia, the Netherlands East Indies, Mexico, and several South American countries. The details of the aid and advice rendered by the State Department to individual companies have been treated extensively in other studies. Hence, no attempt will be made here to chronicle all of the correspondence and meetings between representatives of foreign governments, foreign companies, Washington officials, and American firms. Instead, the general characteristics of the oil diplomacy of the United States government will be discussed, with special attention given to the attitudes and actions of the Commerce Department.

The fact that the United States had not joined the League of Nations complicated the task of the Republicans, for it placed them in the position of demanding economic rights and privileges in certain mandates and other areas where the country had technically refused to accept political responsibilities. This meant that much of their oil diplomacy had to be conducted unofficially through private individuals rather than through public officials. Such methods suited those connected with the oil industry

who had been looking forward to the day when businessmen
rather than "uninformed politicians and so-called diplomats"
would make "fact and science . . . the basis for national laws
and international agreements" in the petroleum field. Hughes and
Hoover agreed with this point of view, and, as they had with the
question of reparations, once again contributed to confusing
rather than clarifying the roles of public and private authority in
the area of economic foreign policy. They began by conferring
with oilmen and engineers about obtaining new fields, asked
their advice about formulating an international oil policy, and
finally allowed businessmen to conduct the oil diplomacy of the
United States. Thus, in the spring of 1921, while Hughes discussed
the complaints of American firms in Mesopotamia with representatives of the British government, he and Hoover were simultaneously meeting with the "best authorities . . . in the petroleum industry" in order to determine what diplomatic action
should be taken. The secretary of commerce finally concluded
the individual sessions with engineers and oil groups with a general
conference on May 16, 1921. At that time Hoover informed the
oil delegations that if the government went all out to open the
door for them in Mesopotamia, their companies must be prepared
to act in a collective fashion.[9]

There was some reluctance among the large oil companies to
accept the Hughes-Hoover policy of a complete Open Door with
equality of opportunity for all American companies. Such an
arrangement was not necessarily in the best interests of those oil
producers who could afford to compete independently abroad.
Nonetheless, State Department backing could not be obtained in
the early 1920s without paying at least lip-service to the Hughes-
Hoover position. In 1921 one executive of Jersey Standard explained his company's strategy to secure Mesopotamian oil in the
following manner:

> The Standard Oil Company cannot hope to get the serious back-
> ing from the State Department if it attempts to enter the Mesopo-
> tamian field alone.
>
> I believe it will be necessary to take some other interests with us
> and a part of whom, at least, should be outside of the subsidiaries.
> I also think that we should select the associates carefully and keep

the list as small as possible. Personally, my suggestion would be Standard Oil Company of New York, Sinclair, Doheny, Texas, and it seems to me necessarily, the Gulf.

I think the effect of any success in Mesopotamia would result in bringing all these people into competition with us in the Mediterranean and that the association is highly undesirable except to gain the support of the State Department.

Thus, an American group of seven large companies under the leadership of Jersey Standard was formed in 1921 and initially led Washington officials to believe it was interested in an independent joint American venture in Mesopotamia. But by the end of the year the American group had obtained the tacit approval of the State and Commerce departments to form a consortium with the British-controlled Turkish Petroleum Company for a share of the Mesopotamian fields.[10]

Having been subtly outmaneuvered by the oil companies the government should have modified its original diplomatic position to fit the altered situation in the Middle East. Yet in communications with the English the State Department continued to oppose the 1920 San Remo Oil Agreement, which divided the fields in Mesopotamia between French and British interests, and also to oppose the prewar claims of the Turkish Petroleum Company in the provinces of Mosul and Bagdad.[11] To say the least, the initial oil diplomacy of Hughes and Hoover appeared compromised at two levels: 1) the United States was on questionable political ground in the Middle East because it had not signed the Peace Treaty of Sèvres with the Turks or accepted a mandate for Armenia; 2) the government publicly insisted on a complete Open Door in Mesopotamia for all nations and all companies while privately it facilitated negotiations so that seven privileged American companies could obtain a share of the monopolistic concession claimed by the Turkish Petroleum Company. By the end of 1921 a coordinated economic and political foreign policy for oil development had not emerged because public officials were not conducting their own diplomacy and the businessmen who were conducting it were not in agreement with the idea of a complete Open Door.

In the next two years the United States unofficially participated in three international conferences at Genoa, The Hague, and Lausanne, all of which touched peripherally on the various oil disputes in the Middle East and Russia.[12] The most significant oil discussions during 1922 and 1923, however, took place outside the framework of these conferences, between American interests and foreign representatives. Ostensibly within the general guidelines established by Hughes and Hoover, oil diplomacy was initiated and conducted by private citizens with a vested interest in the particular controversy. For example, in the contest over concessions in Mesopotamia the American group, headed by officials of Jersey Standard, consulted with the State Department in June 1922 about its negotiations with the Turkish Petroleum Company. They did not want to proceed any further in drafting a preliminary arrangement until it had the approval of Washington officials. In reply to members of the oil consortium, Hughes said he did not want to hamper needlessly or prolong a diplomatic and economic settlement in the Middle East, but insisted that two conditions be met: 1) the principle of a complete Open Door had to be affirmed by allowing all reputable American companies the opportunity to participate in any final oil agreement; and 2) the claims of the Turkish Petroleum Company were not to be recognized until a new concession grant was obtained from the current leaders of Mesopotamia. Earlier in talks with the foreign trade adviser of the State Department, a Standard Oil of New York representative from the American group, had prophetically asserted that the first prerequisite of the State Department, namely, complete equality of opportunity for all countries and companies, was "impractical since Japanese, Italian, French and other nationalities would want to participate." But now A. C. Bedford, chairman of the board of Jersey Standard, passed over the issue by assuring the secretary of state that the seven companies currently in the American group were all those interested, and he did not indicate that any additional foreign nations had expressed a desire to develop oil fields in Mesopotamia. So the private economic negotiations continued with the principle of a complete Open Door circuitously accepted by the oil interests.[13]

By August 1922 the American group had not been able to negotiate an agreement which met with the government's conditions or to obtain a satisfactory percentage of the concession. The San Remo agreement had originally designated 25 percent interest to the French and to Royal Dutch-Shell, with the Anglo-Persian Company, which was controlled by the British government, receiving 50 percent. In August the Americans were offered 12 percent, but they wanted 20 percent of the Anglo-Persian share in addition to equal voice in the management and control of the company. In accordance with the government's Open Door policy, the Americans were also holding out for a plan which would allow subleasing of certain areas inside the concession to other companies. Hughes asked Hoover his opinion of the American position and the secretary of commerce expressed no dissatisfaction except with the percentage the Americans were to receive. As a "matter of national pride," Hoover said, the United States should have at least 25 percent of the concession. Although Hughes had specifically requested Hoover to comment on whether this proposed division amounted to a monopoly for the American and foreign interests involved, Hoover avoided the question in his August correspondence with the secretary of state. Hoover apparently was less concerned than Hughes with the fear of oligarchic control of Mesopotamian oil as long as the United States had a respectable percentage of the operation, and so he confined his remarks to praise for the way in which Hughes was handling the affair. As a result Hughes simply reiterated on August 22 to the president of Jersey Standard, W. C. Teagle, the now familiar position of the State Department; namely, that if all interested American companies had been contacted and invited to participate and if the oilmen thought the United States was being offered a fair share, and if no attempt was being made to establish a monopoly in favor of the Turkish Petroleum Company, then the proposed agreement did not violate the spirit of the complete Open Door principle.[14]

Accordingly, in November 1922, the State Department refused to endorse provisions which called for the recognition of the prewar rights of the Turkish Petroleum Company and the exclusion of any more American companies from participation in the concession. The first would have placed the United States unofficially in opposition to the concession claims of Admiral

Colby M. Chester,[15] and both were a direct challenge to the Hughes-Hoover concept of a complete Open Door in the Middle East. The Europeans involved in the negotiations found it difficult to understand why the United States government would permit negotiations with a concessionaire it refused to recognize, why it would not accept closing the door to Middle Eastern oil after the American group was admitted, and why it was giving half-hearted support to the Chester concession, which involved some of the same territory the American group wanted to share with the Turkish Petroleum Company. Despite these glaring inconsistencies in the American position, the oil interests at Hughes's insistence held firm and the objectionable terms were withdrawn in January 1923. Subsequently in April the subleasing provisions were re-inserted to comply with the expanded Open Door principle of the Harding administration.[16]

It was at this point in the private negotiations that serious objections were raised from within the Commerce and State departments about the latest arrangement with the Turkish Petroleum Company. It is possible but not too probable that these objections were partially a reaction to the Turkish confirmation on April 9, 1923, of the new Chester concession, which was substantially the same as the original one of 1910. Since the internal and financial weaknesses of the Chester project were well known in government circles (it collapsed at the end of the year), the objections to the new American group agreement appear to be of a more fundamental nature and not simply an expedient reaction to the unexpected renewal of the Chester concession. Within the State Department both the Office of the Economic Adviser and the Far Eastern expert, Dr. Stanley K. Hornbeck, complained that even with the subleasing provisions the proposed oil arrangement created a monopoly of American and English interests in Mesopotamia because anyone interested in obtaining a lease had to apply to the Turkish Petroleum Company, which reserved the right to reject bids. "It would, I think," Hornbeck concluded, "be unfortunate if the impression were to become established that this formula falls within and satisfies the theory of open door and equality of opportunity." Later in the year H. C. Morris, chief of the Petroleum Division of the BFDC, criticized American participation in the Turkish Petroleum Company as an "evasion and not a confirmation (satisfaction) of our open-door policy." He continued:

> It seems to me that the State Department could be severely and justly criticized for giving even tacit approval to such a plan for while I know of many plausible arguments in favor of the attempt, nevertheless none of them meet the imputation of bad faith and wholly selfish interest which might be launched at us from other quarters of the world.
>
> Fundamentally, the United States having repeatedly denied the legality of the Turkish Petroleum Concession, the project, so far as we are concerned is dead. Why therefore should we indorse the attempt of a small group of our oil companies, which has gotten together supposedly and originally to gain the support of the United States government for an attempt to obtain an independent concession in Mesopotamia, to force its way into the Turkish Petroleum Company as the easiest means to an, at best, only partially satisfactory end.
>
> American participation in the Turkish Petroleum Company is an admission to the world that our prime interest in the open-door in Mesopotamia was merely to force our participation in the oil development of that country and is, in my opinion, in no way excused by the vague possibility that subleases may be granted to citizens of companies of any nationality.
>
> Politically it may be expedient but ethically it is open to grave dispute.

It does not appear that Hughes or Hoover wavered in support of the American group despite this unequivocal criticism within their own departments.[17]

The concession agreement of 1925, even more clearly than that of 1923, granted the Turkish Petroleum Company absolute jurisdiction over new leases. Praised by Standard Oil officials as representing a "practical open-door policy," it was clear that the principle of a complete Open Door had been whittled away with each successive proposal. When in 1928 the final compromise agreement was reached there were only five American companies still in the consortium and the subleasing plan had been further weakened by the so-called Red Line Agreement which for all intents and purposes excluded nonsignatories from oil activities in

Iraq. In 1930 the general manager of the Iraq Petroleum Company, formerly the Turkish Petroleum Company, told the American consul at Bagdad that his firm had never taken seriously the official protestations from Washington about a complete Open Door once the American group had been given permission to participate in negotiations at the beginning of the decade. One of the key European businessmen involved in the protracted discussions later characterized the attempt by Washington to include the entire world in the exploitation of Middle Eastern oil as so much "eyewash." The *coup de grace* was delivered to the idea of a complete Open Door in 1931 when it was announced that only two American companies remained in the original consortium—Standard Oil of New York and that of New Jersey.[18] By that time Hughes had long since been out of office and Hoover, as a depression president, had little time to bemoan the demise of the Open Door in the Middle East as long as American interests remained secure.

The government's Open Door doctrine met with a similarly compromised fate in the controversy over Russian oil, and once again the Hughes-Hoover policy was all too easily undermined by the very oil interests it was designed to protect. With respect to Russia the call for an Open Door was specifically meant to prevent all foreign oil firms from producing or buying Soviet oil until Jersey Standard received compensation for petroleum property nationalized by the Bolsheviks.[19] This position appeared to emerge victorious from both the Genoa and the Hague conferences of 1922 where the nations agreed for the time being not to make separate agreements with the Soviets for acquiring rights to confiscated property. While these conferences were going on the Royal Dutch-Shell and Jersey-Nobel interests agreed privately and very informally not to deal independently with Russia and to hold out for indemnification. This unsigned "London Memo" of July 24, 1922, was formalized in Paris on September 19, 1922, by sixteen oil companies. Known as the *Front Uni,* the agreement was too negative and vague to be of long-lasting significance. It almost immediately began to disintegrate as the Soviets continued to play upon the self-interests of the larger firms.[20] By the end of 1922, therefore, the Open Door position of the United States had produced a temporary stalemate over Russian oil reserves which the major international companies almost immediately tried to break.

In May 1923, for example, Teagle and Bedford of Jersey Standard presented a plan to the State Department. It called for an agreement between three giant oil groups—Standard Oil, Royal Dutch-Shell, and the Anglo-Persian Oil Company—to market all "the oil which the Soviet people might be able to produce," since nationalization had removed any "basis for investment in Russia at this time." Such a combination of forces, according to the officials of Jersey Standard, would prevent any one of the three from taking advantage of the others. In keeping with his determination to keep economic and political foreign policy separated, Secretary of State Hughes initially refused to commit his department to the plan, saying "it was purely an economic and business matter" for the companies involved to work out. He did intimate, however, that the pooling arrangement might be contrary to the Sherman Anti-Trust Act. At a second meeting between Bedford and Hughes on July 6, 1923, a more detailed draft of the big-three proposal was presented. Hughes, having had more time to study the idea, now made three negative observations about the proposal: 1) in all likelihood the pooling arrangement would "affect the freedom of trade in foreign commerce of the United States" and was therefore "contrary to the Sherman Act"; 2) the combination would play into the hands of Soviet propagandists because it appeared monopolistic and "unpleasant reaction" to it would "do much to offset the moral strength of the position [of the United States] with respect to the confiscation of property"; 3) the agreement appeared to allow for the use of confiscated property by other than its original owners and, therefore, rather than "recognizing private property as sacrosanct," it seemed "to provide for its exploitation." Bedford replied that he had anticipated the secretary's position, "was personally in accord with it," and promised his company would not do anything "which would impair the policy of the Department."[21]

This State Department opposition squelched the marketing deal between Jersey Standard, Royal Dutch-Shell, and Anglo-Persian for the time being, but a marketing combination including these

three oil groups and some of the smaller foreign oil companies did
exist for a few months in 1923. The reason given publicly for its
discontinuance was the desire of the companies involved to force
the Soviets to compensate for their nationalization policies.
Privately, however, one of the participants, Vacuum Oil Company,
informed the State Department that it believed the real reason
behind the dissolution of the combination was the desire of the
larger companies to monopolize Russian oil exports by negotiating
independent agreements with the Soviets.[22]

No agreement for the marketing of Russian oil was reached
among the big three companies until 1929, but a number of
minor agreements were negotiated by the Vacuum Oil Company
and Standard Oil of New York during the 1920s. Braving the less
than altruistic protests of Jersey Standard and Royal Dutch-Shell
about selling "stolen property," these two firms, which were to
merge into Socony-Vacuum at the end of the decade, obtained a
series of small contracts beginning in 1923, and then proceeded
in 1926 to negotiate a five-year contract for the purchase of
approximately ten million dollars' worth of oil annually from the
Soviet Oil Syndicate. President George P. Whaley of the Vacuum
Company answered his critics by pointing out that "if the view
should generally prevail that it would be unrighteous to buy
petroleum from Russia on the theory that to do so would be to
buy goods wrongfully confiscated from Russian subjects, Russia
could export nothing." Referring to the increasing amount of
trade between the United States and the USSR, he questioned
whether it was "more righteous to buy from Russia than to sell
to it."[23]

During 1928 a private truce was effected between Jersey
Standard, Royal Dutch-Shell, and Socony-Vacuum, and the
following year on February 27 the Anglo-American Company
(representing Jersey Standard, Royal Dutch-Shell and Anglo-
Persian) signed a three-year contract with Russian Oil Products,
Ltd. It guaranteed the Soviets 12.5 percent of the British oil
market in return for the right of Anglo-American to buy "considerable quantities" (estimated at $20 million annually) of
Russian oil at 5 percent below the market price. Although the
terms of the contract did not mention compensation it was under-

stood that the 5 percent would be put aside for payment to those whose property had been nationalized. The agreement was described by a member of the foreign service as one which would "virtually eliminate Soviet Russia as an independent competitor from Europe and the Near East markets," by allowing Anglo-American to monopolize the sale of Russian oil in these areas. This time there were no objections raised by the State Department even though this contract was part of a comprehensive understanding between Jersey Standard and Royal Dutch-Shell to allocate the international petroleum markets in violation of the Open Door principle and to control oil prices everywhere except in the United States.[24]

The government's call for an Open Door in the international oil fields also rang hollow in the Netherlands East Indies. As retaliation against oil legislation which discriminated against foreigners, the Department of the Interior had declared the Netherlands a nonreciprocating country in 1922. This was in accordance with the General Leasing Act of 1920 and consequently relations remained strained until 1927, when the Dutch government began to change its oil concession policy in Indonesia. Although Secretary of State Kellogg received permission from Secretary of the Interior Hubert Work in 1927 to reinstate the Netherlands as a reciprocating nation, he refused to do so until 1928 after the Dutch government passed legislation insuring there would be no further discrimination against American companies. In the intervening years both Jersey Standard and the Sinclair Consolidated Oil Corporation displayed an interest in the Djambi fields in Sumatra, but by 1928 only the former was in a position to take advantage of the changed attitude of the Dutch government. It was, in fact, the approval of concessions for a subsidiary of Jersey Standard which prompted Kellogg to announce his statement of reciprocity. By 1939 United States interests, dominated by Jersey Standard, accounted for 28 percent of the total Indonesian oil output, whereas in 1924 Jersey Standard had accounted for only 5 percent.[25]

Thus, the oil diplomacy of the United States government in the late 1920s laid the foundation for the advantage Jersey Standard held over all other American companies in the Indonesian and other international oil fields by World War II. This is not to say that Jersey Standard's advantage resulted from a conspiracy between the State Department and company officials. Rather, it was in large measure due to the government's policy of assuming an impartial attitude in promoting American oil interests. Inevitably the policy of impartiality favored the largest of those interests, the one in the best position to compete abroad for foreign oil fields. Being impartial toward unequals was equivalent, as far as oil diplomacy was concerned, to being partial toward the strongest. This was particularly evident in the crucial years at the beginning of the decade when the State Department refused to take sides in Mesopotamia between Admiral Chester's claims and those of Jersey Standard, and in northern Persia, where Henry Sinclair was competing with Jersey Standard for concessions in the same provinces.[26] Although the stated objective of the government's impartiality and Open Door policy was not to aid the cause of Jersey Standard over that of other American companies, it was, nonetheless, the end result of that policy because the State and Commerce departments acquiesced to oligarchic or monopolistic arrangements negotiated by Jersey Standard in the oil fields of the Middle East, Russia, and Indonesia at the end of the decade.

Finally, in Latin America, where the economic goals of the United States were accompanied by greater political and military influence than in other parts of the world, little attempt was made to uphold any, let alone a complete, Open Door for the companies of all nations. This was evidenced by the steadily mounting American domination of the new oil fields after World War I. Spreading from Mexico, where United States interests controlled 70 percent of the production in 1919, American oilmen moved into Colombia, Chile, Ecuador, Bolivia, Argentina, Peru, and most importantly, Venezuela. A distinguishing feature of the exploitation of Latin American fields in the first half of the decade was the large number of competing American firms. In Mexico, for example, before 1925 there were over twenty-five independent companies operating, and in Venezuela by 1925 there were about thirty-five. Such competition was short-lived, however. After 1925 one American concern, Standard Oil of Indiana, controlled 57 percent of all Mexican oil. In Venezuela, where the British were the first to develop the oil fields, the same thing happened. Numerous American firms moved in after World War I, but by the end of the decade subsidiaries of Jersey Standard and the Gulf Oil Company controlled 46 percent of all oil production. By 1929 Venezuela was second only to the United States in the production of crude oil, and despite earlier fears about depletion of the Mexican fields, that country still ranked third.[27] Because the political influence of the United States was more commensurate with its economic goals in Latin America, the success of its oil diplomacy was more easily achieved there than in some of the other areas discussed above. This success, however, had little to do with adherence to the Open Door policy.

Despite the protestations of Hughes, Hoover, and Kellogg on behalf of the Open Door, their oil diplomacy, it must never be forgotten, was based on the belief that the procurement of oil was absolutely necessary for the security of the United States. They also believed in the necessity of general economic expansion abroad by Americans. If in the short run Jersey Standard or some other company was able to help the government secure these long-term goals, then a compromised Open Door was better than none. Consequently, wherever the door was opened for American interests, it was soon closed by those same interests with little objection from the government. As far as monopolistic or oligarchic practices were concerned, Hoover, at least, had never been averse to bypassing the country's antitrust laws to aid American businessmen abroad. And the secretaries of state and commerce during the 1920s had few compunctions about supporting reactionary regimes which granted generous concessions to American nationals. If anything, the evolution of the Open Door into a Closed Door in the international oil fields was the logical outcome of the original philosophy behind the Hughes-Hoover oil diplomacy.

When we turn to a consideration of the Open Door in the Far East, it becomes immediately evident that the foreign policy of the United States in this part of the world, next to that in Latin America, best epitomizes cooperation between the government and the business community. However, nowhere near as many tangible economic benefits accrued from such cooperation in the Orient as in the Southern Hemisphere. For example, in terms of total American trade and investment, the enormous potential of China remained almost as untapped a myth by 1930 as it had been in 1900 despite the fact that the original Open Door Doctrine had been conceived to guarantee a significant role for American businessmen in China's economic development, as well as to protect the country's territorial and administrative integrity. The outright failures or barren victories which the United States experienced in its erratic attempts to implement various interpretations of the dual principles of the Open Door between 1900 and 1914 should have led to an abandonment of the policy by any rational standards. But such was not to be the case. If anything, in the postwar era the government, to a greater degree than the business community, renewed its commitment to the illusive goals of protecting China while capturing her market. This was done in the face of considerable business apathy which since 1900 had consistently belied business rhetoric about China. In contrast, American businessmen strengthened their economic ties with Japan in the 1920s without undue government prompting, only to find Washington officials beginning to forget that the preservation of China's integrity had never been considered by their predecessors or the business community as worth a major American-Japanese confrontation in the Far East. Originally conceived as an altruistic guideline, the political portion of the Open Door began to be transformed during the decade into a dogmatic policy directed against our best Oriental customer, Japan.[28]

The process began when the dual concepts of the Open Door were associated with the postwar reorganization of a group of international banking firms, known as the China Consortium. Then, as noted in chapter 2, the doctrine was codified in the Nine Power Treaty of the 1922 Washington Disarmament Conference, whose significance was disputed by government officials for the rest of the decade. After the Kellogg-Briand Pact and the Stimson Doctrine failed to give substance to the Open Door in the early 1930s, that policy remained in a semidormant state until 1938. Subsequently, the first, and to date only, unequivocal stand in defense of the policy was taken in 1941 against Japan. The responsibility for the bankruptcy of American diplomacy in the Far East for most of the twentieth century lies not with the men who originated and initially tried to implement the Open Door policy at the turn of the century, but with those who made increasingly indiscriminate attempts to enforce it against the realities of economic and political power in the Far East between the two world wars.

For a brief period during the first Wilson administration it looked as though the pitfalls of the expanded interpretation of the Open Door which had taken place under Taft and Knox were going to be avoided. Not only did Wilson insist upon an American withdrawal from the China Consortium in 1913, but Robert Lansing, as counsel for the State Department, noted in 1914 that "it would be quixotic in the extreme to allow the question of China's territorial integrity to entangle the United States in international difficulties." A scant three years later, however, the Democrats found themselves forced to consider reorganizing and enlarging the group of American bankers who had participated in the prewar consortium because of the enhanced financial and military position of Japan in the Far East. After protracted negotiations the New or Second China Consortium was officially established in October 1920, when certain Japanese objections were finally overcome through the quasi-official diplomatic efforts of banker Thomas W. Lamont.[29]

This renewed participation in the consortium by the American Group represented both the close working relationship between the State Department and international bankers in the last years of the Wilson administration, and the idea of "joining with Japan" in the hope of establishing the "principle of international cooperation in the development of great public enterprises in China." As such, it was viewed by the American Group as a "public service entered upon at the request of the Government to the end of assisting to maintain the Government's traditional policy of the 'Open Door' for China." And to the State Department it seemed the best way at the time to preserve the Far East from Japanese economic domination without resorting to force and without coming to terms with either the revolutionary nationalists in China or the Bolsheviks in Russia. In addition,

Lamont and later Hughes and Hoover realized that although Japan would be a "difficult partner" it might be possible through the New Consortium and Japan's own "economic necessities" to undermine the militarists and convince the moderates they should "swing into line and learn table manners from [the] Western Groups." Finally as the financial counterpart of the Lansing-Ishii understanding of 1917, the New Consortium recognized the special railroad interests of the Japanese in China, thus temporarily smoothing over some of the economic friction between the United States and Japan before the Washington Conference.[30]

Although Lamont announced at the beginning of the decade that the Second China Consortium represented a "Far Eastern League of Nations," its full potential as a means for controlling Japan while rehabilitating China and maintaining the Open Door in the Far East was never realized. This was only partially due to Chinese Nationalist opposition to the financial and political control implicit in the consortium. It was also attributable to the refusal of the consortium to undertake any loans for China in the 1920s. Arguing that China was a poor credit risk because of internal political chaos, the American Group continued to view the consortium as a public service designed to substitute cooperation for competition in China, but said that it was never intended to operate without profit. To the American Group and the State Department, therefore, it was not necessary for the consortium to actually make loans to China in order to justify its re-creation. The very existence of the consortium, according to Hughes and the House of Morgan, confirmed the principle of the Open Door, enhanced the prestige of the United States in the Far East, and preserved the area for future expansion by American businessmen. As Hughes said, "Even a protracted unremunerative period of delay before the Consortium can begin active function, would in the long run prove amply justified by the ultimate benefits to the commercial and financial conditions of our country." In other words, as long as the consortium preserved China in principle from "baneful spheres of influence," there was no immediate need to worry about the inactivity of the American Group.[31]

As it turned out, the Japanese opposed all consortium loans

until previous Chinese foreign debts were consolidated and a comprehensive program for liquidating them was reached among the major Washington Conference powers. England and the United States steadfastly refused to approve debt consolidations or any other collective economic settlement with China in the 1920s. From time to time the banking representatives of the three nations did give perfunctory consideration to consortium loans and their respective governments occasionally issued joint protests over violations of extraterritorial rights, but no significant action was taken by the consortium even after the 1929 depression exacerbated the already hopeless financial condition of China.[32]

The failure of the Second Consortium in general and the American Group in particular to support large, long-term loans to the Chinese government soon became the subject of bitter debate between officials in Washington and those in China, as well as between different segments of the business community. Among the most extreme Sinophiles within the official family were Julean Arnold, commercial attaché in Peking, and the American trade commissioners also assigned to the Chinese capital, Frank Rhea and Paul Whitham. These men in turn were supported by the small group of American businessmen in China represented by the American Chamber of Commerce at Shanghai. Unofficially the Department of Commerce agreed with some of the criticism leveled against the negative role of the Second Consortium, but officially the department defended the inactivity because it was allowing native Chinese bankers to obtain "more and more control of the political affairs in China," and because it was acting as a "blockade on indiscriminate loans to irresponsible Chinese officials." Thus, Julius Klein, director of the BFDC, assured his impatient commercial attaché, Julean Arnold, that in the long run the negative and cautious policy of the consortium would encourage sound American capital to invest in China. "Unless," he added, "there is some assurance that money advanced either to private industrial or public loan purposes in China is not misappropriated there can be no real incentive toward the encouragement of American participation in the industrial development of China." And so Commerce officials aided the State Department in discouraging loans to the Chinese government and in determining whether proposed business transactions fell under the authority of the consortium.[33]

This cooperation with the State Department did not prevent Commerce officials from becoming impatient with the lack of financing for American enterprises doing business in China. It was not that the Commerce Department had any illusions about the stability or honesty of the Peking government, but it did believe that trade and private investment could help to create order in China. The State Department, on the other hand, agreed with the American Group that political unification must precede all major loans. Since the American Group now consisted of thirty-seven prominent banking houses, most loan requests for Chinese development projects were refused by nonconsortium bankers unless the consortium had approved of them. Many of the projects were technically outside the jurisdiction of the consortium. Naturally Commerce officials and businessmen in China resented the indirect financial control which the consortium exercised over ordinary American business ventures in China.[34] A high point of disagreement was reached in 1921 over the way the State Department and the American Group handled the petition by the Federal Telegraph Company for financial assistance to fulfill a contract with the Peking government to build twenty wireless stations. By forcing the British and Japanese interests to recognize the legitimacy of the company's contract, Secretary Hughes struck a blow for the Open Door, but his department could not force the American Group to either support the company or allow it to obtain financial assistance elsewhere. No wireless stations were ever built by the Federal Telegraph Company and so in the eyes of the Commerce Department and American businessmen in China the affair represented at best a dubious victory for the principle of the Open Door.[35] If anything, the American Group appeared to be uninterested in keeping the door open or in helping to improve conditions in China. It had, despite an early warning from Norman H. Davis, created the impression in certain government and business circles that it was in alliance with "foreign financial interests seeking to establish for itself a privileged position."[36]

As a result of the dispute over a loan for the Federal Telegraph Company, the Commerce Department began to consider other means, outside the consortium, for promoting American trade and investment in China in order to counter what seemed to be unnecessary restriction of private investment and initiative by American financiers. Vague hope was expressed from time to time that the Washington Disarmament Conference would improve financial and political conditions in China, but the first concrete proposal concerned the creation of an independent industrial consortium. Although there was some disagreement between Arnold and Rhea in China and officials in Washington about the details of such a banking corporation, the idea was given close consideration, especially after banker Frederick Stevens toured China for the American Group in the spring of 1921. Commerce officials in China were convinced that Stevens was returning to the United States with an overly gloomy impression of conditions. They feared his report to the banking community might so harm "American prospects in China . . . [it] would take years to eradicate" the effects. Consequently Arnold, Rhea, Whitham, and the American Chamber of Commerce at Shanghai came out for the formation of an industrial consortium to aid American businessmen in China. When some members of the American Group were polled by the Commerce Department about the idea in July 1921, first replies indicated the plan was "impracticable."[37] The American Group through Stevens criticized Arnold and Rhea of being so obsessed with furthering trade and commerce that they seldom gave serious consideration to ideas which would succeed as banking proposals. On this point the acting chief of the Far Eastern Division of the BFDC agreed, but he continued to support the "formation of a company with capital drawn either exclusively from American residents in China or a joint enterprise with Chinese bankers."[38]

The split between Arnold and his superiors was one of degree rather than kind, as the Commerce Department's efforts to promote an industrial consortium indicated. Throughout the decade, often to the embarrassment of Commerce officials in Washington and to the irritation of the State Department, the commercial attachés and trade commissioners in the Far East painted exaggerated pictures of favorable conditions in China, excessively criticized American bankers, and passed on confidential information in their eagerness to stimulate trade and development projects.[39] No industrial consortium was ever formed, but the disagreements over it constitute another example of the general conflict within the business community between financial and commercial interests when it came to economic foreign policy, and of the difficult position in which the Commerce Department was placed when this occurred.

The most concerted effort by the Commerce Department to overcome the inactivity of the Second Consortium was its promotion of the various China Trade Acts between 1921 and 1933. The idea behind the legislation was to encourage trade and investment by providing federal incorporation for companies operating in China and by exempting them from most federal taxation.[40] As secretary of commerce, Hoover personally directed the many attempts to achieve a satisfactory China Trade bill, and to this end he worked particularly closely with Representative Leonidas C. Dyer from Missouri. At Dyer's suggestion Hoover wrote to President Harding about the importance of the bill in 1921 and 1922, brought it up before cabinet meetings, and pressured congressmen for early passage.[41] In their well-coordinated efforts, Hoover and Dyer were solidly backed by small businessmen across the country, especially on the West Coast, a few of whom were already trading in the Far East, but most of whom were simply mesmerized by their own and the government's China market dreams.[42] The China Trade legislation probably is the best example during the decade of the determination of the Commerce Department to facilitate trade and investment in China and thereby overcome both the general business apathy and the absence of financial support from the American banking community. As such it represents only one of a series of attempts by the government to artificially stimulate economic relations with an area of the world that businessmen talked a great deal about but shunned because of its internal instability.

Neither the State nor the Treasury Department was as enthusiastic about the 1921 China Trade bill as was the Department of Commerce. Treasury Secretary Mellon, for example, objected to the vague wording of the tax-exemption section and indicated that the entire matter could be dealt with more effectively by a general revision of the Internal Revenue laws. Mellon's idea was to exempt all companies incorporated to carry on trade abroad from corporate and dividend taxes, not simply those doing business in China. He wanted all corporations engaged principally in foreign trade to be taxed only on incomes derived from transactions within the United States. After all, Mellon told Dyer and Hoover, "the tax problems presented by corporations engaged in the China trade are less important in volume and not essentially different in kind from the similar problems presented by corporations engaged exclusively or mainly in business in the Philippine Islands, Porto Rico, and foreign countries." Hoover insisted, however, that China was a special case at the moment because Americans were being driven out of business in China as a result of new British Orders in Council which required that a majority of the directors and executives of any company incorporated under British law had to be English citizens. Before the war Americans had tended to incorporate their businesses under English law because of the inadequacy and lack of prestige of American foreign incorporation permitted by various state laws, the Philippine Incorporation Law, and the Alaskan Code of 1917.[43]

Mellon finally acceded to Hoover's point of view, but the China Trade Act which finally became law in September 1922 proved inadequate because the tax exemption provisions were emasculated before passage by both houses. So within a year after he publicly praised the first China Trade Act, Hoover was working behind the scenes to get its tax section amended. By the beginning of 1923 there were over 400 American firms doing business in China, only 2 of which had incorporated under the China Trade Act. Before amendments were introduced in 1924 only 9 companies had taken advantage of it. During the two-year struggle for satisfactory amendments Hoover once again had to convince the reluctant treasury secretary to support his efforts, but this time the State Department, which had cooperated with Commerce officials in administering the 1922 act, did not raise any objections.

Pacific coast trading companies were as usual actively supporting amendments.[44] Despite these greater tax exemptions, further amendments were suggested in 1927, 1928, and again in 1932. The reason remained the same—the benefits under the law still did not compare favorably with those received by British and other foreign nationals operating in China. Despite these inadequacies the Federal Incorporation Act of 1935 retained essentially the tax provisions of the original China Trade Act as amended in 1925.[45]

What is most interesting about the China Trade legislation in terms of economic foreign policy is that it was more closely identified with the concepts of extraterritoriality and spheres of influence than with the Open Door. If the United States had not been enjoying extraterritorial rights and privileges in China, in all likelihood the China Trade Act, which according to the Chinese Nationalists deprived China of the power "to tax her own capital within her own territory," would not have been proposed in the first place. Procedurally, therefore, the act violated the sovereignty of China and was contrary to the spirit of the Open Door. It is difficult, however, to document any substantive harm resulting from the legislation since it represented a relatively insignificant aspect of the entire question of extraterritoriality and few American companies made use of it. By 1930 there were seventy-four active companies incorporated under the amended China Trade Act with a total authorized capitalization of approximately $24 million. But by that time there were over 500 American firms operating in China and direct business investments there amounted to at least $155 million.[46]

Any consideration of the economic significance of the China Trade Act leads naturally to a discussion of the general characteristics of the commercial and financial activities of the United States in the Far East during the 1920s. Statistics reveal significant differences in the economic relations of the United States with China and Japan. For, despite the Open Door policy and Washington's initiation of the Second China Consortium and the China Trade Act, the economic involvement of the United States with China trailed that of Japan in the categories of trade, shipping, and investments between 1899 and 1930.[47] While the

Chinese share of total American trade and investment remained minuscule, China played a role of increasing importance in the economic life of Japan. For example, exports to China averaged only 3 percent of all American exports between 1923 and 1931. Although this represented between 16 and 18 percent of China's total imports, Japan dominated the field for those years by supplying approximately 27 percent of Chinese imports, which constituted 22 percent of all Japanese exports. Although the American trade balance remained unfavorable with both countries throughout the 1920s, exports from the United States to Japan were on the average double those to China. In 1932 Japan was the fourth largest purchaser of American goods, accounting for 9 percent of the total world trade of the United States by consuming 8 percent of all American exports and providing 10 percent of all American imports. This meant the United States was supplying a little less than one-third of all Japanese imports and receiving a little more than one-third of Japanese exports. The pattern of commercial interdependence which emerged by the end of the decade revealed the United States as the best customer of Japan, while Japan rather than America was China's best customer.[48]

A similar pattern can be seen in the field of investments. By 1932 the United States had invested approximately $466 million in Japan, compared with $250 million in China. (Both figures include missionary property as well as private business investments and public loans.) Because the Japanese government strictly supervised direct investments by foreigners, there were only 50 undertakings in Japan by the end of the decade which were either controlled or heavily contributed to by Americans. While this represented business investments of scarcely $62 million, compared with the larger figure of $155 million for China, it was supplemented by over $400 million in portfolio loans from the United States between 1920 and 1930. China was able to obtain slightly less than $2 million in portfolio loans for the same period. By 1932 the total foreign investment in China amounted to $3.5 billion, of which 7 percent came from the United States and 33 percent from Japan. The American share of Chinese investments constituted slightly over 1 percent of the total foreign investments of the United States, while Japan's share was over 80 percent of that country's total foreign investments.[49]

These statistics reveal a discrepancy in the political and economic postures of the United States in the Far East. The traditional American desire for political and economic equality in the Far East had been reaffirmed at the Washington Conference, but in the course of the decade the economic stake of the United States in China continued to lag far behind those of Japan and England. This economic imbalance worked to undermine the Open Door aspirations of the United States and was the product of an uncoordinated economic and political diplomacy in the Far East. In part the lack of coordination was the result of the loan policy emanating from Washington, which contributed to Japan's expansion in China, sometimes at the expense of American businessmen. The obvious reluctance of the American Group and the State Department to approve loans to China has already been discussed; however, the loan policy toward Japan was both more positive and more complicated.

When the Second Consortium was finally organized in 1920 Thomas W. Lamont anticipated that Japan's military and economic ambitions could be contained by her need for American loans. At the time of the Washington Conference, Hughes believed Japanese adherence to the disarmament and Open Door agreements could be insured by the loan policy of the United States, and in 1930 Stimson expressed the conviction that Japan's economic difficulties made it imperative for her to sign the London Naval Treaty in order to obtain further American financing.[50] But the potential financial power of the United States over Japan was never effectively transformed into economic diplomacy between 1920 and 1933. The only loan restrictions enforced by the United States against Japan were based on the general principle that it was not desirable for "American credit [to] be made available to foreign interests for investment or enterprises in third countries in cases in which the use of such American credit would tend to prejudice or circumscribe the opportunities for American enterprises or to further the organization of competition therewith."[51]

This policy about loans for third-country developments was obviously aimed at preventing Japan from using American money to develop Manchuria, out of the suspicion that the Japanese would not honor the Open Door there. Thus, in 1922 National City Bank tried unsuccessfully to obtain approval for a $20 million loan to the Oriental Development Company. The same firm met with government objections again in 1923 when it tried to float a portion of a British loan to the South Manchurian Railway Company. A 1927 proposal by National City and the House of Morgan for a $30 million loan to the South Manchurian Railway Company also failed to materialize even though Thomas W. Lamont told the State Department he did not think Japan was violating the Open Door in Manchuria or contemplating the use of force in the area. Lamont stressed that the presence of the Japanese in Manchuria had made it the only stable territory in China. In this case the banking houses never officially asked for government approval and so the State Department was saved the embarrassment of having to comment one way or the other on the proposal. To have publicly disapproved of the loan would have placed the United States unequivocally on the side of the Chinese in Manchuria, while approval could have been interpreted as an endorsement of financial cooperation between Japan and the United States in Manchuria. Officials within the department were divided on what to do. Consequently it was finally decided to do nothing, for strong positive or negative action required that the government consciously adjust its stated political goals in Manchuria to fit its economic position or vice versa. Instead, Washington took advantage of the adverse publicity about the loan in China to indirectly discourage bankers from proceeding with it at that time.[52]

With these exceptions, however, most Japanese loans were readily floated in this country, especially those for public utility companies and municipalities. Even a $20 million loan to the Oriental Development Company was approved in 1923 after Japanese officials, the United States ambassador in Japan, and National City all assured the State Department that the money would be spent in Japan and its colonies (primarily Korea) rather than in Manchuria, Mongolia, the South Sea Islands, Singapore, or the Straits Settlements as the original prospectus for the 1922 loan had stated. Even so, some of this money soon found its way into South Manchuria. Another loan whose funds were not all spent for declared purposes was made to the Japanese government in 1924 for the repair of severe earthquake damage. This $150 million loan (of which only about $60 million was new capital, the balance being a refunding operation) represented the epitome of cooperation between government officials and the House of Morgan. In order to insure a favorable acceptance of the loan by the American business community, Lamont asked Hughes not only to give strong public endorsement to the transaction, but also to stress that most of the proceeds would be spent in the United States.[53] In letters to both Hughes and Hoover, Lamont emphasized the difficulty his firm was having in "placing this large loan." Apparently the anti-Japanese sentiment represented in the exclusion provision of the 1924 immigration bill complicated its acceptance, as did the rumor that the earthquake had basically weakened the Japanese economy. Hughes and Hoover promptly accommodated Lamont's request for statements promoting the loan in which they avoided references to the disaster and concentrated on the purchase of American goods. Hughes actually allowed Lamont to rewrite the last paragraph of his letter approving the loan so that it read in part, ". . . it would be a source of great satisfaction, if in view of the apparent heavy requirements of the Japanese Government for supplies and materials procurable in this country, it should be found possible to make this market available to the government and people of Japan on the most favorable terms practicable."[54]

Several months after the Japanese earthquake loan went through, National City obtained approval to loan $22 million to the government-controlled Industrial Bank of Japan. Although it was also supposed to be used for earthquake relief, the loan became the subject of criticism when it was learned that some of the proceeds had been diverted to reduce the indebtedness incurred by the Japanese government in 1916 when almost $90 million in unsecured loans had been made to the Chinese Communications Ministry. Despite this and other claims of misuse of American money for trade and investment purposes in third countries, and even though the country experienced "an acute banking crisis" in the late 1920s, loans continued to be made to

Japan. Perhaps the most blatant violation of the State Department's loan policy was the refinancing of the South Manchurian Railway Company, which took place when loans were made to the Japanese government in 1928 and 1930. In addition, more municipal and public utility loans were floated and the Oriental Development Company received another major loan in the last half of the decade.[55]

In view of the relative ease with which Japan obtained loans from the United States in the 1920s and the fact that the Japanese government never entirely relinquished its domestic control over foreign investments and borrowing after World War I, it is now evident that the hope expressed by American bankers and government officials about deploying the financial power of the United States to keep Japan in line with the principles of the Open Door was doomed to failure. Japan simply did not become excessively dependent upon American loans, and no attempt was ever made by the State or Commerce Department to curb economic activity in the area where there was increasing dependence, that is, trade. In essence the economic foreign policy of the United States reflected a "negative acquiescence" to Japanese expansion which had the approval of leading American financiers.[56] This was particularly true in Manchuria, where the political commitment of the United States to the Open Door was steadily undermined by loans to Japan while China remained on the periphery of the magic circle of international finance between 1920 and 1933.

Aside from American loan policy, another reason for the uncoordinated economic and political diplomacy in the Far East can be found in the two conflicting interpretations within the State Department of the meaning of the Washington Conference. The opposing positions which emerged in the 1920s have become associated with the names of two career diplomats, both of whom served successively as chief of the Division of Far Eastern Affairs of the State Department and as minister to China between 1919 and 1933, John Van Antwerp MacMurray and Nelson Johnson.[57] MacMurray, who became a close adviser of Secretary Hughes between 1919 and 1925 as division chief, thought the Washington treaties bound the United States, Japan, and England to deal jointly with China. Furthermore MacMurray

contended that the Chinese were obligated by the treaties to improve their country. In return the major nations would gradually
abolish the extraterritorial and tariff privileges they enjoyed and
which they had refused to abandon at the Washington Conference. If, however, the internal situation in China continued to
disintegrate and threaten foreign nationals and their property,
then the major nations, individually or collectively according to
MacMurray, had every right to continue to enforce their unequal treaties with military intervention.[58] This independent internationalist course of action favored the Japanese over the Chinese
because it posited Japanese-American cooperation in the Far
East while it perpetuated the relegation of China to an inferior
status among nations and implicitly denied the Chinese people
the right to work out their own problems free from the possibility
of foreign interference.

Although Hughes maintained that the Washington Conference had in fact freed China to determine its own future, his
actions were more in keeping with MacMurray's ideas than with
the spirit of Chinese sovereignty contained in the Nine Power
Treaty. It was on MacMurray's advice, for example, that Hughes
successfully negotiated with England and France to deny China
aid in building up a navy. He also refused to consider consortium
loans opposed by the Japanese and he rejected the Chinese suggestion that the United States inform Japan of its opposition to
intervention. "Such a suggestion," Hughes explained to the
Chinese minister, "would be gratuitous as we have been assured
that intervention was not contemplated by the Japanese Government." Finally, the secretary of state justified the delay in a
conference to reconsider extraterritoriality on the grounds that
the Chinese did not appear to be "taking advantage of the opportunity afforded by the Washington Conference," "had not been
able to give protection to foreigners," and had "utterly failed to
discharge their international obligations."[59] Thus, nothing was
done by the State Department under Hughes to eliminate or
modify the unequal treaties. His most positive action toward the
Chinese after the Washington Conference came when he supported the unconditional remission for educational purposes of
the remaining American portion of the Boxer indemnity. He did

so over the objections of Hoover, Representative Dyer, and a number of businessmen supporting the China Trade Act, who preferred a conditional remission guaranteeing the purchase of a certain amount of American goods.[60]

A more pro-Chinese, but no less independent internationalist, interpretation of the Washington Conference emerged under Frank B. Kellogg and his Far Eastern Division chief, Nelson Johnson. The failure of the major nations to cooperate in aiding China plus rising Chinese nationalism had convinced such men as Kellogg, Johnson, and Senator William Borah by the middle of the decade that certain premises of the Washington treaty system were no longer relevant to the changing scene in China. In particular, Johnson believed the United States should initiate independent negotiations to eliminate tariff and extraterritorial privileges, although he never ruled out the possibility of a collective settlement. Rather than stressing Chinese obligations and duties, the policies of Kellogg and Johnson appeared to be guided by the desire to give China's new leaders a chance to develop their country, however inefficiently, unencumbered by the constant threat of foreign intervention. Although a minimum number of marines were sent to Shanghai to protect American nationals, patience and moderation generally characterized the attitude of the State Department during the critical years of the Nationalist Revolution between 1925 and 1928. As minister to China during this period, MacMurray opposed what he thought to be the inadequate number of American troops in China and all actions which seemed to contradict the Far Eastern policy he had tried to establish prior to 1925. Nonetheless, after a Nationalist Chinese government was established under Chiang Kai-shek and some semblance of order prevailed, MacMurray carried out orders to negotiate the 1928 agreement which granted tariff autonomy to the Chinese. Kellogg and Johnson also favored the gradual abolition of extraterritoriality, but the talks broke down because of the Chinese demand for immediate and unconditional surrender of these privileges.[61]

This "soft policy" toward China had the support of the general public and the business community in the United States, but not of American businessmen in China. Represented primarily by the American Chamber of Commerce at Shanghai and supported by Minister MacMurray, spokesmen for these businessmen accused the government of allowing the "uplifters" to dictate Chinese policy at the expense of American lives and property and of subordinating the Open Door to charity. In addition they censured their business colleagues in the United States for not speaking out on their behalf and for not supporting a greater use of force to quell disturbances resulting from the civil war. Neither the State nor the Commerce Department officially answered these charges. Hoover's personal replies to all of the attempts by the Shanghai Chamber of Commerce to gain his sympathy were very noncommittal, even though commercial attaché Arnold and the chamber tried to impress him with the role the communists were supposedly playing in the Nationalist Revolution. Instead of taking action to protect Americans from excessive taxation and other harassment by the Nationalists, the Commerce Department simply assumed a more cautious attitude toward future business prospects in China in the last half of the decade. On the advice of Nelson Johnson, for example, Hoover rejected a proposal by the Rev. Hugh W. White for the development of a port and industrial project at Tungchow by saying, "While I am, of course, sympathetic to every form of development in China I do not see that there is very much our Government can do . . . in the promotion of private enterprise." Even before the Nationalist Revolution occurred, he had told a correspondent that China needed "cohesion at that end before anything can really be developed." By September 1929 the acting director of the BFDC told Arnold that the reappearance of "business as usual" in China was more superficial than substantial and therefore the State and Commerce departments were "not anxious to overemphasize China in our promotional activities at this time." Accordingly, despite the protests of certain western senators including Key Pittman, the Silver Producers Association of America, and businessmen in China, Nelson and officials of the Commerce Department refused to support a silver loan to China in 1930.[62]

Thus, despite all of its professed political sympathy for the independent development of a sovereign China, the moderate policy of Kellogg and Nelson failed to stabilize China under

Chiang Kai-shek or any other Nationalist leader because it was at no time backed by sufficient economic aid from private or public sources. Not only were American businessmen in the Shanghai Chamber of Commerce working at cross purposes with the Nationalists, but government officials who supported the political conservatism of Chiang Kai-shek nonetheless could not condone the antiforeign fiscal and monetary policies of his Nationalists. Thomas W. Lamont and the American Group continued to disparage Chinese credit and discourage consortium loans, while American journalists sent to China under the auspices of the Carnegie Endowment for International Peace in the summer of 1929 issued unfavorable accounts of the claims of progress by the Nanking government. Even the American Red Cross concluded at the end of the decade that additional foreign aid for famine relief in China "would do more harm than good" because "famine conditions are chiefly due to the absence of a strong central government in China, to the exactions of warlords, the depredations of bandits, and confiscatory taxation."[63] Once again, therefore, the lack of a coordinated economic and political foreign policy thwarted the goals of the United States in the Far East. Nationalist China may have had the moral support of the American government and people, but that was not enough.

Chapter Eight

A Glimpse of the Future:
Manchuria, 1931–1933

By the time Hoover became president the government had followed one basic economic policy and two rival political courses in the Far East for a number of years. Hoover's own 1929 position on the subject reflected this ambiguity, as discussed in the previous chapter. While he had supported the efforts of Charles Evans Hughes at the Washington Conference, he had warned the secretary of state at the time that a "negative hands-off policy" would not be enough to strengthen China internally. What was needed, Hoover had advised Hughes, was foreign aid in the form of a $250 million bankers' loan. Later he noted in his memoirs that after the disarmament conference of 1921–1922 not enough financial aid was ever undertaken for China. But this was a condition, it must be remembered, for which he, as secretary of commerce, was partially responsible; he considered himself an expert on China and was often consulted as such by businessmen. Having spent the years 1899–1902 in China as an engineer, he never completely overcame his initial negative opinions about China's potential for trade, investment, resource development, industrialization, and democratization.[1] Although he did modify his original views about the commercial possibilities in China during the 1920s, Hoover's business orientation led him to prefer the political and economic stability of Japan to the opposite conditions prevailing in China. Consequently, while he worked for the passage of the China Trade Act, he also tacitly assented to the anti-Chinese loan policy of the State Department and the American Group of the Second China Consortium.

Yet, unlike Secretary Hughes, Hoover did not oppose Japanese exclusion in 1924. His position here seems to have been largely determined by his association with California politics and by a racial bias not uncommon for the period. "It is my own belief," he told his friend Mark Requa, "that a definite exclusion law would make in the long run for better relations between our own and the Japanese people. . . . The biological fact makes mixture of bloods disadvantageous." On this question, Hoover found himself in opposition to a large number of bankers and exporters (especially in the lumber industry) outside of California, who feared the negative effects exclusion would have on the growing trade between Japan and the United States. Also in opposition to such an immigration restriction were some engineers, land companies, and large manufacturers (especially in the iron and steel industry) who were concerned with insuring an adequate supply of agriculturists and laborers for domestic needs.[2]

With the exception of this exclusion issue, Hoover appears to have supported most of the independent internationalist methods applied to the Far East by Secretaries of State Hughes and Frank B. Kellogg without discriminating between the conflicting positions of their respective advisers, John V. A. MacMurray and Nelson T. Johnson. Not surprisingly, therefore, his own advisers came from both camps. His first appointments, Johnson as minister to China, Henry L. Stimson as secretary of state, and Stanley K. Hornbeck as chief of the Far Eastern Division of the State Department, were in keeping with the Kellogg approach. These men did not believe the Washington treaties had established any binding cooperative system which prevented the United States from taking unilateral action in upholding the Open Door or otherwise aiding China. However, the man he hand-picked to be under-secretary of state in 1931, William R. Castle, Jr., was sympathetic with the earlier hard-line policy toward China developed by Hughes and MacMurray. Castle believed the United States "ought to be willing to play pretty closely with Japan" because "selfish interests make it imperative that we have Japan as a friend in the western Pacific."[3]

Given Hoover's own lack of a consistent Far Eastern policy and the division of opinion among his advisers, his administration tended to straddle issues in the Orient. For example, contrary to the expectations of the Chinese Nationalists, Hoover's administration did not extend the scope of the policy initiated by Kellogg and Johnson. That is, no more progress was made toward ending extraterritoriality, and during the 1929 Sino-Soviet crisis over the Chinese Eastern Railway, Stimson scrupulously assumed a policy which favored neither side, although his invocation of the Kellogg-Briand Pact was resented by Soviet officials and Russophiles in the United States as being unnecessary and designed to aid China.[4]

Likewise in the Manchurian crisis of 1931–1932, the policy of the United States was intended not to alienate the Japanese as much as to prevent aggression against the Chinese. In this last instance it proved impossible to achieve both goals and in attempting to do so the Hoover-Stimson policy reflected the common defect of the policies of their predecessors, namely, the refusal to help China directly by backing the Open Door with sufficient military and/or economic aid. The two obvious alternatives skirted by American diplomatists in the 1920s consisted of protecting China by playing Japan and Russia off against one another (which would have required the recognition of the USSR), or of candidly joining with Japan at the expense of both China and Russia. Instead of devising a strategy which consistently followed any of these alternatives, the United States between 1920 and 1933 continued to call for the protection of China without any concrete means for deterring Japan. Hoover once said that "words without action are the assassins of idealism." In these terms, the ideal of the Open Door in the Far East had all but been killed before the Manchurian crisis of the early 1930s delivered the *coup de grace*.

This crisis, which ended in the creation of the puppet state of Manchukuo in Southern Manchuria, provoked several major policy statements by Secretary of State Stimson in 1932. They included the proclamation on January 7 of the nonrecognition of the fruits of aggression, commonly known as the Stimson Doctrine; two public letters written to Senator Borah in February and September; and an address before the Council on Foreign Relations on August 8. Since the formulation of the Hoover-Stimson policy has been examined at length in other studies, it will simply be summarized here in relation to business and mass opinion.

By 1930 businessmen usually conceded that Japan had special interests in Manchuria, and, like Under-Secretary of State Castle, tended to think there was "even less danger that Japan will annex Manchuria than that we might sometime annex Cuba." On the eve of the outbreak of hostilities, the *Bankers Magazine* predicted that the Japanese wanted no disruption in Manchuria because of their economically devastating experience there during the war with Russia early in the century. In the fall of 1931 the most immediate concern of businessmen dealing in the Far East was the effect of certain taxes imposed by the Nationalists, along with violations of extraterritorial privileges and the impact the depression was having on commercial relations. Wheat farmers and flour millers in particular had been attempting for several years to sell their surpluses to China to relieve the famine there and the depression here. In August 1931, the Federal Farm Board in cooperation with the China Famine Relief Association concluded an agreement with China for the purchase of 450,000 tons of wheat and flour, and shipments began in September. Hoover supported this transaction, but subsequent attempts to negotiate the sale of wheat and cotton surpluses failed until an RFC loan was obtained in June 1933.[5]

When the Mukden incident occurred on September 18, 1931, this country's greater commercial and financial involvement with Japan automatically placed most businessmen with Far Eastern interests tacitly on the side of the Japanese, with the exception of those few in Manchuria who actually suffered physical damage. It was generally assumed that Japanese control of the area would provide greater economic stability and possibly greater economic opportunity in the long run. Although some fear was expressed about the future of the Open Door in Manchuria, it should be noted that the Far Eastern expert in the Commerce Department was informing concerned businessmen at the end of the 1920s that in the event Manchuria became a Japanese protectorate, "there was no evidence to indicate that a nullification of the 'Open Door' policy would necessarily follow." In addition, increasing doubts were expressed within the business community about the practicality of continuing to insist "that China be kept intact and wide open as a free commercial field." In other words, a decade of increasing economic interdependence with Japan and the failure of the Washington Conference treaties to strengthen China had begun to weaken business commitment to the original principles of the Open Door as embodied in the Nine Power Treaty.[6]

After all, little of the $155 million invested by American businessmen in China was actually in Manchuria. Sixty-five percent of this direct investment was in Shanghai alone, while another 27 percent could be found in Tienstsin, Hong Kong, and the rest of China excluding Manchuria, where only 8 percent, or some $13 million, was invested by 1931. Despite the interest in Manchurian railroads expressed by bankers and government officials when the First and Second Consortiums were created, and aside from the diversion of some American funds to the area by the Japanese government, American portfolio investments in the area remained small throughout the decade. However, the United States did enjoy a favorable trade balance with Manchuria, in contrast to that with the China mainland. The American share of Manchurian imports during the 1920s remained stationary at between 10 and 12 percent, while Manchurian exports to the United States amounted to approximately 3 percent of its total foreign exports. In 1929, for example, commercial transactions with Manchuria came to $23 million, of which $16 million represented American exports. Total United States trade with all of China in 1929 was in the neighborhood of $339 million, making the Manchurian portion no more than 7 percent. Given these figures it is difficult to explain the intense interest Washington officials periodically demonstrated in Manchuria, except that the area represented a political testing ground for the Open Door rather than an actual outlet for American economic expansion.[7]

Within a week after the Mukden incident the Radio Corporation of America complained to Stimson that their radio service for business interests in Manchuria had been disrupted on September 19. The State Department in turn notified the Japanese government of the complaint and was assured by Foreign Minister Baron

Kijuro Shidehara that the damage was minimal and operation of the station would be resumed promptly.[8] Thirteen other companies had reported damages to Stimson by the beginning of 1932 in the wake of continued military action. In April 1932 the consul general at Mukden, Myrl S. Myers, reviewed the various adverse effects Japanese occupation was having on individual firms and concluded that there was a general economic paralysis of American business. Since these complaints and negative reports did not receive widespread publicity, businessmen in the United States, like the public in general, were not moved to condemn the Japanese invasion of Manchuria on economic grounds. After repeated government protests to Tokyo produced no significant results, the injured firms simply began to make their own adjustments to Japanese control. Some of the other American companies affected were Standard Oil of New York, Texas Company, Ford Motor, American Harvester, General Motors, National City Bank, British-American Tobacco Company, Anderson, Meyer and Company, and Frazer-Federal Incorporated.[9]

The lack of extensive criticism from the American business community can be explained not only in terms of economic ties, but also by the fact that the expansionist policies of Japan in Asia were often equated with those of the United States in Canada and Latin America. As early as 1921, A. Barton Hepburn, chairman of the advisory board for the Chase National Bank, described Japan's ambitions in Manchuria as "perfectly legitimate" since "her economic development is naturally on the mainland of Asia. Propinquity would dictate this." He also noted that since the United States would not allow the Japanese to migrate freely to the Western Hemisphere, they had to move into Asia and the American government should allow them to do this without "continuous nagging." There was no danger that the United States would go to war with Japan over Shantung or to preserve the Open Door, Hepburn prophetically asserted, as long as France and England also remained offenders of American principles in the Far East. Since Japan had simply taken over the Oriental rights of Russia and Germany, her newly acquired power indisputably represented the fruits of war. The key distinction Hepburn made between Japan and China was that the former represented law, order, and peace, while the latter did not. Like many international bankers in the postwar period, he was convinced that Japan was "very human and motivated by the same impulses that . . . actuate our nation." Therefore, the two countries should "work in unison for the welfare of the world and ourselves." This attitude gained strength within the business community in the 1920s, among nationalists and internationalists alike, until by 1931 it was common to find businessmen justifying Japan's initial military action in Manchuria in terms of past American interventions in Cuba, Mexico, Nicaragua, and Shanghai, and comparing the special interests of Japan in that area of the world to those of the United States in Latin America. It was also suggested by some businessmen that Japan was doing this country and the world an ideological favor in the Far East by opposing communism as she expanded.[10]

Mass opinion followed a somewhat different course from business attitudes during the initial stages of the Manchurian affair. The average American traditionally displayed little interest in the Far East except in times of crisis. Following World War I, racial prejudice directed against the Japanese via immigration legislation overshadowed the moral platitudes expressing friendliness toward the Chinese in the popular mind. Between the outbreak of fighting on September 18, 1931, and the Japanese bombing of a section of Shanghai on January 29, 1932, there was passive support for the administration's actions and policies. These policies included, first, qualified cooperation with the League of Nations, then the unilateral declaration of the Stimson Doctrine of nonrecognition on January 7, 1932.[11] After the invasion of Shanghai, however, mass opinion became more emotionally aroused and critical of Japan. At the same time, rational ideas about a commercial or financial boycott against Japan, although discussed earlier in the crisis, now took the more concrete form of petitions, resolutions, and rallies. Support for economic sanctions came largely from a coterie of college professors, clergymen, lawyers, liberal editors, and civic leaders across the country, many of whom had long been associated with world peace and disarmament groups. Early in 1932 Dr. Abbott Lawrence Lowell, president of Harvard University, former Secre-

tary of War Newton D. Baker, and Raymond Rich of the World
Peace Foundation emerged as the major spokesmen of the
movement. Ultimately over 17,000 individuals, including an impressive number of community opinion leaders, signed the Lowell-
Baker petition or similar ones asking Hoover and Congress to
pledge the support of the United States for any economic sanctions
the League might undertake against Japan.[12]

At no time before or after the attack on Shanghai did the idea
of collective, let alone unilateral, economic action enjoy the support of a majority of the nation's press or widespread mass approval. According to *Literary Digest,* the newspaper proponents
of a boycott constituted a small minority throughout the winter
and spring of 1931–1932. Strongest editorial opposition to economic sanctions came from newspapers on the Pacific Coast, in
the Midwest, in New England, and in Texas. Ironically, with the
exception of the West Coast, these were the same areas where the
largest number of professional people had signed the boycott
petitions. To confuse matters further, many newspapers of the
South and Far West, where exports to the Orient were important to
the economy, remained discreetly silent on the issue. When business publications commented on the boycott their remarks were
invariably negative, but they too displayed a reticence to speak out
against the idea, not only because they could be so easily accused
of crass self-interest, but also because the depression had de-
flated temporarily the image and influence of the business community. Thus the wisest course under the circumstances seemed
to be passive resistance to economic embargoes of any kind.
Published opinion in the mass media and business journals,
therefore, did not accurately reflect either the organized pressure
which existed for economic sanctions or the myriad of opposing
views, especially from farmers, bankers, import-export firms, and
manufacturers.[13]

On March 5, 1932, *Literary Digest* described the collapse of
the boycott movement, scarcely a month after the petition drive
had reached its peak. Later in March the magazine noted the
formation of the American Boycott Association to conduct a
private, voluntary consumer boycott of Japanese goods in order
to preserve the Open Door and to force arbitration of the Sino-

Japanese dispute in the face of the unwillingness of the United States government or the League of Nations to take action. Simultaneously, the Committee on Economic Sanctions, created by the Twentieth Century Fund and headed by Nicholas Murray Butler, recommended adding to the Kellogg-Briand Pact provision for embargoes against aggressor nations. Despite the prominence of some members of this committee and others in favor of economic sanctions, the fear that such action could precipitate war or worsen the depression was not overcome in the public at large during the various phases of the boycott movement, nor was the general lack of popular support for continued involvement in Asian problems. The latter was best illustrated by public willingness to relinquish American sovereignty over the Philippines against the wishes of the executive branch of government in 1932 and 1933.[14] Most significant, of course, was the fact that official policy did not reflect the activities of the well-organized minority in favor of a boycott.

The president, his cabinet, the Department of Commerce, and most senators, including the influential Senator Borah, opposed collective or unilateral economic sanctions from the beginning of the Manchurian crisis. Early in December 1931 there was some vacillation within the State Department on the part of Stimson, Hornbeck, and their advisers, Allen T. Klots and James Grafton Rogers, but the firm opposition of Hoover, Castle, and Nelson Johnson prevailed. By the end of the year the secretary of state had unofficially informed Geneva that the United States would "probably" not use its fleet to interfere with any economic blockade established by the League of Nations, but would take no action to initiate an independent one, nor would it participate in council discussions of a boycott.[15] This position of the government did not change as organized pressure for economic sanctions gained strength in the spring of 1932, even though both the president and the secretary of state were less inclined to continue giving Japan the benefit of the doubt in light of the capture of Chinchow and military operations at Shanghai.[16]

As Japanese aggression intensified in 1932, a tactical division arose between Hoover and Stimson which had been temporarily settled in the last months of 1931. The two men found themselves at odds not over the principles contained in the January 7 proclamation of nonrecognition nor over the letter to Senator Borah of February 23, stressing the applicability of the Nine Power Treaty as well as that of the Kellogg-Briand Pact to the Manchurian situation. Rather, their misunderstanding was rooted in their personal estimations of one another and their temperamental differences. Generally speaking, Hoover thought Stimson was acting more like a "warrior than a diplomat" when he tried to put teeth into nonrecognition and the Nine Power Treaty through the use of veiled threats about military and economic sanctions. Stimson, for his part, thought Hoover lacked combativeness because of his Quaker background, and was not firmly enough committed to the Open Door to try to "bluff" Japan into compliance with it. In other words, neither man was prepared to "go it alone" against Japan in view of the reluctance of England and France to take decisive action in the League of Nations, and both agreed that moral sanctions were all the United States could bring to bear in the Far East. Nonetheless, Stimson was definitely more disposed toward a bellicose public posture than Hoover. According to Stimson the only difference between his views and the president's "was the reliance which I felt we could put upon America's strength both economically and militarily. . . . I thought we had a right to rely upon the unconscious elements of our great size and military strength; that I knew Japan was afraid of that, and I was willing to let her be afraid of that without telling her that we were not going to use it against her."[17]

Consequently, the secretary of state was angered in May 1932 to find that Hoover and Castle had taken advantage of his absence from Washington to attend the Geneva Disarmament Conference, to announce that the United States had no intention of supporting an independent boycott against Japan nor of pursuing by other than peaceful means a settlement of the Sino-Japanese conflict. Stimson resented this public denial of all sanctions because it undermined the implicit threat he had made in his letter to Borah about fortifying Guam and the Philippines if Japan continued to violate the Nine Power Treaty. Hoover's and Castle's collusion, however, did not prevent Stimson from privately telling Walter Lippmann he was in "full agreement with the essentials of the President's position," and recognized "all the evils of a boycott; the danger of its leading to war blindly and unwisely." He said the movement headed by Dr. Lowell was "unfair" because the League had no intention of approving economic sanctions. He added, however, that he was not opposed to the idea of an unofficial boycott on the part of individual citizens. "I have regarded such an unofficial boycott," he said to Lippmann, "as an expression of the same world public opinion which I regard as the sanction, the real sanction behind the peace treaties we are trying to develop and encourage." The difference between an official boycott imposed by the government and an unofficial one voluntarily participated in by private citizens was a crucial one to Stimson, but as Armin Rappaport has pointed out, it was a distinction which has largely been obscured. This has been due to Hoover's insistence in his memoirs that his secretary of state wanted an official boycott, to Stimson's own obtuseness on the subject at the time, and his later admission that his doctrine of nonrecognition enforced by moral condemnation alone had proven inadequate in the face of aggression.[18]

Whatever second thoughts Stimson may have had about appeasement as a result of World War II, the fact remains that in 1931–1932 he was as convinced as Hoover of the foolishness of pushing ahead with unilateral sanctions. And both men realized there was no chance of collective action by the League or unilateral action by England or France. Their individual estimations of the situation were, therefore, neither unrealistic nor naive; compounded by the worldwide depression, the situation simply defied either an independent or an international solution. There is little doubt, however, that Stimson was willing to endorse the use of sanctions as a diplomatic ploy, while Hoover was not. In this sense their misunderstanding, although of relatively minor significance during the Manchurian crisis, became enormously important in terms of the subsequent application of the Stimson Doctrine and the Open Door it was intended to protect. The policy of nonrecognition of the fruits of aggression was significant to Hoover as an end in itself (so much so that he tried to insist upon calling it the Hoover Doctrine), but to Stimson it

was simply a means to an end which required concrete implementation. Thus, Hoover continued to praise the doctrine because it "avoids precipitant action and allows time to work out
proper solutions," while Stimson thought of it as not yet an
"effective living reality" and ultimately as an ideological justification for war.[19] The significance of their basically conflicting interpretations was lost on all but a handful of Americans in the
early 1930s, some of whom came from the ranks of business.

Although business tempers had also risen after the invasion
of Shanghai, even among the Sinophiles it was difficult to find
anyone who favored war or strong retaliatory policies. Approximately three out of every four businessmen who were sent a
questionnaire in 1934 responded that they believed the economic
interests of Japan in Manchuria did not justify its recent actions
there. But within the 1932 boycott movement the average Republican businessman was not very prominent. He may not have
approved of Japan's conduct, but trade relations were too basic to
tamper with for political reasons, unless the country happened
to be communist, and even here the depression was breeding
resistance to government restrictions on trade with the Soviet
Union.[20] Most of the businessmen who were actively involved in
the campaign for economic sanctions were former Wilsonian
internationalists, such as Newton D. Baker, Norman H. Davis,
and Edward A. Filene. These men not only urged that the
United States participate in a collective boycott against Japan
to enforce the Stimson Doctrine, but they also hoped cooperation
with the League would increase the chances of American membership in the near future. While these Wilsonians denied that a
boycott would provoke war with Japan, they were not basically
hostile to Japan's aspirations in the Far East so much as they
were bewildered and exasperated by the methods she chose to
achieve them.[21]

When the State Department informally encouraged a partisan
rebuttal of this Wilsonian position, it found itself with the solid
backing of most international bankers. Led by Thomas W. Lamont, this segment of the business community had remained
pro-Japanese even after others had been aroused by the Chinchow
and Shanghai incidents. These bankers tried to offset the un-

favorable image of Japan in the mass media by privately keeping
Hoover and Stimson informed of the Japanese point of view during the spring and summer of 1932. Rather than looking upon
the Stimson Doctrine and the February letter to Borah as requiring
enforcement through sanctions or as vehicles for bringing the
United States into closer cooperation with the League, Lamont
interpreted the Hoover-Stimson policy to mean the United States
would allow Japan and China to settle their difficulties by themselves without outside interference. Lamont, therefore, opposed
collective economic action against Japan as being "practically
tantamount to war," and told Stimson the Manchurian situation
was far too complex to be solved by private pressure groups,
such as the one headed by Dr. Lowell. These sentiments were
echoed by another prominent financier, Fred I. Kent, in a letter
to Toyotaro Yuki of the Industrial Bank of Japan. "It is incon-
ceivable to me," wrote Kent, "that those who signed the [Lowell]
document had any conception of how far-reaching it might be if
their ideas prevailed and how much unnecessary hardship would
be created. In other words, it was merely an academic demonstra-
tion of a theoretical notion from a pacifist point of view." Kent
also discounted the numerous women's groups supporting a
voluntary boycott (the wives of several New York financiers, including the daughter-in-law of Thomas W. Lamont, were members of the American Boycott Association) by saying they were
following the academicians without any understanding of the
situation.[22]

Both Lamont and Kent in their private correspondence with
Japanese bankers insisted that the signers of the petitions did not
represent the opinion of the American government or the mass of
the American people. On both counts Lamont and Kent correctly
judged the temper of Washington and most citizens as evidenced
by the rapid demise of the boycott movement. They also assured
their Japanese friends that they were personally convinced the
situation did not warrant any drastic action. In general, then,
throughout the spring, summer, and fall of 1932, powerful
Wall Street figures warned the government against doing anything
which would further inflame public opinion. Lamont in particular
was critical of the League of Nations' "attempting to pontificate"

and told Stimson the best course for both the United States and the League was to lie low and follow a hands-off policy.[23] Except, as will be noted, for a few inflammatory remarks by the secretary of state, this is exactly what the government did, and in all likelihood would have done without urging from financiers. There is little doubt, however, that Hoover was more comfortable with this advice from the international bankers than Stimson was because, like Hoover, they viewed the doctrine of nonrecognition as an end rather than a means.

This is not to say that government officials and the international bankers refused to consider other means of bringing unilateral pressure to bear upon Japan in 1931 and 1932. State Department records indicate behind-the-scenes activity to prevent Japan from profiting from her aggressive actions in the Far East. According to Stanley K. Hornbeck, chief of the Far Eastern Division, Herbert Feis, economic adviser to the State Department, and Thomas W. Lamont, this could be accomplished without resorting to an economic boycott or to military action. These men argued that Japan's future need for credit and loans gave the United States a powerful diplomatic advantage in dealing with the Manchurian situation. It was generally agreed by bankers and government officials that Japan's military effort was seriously impairing her economic stability, making her a greater credit risk than at any time since World War I. Obviously the Japanese economy was also being adversely affected by the worldwide depression and the Chinese boycott of Japanese merchants in Shanghai, which had begun before the invasion of Manchuria. With the war aggravating her financial difficulties, Hornbeck, Lamont, and others believed credit was the strongest weapon the United States possessed against Japan. Even so, none of these government officials or businessmen wanted to see Japan bankrupted by her Manchurian adventure for fear of what that would do to American trade and the civilian government in Japan.[24]

Accordingly, Hornbeck simply recommended in January 1932 that "no encouragement be given to American financiers to make loans to the Japanese until the development of more satisfactory evidence concerning their intentions in Manchuria." A few days later Feis warned the State Department to be on the alert for at-

tempts by Japan to obtain construction loans for the South Manchurian Railroad. Stimson approved of this unofficial loan ban, as
did Lamont when he told Under-Secretary William Castle that
Japan was "up against it financially" and looking around for
loans, but New York was "not going to lend any money whatsoever to Japan at the present time." Lamont also noted that since
Japan's trade had so greatly declined and the nation had gone off
the gold standard, it was "at the moment anything but good security."[25] On the heels of this decision by the Department of
State and Wall Street, rumors developed about the possibility of
the Japanese obtaining loans from the English or French. Stimson investigated every rumor and reported in February to Representative Louis T. McFadden that his department was convinced no direct or indirect loans to the Japanese were being
contemplated by European nations. Nonetheless, he took the
precaution of making it known abroad that the United States opposed all such transactions under the circumstances.[26]

In the first months of 1932 Lamont remained Stimson's best
source of information about Japan's financial activities and intentions, but his advisory position became somewhat compromised
for a time in March when Herbert Feis pointed out that an earlier
short-term loan to Japan by American bankers, notably the House
of Morgan, had fallen due in January and had been renewed
until April. This advance of 127 million yen was made to the
Yokohama Specie Bank through a banking group headed by
Morgan and Company three days after the proclamation of
Stimson's nonrecognition doctrine. The loan had originally been
made in November 1931 during the first phase of Japan's invasion of Manchuria. Lamont confirmed the advance on March
18, explaining the loan had since been "liquidated in full by
the [Japanese] Government and by the Bank of Japan through
the shipment of gold and otherwise." This liquidation technically
ended the violation of the Department's unofficial ban against
further Japanese credit, but a transgression of the policy had taken
place, nonetheless. Feis, in explicitly pointing out in a January
memorandum on Japanese loans that a total of 300 million yen
would fall due in the spring and summer of 1932, had commented: "If the Japanese Government is compelled to pay off

these loans and advances, it would certainly be a difficult problem, as current merchandise trade is probably running against Japan and as the total of gold reserves in Japan has now fallen to 430 million yen."[27] While no new long-term loans were forthcoming for the Japanese from the United States or Europe during the rest of 1932, Japan was not "compelled" by her American and European creditors to pay off old loans which fell due during the Manchurian crisis, and thus the efforts of the State Department to capitalize on the economic problems of Japan in order to gain compliance with the Stimson Doctrine and adherence to the Open Door principles failed. Possibly the department had placed too much emphasis on preventing new loans and not enough on renewals. Bankers, of course, were willing to forego new loans in time of depression, but short-term renewals were viewed as an entirely different matter. In any event this attempt to bring financial pressure to bear on Japan would never have been carried to the point of bankrupting such a valuable foreign customer.

Although the House of Morgan continued to deal with Japan normally, at least on a short-term basis, the firm through Lamont did issue several friendly warnings to the Japanese financial minister, Korekiyo Takahashi. In particular Lamont wrote to the New York manager of the Yokohama Specie Bank (for transmission to Takahashi) that all of Japan's friends in the United States were alarmed by the change in public opinion which occurred after Shanghai. "While I do not attach too much importance to the talk of governmental boycotts," Lamont said, "nevertheless, so far as the effect upon Japan is concerned private action might be equally or more detrimental. One never can tell how far an aroused public opinion will move. Fortunately for Japan her government requires no present foreign credit. If it did, of course it would be quite impossible to arrange any credit either through investment or banking circles. The effect which the Shanghai disturbance has had upon outstanding Japanese obligations here is only too obvious." In later communications Lamont became more explicit and reminded the Japanese foreign minister of the past service the House of Morgan had rendered his government in securing loans in the United States which had fostered trade and built up the international credit of Japan. He concluded one letter with the mild admonishment: "There will come a time in the future when the Japanese Government perhaps and certainly some of your public utility or industrial corporations will again desire to arrange credits in the American markets. But naturally for any such future developments there will have to be a great change in the picture." Takahashi answered Lamont with perfunctory defenses of Japanese action similar to those Kent was receiving from Japanese bankers; both Americans passed these on to their own government.[28]

By August 1932 it was evident that the Stimson Doctrine, the first Borah letter, and the unofficial loan ban were not preventing Japan from taking over Manchuria. One of Stimson's last attempts at diplomatic bluffing occurred in the summer of that year when he talked Hoover into retaining a portion of the fleet in the Pacific instead of returning all of it to the Atlantic after the annual war game maneuvers. Simultaneously, however, Hoover went ahead, over Stimson's objections, to propose a 30-percent overall reduction in armaments at the Geneva Disarmament Conference, once again undercutting the impact of Stimson's bellicose gesture. It was at this point that the secretary of state made his last major bid to "implement the Kellogg Pact with a declaration" of cooperation with the League against aggressor nations. He did so in a far-reaching public pronouncement on the meaning of the Paris Pact before the Council on Foreign Relations in New York on August 8. For political as well as philosophical reasons Hoover censored the last three pages of the speech in which Stimson had said the United States was willing to join in League sanctions. Nonetheless, the secretary's remarks remained controversial because he forthrightly denied the validity of traditional American isolationism and neutrality in the face of an increasingly interdependent world. He now suggested publicly what he had said privately in 1929 during the Sino-Soviet crisis, that the Kellogg-Briand Pact carried with it the implied obligation of its signatories to consult in order to clarify public opinion and denounce aggressors. He went on to condemn Japan implicitly for harboring imperialistic designs and to reaffirm the principle of "sympathetic cooperation" between the League and the United States.[29]

Yet throughout the speech Stimson's often intemperate rhetoric was muted by his exclusive reliance upon the power of world opinion to enforce the provisions of the Pact of Paris and the doctrine of the nonrecognition of the fruits of aggression. "The sanction of public opinion," he said, "can be made one of the most potent sanctions in the world. . . . Moral disapproval, when it becomes the disapproval of the whole world takes on a significance hitherto unknown in international law." Although Stimson later maintained that he never accepted in 1932 the idea that public opinion alone was sufficient to enforce the principles of the pact, there was no indication of this in the speech; indeed, there was no other possibility of enforcement in view of Hoover's position, the depression, and popular as well as official resistance to the idea of sanctions at home and abroad.

No sooner had the secretary of state delivered this address than the president further weakened its impact when he accepted his party's renomination for the presidency on August 11. Hoover took the occasion to agree with Stimson that the United States was obliged by the terms of the Kellogg-Briand Pact to consult with other nations, but at the same time he reiterated that the United States would not use "force to preserve peace." He also narrowed the scope of the Stimson Doctrine by limiting nonrecognition to simply the "title to possession of territory," whereas the original January 7 proclamation had encompassed "any situation, treaty or agreement" in violation of the pact. Hoover's initial editing of Stimson's August 8 speech and his subsequent modification of it on August 11 did not prevent the secretary's remarks from worsening public relations with Japan. In fact, Stimson's address placed the United States in the very position Hornbeck had warned against back in January; namely, the United States was too far ahead of the League and world sentiment. In view of this, Hornbeck and Stimson himself privately informed the Chinese and the League Council not to count on America to take any initiative against Japan. Domestic politics geared to the forthcoming presidential election, and practical military and economic considerations, as well as strong domestic opposition to war, determined this strategic retreat from the August 8 speech.[80] The bluff and bluster tactics of Stimsonianism would ultimately lead to conflict between the United States and

Japan under the third administration of Franklin D. Roosevelt, but in 1932 Stimson's extreme rhetorical belligerence was not supported by the navy, peace groups, Wilsonian internationalists such as Newton D. Baker, those in favor of economic sanctions, or the business community.

In September, Stimson added the final dimension to his policy when he answered Senator Borah, who had requested a reconsideration of Russian recognition in light of the Far Eastern crisis. Admitting that he had considered the subject of recognition while attending the Geneva Disarmament Conference, Stimson said he had rejected the idea because the position of the United States concerning Manchuria and recognition rested on the integrity of international obligations. Drawing extensively from a memorandum prepared by Hornbeck, Stimson told Borah the United States could not risk the loss of moral standing which would result if the Soviet Union was recognized in violation of long-standing American principles, for as the Hornbeck memorandum more candidly noted, recognition in the name of expediency would be tantamount to a diplomatic defeat for the United States. Rather than admit the failure of the policy in the Far East and follow the alternative of recognizing the Soviet Union in an attempt to restrain Japan, Stimson retreated to the traditional moral and ideological position of his predecessors. Finally, when the Lytton Commission report on Manchuria was made public on October 2, 1932, Stimson avoided making any precipitous statements about what the League and Japan should do with it, clearly indicating that the United States was no longer trying to influence world opinion.[31]

Faced with continued Japanese implacability, Stimson further retreated from his August speech until, by the beginning of 1933, he was considering a peace "gesture" toward Japan before going out of office. It involved, he told his Far Eastern adviser, Stanley Hornbeck, the possibility of recommending to Congress a change in the immigration law and a meeting with Japanese representatives. Hornbeck dismissed both suggestions, noting that the Japanese ambassador had already been "repeatedly" assured that the United States was not going to support its position with force. In particular he feared a meeting with the Japanese by a lame duck administration might result in another "ill-advised" and "much abused" Lansing-Ishii agreement. Convinced that the differences between the two countries would remain irreconcilable until one side surrendered, Hornbeck thought no action should be taken at this time. Stimson agreed that there was probably little point in a meeting because "the depth of the cleavage between American and Japanese policy on the issues involved in the Manchurian trouble is far too great to be bridged . . . and the character of the Japanese Government now in control of Japan precludes any hope of solution by that means." He still insisted, however, that a change in the immigration law would remove the Japanese belief that American policy had been motivated by "personal hostility." The secretary said he had been considering such action before the "Japanese army ran amuck in September 1931." Nothing came of this suggestion before the end of Hoover's administration.[32]

When Roosevelt and Hull came to office they publicly acceded to the Stimson Doctrine, but privately followed Hornbeck's no-action advice for the rest of the year. As a result, political relations with Japan appeared to return to a normal state, but in fact increasing Anglo-American cooperation in the Far East gradually left Japan isolated in a political sense.[33] From an economic standpoint, however, the American business community under the leadership of a few international financiers, quickly resumed its formerly friendly stance toward the country which remained the best Oriental customer of the United States. No greater effort was made by the Democrats in the early 1930s than by the Republicans in the late 1920s to resolve the contradiction between economic and political foreign policy in the Far East.

Hornbeck, Elihu Root, and others sanguinely continued to note (both before and after the Manchurian affair) that although the United States had never used force to uphold the Open Door in China and had no intention of ever doing so, it still adhered to the principles involved. In spite of such assurances the Open Door was far from what it had been in 1900 or on the eve of World War I. It had been codified in 1922 and unsuccessfully defended in Manchuria in the late 1920s and early 1930s, and was gradually being transformed into a sacrosanct concept for which America finally did fight. Nonetheless, the pragmatic denial of force to protect abstract principles in an area of the world where material interests were of negligible proportions prevailed until the late 1930s, when there developed a moralistic policy of nonrecognition (which the Hoover and Roosevelt administrations had sensibly abandoned for Latin America) and American political leaders no longer acknowledged any similarities between the sphere of influence which they so jealously guarded in the Southern Hemisphere and the one the Japanese were determined to establish in the Far East.[34]

Perhaps the greatest significance of the Manchurian incident and of all various attempts by the United States to open and close doors in different parts of the world between 1920 and 1933 lay in the fact that this appeared at the time to be one of the most realistic ways to pursue peace and economic expansion with a minimum of political commitment. For the same reason, the policy makers of this period also endorsed, with varying degrees of success, disarmament, the outlawry of war, membership in the World Court, indirect cooperation with the League of Nations, and the scaling down of Allied debt and German reparation payments. On numerous occasions Herbert Hoover's economic and political foreign policy best reflected all of these attempts to promote peace, capitalism, and democracy abroad under an American mantle. The fact that he occupied high public office during twelve of the thirteen years covered in this study put him in a position to influence foreign relations longer than any other single individual within the government. At the same time his intimate relationship with the business community provided ample opportunity for the investigation of the influence certain economic groups had on the formulation of foreign policy.

In an age of Cold War, limited war of massive proportions, and a nuclear arms race, it is difficult to empathize with Hoover and others of the 1920s and early 1930s who were openly skeptical about the use of force as a means for preserving peace or building a permanent American economic empire. It is also difficult to see what diplomatic assumptions we continue to share with that generation of Americans. In moving from their negotiate-rather-than-annihilate frame of reference to the overkill theories of the present, the men and women of the decade following World War I often appear hopelessly naive and overly optimistic, when in all probability they were simply being more rational (and humane) about the limitations of force as a diplomatic tool than is now thought practicable. Obviously we are today as much victims of the belief in ever-expanding foreign economic activity as they were, but lack their compensating emphasis on good faith in international affairs, and, until most recently, on political disengagement.

In retrospect it would appear that the following features of the independent internationalist practices of the Hoover era were preserved and reinforced following 1933: 1) An ideological insistence on the superiority of the American economic and political system which has led to the equation of capitalism with democracy, and the attempt to apply it universally. 2) An anticommunist paranoia which has developed into a suspicion of all revolutionary situations. 3) A blurring of public and private responsibilities and values, particularly in the area of economic foreign policy, because of the development of a corporate ideology which has often defied political realities abroad and humanitarian considerations at home. 4) A selective dependence upon public opinion in the formulation of policy, when it coincides with the private views of those in leadership positions, which has perpetuated an illusion about the impact of popular attitudes on foreign affairs. 5) An increasing acceptance of unproductive foreign loans which has helped to discredit the American foreign aid program here and overseas. 6) A growing preference for Stimsonianism rather than Hooverism as a means for implementing the Open and Closed Door policies and for containing aggression whereever deemed necessary for ideological reasons.[35]

Other diplomatic features of the post-World War I period are now emerging for reconsideration, however. They are: 1) A renewed interest in disarmament. 2) Gradual acknowledgment of the necessity for greater coordination between economic and political foreign policy at the federal level. 3) Recognition of the importance of promoting self-sufficiency and internal reforms in unstable, underdeveloped nations. (As in the 1920s, however, this goal is seldom pursued at the expense of American economic expansion.) 4) Some recognition of the limitations of this country's vast military power and the futility of attritional wars based on ideological considerations. 5) Tacit admission that corporate ideology cannot be allowed to dominate American foreign relations. 6) A strengthened realization of the importance of tending to domestic problems before setting out to remake the world in America's image.[36]

As for the dream of a mutually beneficial world community based on international cooperation and American leadership, it remains unrealized. Independent internationalism is still the means by which American foreign policy is conducted because it remains an eminently practical way to operate and has maintained American leadership in the world since 1920, although it has failed to establish a cooperative economic community. The method today, as in Hoover's time, is only as effective as the specific policies which it is supposed to implement. By itself it is no guarantee of success, as the record of the years 1920–1933 clearly shows. But an examination of the period does provide valuable insights into the increasingly complicated relationship between government and business in the formulation of modern diplomacy, a relationship which remains, despite Hoover's warnings and efforts, poorly defined and inadequately controlled.

Finally, it appears that the peace and disarmament movement and the attempts of isolated individuals to rationally limit the commitments and expansion of the United States—that is, the idea of disengaging without retreating to an obsolete brand of nationalism—has assumed new relevance and meaning, as have the ideas of the internationalists of the 1920s about how to create a world community without resorting to force. It can only be hoped that the constructive aspects of the diplomacy of the 1920–1933 period will begin to receive the positive consideration they have long deserved, rather than the opprobrium they have traditionally been accorded.

The following abbreviations are used in the notes to refer to the files in the Herbert Hoover Presidential Library, West Branch, Iowa.

HHCD: Herbert Hoover Commerce Department Papers, Official File (unless designated PF for Personal File).

The following are files within the Commerce Papers:

AF:	Achievements File (followed by appropriate years)
BFDC:	Bureau of Foreign and Domestic Commerce File
CF:	Commerce File (followed by subtitle, e.g., CF-American Businessman)
FLF:	Foreign Loans File
IAHC:	Inter-American High Commission File
JF:	Japan File
OF:	Oil File
PF-Loans:	Personal File-Foreign Loans
TF:	Tariff File

HHPP: Herbert Hoover Presidential Papers, Official File (unless designated HHPPF for President's Personal File).

The following are files within the Presidential Papers:

CF:	Countries File (followed by specific country, e.g., CF-Brazil)
DF:	Disarmament File (sometimes followed by specific years)
DF:	Debts File (followed by subtitle, e.g., DF-Moratorium)
DF-Drafts:	Debts File-Speech Drafts
Diary:	Outline Diary of Events Leading to Moratorium, in FLF
ED-State:	Executive Departments File-State Department
FA:	Foreign Affairs File (followed by subtitle, e.g., FA-Diplomats)
FA-Disarm.:	Foreign Affairs File-Disarmament
FLF:	Foreign Loans File
TF:	Tariff File

Notes

Introduction

[1] In addition to my own research, the following works were utilized in preparing the introduction: Raymond Bauer, et al., *American Business and Public Policy**; A. D. H. Kaplan, *Small Business: Its Place and Problems;* idem, *Big Enterprise in a Competitive System;* Alfred D. Chandler, Jr., *Strategy and Structure;* Robert H. Wiebe, *Businessmen and Reform;* Francis X. Sutton, et al., *The American Business Creed;* Adolf A. Berle, Jr., and Gardiner C. Means, *The Modern Corporation and Private Property* (New York, 1948); Benjamin H. Williams, *Economic Foreign Policy of the United States;* President's Research Committee on Social Trends, *Recent Social Trends in the United States* (New York, 1934).

Chapter One

[1] Joseph Dorfman, *The Economic Mind in American Civilization,* 4: 22.

[2] Ibid., 3: 474; Ernest R. May, *The World War and American Isolation, 1914–1917* (Cambridge, Mass., 1959), pp. 339–40, 343, 346; Charles C. Tansill, *America Goes to War* (Boston, 1938), p. 55; Paul Studenski and Herman E. Krooss, *Financial History of the United States,* pp. 281–85; Frank H. Simonds, *American Foreign Policy in the Post-War Years,* p. 23; John Hays Hammond, "Lessons Americans Have Learned from the War with Respect to National Problems," address delivered 5 June 1916, Box 20, John Hays Hammond Papers, Yale University (hereafter cited as Hammond Papers); Conference on Unemployment, *Recent Economic Changes in the United States* (hereafter cited as *Recent Economic Changes*), 2: 847.

[3] In describing the Progressive movement as nationalistic I do not mean to imply that there was a single Progressive attitude toward foreign policy. No

---

* For facts of publication where not given in the notes, see bibliography, pp. 313–29.

imperialist or isolationist or any other kind of consensus existed among leading Progressives. They disagreed over individual foreign policy issues prior
to 1914 and between 1915 and 1920, just as most political conservatives did.
Nationalism in the broad sense of the belief in American patriotism, economic expansion, and moral mission was not the monopoly of any particular
political grouping, nor were interventionist and antiexpansionist predilections
in foreign affairs. For a discussion of the differences among Progressives on
foreign policy issues, including intervention in World War I, see: Walter I.
Trattner, "Progressivism and World War I: A Reappraisal," *Mid-America* 44
(July 1962): 131–45; Howard W. Allen, "Republican Reformers and Foreign Policy, 1913–1917," *Mid-America* 44 (Oct. 1962): 222–29; Walter A.
Sutton, "Progressive Republican Senators and the Submarine Crisis, 1915–
1916," *Mid-America* 47 (Apr. 1965): 75–88; idem, "Republican Progressive Senators and Preparedness, 1915–1916," *Mid-America* 52 (July 1970):
155–76; Barton J. Bernstein and Franklin A. Leib, "Progressive Republican
Senators and American Imperialism, 1898–1916: A Reappraisal," *Mid-
America* 50 (July 1968): 163–206; John Milton Cooper, Jr., "Progressivism
and American Foreign Policy: A Reconsideration," *Mid-America* 51 (Oct.
1969): 260–77.

[4] Robert H. Wiebe, *Businessmen and Reform,* pp. 98–100, 144, 210–12;
idem, *The Search for Order, 1877–1920,* pp. 167–68, 188, 201, 236, 229–
55; Gabriel Kolko, *The Triumph of Conservatism,* pp. 1–10, 279–86, and
passim; James Weinstein, *The Corporate Ideal in the Liberal State, 1900–
1918,* pp. 40–91. While these three authors disagree over the value of the
business contribution to the reforms of the Progressive era, they concur that
business was deeply involved in the movement.

[5] John W. Rollins, "The Anti-Imperialists and Twentieth Century Amer-
ican Foreign Policy," *Studies on the Left* 3, no. 1 (1962): 9–24; John P.
Campbell, "Taft, Roosevelt, and the Arbitration Treaties of 1911," *Journal
of American History* 53 (Sept. 1966): 288, 290; William E. Leuchtenburg,
"The Progressive Movement and American Foreign Policy," *Mississippi
Valley Historical Review* 39 (Dec. 1952): 483–504; William Appleman
Williams, *The Contours of American History,* pp. 363–70, 376–77, 395,
413–24; idem, *The Tragedy of American Diplomacy,* pp. 18–63; Gabriel
Almond, *The American People and Foreign Policy* (New York, 1960; re-
print of 1950 Harcourt Brace ed.), p. 52.

[6] For representative examples see: *Nation's Business* 6 (May 1918): 32,
74; *Iron Age* 102 (24 Oct. 1918): 1038; 104 (14 Aug. 1919): 454; 104 (11
Dec. 1919): 1218–19; 105 (5 Feb. 1920): 419; *Journal of the American
Bankers Association* (hereafter cited as *ABA Journal*) 11 (Sept. 1918): 193;
12 (Nov. 1919): 250; 13 (Sept. 1920): 136; 13 (Nov. 1920): 268, 277–81;
Coast Banker 25 (Dec. 1920): 669; Frank A. Vanderlip, Abstract of Speech
before the Economic Club of New York, 25 Feb. 1920, Frank A. Vanderlip
Papers, Columbia University (hereafter cited as Vanderlip Papers); Paul M.
Warburg to Asst. Sec. of Treasury Russell Leffingwell, 4 Feb. 1920, and ad-

dresses delivered 6 Dec. 1918 and 2 Apr. 1919, Box Aug. 1918–1931, Paul
M. Warburg Papers, Yale University Library (hereafter cited as Paul M.
Warburg Papers); Morrell Heald, "Business Thought in the Twenties: Social
Responsibility," *American Quarterly* 13 (Summer 1961): 127, fn. 3; Wein-
stein, *Corporate Ideal*, pp. x–xi.

  [7] Edward Chase Kirkland, *Dream and Thought in the Business Community, 1860–1900* (Chicago, 1964; reprint of 1954 Cornell Univ. Press
ed.), pp. 145–67; John G. Cawelti, *Apostles of the Self-Made Man* (Chicago,
1965), pp. 184–99; James W. Prothro, *The Dollar Decade*, pp. 54–59;
Charles Norman Fay, *Business in Politics: Considerations for Business Leaders,* pp. vii–xi, 157, 166–74; Heald, "Business Thought," pp. 126–39; idem,
"Management's Responsibility to Society: The Growth of an Idea," *Business
History Review* 31 (Winter 1957): 375–84; *Wall Street Journal*, 14 May
1920, p. 1.

  [8] *Coast Banker* 23 (Sept. 1919): 292; Paul M. Warburg, "Some Phases of
Financial Reconstruction," address delivered 6 Dec. 1918, p. 3, Box Aug.
1918–1931, Paul M. Warburg Papers; *Recent Economic Changes,* 2: 849.

  [9] The following citations refer to statements which can be considered atypical or antinormal according to the definition given in the text. Because such
references in business journals were so numerous between 1919 and 1921,
only the most representative samples will be cited here: *American Industries* 19 (June 1919): 18; 20 (Aug. 1919): 41; 21 (Jan. 1921): 22;
Annalist 15 (24 Jan. 1920): 69; 15 (26 Jan. 1920): 147–48; 15 (21 June
1920): 821; *Coast Banker* 24 (May 1920): 579; 24 (June 1920): 694; 25
(Aug. 1920): 153; *Iron Age* 105 (13 May 1920): 1389; 106 (29 July
1920): 273; *Nation's Business* 7 (Feb. 1919): 10; 7 (Apr. 1919): 34; 8
(Apr. 1920): 21; Philadelphia Board of Trade, *88th Annual Report*, 24 Jan.
1921, p. 33; *Wall Street Journal*, 1 March 1919, p. 1; 6 Jan. 1920, p. 1; 2
Nov. 1921, p. 3; George W. Perkins, "The Man of the Future," Columbia
University speech, 9 Dec. 1919, Box 31, George W. Perkins Papers, Columbia University (hereafter cited as Perkins Papers); Henry Morgenthau, Sr.,
address, 2 Mar. 1919, p. 4, Box 23, Henry Morgenthau, Sr., Papers, Library
of Congress (hereafter cited as Morgenthau, Sr., Papers); Mary Jane Matz,
The Many Lives of Otto Kahn, p. 207; John Hays Hammond, "Enlightened
Self-Interest Most Effective Surety of Peace," *Annalist* 17 (7 Mar. 1921):
302; Herbert Hoover, "Momentous Conference," *ABA Journal* 13 (Jan.
1921): 462–63.

  [10] F. G. Young, "Oregon's Abundant Energy in War Work to Be Turned
to Oregon Planning and Development," *Commonwealth Review* 1 (Apr.
1920): 48; *Iron Age* 101 (2 May 1918): 1150; 103 (9 Jan. 1919): 116; 103
(27 Feb. 1919): 551; *Coast Banker* 21 (Dec. 1918): 550; 25 (Aug. 1920):
153; *Pacific Banker* editorials for 2, 9, and 16 Nov. 1918, p. 1; Newton D.
Baker to Julius Rosenwald, 29 July 1918, "Letters and Documents in Time
of Peace and War," p. 10, Julius Rosenwald Papers, American Jewish Archives (hereafter cited as Rosenwald Papers).

[11] *Iron Age* 102 (4 July 1918): 11; 103 (27 Mar. 1919): 821; 103 (1 May 1919): 1153; *Wall Street Journal*, 26 Jan. 1918, p. 1; *Magazine of Wall Street* 21 (2 Feb. 1918): 619; National Association of Manufacturers (hereafter cited as NAM), *Proceedings*, 1918, p. 242.

[12] *Bankers Magazine* 99 (July 1919): 41–42; *ABA Journal* 11 (Feb. 1919): 416; 13 (Jan. 1921): 463; *Coast Banker* 22 (Sept. 1919): 9; *Iron Age* 102 (18 July 1918): 138–39; 102 (26 Dec. 1918): 1593; *American Industries* 19 (June 1919): 35; 19 (July 1919): 17–18; 20 (Aug. 1919): 22; 21 (Oct. 1920): 22–23; Cleveland Chamber of Commerce, *Annual*, 17 Apr. 1917, p. 64; 19 Apr. 1921, p. 21; *Nation's Business* 6 (May 1918): 23; 8 (Mar. 1920): 81–82, 84; *Pacific Banker*, 1 Nov. 1919, p. 2; David Brody, "The Rise and Decline of Welfare Capitalism," in *Change and Continuity in Twentieth-Century America: The 1920's*, ed. John Braeman, Robert H. Bremner, and David Brody, pp. 147–60; Otis Pease, *The Responsibilities of American Advertising: Private Control and Public Influence, 1920–1940* (New Haven, 1958), pp. 1–86, passim; Merle Curti, "The Changing Concept of 'Human Nature' in the Literature of American Advertising," *Business History Review* 41 (Winter 1967): 335–57; Fay, *Business in Politics*, pp. 34–46; Albert K. Steigerwalt, *The National Association of Manufacturers, 1895–1914: A Study in Business Leadership* (hereafter cited as Steigerwalt, *NAM*), pp. 103–17, 170–71; Wiebe, *Search for Order*, pp. 209–10; Heald, "Business Thought," pp. 126–39; Alfred P. Sloan, Jr., *Adventures of a White Collar Man*, pp. 145–54; Matz, *Otto Kahn*, pp. 205–6; Otto Kahn, *Of Many Things*, pp. 267–70; Williams, *Tragedy*, pp. 128–32; Albert U. Romasco, *The Poverty of Abundance: Hoover, the Nation, the Depression* (New York, 1964), pp. 20–23, 97–105; Hoover, *Memoirs*, 2: 101–8; John D. Rockefeller, Jr., *The Personal Relation in Industry*, pp. 9–12; Henry Ford, *My Philosophy of Industry*, pp. 100–107.

[13] *Wall Street Journal*, 9 Nov. 1918, p. 1; 18 Dec. 1918, p. 1; *Magazine of Wall Street* 23 (7 Dec. 1918): 257; *Annalist* 13 (12 May 1919): 475; 17 (17 Jan. 1921): 108; Philadelphia Board of Trade, *87th Annual Report*, 26 Jan. 1920, pp. 21, 30, 32; *Nation's Business* 8 (July 1920): 17; Prothro, *Dollar Decade*, pp. 87–91, 111–12, 141–50, 157–64, 189–92, 197–203; John Nellis Stalker, Jr., "The National Association of Manufacturers: A Study in Ideology" (Ph.D. dissertation, University of Wisconsin, 1950), pp. 276–85, 292–96, 313–20, 420–24 (hereafter cited as Stalker, "NAM"); Fay, *Business in Politics*, pp. 1–21, 135–53; Weinstein, *Corporate Ideal*, pp. 251–52.

[14] Wiebe, *Search for Order*, pp. 222–23, 235–36, 295–302; Kolko, *Triumph of Conservatism*, pp. 286–87; Robert D. Cuff, "A 'Dollar-a-Year Man' in Government: George N. Peek and the War Industries Board," *Business History Review* 41 (Winter 1967): 404–20; Paul A. Koistinen, "The 'Industrial-Military Complex' in Historical Perspective: World War I," *Business History Review* 41 (Winter 1967), pp. 378–403; idem, "The 'Industrial-Military Complex' in Historical Perspective: The InterWar Years," *Journal of American History* 56 (Mar. 1970): 819–35; Gerald D. Nash, "Experiments

in Industrial Mobilization: WIB and NRA," *Mid-America* 45 (July 1963): 157–67; J. Richard Snyder, "Coolidge, Costigan and the Tariff Commission," *Mid-America* 50 (April 1968): 131–48; Thomas C. Blaisdell, Jr., *The Federal Trade Commission: An Experiment in the Control of Business* (New York, 1932), pp. 287–311; G. Cullom Davis, "The Transformation of the Federal Trade Commission, 1914–1929," *MVHR* 49 (Dec. 1962): 437–55; Warren G. Harding, "Less Government in Business and More Business in Government," *The World's Work,* Nov. 1920, pp. 25–27.

[15] H. W. Arndt, *The Economic Lessons of the Nineteen-Thirties,* pp. 10–12, 228.

[16] Historians and economists have referred to this attempt on the part of leading American businessmen and politicians by a variety of terms ranging from liberal-capitalist internationalism, American corporatism, world community of interest, and the internationalization of business, to simply Yankee imperialism.

[17] The basic long-term economic trend which escaped notice at the time was the gradually increasing stagnation and rigidity of the advanced capitalist economies in this century. Using the U.S. as an example it has been argued that only a series of wars and certain external stimuli such as technological innovations represented primarily by the growth of the automobile industry have prevented a steady decline in American economic expansion since 1900. The periodic appearance of relatively high unemployment figures (the average for the "prosperous" 1920s was 5 percent), perennial surplus marketing problems, the shrinking rate of net capital formation after 1925 (except for war-related periods) as manifested in declining investment and growth rates and declining utilization of manufacturing capacity—all have been cited as evidence of the "creeping stagnation" of the American economy. And for the world as a whole "the decline in the long-term rate of expansion . . . has tended to diminish the mobility of resources." This has meant an increased rigidity within capitalist economies in terms of the price/income levels, the mobility of labor, and the amount of capital necessary to initiate new enterprises. Since World War I such rigidity has contributed to the continuous malfunctioning of the international gold standard system by rendering less and less effective its built-in price and market mechanism for making economic adjustments within and between nations. For further details about these theories concerning economic stagnation and rigidity, see: Arndt, *Economic Lessons,* pp. 284–85, 289–91 (fn. 1), 293, and passim; Paul A. Baran and Paul M. Sweezy, *Monopoly Capitalism: An Essay on the American Economic and Social Order,* pp. 218–48; Peter d'A. Jones, *The Consumer Society: A History of American Capitalism* (New York, 1965), pp. 281–300.

[18] For example, this would have required the United States, as the world's leading creditor and surplus exporter, to inflate greatly its domestic credit structure, especially between 1927 and 1929, in order to encourage imports and shift labor and capital away from industries competing with foreign imports. Aside from the general failure of the United States to adapt its

economy to its new world position through a policy of conscious inflation and productive (self-liquidating) loans abroad, a number of factors prevented the "automatic" functioning of the gold standard system after the war, in addition to the long-term economic trend discussed in note 17. They included: the problem of "hot money" (the rapid and erratic transfer of short-term capital), a new feature of international finance following the war; inadequate exchange rates for national currencies; and the massive economic maladjustments between nations as represented by the Allied war debts and German reparations. See: Arndt, *Economic Lessons,* pp. 13–14, 223, 232, 283–87, 290, 292–95; Elmus R. Wicker, "Federal Reserve Monetary Policy, 1922–33: A Reinterpretation," *Journal of Political Economy* 73 (Aug. 1963): 337–43.

[19] Arndt, *Economic Lessons,* pp. 12, 234, 283, 289; Wicker, "Federal Reserve Monetary Policy," pp. 235–38; Giulio Pontecorvo, "Investment Banking and Speculation in the Late 1920's," *Business History Review* 32 (Summer 1958): 166–68, 170, 188.

[20] Arndt, *Economic Lessons,* pp. 221–34. See my chapters 3–5 for further details.

[21] Arndt, *Economic Lessons,* pp. 224, 229, 234, 289–90, 294; Carl P. Parrini, *Heir to Empire: United States Economic Diplomacy, 1916–1923,* pp. 40–71.

[22] Cleona Lewis, *The United States and Foreign Investment Problems,* p. 24; idem, *America's Stake in International Investments,* pp. 449–52; Raymond F. Mikesell, *United States Economic Policy and International Relations,* pp. 8–10, 12–13, 18–20; William B. Kelly, Jr., "Antecedents of Present Commercial Policy, 1922–1934," in *Studies in United States Commercial Policy,* ed. William B. Kelly, Jr., p. 5; Arndt, *Economic Lessons,* pp. 13, 19, 31.

[23] In the nineteenth century most international loans had been self-liquidating, but after World War I reconstruction loans, whether sponsored by private banking houses in the United States and other nations or by the League of Nations, were not because they were often "used to cover budget deficits and to provide the basis for currency stabilization," rather than the positive economic development necessary for future interest and amortization payments. See Arndt, *Economic Lessons,* pp. 226–27, 293; Parrini, *Heir to Empire,* pp. 189–90; and my chapters 3 and 4.

[24] Vanderlip, 10 Feb. 1920 statement, handwritten manuscript, probably dating from 1922, Vanderlip Papers; Vanderlip statements in *Iron Age* 103 (15 May 1919): 1315; 103 (18 Sept. 1919): 793; Warburg, addresses delivered 6 Dec. 1918, 2 Apr. 1919, and 30 Apr. 1920, Box 1918–1931, Paul M. Warburg Papers; Hoover, statements and memoranda in "Financial Cooperation between the U.S. and Europe" folder 5 (hereafter cited as Financial Coop. folder), Hoover Papers, Stanford Univ.; Hoover, quoted in *Wall Street Journal,* 25 Apr. 1921, p. 2. It should be noted that these complexities and dangers became apparent to later generations only after extensive research and hindsight. No attempt will be made therefore to dwell on the

fallacious aspects of economic thought from 1920 and 1933, or to stress the domestic economic considerations which tempered Hoover's internationalism, distinguishing it from that of eastern financiers, such as his concern for obtaining as much American economic self-sufficiency as possible.

[25] In the period 1918–1920 the NAM officially supported high tariffs to protect the domestic market and looked forward to American domination of world trade, ignoring the ideas of cooperation and economic interdependence. To an even greater degree this narrow, nationalistic point of view was also held by the American Protective Tariff League and the New England Home Market Club. All three groups represented the small or medium-sized manufacturer. See Stalker, "NAM," pp. 283–84; Carl Philip Parrini, "American Empire and Creating a Community of Interest" (Ph.D. dissertation, Univ. of Wisconsin, 1963), p. 266.

[26] Vanderlip, address delivered 25 Apr. 1920, and undated 15-page statement (beginning with words "another momentous inheritance of the World War. . . ."), Vanderlip Papers; Lester V. Chandler, *Benjamin Strong: Central Banker*, p. 250; *Magazine of Wall Street* 26 (30 Oct. 1920): 892; 27 (19 Mar. 1921): 665; 28 (9 July 1921): 303; *Iron Age* 103 (2 Jan. 1919): 73–74; 103 (1 May 1919): 1180–81; Parrini, "American Empire," pp. 80–82, 236, 266; Davis to James M. Cox, 17 Sept. 1920, Box 10, Norman H. Davis Papers, Library of Congress (hereafter cited as Davis Papers); Hoover, interview in *Chicago Daily News*, 15 Sept. 1920, Hoover Speeches and Addresses, 1915–1923, Hoover Papers, Stanford Univ.; Williams, *Contours*, pp. 425–26; U.S. Chamber of Commerce, *9th Annual Board of Directors Report*, Apr. 1921, p. 8; *Nation's Business* 7 (Jan. 1919): 11–12, 61; 7 (May 1919): 24, 56, 59; 7 (Nov. 1919): 21; 7 (Dec. 1919): 12, 19.

[27] Paul P. Abrahams, "American Bankers and the Economic Tactics of Peace: 1919," *Journal of American History* 56 (Dec. 1969): 572–83.

[28] Parrini, *Heir To Empire*, pp. 55–57; idem, "American Empire," pp. 45–48, 54, 70, 74, 76, 94, 113, 136.

[29] Parrini, *Heir To Empire*, pp. 55–62; *ABA Journal* 11 (Aug. 1918): 68–70; *Iron Age* 102 (7 Nov. 1918): 1141; Vanderlip, press statement, 10 Feb. 1920, abstract of speech before the Economic Club of New York, 25 Feb. 1920, undated 15-page statement, undated speech (beginning "The great war increased the internal debts of the belligerents. . . .")—all in Vanderlip Papers; Vanderlip to Col. Edward M. House, 29 Apr. 1919, Norman H. Davis and Thomas W. Lamont to Asst. Sec. of Treasury Russell Leffingwell, 27 May 1919, secret report of economic advisers to President Wilson, 9 May 1919—all in Box 16a, Davis Papers; Hoover, Financial Coop. Folder, Hoover Papers, Stanford Univ.; *Wall Street Journal*, 23 Aug. 1920, p. 2; Paul M. Warburg, addresses delivered 6 Dec. 1918, and 2 Apr. 1919, Box 1918–1931, Paul M. Warburg Papers; John Hays Hammond, address delivered 5 Mar. 1919, Hammond Papers.

[30] Parrini, *Heir To Empire*, pp. 63–65, 101–37; Charles H. Sabin, "Should Act Promptly," *Coast Banker* 23 (Aug. 1919): 113.

[31] For details see Parrini, *Heir To Empire*, pp. 72–100. Two types of for-

eign-trade financing corporations were established under the Edge Act: one kind would function as short-term acceptance corporations and the other as long-term debenture issue corporations. Under the influence of the House of Morgan, however, most investment bankers before the 1920–1921 depression assumed an indifferent or cautious attitude toward the latter. The results of the act prior to 1922 clearly represented a temporary victory for the interests represented by the House of Morgan over those represented by the National City Bank.

[32] Abrahams, "American Bankers," pp. 579–83; Hoover, addresses delivered 23 Feb. 1920, and 7 June 1920, in Hoover Speeches and Addresses, 1915–1923, Hoover Papers, Stanford Univ.; Hoover, *Memoirs,* 2: 13–14; *ABA Journal* 12 (Mar. 1920): 520–21; 13 (Jan. 1921): 457–69; *Magazine of Wall Street* 27 (Mar. 1921): 733; *Iron Age* 105 (12 Feb. 1920): 490–91. The Wilson administration ended most government loans to Europe by September 1919, suspended the export credits of the War Finance Corporation against the wishes of large manufacturers, export-import groups, and most bankers, and discontinued the War Industries Board before it had an opportunity to supervise the economic demobilization of the country. Only with respect to the rehabilitation of foreign currencies did the United States assume a major cooperative economic function in the postwar world and this was through the Federal Reserve Board which was legally independent of the government. See Wicker, "Federal Reserve Monetary Policy," pp. 325, 334–37; Arndt, *Economic Lessons,* p. 232; Herbert Stein, *The Fiscal Revolution in America,* p. 15.

[33] Parrini, *Heir to Empire,* pp. 252–54; N. Gordon Levin, Jr., *Woodrow Wilson and World Politics,* pp. 1–3.

[34] Kolko, *Triumph of Conservatism,* pp. 2–3, 58–60; Williams, *Contours,* pp. 420–38; Richard N. Gardner, *Sterling-Dollar Diplomacy: Anglo-American Collaboration in the Reconstruction of Multilateral Trade* (Oxford, 1956), pp. 2–9; Levin, *Woodrow Wilson,* pp. 4–10. Although Wilson began to perceive the prerequisites for an integrated economic and political foreign policy during the war, they were not highly developed in the minds of most politicians and businessmen by 1920 with the possible exception of Hoover and a few international financiers, some of whom were former Wilsonians.

[35] *ABA Journal* 11 (Aug. 1918): 69; *American Industries* 19 (July 1919): 7–8; *Annalist* 14 (24 Nov. 1919): 664; *Bankers Magazine* 98 (Apr. 1919): 407; 98 (June 1919): 655; *Bradstreet's* 48 (1 May 1920): 288; 48 (8 May 1920): 304; Cleveland Chamber of Commerce, *Annual,* 20 Apr. 1920, p. 109; *Coast Banker* 22 (Apr. 1919): 343; 23 (May 1919): 351; 23 (Aug. 1919): 118; 23 (Sept. 1919): 227; *Iron Age* 103 (29 May 1919): 1416; 104 (11 Sept. 1919): 730; *Magazine of Wall Street* 25 (Feb. 1920): 521; 26 (15 May 1920): 3; *Nation's Business* 6 (Dec. 1918): 16–17; 7 (Mar. 1919): 21; 7 (Dec. 1919): 64; Newton D. Baker to George Foster Peabody, 20 Jan. 1920, Box 185, Newton D. Baker Papers, Library of Congress (hereafter cited as Baker Papers); Bernard Baruch, *The Public Years,* pp. 131, 134,

138; Norman H. Davis to President Wilson, 26 Nov. 1919, and Davis to Arthur Sweetser, 3 Sept. 1920, Box 62, Davis to Joseph Tumulty, 1 Dec. 1919, Box 63, Davis to Albert Rathbone, 21, 29 Oct. 1919, 10 Jan. 1920, Box 48, Davis to Governor Cox, 17 Sept. 1920, Box 10—all in Davis Papers; Allan Nevins and Frank Ernest Hill, *Ford*, vol. 2, *Expansion and Challenge, 1915–1933*, pp. 129, 300; Hoover to President Wilson, 12 Nov. 1919, in Hoover-Wilson Correspondence, 1918–1920, addresses delivered 16 Sept. 1919 and 23 Feb. 1920, interview in *Washington Star*, 18 Mar. 1920, in Speeches and Addresses—all in Hoover Papers, Stanford Univ.; Thomas W. Lamont, *Across World Frontiers*, pp. 194, 218; Vance McCormick, statement, 17 July 1919, and R. S. Brewster to L. P. Sheldon, 4 Apr. 1919, Box 39, Vance McCormick Papers, Yale University (hereafter cited as McCormick Papers); Henry Morgenthau, Sr., "An Appeal to Our Fellow Citizens," 23 Feb. 1919, Box 18, undated two-page statement on League, Box 19, addresses delivered 2 Mar. 1919, and 17 Oct. 1920, and Oscar S. Straus, address delivered 10 Jan. 1919—all in Morgenthau, Sr., Papers; George Foster Peabody to Newton D. Baker, 16 Dec. 1918, 25 Nov. 1919, Box 74, Peabody to Joseph Tumulty, 26 July and 17 Nov. 1919, Peabody to editor of *New York Times*, Box 75—all in George Foster Peabody Papers, Library of Congress (hereafter cited as Peabody Papers); Louise Ware, *George Foster Peabody*, pp. 178, 183–85, 195; John H. Garraty, *Right-Hand Man: The Life of George W. Perkins*, p. 385; Elihu Root to Henry Cabot Lodge, 7 Mar. 1919, and 26 Sept. 1919, Box 161, Elihu Root Papers, Library of Congress (hereafter cited as Root Papers); Julius Rosenwald, *Denver Express* clipping for 27 Oct. 1919, Microfilm SB/5/28, Rosenwald Papers; Cyrus Adler, *Jacob H. Schiff* (London, 1929), 2: 196–97, 208; William Howard Taft to Oscar S. Straus, 19 Jan. 1919, Straus to Bainbridge Colby, 5 Apr. 1920, and Straus to President Wilson, 4 Mar. 1920, Box 15, Straus Diary, Box 24—all in Oscar S. Straus Papers; Chandler, *Strong*, pp. 146, 263; Frank A. Vanderlip, interview with International News Service, 21 Aug. 1920, Vanderlip Papers; Paul M. Warburg to Norman H. Davis, and undated letter on world situation, Box Aug. 1918–1931, Paul M. Warburg Papers.

[36] Selig Adler, *The Isolationist Impulse*, pp. 55–112; Harold Tiffany Butler, "Partisan Positions on Isolationism vs. Internationalism, 1918–1933" (D.S.S. dissertation, Syracuse Univ., 1963), pp. 48, 50–56, 603–6, 653, 667; Harvey O'Connor, *Mellon's Millions*, pp. 115–16; Robert James Maddox, *William E. Borah and American Foreign Policy*, pp. 56, 59–60, 69–70.

[37] Those sections of the treaty that particularly irked this segment of the business community included the one on reparations (no reasonable sum had been set for Germany to pay), the one establishing mandates, especially those in oil-rich areas, and most of the articles in Part 10 placing numerous economic restrictions on Germany. See: Hoover, *Memoirs*, 1: 459, 461–72; Vanderlip, address delivered to American Manufacturers Export Association, 30 Oct. 1918, reported in *Iron Age* 102 (7 Nov. 1918): 1141; abstract of Vanderlip's speech before the Economic Club of New York, 25 Feb. 1920,

Vanderlip Papers; Vanderlip, *What Next in Europe?* pp. 64–84; idem, *From Farm Boy to Financier,* p. 301; Otto Kahn, *Of Many Things,* pp. 277, 285, 322, 332; idem, *Our Economic and Other Problems,* pp. 359, 363–67; Stephen Birmingham, *Our Crowd: The Great Jewish Families of New York* (New York, 1967), pp. 317–23; Matz, *Otto Kahn,* pp. 196–99; Committee of American Business Men (including 29 Nov. 1919 letter from Kahn to Senator Poindexter) to State Dept., 22 Dec. 1919, File 763.72119/8543, National Archives, Record Group 59 (hereafter cited as NA, RG); Lamont, *Across World Frontiers,* p. 220; Lamont to Norman H. Davis, 26 Jan. 1939, Box 33, and Vanderlip to Colonel Edward M. House, 29 Apr. 1919, Box 16a, Davis Papers; Chandler, *Strong,* pp. 143–45; Parrini, "American Empire," pp. 237, 239, 266 (fn. 270); idem, *Heir to Empire,* pp. 14, 138–41; *Wall Street Journal,* 23 Aug. 1920, p. 2; 1 Sept. 1921, p. 1; *Magazine of Wall Street* 26 (24 July 1920): 373–74; *Pacific Banker,* 9 Oct., 2 Dec. 1920, p. 1; *Bankers Magazine* 98 (Apr. 1919): 405–13; 99 (Dec. 1919): 754; 100 (Feb. 1920): 209.

[38] So in the name of American "freedom of action," Wilson's business advisers at Paris insisted on liquidating the intergovernmental economic controls, the only existing machinery for international cooperation which had survived the armistice, and rejected John Maynard Keynes's plan for cooperative reconstruction financing based on government guaranteed bonds. See: Arndt, *Economic Lessons,* pp. 222–23; William Diamond, *The Economic Thought of Woodrow Wilson* (Baltimore, 1943), pp. 166–67, 184–87; Hoover, *Memoirs,* 1: 456–57, 466; Hoover to Wilson, 11 Apr. 1919, Hoover-Wilson Correspondence, Hoover Papers, Stanford Univ.; Norman H. Davis, Thomas W. Lamont, Bernard Baruch, and Vance McCormick to Wilson, "Observations upon the European Economic Situation," Apr. 1919, Davis and Lamont to Leffingwell, 28 Apr. and 27 May 1919, Wilson to Lloyd George, 5 May 1919—all in Box 16a, Davis Papers; Baruch, *Public Years,* pp. 98–99.

[39] Parrini, *Heir to Empire,* pp. 138–41; Davis to John Maynard Keynes, 19 Mar. 1920, Box 32, Davis Papers; Baruch, *Public Years,* p. 134; Margaret L. Coit, *Mr. Baruch,* p. 289.

[40] Hoover to Wilson, 14 May, 3 June (oral remarks), 5 June 1919—all cited in Hoover, *Memoirs,* 1: 463–67; Coit, *Mr. Baruch,* pp. 269, 279; Elting E. Morison, *Turmoil and Tradition,* p. 207; Daniel M. Smith, *Aftermath of War,* p. 22 (fn. 56).

[41] See notes 35, 37 to this chapter.

[42] A total of twenty-one pro-League communiqués from individual businessmen and business groups were entered into the *Congressional Record* by Republican and Democratic senators between 1919 and 1920. Only one was in opposition to the League, according to Butler, "Partisan Positions," pp. 576–77. This by no means represented all of the business opinions sent to the Senate, but it is significant that only one negative business opinion was recorded by Republican senators. Belated attempts by financial interests to

bring pressure to bear upon the Senate were reported only in the *Annalist* 14 (24 Nov. 1919): 664.

[43] Davis to Keynes, 19 Mar. 1920, Box 32, Davis Papers; Baruch, *Public Years,* p. 124.

[44] See note 35 to this chapter.

[45] Wiebe, *Businessmen and Reform,* pp. 117–18. It is Wiebe's contention that the only large group of "big and moderately prosperous businessmen" who were not Republicans were southerners and "they deferred to the dominant Republican sentiment when they did speak." He also notes (p. 252) that "no business journal was avowedly Democratic; many were Republican."

[46] See note 35 above with particular reference to *Bradstreet's, Bankers Magazine,* Cleveland Chamber of Commerce, *Magazine of Wall Street,* Peabody, Morgenthau, Davis, Taft, Hoover, Vanderlip, and Straus.

[47] See note 35 above.

[48] See notes 35 and 37 above, plus Hoover to Warren G. Harding, 2 Aug. 1920, Hoover Correspondence, Jan.–Aug. 1920, and statement in *Chicago Daily News,* 15 Sept. 1920, Speeches and Addresses, Hoover to William Allen White, 13 June 1924, Hoover-Wilson Correspondence—all in Hoover Papers, Stanford Univ.; Hoover to Warren Gregory, 30 Mar. 1920, Box 7, Irving Fisher Papers, Yale Univ. (hereafter cited as Fisher Papers); Hoover, *Memoirs,* 2: 11–13; idem, *The Ordeal of Woodrow Wilson* (New York, 1958), pp. 268, 282–83.

[49] Hoover, *Memoirs,* 2: 352, 378 (fn. 8); Vanderlip, *What Next in Europe?* pp. 64–84; Kahn, *Of Many Things,* pp. 356–77; Henry Ford, *Today and Tomorrow,* pp. 24–25, 250; Butler, "Partisan Positions," pp. 384–86, 666; *Coast Banker* 29 (Nov. 1922): 43–44; *Wall Street Journal,* 17 July 1923, p. 2; 17 Sept. 1924, p. 11; 14 Apr. 1925, p. 1; 29 Mar. 1926, p. 9; *Chicago Journal of Commerce,* 8 Jan. 1923, p. 4; 21 Nov. 1933, p. 16.

[50] For an example of Democratic bitterness, see: Newton D. Baker to Judge John H. Clarke, 8 Nov. 1922, and Baker to Josephus Daniels, 17 Nov. 1927, 29 Feb. 1932, Box 59, Baker Papers.

[51] Norman A. Graebner, ed., *Ideas and Diplomacy* (New York, 1964), p. ix; Robert Endicott Osgood, *Ideals and Self-Interest in America's Foreign Relations,* pp. 88, 278; Butler, "Partisan Positions," pp. 550–72; John P. Campbell, "Taft, Roosevelt and the Arbitration Treaties of 1911," *JAH* 53 (Sept. 1966): 279–98.

[52] Adler, *Isolationist Impulse,* pp. 31–32, 111–12; Edwin L. James, "Our World Power and Moral Influence," *International Digest* 1 (Oct. 1930): 21–24; Williams, "Legend of Isolationism," pp. 5–7; idem, *The Shaping of American Diplomacy* (Chicago, 1956), 2:652–56; Albert K. Weinberg, "The Historical Meaning of the American Doctrine of Isolation," *American Political Science Review* 34 (June 1940): 539–47; President's Research Committee on Social Trends, *Recent Social Trends in the United States* (New York, 1934), 1: lxix (hereafter cited as *Recent Social Trends*).

[53] Osgood, *Ideals,* pp. 262, 264; Graebner, *Ideas and Diplomacy,* pp. 462,

464, 487–99; Levin, *Woodrow Wilson,* pp. 13–14, 16; Williams, *Tragedy,* pp. 106–23; Richard Coke Lower, "Hiram Johnson and the Progressive Denouement" (Ph.D. dissertation, Univ. of California at Berkeley, 1969), Chapter 7; Maddox, *Borah,* pp. xvii–xviii, 6–9, 26, 44–45, 50–51, 120–21, 152. The Borah-Johnson irreconcilable faction has been singled out because it was the best known at the time. However, there were differing points of view even among these bitter-end opponents of the League, as Ralph A. Stone points out in "The 'Irreconcilables' Alternatives to the League of Nations," *Mid-America* 49 (July 1967): 163–73.

⁵⁴ Hoover, address delivered 23 Feb. 1920, in Speeches and Addresses, Hoover Papers, Stanford Univ.; italics added.

Chapter Two

¹ William Allen White, *The Autobiography of William Allen White,* p. 602; John Chalmers Vinson, *The Parchment Peace,* p. 45; C. Leonard Hoag, *Preface to Preparedness,* p. 1; Herbert Hoover to U.S. Senate, 7 July 1930, Disarmament File-Speech Drafts (hereafter cited as DF-Drafts) and Hoover to Henry Stimson, 24 May 1932, Foreign Affairs File-Disarmament (hereafter cited as FA-Disarm.), both in Herbert Hoover Presidential Papers, Official File (hereafter cited as HHPP), Hoover Library, West Branch, Iowa.

² In addition to insisting that disarmament agreements must rest on good faith rather than inspection and control machinery, the U.S. brought four other principles to every international disarmament meeting. They were: 1) arms limitation agreements should be negotiated "without awaiting complicated measures for providing security"; 2) reduction of land, sea, and air armaments should not be considered together at the same conference; 3) only peacetime levels of armaments should be considered because "any scheme involving the complicated and variable industrial, financial and economic factors" simply complicates the problem; 4) naval disarmament should be dealt with separately by a limited number of naval powers, while land and air disarmament constitutes a regional problem which varies from area to area. See U.S. Dept. of State, *Papers Relating to the Foreign Relations of the United States* (hereafter cited as *FRP*), *1927,* 1 (Washington, 1942): 164–65.

³ Frederick L. Schuman, "The Impasse of Disarmament," *Current History* 41 (Nov. 1961): 268–69; Walter Millis, "On Disarmament," *The Center Magazine* 1 (Jan. 1968): 38–43. In retrospect Schuman defends the Washington Conference treaties because he thinks it is psychologically and politically impossible to "institutionalize mutual distrust" through international inspection plans. See Schuman, "The Wasted Decades: 1899–1939," *Current History* 46 (June 1964): 326–30.

⁴ Hoag, *Preparedness,* pp. 78–79. The text of the San Francisco resolution is noteworthy because of the predominance of economic arguments.

RESOLVED: That this Chamber of Commerce attributes the decline of our foreign trade and the reduced domestic consumption of manufactures and luxuries to excessive taxation and to the exhaustion of capital and credit. It places hope of a substantial and world-wide recovery upon the success of the Conference for the Limitation of Armaments and urges the Administration to use every effort to bring about a drastic reduction of naval and military expenditure, so that all countries and all classes may be relieved of a staggering burden which threatens some with insolvency and confiscation and all with trade stagnation and unemployment.

Also see Vinson, *Parchment Peace,* p. 84.

[5] Both Vinson and Sprout briefly mention the lack of early business participation in the disarmament movement, but neither attempts to document or analyze the nature or the significance of business attitudes in relation to the movement. See Vinson, *Parchment Peace,* p. 84; Harold and Margaret Sprout, *Toward a New Order of Sea Power,* p. 112. Hoag, on the contrary, maintains that the action taken by the San Francisco Chamber of Commerce on 27 Sept. 1921 was "the single most important action taken by any business organization in the period before the disarmament conference. Various groups had been urging that a convention be called. The San Francisco Chamber of Commerce took the initiative in arranging it." (*Preparedness,* p. 78.) This interpretation simply does not correspond to the facts. It may well be that the San Francisco action was the most important one taken by a business group, but given the date of this action it cannot be considered influential in bringing about the conference, since the conference had been announced in July and formally confirmed in August. It had in fact been "arranged" before the San Francisco resolution was passed.

[6] Memoranda of Conversations of the Secretary of State, 1921–1923, National Archives, Record Group 59.

[7] 49 (12 Feb. 1921): 116; 49 (19 Feb. 1921): 132.

[8] 102 (Mar. 1921): 377–79; 103 (Oct. 1921): 619–20.

[9] 30 Dec. 1920; 1 Jan. 1921; 4 Jan 1921; 13 Jan. 1921; 12 July 1921; 15 Nov. 1921; 8 Mar. 1922; 1 Aug. 1927; 3 Aug. 1928; 10 Dec. 1928 (all on page 1).

[10] 9 (May 1921): 36–38.

[11] *New York World,* 26 Dec. 1920, p. 2; 27 Dec. 1920, p. 2; 28 Dec. 1920, pp. 1–2; 30 Dec. 1920, p. 2; 4 Jan. 1921, p. 2; 11 Jan. 1921, p. 2. In this series the statements by religious spokesmen far outnumbered those by businessmen.

[12] Los Angeles Chamber of Commerce, *1922 Members' Annual,* p. 64; resolution passed by Commerce and Marine Commission of ABA, included in Fred I. Kent to Hughes, 10 Mar. 1922, File 500A 4/389, NA, RG 59; *Magazine of Wall Street* 28 (6 Aug. 1921): 449; 29 (26 Nov. 1921): 79; for Lamont, Goodrich, Warburg, and T. Coleman du Pont, see Files 500A 4/471, 500A 4P81/166, 396, 401—all in NA, RG 59; *Nation's Business* 9 (Oct. 1921): 9–10; 9 (Dec. 1921): 11–12; 10 (June 1922): 20; John Hays Hammond, "Function of International Courts and Means of Enforcing

Their Decisions," speech delivered 14 May 1921, Box 20, Hammond Papers; numerous statements of less-well-known businessmen who publicly supported disarmament can be found in *American Industries* 22 (Nov., Dec. 1921).

[13] American Manufacturers Export Assoc. to Hoover, 23 Nov. 1921, and Hoover to John S. Drum, 19 Sept. 1921, Disarmament Conferences File, 1921–1924 (hereafter cited as DCF-1921–1924); Hoover, "Summary of Achievements of the Dept. of Commerce," 25 July 1924, p. 15, Achievements File-1924 (1)—all in Herbert Hoover Commerce Department Papers, Official File (hereafter cited as HHCD), Hoover Library, West Branch, Iowa.

[14] This lack of functional and sectional divisions is an exception to the idea expressed earlier that the business world tended to unite on foreign policy issues in the 1920s only when an ideological threat was present. Since divisions did appear on the issue of disarmament in the late 1920s and early 1930s, the unity displayed on the Washington Conference must be considered a temporary aberration due to immediate postwar conditions.

[15] There was not a single editorial in the *Nation's Business* during 1921–1922 on the question of disarmament, although the journal did publish a few articles on the subject.

[16] Bethlehem Steel was, by Schwab's own admission, the "largest war materials manufacturing works in the world." See: *Magazine of Wall Street* 29 (26 Nov. 1921): 79; *Iron Age* 108 (24 Nov. 1921): 1344.

[17] *Iron Age* 108 (17 Nov. 1921): 1284–85; *New York World,* 5 Jan. 1921, p. 1; M. O. Hudson, "Private Enterprise and Public War," in *New Republic* pamphlet, *Roads to Peace: A Handbook to the Washington Conference* (New York, 1921), pp. 44–47; Vinson, *Parchment Peace,* p. 229, fn. 5.

[18] Washburn, "Points to Actual Necessity for Limitation," *American Industries* 22 (Nov. 1921): 20.

[19] *Literary Digest* 71 (12 Nov. 1921): 16–17; Sisley Huddleston, "What France Wants," in *Roads to Peace,* p. 37.

[20] 27 (Aug. 1921): 129–30.

[21] 22 (Sept. 1921): 22. For similar statements, see: Philadelphia Board of Trade, *Proceedings,* 23 Jan. 1922, pp. 9–10; Cleveland Chamber of Commerce, *Annual,* 18 Apr. 1922, p. 123; *Coast Banker* 27 (Dec. 1921): 562; 28 (Jan. 1922): 34; *Nation's Business* 9 (May 1921): 36; *Iron Age* 108 (17 Nov. 1921): 1284; *Annalist* 19 (9 Jan. 1922): 41; *Bankers Magazine* 103 (Dec. 1921): 1045–46; 104 (Jan. 1922): 2–3; *Magazine of Wall Street* 19 (7 Jan. 1922): 306–7; *Pacific Banker,* 11 Aug. 1921, p. 1; *Wall Street Journal,* 12 July 1921, p. 1.

[22] *Nation's Business* 9 (Sept. 1921): 7–8; *Coast Banker* 27 (Dec. 1921): 562; Huddleston, "What France Wants," p. 37; George L. Ridgeway, *Merchants of Peace,* pp. 93–94, 150–51.

[23] *New York World,* 26 Dec. 1920, p. 2; 27 Dec. 1920, p. 2; *Nation's Business* 9 (Dec. 1921): 11–12; 10 (5 June 1922): 12–14, 20; *Annalist* 19 (13 Mar. 1922: 315; Hoover, Interview with *Washington Star,* 18 Mar. 1920, in Speeches and Addresses, 1915–1923, Hoover Papers, Stanford

Univ.; John Hays Hammond, "Function of International Courts," 14 May 1921, Hammond Papers; *ABA Journal* 14 (Jan. 1922): 512–13.

[24] *Magazine of Wall Street* 29 (26 Nov. 1921): 77.

[25] Philadelphia Board of Trade, *Proceedings*, 26 Jan. 1923, pp. 11–12; *ABA Journal* 15 (Nov. 1922): 267; *Coast Banker* 27 (Aug. 1921): 129; 27 (Nov. 1921): 451; 28 (Mar. 1922): 263; *Magazine of Wall Street* 28 (3 Sept. 1921): 594; 29 (12 Nov. 1921): 1; 29 (7 Jan. 1922): 299; 29 (18 Feb. 1922): 515; 29 (18 Mar. 1922): 659; *Chicago Journal of Commerce*, 3 Jan. 1922, p. 4; 2 Feb. 1922, p. 1; 6 Feb. 1922, p. 4; *Nation's Business* 10 (June 1922): 14; *American Industries*, 22 (Feb. 1922): 22; *Annalist* 18 (21 Nov. 1921): 483; 18 (5 Dec. 1921): 531, 534; 18 (19 Dec. 1921): 579; 19 (9 Jan. 1922): 108; *Pacific Banker*, 21 July 1921, p. 6; editorial and financial columns, 8 Dec. 1921, p. 1; 15 Dec. 1921, p. 1; *Bradstreet's* 103 (16 July 1921): 469; *Wall Street Journal*, 11 Nov. 1921, p. 8; 22 Nov. 1921, p. 2.

[26] Sprout, *New Order of Sea Power*, p. 101; *Pacific Banker*, 25 Aug. 1921, p. 1.

[27] *Wall Street Journal*, 11 Nov. 1921, p. 8; 22 Nov. 1921, p. 2; 23 Nov. 1921, p. 1.

[28] *Nation's Business* 9 (Nov. 1921): 16–17.

[29] Contemporary business journals never clearly explained how expansion of trade with China would benefit the average American businessman. The implication was that expanding trade meant greater prosperity at home. Exaggerations about the potential of the China market were as rampant after the war as they had been before. See Paul A. Varg, "The Myth of the China Market, 1890–1914," *AHR* 73 (Feb. 1968): 742–58.

[30] Pauline Tompkins, *American-Russian Relations in the Far East*, pp. 164–65, 170–71, 174, 188; Charles Vivier, "The Open Door: An Idea in Action, 1906–1913," *Pacific Historical Review* 24 (Feb. 1955): 49–62; Raymond A. Esthus, "The Changing Concept of the Open Door, 1899–1910," *MVHR* 46 (Dec. 1959): 435–54; William Appleman Williams, *American-Russian Relations, 1781–1947* (New York, 1952), pp. 183–84, 186–89; Betty Glad, *Charles Evans Hughes and the Illusions of Innocence*, pp. 292–96; Carl P. Parrini, *Heir to Empire*, pp. 1–39; Noel Pugach, "Making the Open Door Work: Paul S. Reinsch in China, 1913–1919," *Pacific Historical Review* 38 (May 1969): 157–76.

[31] Tompkins, *American-Russian Relations*, pp. 171–74, 178; Raymond Leslie Buell, *The Washington Conference* (New York, 1922), pp. 299–300, 311–13; Glad, *Hughes*, p. 297; Robert T. Pollard, *China's Foreign Relations, 1917–1931* (New York, 1933), pp. 239–47; Russell H. Fifield, "Secretary Hughes and the Shantung Question," *Pacific Historical Review* 23 (Nov. 1954): 373–85.

[32] Dorothy Borg, *American Policy and the Chinese Revolution, 1925–1928*, pp. 8–13; Richard Dean Burns, "Inspection of the Mandates, 1919–1941," *Pacific Historical Review* 37 (Nov. 1968): 447, 449, 451; Schuman,

"Impasse of Disarmament," pp. 268–69. Both Burns and Schuman agree that when the United States finally did endorse the idea of international inspection this was a negative diplomatic step reflecting a deteriorating world situation, in which ideological considerations were playing an ever-increasing role.

· [33] For the standard set of American disarmament principles see n. 2 of this chapter; Robert K. Murray, *The Harding Era,* pp. 163–64; Parrini, *Heir to Empire,* p. 263.

[34] Carl P. Parrini, "American Empire and Creating a Community of Interest" (Ph.D. dissertation, Univ. of Wisconsin, 1963), pp. 283–84; idem, *Heir to Empire,* p. 253 (fn. 8); Glad, *Hughes,* pp. 297–99; Hughes, quoted in Fifield, "Shantung Question," p. 374.

[35] Murray, *Harding Era,* p. 163; *FRP, 1928,* 1: 235–51. Major European nations had advocated a system of inspection and control during the entire decade, but unlike Soviet Russia they did not call also for complete disarmament. It is interesting to note that as ideological tension increased between the U.S. and the USSR after World War II, they reversed the positions they had originally assumed in the 1920s on the question of international supervision of disarmament agreements.

[36] Davis to Ray Stannard Baker, 3 Mar. 1922, Davis to James M. Cox, 17 Sept. 1920, Davis to Senator Carter Glass, 16 Feb. 1922, Davis to Cordell Hull, 19, 20 Dec. 1921, 23 Feb. 1922, Davis to William G. McAdoo, 11 Feb., 17, 25 April 1922, Davis to Senator Key Pittman, 7 Mar. 1922, Davis to George W. Wickersham, 9, 10, 15, 17 Mar. 1922, and replies from these men, Boxes 3, 10, 26, 40, 47, 67, Davis Papers; Davis, "American Foreign Policy: A Democratic View," *Foreign Affairs* 3 (15 Sept. 1924): 27–29; Bernard Baruch, *The Public Years,* pp. 265–66.

[37] Robert James Maddox, *William E. Borah and American Foreign Policy,* pp. 107–17; Selig Adler, *The Isolationist Impulse,* p. 142; Harold Tiffany Butler, "Partisan Positions on Isolationism vs. Internationalism, 1918–1933" (D.S.S. dissertation, Syracuse Univ., 1963), pp. 118–19, 125; Newton D. Baker to Raymond B. Fosdick, 28 Mar. 1922, Box 99, Baker Papers; Murray, *Harding Era,* p. 165.

[38] Perhaps the best defense that can be made of the demand for parity is that it was an attempt to insure that the stability provided by British sea power before the war would not be destroyed in a multinational postwar struggle for control of the seas. It was logical from the English and American points of view to share that power rather than compete for it. This was essentially how Secretary Henry Stimson explained the parity issue to President Hoover in 1929; see Stimson to Hoover, 1 May 1929, FA-Disarm., HHPP.

[39] George L. Grassmuck, *Sectional Biases in Congress on Foreign Policy,* pp. 32–33, 54; Butler, "Partisan Positions," p. 465; *American Industries* 22 (Nov. 1921): 7; *Magazine of Wall Street* 28 (29 Oct. 1921): 890–91; U.S. Chamber of Commerce to Hoover, 1 July 1930, FA-Disarm., HHPP.

[40] Hoag, *Preparedness,* p. 172; *Nation's Business* 10 (5 June 1922): 33–

34. The War Department assumed an almost identical position throughout the period under discussion. See Fred H. Winkler, "The War Department and Disarmament, 1926–1935," *Historian* 28 (May 1966): 426–46.

[41] Hoag, *Preparedness,* pp. 172–73.

[42] Grassmuck, *Sectional Biases,* pp. 36, 39, 45–49, 54–55; Butler, "Partisan Positions," pp. 119–20, 131–32. Grassmuck and Butler use the same geographical divisions in their studies. The Lake States include Illinois, Indiana, Michigan, and Ohio. The Great Plains area consists of Iowa, Kansas, Minnesota, Nebraska, Wisconsin, and North and South Dakota.

[43] *American Industries* 22 (May 1922): 24; Stalker, "NAM," pp. 278–79.

[44] Rappaport, *Navy League,* p. 98; Hoag, *Preparedness,* pp. 183–84.

[45] *Magazine of Wall Street* 29 (7 Jan. 1922): 307, 515: "Unfortunately, the direct results of the conference up to the present time have not been for practical economy and improvement in national conditions. There seems to have been a grave mis-conception of the economics of the situation." These early suspicions about the tax-reducing power of disarmament were later confirmed.

[46] Contrary to American advice the Chinese negotiated a treaty with the Soviet Union in May 1924 which gave these two countries joint control of the Chinese Eastern Railway. Although these two nations continued to fight between themselves over the line, the issue was beyond the influence of the U.S. by 1924. The issue of Japan's occupation of Siberia was settled by the Karakhan-Yoshizava treaty of January 1925, which was negotiated between Russian and Japanese delegates on mutually beneficial terms. Although Japan had promised to withdraw from Siberia at the time of the Washington Conference, this was not accomplished until 1925. If anything, American-Japanese enmity following the Washington Conference first delayed withdrawal and later drove Japan into an independent agreement with the Soviet Union, contrary to the original intention of Secretary Hughes. See Louis Fischer, *The Soviets in World Affairs* (London, 1930), 2: 544–60; Williams, *American-Russian Relations,* pp. 187–91.

[47] *American Industries* 26 (Jan. 1926): 5–6; *ABA Journal* 25 (Mar. 1933): 28–29, 48; *Nation's Business* 17 (May 1929): 21–22, 126, 128; Stalker, "NAM," pp. 278–79.

[48] During the preparatory sessions for the 1927 conference, the U.S. government consistently opposed monetary limitations as a means for reducing armaments, military and economic blockades for enforcing any disarmament agreements, and federal supervision of private munitions manufacturers—positions with which the business community was in essential agreement. See *FRP, 1927,* 1: 172–73, 177, 208–9, 232–34.

[49] *Iron Age* 120 (15 Sept. 1927): 736–37; *Cotton* 91 (Sept. 1927): 1098.

[50] *Bradstreet's* 55 (5 Mar. 1928): 168; *Bankers Magazine* 114 (May 1927): 647–48; *Wall Street Journal,* 8 Oct. 1925, p. 1; 1 Aug. 1927, p. 1; 25 Aug. 1928, p. 1; *ABA Journal* 22 (Nov. 1929): 462; secretary of Foreign Affairs Committee to Felix Warburg, 7 May 1926, Felix Warburg Papers.

For a discussion of the technical points over which England and the United States could not agree, see David Carlton, "Great Britain and the Coolidge Naval Disarmament Conference of 1927," *Political Science Quarterly* 83 (Dec. 1968): 573–98.

[51] 39 (20 Dec. 1927): 660–62.

[52] *Chicago Journal of Commerce,* 16 Apr. 1924, p. 14; *American Industries* 24 (May 1924): 5–8; 26 (Jan. 1926): 5–6; *Pocket Bulletin* 26 (Apr. 1926): 3–6; 27 (Dec. 1926): 1–4; 27 (Feb. 1927): 3–4; *Nation's Business* 18 (Mar. 1930): 142, 144, 146, 154, 156; *Wall Street Journal,* 12 Mar., 10, 14, 17 July, 13 Aug., 22 Dec. 1928, all on page 1; *ABA Journal* 25 (Mar. 1933): 28–29, 48; Stalker, "NAM," pp. 278–79; Lester H. Brune, "Foreign Policy and the Air Power Dispute, 1919–1932," *Historian* 23 (Aug. 1961): 450–52, 464.

[53] Winkler, "War Department," p. 431; *FRP, 1927,* 1: 232–34.

[54] Paul A. C. Koistinen, "The 'Industrial-Military Complex' in Historical Perspective: World War I," *Business History Review* 41 (Winter 1967): 378–403; idem, "The 'Industrial-Military Complex,' in Historical Perspective: The Inter-War Years," *JAH* 46 (March 1970): 819–34; Bernard L. Boylan, "Army Reorganization, 1920: The Legislative Story," *Mid-America* 49 (Apr. 1967): 115–28; Winkler, "War Department," p. 431; U.S., Congress, House, *Documents by War Policies Commission: Analysis of Testimony,* House Doc. 271, 72d Cong., 1st sess., pp. 26–33; U.S., Congress, House, *Hearings before War Policies Commission,* House Doc. 163, 72d Cong., 1st sess., 12 Mar. 1932, pp. 30–72, 121–44, 169–205, 221–51, 286–88; U.S., Congress, Senate, Special Committee, *Hearings on S. R. 206: A Resolution to Make Certain Investigations Concerning the Manufacture and Sale of Arms and Other War Munitions,* 73d Cong., 2d sess., Dec. 1934 (hereafter cited as U.S. Senate, *Munitions Industry Hearing*), pts. 15, 16, 17, 24, passim.

[55] *Cotton* 92 (Aug. 1928): 1022; *Chicago Journal of Commerce,* 9 Apr. 1924, p. 14; 27 Aug. 1928, p. 14; 22 Dec. 1928, p. 12; 24 Dec. 1928, p. 12. Members of the National Economic League, whose executive council included a number of prominent businessmen, voted 1,617 to 45 in favor of ratification of the Kellogg-Briand Pact. *Wall Street Journal,* 22 Dec. 1928, p. 1; *Coast Banker* 38 (June 1927): 591–93; 41 (Sept. 1928): 389; 42 (Feb. 1929): 128–29; *Bankers Magazine* 117 (Sept. 1928): 328–39; 117 (Oct. 1928): 501–2; *Nation's Business* 17 (25 May 1929): 31.

[56] John P. Campbell, "Taft, Roosevelt, and the Arbitration Treaties of 1911," *JAH* 53 (Sept. 1966): 288–91. According to Campbell, the term "international arbitration" as it was used by the prewar peace societies meant "every remotely judicial contrivance to settle international disputes." Republicans had been advocating a world court since the turn of the century. See memorandum to Hoover from Division of Western European Affairs, 2 Nov. 1929, File 500. C114/904½, NA, RG 59.

[57] American Manufacturers' Export Association to Frank B. Kellogg, 18 Nov. 1925, File 102. 1702/166, NA, RG 59; U.S. Chamber of Commerce,

Board of Directors Annual Report, May 1925, p. 18; May 1926, pp. 45–46; *Bradstreet's* 50 (11 Nov. 1922): 724; 51 (10 Mar. 1923): 166; 57 (16 Mar. 1929): 180; *Coast Banker* 29 (Dec. 1922): 617; 30 (Mar. 1923): 255; 33 (July 1924): 206–7; 36 (Feb. 1926): 108–9; 42 (20 Apr. 1929): 336; *Nation's Business* 12 (Dec. 1925): 36; 14 (Jan. 1926): 31.

[58] *Wall Street Journal,* 16 Dec. 1920, 6 Jan., 19 Aug., 11 Dec. 1925, 28 Jan. 1926, all p. 1.

[59] Hoover, *Memoirs,* 2: 50, 332, 337; Frank B. Kellogg to Elihu Root, 28 Nov. 1928, File 500. C114/737A, Root to Henry L. Stimson, 16 May 1929, File -/790½, Stimson to Root, 25 May 1929, File -/791¾, William R. Castle, Jr. to Stimson, 27 May 1929, File -/795, Root to Stimson, 18 Nov. 1929, Stimson to Root, 4 Dec. 1929, File -/910½, Hoover to Senate, 3 Dec. 1930, File -/1186½—all in NA, RG 59; Root to Raymond B. Fosdick, 28 Sept. 1929, Box 62, Kellogg to Root, 23 Sept. 1930, Box 145, Stimson to Root, 17 Mar. 1931, Box 147—all in Elihu Root Papers, Library of Congress.

[60] Maddox, *Borah,* pp. 168–70, 22–24; *Coast Banker* 36 (Feb. 1926): 108–9; *Wall Street Journal,* 11 Dec. 1925, p. 1.

[61] Adler, *Isolationist Impulse,* pp. 187–92, 216–17; Lester W. Milbrath, "Interest Groups and Foreign Policy," *Domestic Sources of Foreign Policy,* ed. James N. Rosenau, p. 249.

[62] Adler, *Isolationist Impulse,* pp. 144, 199–200.

[63] Davis to James G. MacDonald, 11 Jan. 1923, Box 25, Davis to William G. McAdoo, 23 Mar. 1923, and McAdoo to Davis, 31 Dec. 1923, Box 40, Davis to Mrs. Henry James, 21 Oct. 1927, Box 25, Senator Pat Harrison to Davis, 12 Dec. 1928, and Davis to Harrison, 17 Dec. 1928, Box 27, Davis to Arthur Sweetser, 9 Jan. 1929, Box 62, Davis to Hoover, 22 Dec. 1930, Box 27, Davis to Ray Stannard Baker, 21 July 1933, Box 3—all in Davis Papers; Newton D. Baker to George Foster Peabody, 4 Nov. 1925, Box 185, Baker address to Colorado Bar Assoc., 18 Sept. 1927, and Baker to John H. Clarke, 10 Aug. 1928, Box 59, Baker Papers.

[64] Butler, "Partisan Positions," pp. 108–10, 651; Adler, *Isolationist Impulse,* p. 193.

[65] Hoover, *Memoirs,* 2: 343, 366; Hoover to Stimson, 17 Sept. 1929, Hoover, 1930 statement on Kellogg-Briand Pact, Edward A. Filene to Hoover, 24 Feb. 1930, Hoover to Filene, 25 Feb. 1920, FA-Disarm., Hoover to Paul V. McNutt (undated in folder for 1929–1932), DF-Drafts—all in HHPP.

[66] Hoover, 1 Dec. 1929 statement on public opinion, FA-Disarm., and undated handwritten statement on public opinion, DF-Drafts, HHPP.

[67] Most contemporary articles about Hoover commented on his indifference to or inability to respond to public opinion on specific issues, despite his "genius for personal publicity." See: *Harper's* 166 (June 1930): 5; *Colliers,* 9 June 1928, p. 44; *World's Work* 56 (June 1928): 132; Herbert Croly, "How Is Hoover?" in *The Faces of Five Decades: Selections from Fifty Years of the New Republic, 1914–1964,* ed. Robert B. Luce (New York,

1964), pp. 164–69; survey of editorial comment on proposed Ramsay Mac-Donald visit, 20 June–24 July 1929, survey of editorial comment on proposed cruiser suspension, 5–9 Aug. 1929, survey of editorial comment on president's statement about Germany and the disarmament conference, 21–25 Sept. 1932, results of Intercollegiate Disarmament Council national poll, 30 Dec. 1931, tabulation of the Amherst disarmament poll, 12 Dec. 1931, resolutions of Student Volunteer Movement for Foreign Missions, 3 Jan. 1932, and Hoover, 1930 statement on Kellogg-Briand Pact—all in FA-Disarm., HHPP.

[68] *Iron Age*, 125 (10 July 1930): 111; 126 (30 Oct. 1930): 1257; *Chicago Journal of Commerce*, 16 May 1930, p. 1; 21 May 1930, p. 16; 13 June 1930, p. 14; 14 June 1930, p. 12; NAM, *Proceedings*, 16 Oct. 1929, p. 72; *Bradstreet's* 58 (26 Apr. 1930), p. 276; *Wall Street Journal*, 30 Apr. 1920, p. 1; 16 May 1920, p. 1; *Nation's Business* 17 (25 May 1929): 31; Elting E. Morison, *Turmoil and Tradition*, p. 335. Businessmen and business groups who notified Hoover directly of their approval of the London Treaty can be found in FA-Disarm., HHPP.

[69] Raymond G. O'Connor, *Perilous Equilibrium*, pp. 59, 110–11; Benjamin H. Williams, *The United States and Disarmament* (New York, 1931), pp. 183–85. When the Shearer scandal was first exposed in 1927, the shipbuilding interests compromised themselves by immediately denying they knew anything about Shearer. Later Kellogg recalled that he had investigated the situation at the time and "was perfectly satisfied that Shearer's activities in Geneva had no effect whatever on our delegation." But he did not publish the 1927 correspondence with Bethlehem Steel, in which it was admitted that Shearer had been employed by the company, because it "might mislead the public both at home and abroad into placing international significance on his activities, which in my judgment had no influence whatever." Kellogg was convinced that excessive British demands for cruiser tonnage were the major reason the conference had failed. See Charles M. Schwab to Frank B. Kellogg, 19 Dec. 1927, File 500. A15A1 Shearer, William B./39, Kellogg to Joseph P. Cotton, 23 Sept. 1929, File -/39, same to same, 6 Nov. 1929, File -/47, Kellogg to Stimson, 19 Oct. 1929, File -/754—all in NA, RG 59; U.S. Senate, *Munitions Industry Hearing*, 12 Mar. 1935, 74th Cong., 1st sess., pt. 21, pp. 5941–85.

[70] Hoover to U.S. Senate, 7 July 1930, DF-Drafts, HHPP; O'Connor, *Perilous Equilibrium*, pp. 111, 127; Gerald E. Wheeler, "Isolated Japan: Anglo-American Diplomatic Cooperation, 1927–1936," *Pacific Historical Review* 30 (May 1961): 165–70.

[71] *Wall Street Journal*, 16 May 1930, p. 1; *ABA Journal* 23 (Aug. 1930): 94–95, 142; 24 (Oct. 1931): 244; *Chicago Journal of Commerce*, 26 Jan. 1932, p. 12; *Bankers Magazine* 120 (Apr. 1930): 471–72; 120 (June, 1930): 763–65; 124 (Jan. 1932): 10–11; 127 (July 1933): 1–2.

[72] Hoover, *Memoirs*, 2: 353; Hoover, Diary of the Moratorium, 6 May 1931, Foreign Loans File, and Hoover to Stimson, 24 May 1932, FA-Disarm., HHPP.

[73] Norman H. Davis to Hoover, 13 July 1933, Box 27, Davis Papers; memorandum of transatlantic conversation between Hoover, Hugh Gibson, and Norman Davis, 19 June 1932, FA-Disarm., HHPP. See my chapter 4 for the details of the inter-Allied debt problem.

[74] Memoranda of transatlantic conversations between Hoover, Stimson, Gibson, and Davis, 21 June 1932 (2:10 P.M.), 21 June 1932 (5 P.M.), 22 June 1932, Lawrence Richey File-Disarm., HHPP; Hoover, *Memoirs,* 2: 354.

[75] Stimson to Norman Davis, 1 Apr. 1932, Julius Klein to Hoover, 22 Dec. 1932, Charles L. Lawrence to Hoover, 9 Jan. 1933, Aeronautical Chamber of Commerce to Hoover, 9 Jan. 1933, Chamber of Commerce of Connecticut to Hoover, 23 Dec. 1932, Manufacturers Assoc. of Connecticut to Hoover, 23 Dec. 1932—all in FA-Disarm., HHPP; *Iron Age* 120 (July 1932): 117. In terms of popular interest in the issues of disarmament, war debts, and reparations, it is worth noting that articles on these topics cited in *Reader's Guide to Periodical Literature* declined between 1929 and 1932 to a point lower than in any period since 1919. See tables in President's Research Committee on Social Trends, *Recent Social Trends in the United States* (New York, 1934), pp. 436, 439.

Chapter Three

[1] See: above, chapter 1, n. 24; *Bankers Magazine* 104 (Jan. 1922): 288–89; 107 (July 1923): 10; *Wall Street Journal,* 20 June 1921, p. 5; 7 Oct. 1921, p. 1; 31 Oct. 1921, p. 1; 11 Feb. 1928, p. 1; 30 Apr. 1928, p. 1; *Cotton* 89 (Feb. 1925): 339; 90 (Mar. 1926): 422; 90 (Mar. 1927): 415–16; 92 (July 1928): 902; *American Industries* 24 (May 1924): 38–39; NAM, *Proceedings,* 1926, p. 104; *Nation's Business* 12 (May 1924): 110; 18 (20 May 1930): 54; *Iron Age* 109 (11 May 1922): 1286–87; *Oregon Business* 3 (June 1925): 10; NFTC, *Proceedings,* 1922, pp. 47–65, 573; James A. Farrell, "Greater Prosperity through Foreign Trade," *North American Review* 229 (Jan. 1930): 1–6; Herbert Hoover, *The Future of Our Foreign Trade* (Washington, 1926), p. 1; Newton D. Baker to George Foster Peabody, 4 Dec. 1922, Box 185, Baker Papers; "Tariff Problems of the United States," *The Annals of the American Academy of Political and Social Science* 141 (Jan. 1929): 8–9 (hereafter cited as "Tariff Problems").

[2] Lester W. Milbrath, "Interest Groups and Foreign Policy," in *Domestic Sources of Foreign Policy,* ed. James N. Rosenau, p. 231; "Tariff Problems," pp. 40–52, 259–60; Carl P. Parrini, *Heir to Empire,* pp. 212–13, 219–20, 245. Until England returned to the gold standard in 1925, business internationalists logically looked upon American tariff rates as one means of stabilizing domestic prices and the international exchange situation by controlling the movements of gold inside and outside of the country. So it is not surprising that they did not opt for a free trade position (which would have been in keeping with the nation's creditor status according to traditional economic theory) in the immediate postwar years because of the absence of

an international gold standard. Even after 1925, however, business internationalists who advocated free trade (as opposed to simply low rates)
remained a distinct minority. Thus, between 1920 and 1933, the tariff policy
of the United States, as far as duties were concerned, never did conform to
the rules of the gold standard game discussed in chapter 1, above.

³ Arthur S. Link, *Wilson*, vol. 4, *Confusions and Crises, 1915–1916*
(Princeton, 1964), p. 345; NFTC, *Proceedings*, 1917, pp. 104–7; 1918, p.
603; 1919, pp. 75–79; Parrini, *Heir to Empire*, pp. 213–18.

⁴ Joseph F. Kenkel, "The Tariff Commission Movement: The Search for
a Nonpartisan Solution of the Tariff Question" (Ph.D. dissertation, Univ. of
Maryland, 1962), pp. 1–97, and passim; William Diamond, *The Economic
Thought of Woodrow Wilson* (Baltimore, 1943), pp. 98–99; Stalker, "NAM,"
p. 274; William B. Kelly, Jr., "Antecedents of Present Commercial Policy,
1922–1934," in *Studies in United States Commercial Policy*, ed. William B.
Kelly, Jr., p. 15; Frank Burdick, "Woodrow Wilson and the Underwood
Tariff," *Mid-America* 50 (Oct. 1968): 272–90.

⁵ *Annalist* 17 (21 Mar. 1921): 349; *Coast Banker* 29 (Oct. 1922): 366;
29 (Dec. 1922): 587–88; *Pacific Banker*, 28 Sept. 1922, p. 1; 19 Oct. 1922,
p. 1; *Wall Street Journal*, 7 Oct. 1921, p. 1; *Magazine of Wall Street* 30 (19
Aug. 1922): 573; *Cotton* 89 (Nov. 1924): 3; 92 (June 1926): 808; 93 (Jan.
1929): 272; NAM, *Proceedings*, 1922, p. 144; 1923, pp. 107, 315; 1927, pp.
35–36, 65–66, 124; 1929, pp. 75–76; *American Industries* (*Pocket Bulletin*)
29 (Nov. 1928): 5–6; 30 (Aug. 1929): 27–28; 30 (Nov. 1929): 3–5; 30
(Jan. 1930): 3–5; *Nation's Business* 10 (Mar. 1922): 30; 10 (July 1922):
16–18; *Tariff Review* (successor to *American Economist*) 81 (Apr. 1930):
118; 81 (May 1930): 130; 81 (June 1930): 181; J. C. Brady to Fred I.
Kent, 23 Nov. 1929, Box 4, Kent Papers, Princeton Univ. (hereafter cited
as Kent Papers).

⁶ U.S. Tariff Commission, *Reciprocity and Commercial Treaties*, pp. 17,
59; Wallace McClure, *A New American Commercial Policy*, pp. 91–103;
F. W. Taussig, "The Tariff Controversy with France," *Foreign Affairs* 6 (Jan.
1928): 179–80.

⁷ U.S. Tariff Commission, *Reciprocity*, pp. 9, 39 (italics added); Lloyd C.
Gardner, *Economic Aspects of New Deal Diplomacy*, pp. 40–41; Steigerwalt,
NAM, pp. 157, 167. For further details about tariff negotiability and the relative merits of conditional versus unconditional most-favored-nation policies,
see Kelly, "Antecedents," pp. 25–27, 30–36.

⁸ McClure, *Commercial Policy*, pp. 6–72. As originally conceived by
protectionists this kind of flexibility was based exclusively on the imposition
of penalty duties. For example, there were penalty provisions in the 1890
and 1897 tariffs but these were to be used to obtain *preferential* treatment
for United States exports, while those in the 1909 tariff were to obtain *nondiscriminatory* treatment. None of the penalty provisions of 1890, 1897, or
1909 allowed the tariff rates of the United States to be lowered, only raised.
See Kelly, "Antecedents," pp. 26 (fn. 78), 36–37. It is this distinction be-

tween preferential and nondiscriminatory treatment which made the precedent set by the 1909 Payne-Aldrich tariff significant to internationalists
after the war. In addition, they insisted that flexibility should include lowering
as well as raising duties.

[9] U.S. Tariff Commission, *Reciprocity,* p. 13. The various groups within
the American business community were not always precise in their use of
the terms "bargaining" and "flexible." Often out of carelessness or the desire
to be ambiguous the terms would be used interchangeably. Generally, however, during the drafting of the Fordney-McCumber and Hawley-Smoot
tariffs, and House of Representatives, medium-sized manufacturers and businessmen not engaged in exporting or importing, and high protectionists
favored the bargaining provisions which would have allowed the president
to negotiate reciprocity agreements of the limited nineteenth-century variety.
In contrast, the Senate, under the influence of the State Department, the
Federal Tariff Commission, and the National Foreign Trade Council, representing large manufacturing, financial, and export-import interests, succeeded in replacing these negotiable bargaining provisions with nonnegotiable
flexible ones. Under both types of tariffs, however, duties remained high.

[10] NFTC, *Proceedings,* 1917, p. viii; 1919, p. x; 1921, p. xi–xii; 1922, p. xiv.
In the early years of its support for a flexible tariff the NFTC always emphasized that such a tariff was necessary "to insure equality of treatment"
and since flexibility involved "neither the policy of free trade nor the policy
of protection," it could be incorporated into any American tariff, "whatever
its underlying principle."

[11] McClure, *Commercial Policy,* pp. 102–3; "Tariff Problems," pp. 48,
260–61.

[12] NFTC, *Proceedings,* 1916, p. 124; Parrini, *Heir to Empire,* pp. 221–22;
"Tariff Problems," p. 41.

[13] James D. Richardson, ed., *A Compilation of the Messages and Papers
of the Presidents,* 18: 9024, 9137.

[14] George P. Auld, *Rebuilding Trade by Tariff Bargaining* (New York,
1936), p. 7. There was disagreement among internationalists over whether
or not flexible rates could actually equalize domestic and foreign costs of
production. The first chairman of the U.S. Tariff Commission, F. W. Taussig,
maintained that it could not and pointed out that the "notion of equalizing
costs of production had become a sort of fetish among the protectionists."
But internationalists like Hoover followed the lead of another member of the
Tariff Commission, William S. Culbertson, who denied that the difficulty
of ascertaining foreign costs of production made equalization an administrative or economic impossibility. After Taussig's resignation on 21 July 1919,
Culbertson's point of view prevailed among the federal tariff commissioners,
and was embodied in both the 1922 and 1930 tariffs despite widespread
criticism of the "equality-of-cost" principle from economists and some business internationalists. See n. 62, this chapter; McClure, *Commercial Policy,*
58–60; Robert K. Murray, *The Harding Era,* p. 273; U.S. Tariff Commission,

Annual Report, 1921, p. 100; 1922, pp. 2–3; 1929, p. 17; "Tariff Problems," pp. 59, 115–17, 245.

    [15] *American Economist* 47 (11 Mar. 1921): 77–79.

    [16] Ibid., 46 (17 Dec. 1920): 202; Kelly, "Antecedents," pp. 7, 9.

    [17] U.S., Congress, Senate, Committee on Finance, *Hearing on H.R. 2435: An Act Imposing Temporary Duties upon Certain Agricultural Products to Meet Present Emergencies, to Provide Revenue, and for Other Purposes,* 67th Cong., 1st sess., 18–19, 21–23, 26 Apr. 1921 (hereafter cited as U.S. Senate, *Emergency Tariff Hearing,* Apr. 1921), pp. 81–121, 214–15.

    [18] Ibid., pp. 82–86.

    [19] Ibid., p. 87; U.S., Congress, Senate, Committee on Finance, *Hearing on H.R. 15275: An Act Imposing Temporary Duties upon Certain Agricultural Products to Meet Present Emergencies, to Provide Revenue, and for Other Purposes,* 66th Cong., 3d sess., 6–8, 10–11, 13 Jan. 1921 (hereafter cited as U.S. Senate, *Emergency Tariff Hearing,* Jan. 1921), pp. 205–7.

    [20] *Pacific Banker,* 27 Jan. 1921, p. 1; 24 Mar. 1921, p. 1; 23 June 1921 (convention issue), p. 4; *Coast Banker* 26 (Apr. 1921): 435; *Magazine of Wall Street* 28 (25 June 1921): 232–33; *Wall Street Journal,* 12 Jan. 1921, p. 1; 28 Jan. 1921, p. 1; 15 May 1923, p. 1. Beginning with the Emergency Tariff bill even the strongly nationalistic *Wall Street Journal* began to express concern over "changed world conditions" in relation to American tariff policy. Increasingly in the 1920s this newspaper criticized what it called the "limitless protectionist," and stressed that "expanding markets" were more important than "high protection."

    [21] U.S. Senate, *Emergency Tariff Hearing,* Apr. 1921, p. 215.

    [22] 47 (13 May 1921): 151; 47 (3 June 1921): 176; Kelly, "Antecedents," pp. 7–10. Kelly notes that the Tariff Commission never found any correlation between protection and farm price recovery. Instead, the effect on the farmer of the emergency duties was to curtail further his foreign markets and increase the prices of both foreign and domestic goods he wanted to buy. Nonetheless, the debate over how much high duties benefited the farmer continued throughout the decade. For arguments on both sides see "Tariff Problems," pp. 48, 55–56, 120–74.

    [23] Harold Tiffany Butler, "Partisan Positions on Isolationism vs. Internationalism, 1918–1933" (D.S.S. dissertation, Syracuse Univ., 1963), pp. 143–44, 235–36. Butler's figures also show that a much smaller percentage of Democrats voted for the Republican emergency bill of 1921 than had supported a similar bill in the last months of the Wilson administration. The figures for the House and Senate Democrats in support of the first emergency bill were 33.5 and 25 percent, respectively.

    [24] *Magazine of Wall Street* 28 (25 June 1921): 233.

    [25] Milbrath, "Interest Groups," pp. 244, 247–51; Raymond A. Bauer, et al., *American Business and Public Policy,* p. 479.

    [26] J. A. Campbell, president of Youngston Sheet and Tube Co., testified in 1921, and Alfred P. Sloan, Jr., of General Motors Corp., in 1929. I have

used only Senate hearings in this study because this is where opponents of the 1922 and 1930 tariffs testified in greatest number. Such critics were not always informed about House tariff proposals and House hearings.

[27] E. E. Schattschneider, *Politics, Pressures and the Tariff*, p. 185. This is not to say that protectionist policies had not contributed to the development of big business in the past. But as early as 1913 it was apparent that large firms were beginning to look upon high duties as either irrelevant or a threat to their future growth. See Burdick, "Woodrow Wilson and the Underwood Tariff," pp. 278–90.

[28] Kelly, "Antecedents," pp. 44–47; U.S., Congress, Senate, Committee on Finance, *Hearings on H.R. 7456: To Provide Revenue, to Regulate Commerce with Foreign Countries, to Encourage the Industries of the United States and for Other Purposes.* 67th Cong., 1st sess. [hereafter cited as *Hearings on H.R. 7456 (Fordney)*], 5: 1817 Also see note 2, this chapter.

[29] Louis Galambos, *Competition and Cooperation: The Emergence of a National Trade Association* (Baltimore, 1966), pp. 60–61; *Cotton* 90 (Nov. 1925): 14–15; 93 (Mar. 1929): 487.

[30] 47 (1 Apr. 1921): 103.

[31] U.S. Senate, *Emergency Tariff Hearing*, Apr. 1921, pp. 84–85; U.S., Congress, Senate, Subcommittee of the Committee on the Judiciary, *Hearings on S.R. 20: A Resolution to Investigate the Activities of Lobbying Associations and Lobbyists in and around Washington, D.C.*, 71st Cong., 2d sess., 24 Oct.–11 Nov. 1929, pt. 5, p. 2071.

[32] Schattschneider, *Politics, Pressures*, p. 161.

[33] U.S. Senate, *Emergency Tariff Hearing*, Apr. 1921, pp. 36, 104. For documentation and discussion of "insiders" vs. "outsiders" during the 1929 tariff hearings, see Schattschneider, *Politics, Pressures*, pp. 164–213.

[34] *Wall Street Journal*, 17 Sept., 1921, p. 1; Schattschneider, *Politics, Pressures*, p. 161; *American Industries* 22 (Mar. 1922): 8.

[35] U.S. Senate, *Hearings on H.R. 7456 (Fordney)*, 2 (*American Valuation*): 287. Doherty did not consistently practice what he preached in 1921. At the 1929 Senate hearings he represented the American Iron and Steel Institute and advocated higher import duties on finished steel products.

[36] Ibid., p. 130.

[37] Ibid., 4: 990, 995.

[38] Bankers in particular were inaccurately singled out as opposing adequate tariff protection or as actually being free-traders. See: *ABA Journal* 15 (Nov. 1922): 263; *Iron Age* 131 (9 Feb. 1933): 245; Hoover, *Memoirs*, 2: 179; 3: 7–12; *American Industries (Pocket Bulletin)* 28 (Dec. 1927): 2; *Cotton* 92 (Nov. 1927): 25; *American Economist* 67 (11 Feb. 1921): 42; *Nation's Business* 15 (Apr. 1927): 89–90; *New York Journal of Commerce Bulletin*, 16 Mar. 1922, p. 6; James Speyer to Norman H. Davis, 26 May 1932, Box 53, Davis Papers.

[39] Schattschneider, *Politics, Pressures*, pp. 66, 163, 212; Bauer, et al., *American Business and Public Policy*, pp. 17, 25.

[40] *Pacific Banker,* 27 Jan. 1921, p. 1; 24 Mar. 1921, p. 1; 23 June 1921, p. 4; 1 Sept. 1921, p. 6; *Annalist* 16 (Dec. 1920): 712; Otto Kahn, *Of Many Things,* pp. 325–26; *Wall Street Journal,* 1 Sept. 1923, p. 3; 30 Apr. 1928, p. 1; *Iron Age* 102 (1 May 1919): 1181; James D. Mooney, *The New Capitalism,* pp. 137, 153; *Nation's Business* 9 (July 1921): 12; 19 (July 1931): 14; *Bankers Magazine* 105 (Nov. 1922): 807; NFTC, *Proceedings,* 1922, p. 59; Lester V. Chandler, *Benjamin Strong,* pp. 265, 325–26; "Tariff Problems," pp. ix, 27–29, 45–49, 51–54, 260–64.

[41] McClure, *Commercial Policy,* pp. 97–99; Parrini, *Heir to Empire,* pp. 226–30. According to Parrini, on 26 May 1921, six representatives of the State Dept. met with Commissioner Culbertson, Charles E. Herring, acting head of the BFDC, and Louis Domeratsky of the Tariff Division of the BFDC to discuss what recommendations the executive branch should make to Congress concerning the forthcoming tariff revision. Over the objections of the BFDC men it was agreed that only flexible provisions (as opposed to those embodying the idea of reciprocity) should be recommended.

[42] Parrini, *Heir to Empire,* p. 231; NFTC, *Proceedings,* 1919, p. x; 1920, p. ix; 1921, pp. xi–xii; 1922, p. xiv; Murray, *Harding Era,* p. 275; U.S. Chamber of Commerce to Hoover, 26 Jan. 1922, Tariff File (hereafter cited as TF), HHCD; *Nation's Business* 10 (Jan. 1922); 21–22; 10 (Mar. 1922): 30–31.

[43] U.S. Tariff Commission, *Reciprocity,* pp. 9–15; idem, *Annual Report,* 1920, p. 10; Parrini, *Heir to Empire,* p. 232

[44] Parrini, *Heir to Empire,* p. 233; Kelly, "Antecedents," pp. 16, 43.

[45] McClure, *Commercial Policy,* p. 74; Benjamin H. Williams, *Economic Foreign Policy of the United States,* p. 299; Percy W. Bidwell, *The Invisible Tariff,* pp. 118–19. Since the president's power under Section 316 was very similar to those possessed by the Treasury Dept. to prevent dumping or other unfair commercial practices, and since Section 317 provided for retaliatory duties very similar to those contained in the 1909 tariff, it is not surprising that most of the senators who participated in the brief debate on these provisions were unaware that they implied a reversal of the country's 144-year conditional most-favored-nation policy. See Kelly, "Antecedents," pp. 21–22, 38–44; "Tariff Problems," pp. 66–67.

[46] J. Marshall Gersting, *The Flexible Provisions in the United States' Tariff, 1922–1930,* pp. 17–20.

[47] U.S. Senate, *Hearings on H.R. 7456 (Fordney),* 2 (*American Valuation*): index, pp. 195–97; 5 (*Metals and Manufactures of*): 1712, 1720, 1730, 1817; 7 (*Wool and Manufactures of*): 3536–37; Philadelphia Board of Trade, *Proceedings,* 24 Jan. 1922, p. 37; *Nation's Business* 9 (Dec. 1921): 22–23; 10 (Jan. 1922): 22; *American Industries,* 22 (Feb. 1922): 7–8, 41–44; 22 (Mar. 1922): 8–10, 42; 22 (Apr. 1922): 15–16; *Iron Age* 109 (2 Feb. 1922): 363–64; 109 (23 Feb. 1922): 540–41; *American Economist* 67 (6 May 1921): 139; 68 (30 Sept. 1921): 109–10; 68 (11 Nov. 1921): 153–58 (symposium of congressmen in favor of American valua-

tion); 68 (7 Oct. 1921): 113–14 (resolution of the 1921 National Conference of State Manufacturers' Associations); Stalker, "NAM," p. 274; J. Roffe Wike, *The Pennsylvania Manufacturers' Association*, p. 158.

[48] *Nation's Business* 10 (Mar. 1922): 30–31.

[49] *Chicago Journal of Commerce*, 18 Feb. 1922, p. 4; *American Industries* 22 (Mar. 1922): 8–10, 42.

[50] U.S. Senate, *Hearings on H.R. 7456 (Fordney)*, 2 (*American Valuation*): 86, 130, 264–99, and index; 6 (*Flax, Hemp, and Jute, and Manufactures of*): 3486; 9 (*Special and Administrative Provisions and Appendix*): 5108–11, 5364–411, 5417–18; *Nation's Business* 9 (Dec. 1921): 23; *Wall Street Journal*, 18 Apr. 1922, p. 10; *Bradstreet's* 49 (29 Oct. 1921): 718; Cleveland Chamber of Commerce, *Annual*, 18 Apr. 1922, p. 83 (while the board initially opposed American valuation, the chamber as a whole assumed a "position of neutrality" on the issue); *Magazine of Wall Street* 28 (15 Oct. 1921): 819; *Chicago Journal of Commerce*, 5 Jan. 1922, p. 1; 17 Jan. 1921, p. 4; 20 Jan 1922, p. 4; 26 Jan. 1922, p. 1; Kahn, quoted in *Wall Street Journal*, 20 Oct 1921, p. 1; Julius Rosenwald, roll 42, SB5/30, Rosenwald Papers; Gersting, *Flexible Provisions*, pp. 18–19.

[51] U.S. Senate, *Hearings on H.R. 7456 (Fordney)*, 2 (*American Valuation*): 2–85; Page to Hoover, 1 Dec. 1921, Hoover to Page, 3 Dec. 1921, and BFDC to Hoover, 27 Dec. 1921—all in TF, HHCD.

[52] Gersting, *Flexible Provisions*, pp. 25–35.

[53] U.S., Congress, House, *Tariff Act of 1922*, document no. 393, 67th Cong., 2d sess. (hereafter cited as U.S. House, *Tariff Act of 1922*), p. 94.

[54] U.S., Congress, Senate, Committee on Finance, *Minority Report to Accompany H.R. 7456*, 67th Cong., 2d sess., Senate Report 595, 20 Apr. 1922, pt. 2, pp. 1–12; U.S. Tariff Commission, *Annual Report*, 1929, pp. 24–25; U.S. House, *Tariff Act of 1922*, pp. 3–5.

[55] Gersting, *Flexible Provisions*, pp. 36–42.

[56] Wesley Clair Mitchell, "Intelligence and the Guidance of Economic Evolution," in *Authority and the Individual*, Harvard Tercentenary Conference of Arts and Sciences (Cambridge, Mass., 1936), pp. 24, 29; "Tariff Problems," pp. 16–17, 43–48, 124–36, 232, 244–46, 260–61; Parrini, *Heir to Empire*, pp. 219 (fn. 20), 233–34; Bernard Baruch, *Public Years*, pp. 157, 166, 227; Mary Jane Matz, *The Many Lives of Otto Kahn*, pp. 204–5; Chandler, *Strong*, pp. 264–65; Henry Ford, *Today and Tomorrow*, pp. 254–55; Rosenwald, roll 42, SB5/30, Rosenwald Papers; *Wall Street Journal*, 20 Oct. 1921, p. 1; *Magazine of Wall Street* 30 (28 Oct. 1922): 980–81; *Bankers Magazine* 126 (Apr. 1933): 340–42; NFTC, *Proceedings*, 1933, p. 153.

[57] *Cotton* 89 (Nov. 1924): 3; 89 (Oct. 1925): 1224; 92 (June 1928): 808; *Iron Age* 109 (2 Mar. 1922): 600; 110 (6 July 1922): 32; 110 (5 Oct. 1922): 877; *American Economist* 67 (11 Feb. 1921): 42; 67 (22 Apr. 1921): 122; 67 (6 May 1921): 139; 68 (12 Aug. 1921): 51; Southern Tariff Assoc. to Hoover, 13 June 1923, TF, HHCD.

[58] *Bankers Magazine* 105 (Dec. 1922): 985; *Pacific Banker*, 19 Oct. 1922, p. 1; *Wall Street Journal*, 3 Oct. 1922, p. 1; *ABA Journal* 15 (Nov. 1922): 322; *American Industries* 24 (May 1924): 6; Stalker, "NAM," pp. 275, 424; *Protectionist* 36 (May 1924): 44; *American Economist* 70 (29 Sept. 1922): 121; 70 (13 Oct. 1922): 137–38.

[59] The "independents" were all the smaller steel producers who were in competition with U.S. Steel. They had lobbied for low duties on raw materials such as refractories and ferro-alloys and high duties on manufactured steel products such as pig iron, but were dissatisfied with the results.

[60] *Iron Age* 110 (6 July 1922): 32; 110 (5 Oct. 1922): 877; 111 (22 Mar. 1923): 836; 115 (25 June 1925): 1853; U.S., Congress, Senate, Subcommittee on Finance, *Hearings on H.R. 2667: An Act to Provide Revenue, to Regulate Commerce with Foreign Countries, to Encourage the Industries of the U.S., to Protect American Labor and for Other Purposes*, 71st Cong., 1st sess. [hereafter cited as U.S. Senate, *Hearings on H.R. 2667 (Hawley)*], 3: 1, 4, 8. Topping quoted in *Magazine of Wall Street* 30 (28 Oct. 1922): 980–81.

[61] "Tariff Problems," pp. 61–62; U.S. Tariff Commission, *Annual Report*, 1929, p. 23. The third strong proponent of flexibility in 1922—the State Department—continued to defend the provisions in the late 1920s despite their defects because they provided the legal basis of the negotiations being conducted for commercial equality. It would have proved embarrassing to the department to suspend all such negotiations in the immediate future. See *FRP, 1927*, 1: 280; *1929*, 1: 994–97.

[62] U.S. Tariff Commission, *Annual Report*, 1929, pp. 24–25; *Wall Street Journal*, 6 May 1930, p. 1. In addition to administrative difficulties (out of over 600 applications only 47 investigations were conducted), it has been pointed out that Section 315 was economically unsound in the sense that international trade is largely based on cost differences. Tariffs designed to equalize costs would theoretically "stop all trade except in those items where value, special design, or some other feature is paramount irrespective of cost considerations." See Kelly, "Antecedents," pp. 17–18, 22; "Tariff Problems," pp. 59, 115–17, 245.

[63] Bidwell, *The Invisible Tariff*, pp. 4–5, 7–8. The administrative measures which were part of the invisible tariff of the United States in the 1920s included trade mark, antidumping, and unfair competition legislation as well as prohibitions against imports produced by convict labor, laws applying countervailing duties to bounty-fed imports, and laws penalizing imports from countries discriminating against American commerce.

[64] Edward P. Costigan, *Public Ownership of Government*, pp. 259–74 (letter of resignation, 14 Mar. 1928); J. Richard Snyder, "Coolidge, Costigan and the Tariff Commission," *Mid-America* 50 (Apr. 1968): 133–41.

[65] Costigan, *Public Ownership*, pp. 260–66, 271, 273–74. Costigan brought the attention of Congress not only to Coolidge's mistreatment of the commission and his opposition to lowering duties, but also to the inadequate

methods of the commission itself. As a result, a Senate investigating committee recommended in 1928 that Section 315 be abolished and the commission be reconstituted as simply a fact-finding board. When Hoover became president he pressured Congress to ignore these recommendations, except for the one calling for new appointees. See Snyder, "Tariff Commission," pp. 142–48.

⁶⁶ James A. Farrell, president of United States Steel, was another; see Parrini, *Heir to Empire*, pp. 266–67. Most businessmen who supported both positions tried to avoid this theoretical contradiction by integrating U.S. tariff policy into larger plans for the reconstruction of Europe under American leadership.

⁶⁷ Kelly, "Antecedents," p. 16; Snyder, "Tariff Commission," p. 136; Butler, "Partisan Positions," pp. 470–71; Hoover to Warren Harding, 16 Mar. 1923, Tariff File; Gerard Swope to Hoover, 2 Oct. 1927, Personal File (hereafter cited as PF)-Tariff, Hoover to David Lawrence, 29 Dec. 1927, Commerce File (hereafter cited as CF)-American Businessman—all in HHCD; Brandes, *Hoover*, pp. 3–4, 34–35; *FRP, 1929*, 1: 994; *Wall Street Journal*, 25 May 1921, p. 13.

⁶⁸ Hoover, address to U.S. Chamber of Commerce, 7 May 1924, Achievements File (hereafter cited as AF)-1924 (1), and Hoover to Calvin Coolidge, 12 Jan. 1928, PF-Tariff, HHCD; Hoover to Warren D. Smith, 4 Sept. 1930, Tariff File (hereafter cited as TF)-664, Herbert Hoover, President's Personal Papers File (hereafter cited as HHPPF), Hoover Library, West Branch, Iowa; Brandes, *Hoover*, pp. 70–72.

⁶⁹ Hoover to Charles Evans Hughes, 11 Oct. 1923, Hoover to editor of *New York Times*, 18 Mar. 1923, Hoover to editor of *New York World*, 20 Jan. 1923—all in TF, HHCD; Henry Chalmers (chief, Division of Foreign Tariffs) to Secretary of Commerce Robert Lamont, 1 June 1931, Countries File-Argentina, HHPP.

⁷⁰ The degree to which Hoover relied on leading social scientists of the day for theories and techniques has been overlooked until recently. He was particularly interested in the quantitative analytical methods of Wesley Clair Mitchell, and the man he appointed as director of the BFDC in 1921 was a disciple of Edwin F. Gay. Gay helped him reorganize the Commerce Department and Mitchell influenced his ideas on business cycles. See Herbert Heaton, *A Scholar in Action: Edwin F. Gay* (Cambridge, Mass., 1952), 189–91, 196–99, 202–3; Paul T. Homan, *Contemporary Economic Thought*, pp. 385–87; Arthur F. Burns, *Wesley Clair Mitchell: The Economic Scientist* (New York, 1952), 136, 186–90, 309; Herbert Stein, *The Fiscal Revolution in America*, pp. 6–38; Barry D. Karl, "Presidential Planning and Social Science Research: Mr. Hoover's Experts," *Perspectives in American History* 3 (1969): 347–409.

⁷¹ Commerce Dept., "Report on the Repercussion of the Reduced Buying Power of Europe on International Trade," May 1927, Conferences File-Economic, pp. 7–8, and Chalmers to Hoover, 29 Dec. 1925, 18 Jan. 1926,

Foreign Combinations File-Tariffs, HHCD; H. W. Arndt, *The Economic Lessons of the Nineteen-Thirties*, p. 287.

[72] Hoover, *Future of Our Foreign Trade*, pp. 12–13; idem, *Memoirs*, 2: 84; idem, *The New Day*, pp. 132–38; idem, address to U.S. Chamber of Commerce, 8 May 1923, AF-1921–1923, HHCD; "Tariff Problems," p. 8. It is to Hoover's credit, however, that he looked favorably upon an adverse trade balance if it would precipitate a gold flow from the U.S. without causing inflation. For a critique of the value of these "invisible exports" see Williams, *Economic Foreign Policy*, pp. 238–39, and Kelly, "Antecedents," p. 4.

[73] Hoover, *Memoirs*, 2: 331; 3: 4; Arndt, *Economic Lessons*, pp. 14–19.

[74] Hoover to David Lawrence, 29 Dec. 1927, CF-American Businessman, and Hoover, "Summary of Achievements of the Dept. of Commerce," 25 July 1924, AF-1924 (1), HHCD; Herbert Stein, "Pre-revolutionary Fiscal Policy of Herbert Hoover," *Journal of Law and Economics* 9 (Oct. 1966): 190–92, 198; Albert Romasco, *Poverty of Abundance* (New York, 1965), p. 214; "Tariff Problems," p. ix.

[75] For criticisms of Hoover's tariff policy in connection with his activities against foreign cartels, see Owen D. Young to Hoover, 3 May 1926, HHPPF; Brandes, *Hoover*, pp. 70, 98–104, 123–28. Hoover defended himself by saying that American tariff policy was not contrary to the law of supply and demand, while foreign monopolies amounted to government control of "raw materials for price-fixing purposes." See Hoover, *Future of Our Foreign Trade*, p. 8; idem, "America Solemnly Warns Foreign Monopolists of Raw Materials," *Current History* 23 (Dec. 1925): 307–11; idem, address delivered 31 Oct. 1925, and press release, 4 Jan. 1926, Fordney File, HHCD.

[76] What Hoover and both his nationalist and internationalist supporters did not realize at the time was that the successful application of the "equality of cost" and unconditional most-favored-nation principles depended upon the restoration of long-term economic equilibrium between major nations after World War I, and this did not occur for the reasons discussed in chapter 1 above.

[77] *ABA Journal* 19 (Nov. 1926): 294–95; Joseph M. Jones, Jr., *Tariff Retaliation*, pp. 21–22, 247–48; Arndt, *Economic Lessons*, pp. 236–37 (fn. 1); *FRP, 1927*, 1: 243; *1930*, 1: 241–42, 246.

[78] *FRP, 1929*, 1: 990–92; Williams, *Economic Foreign Policy*, pp. 299–302.

[79] Kelly, "Antecedents," pp. 47–53; Parrini, *Heir to Empire*, pp. 241–46; Taussig, "Tariff Controversy with France," pp. 177–79, 185; Henry Chalmers to Hoover, 22 May 1926, TF, HHCD; *FRP, 1927*, 1: 241, 243, 271; *1929*, 1: 985–1004; *1930*, 1: 246–51; 3: 47–50.

[80] *FRP, 1927*, 1: 246–85; *1928*, 1: 366–98; Kelly, "Antecedents," pp. 53–63.

[81] The best indication of the change in internationalist sentiment can be found in the final declarations approved by NFTC conventions for the years 1917–1922 and 1928–1933 and by comparing the speeches made by the

NFTC treasurer Robert H. Patchin and Tariff Commissioner Culbertson in 1919–1920 with those made in 1927–1928 by George C. Davis, customs adviser for the National Council of American Importers and Traders. See NFTC, *Proceedings,* 1917, p. viii; 1918, p. ix; 1919, pp. x, 71–81; 1920, pp. ix, 286–303; 1921, pp. xi–xii; 1922, p. xiv; 1927, pp. 125–29, 228–36; 1928, pp. vi, 198–99; 1929, p. vii; 1930, p. vii; 1931, p. viii; 1932, p. 18.

[82] U.S. Senate, *Hearings on H.R. 2667 (Hawley),* 9: 170, 407–31, 462–64; *American Industries* 29 (Nov. 1928): 5–6; 29 (Dec. 1928): 10–24; 29 (Mar. 1929): 1–32; 29 (May 1929): 3–7; *Tariff Review* 81 (Feb. 1930): 49–50, 52; 81 (Apr. 1930): 104, 118; 81 (May 1930): 145–46, 148, 151; 81 (July 1930): 213, 218, 223–24; John Hays Hammond, Apr. 1930 speech, Box 21, Hammond Papers.

[83] Costigan, *Public Ownership,* p. 260; Hoover, *Memoirs,* 2: 292–96.

[84] James D. Mooney, *New Capitalism,* p. 171; Norman H. Davis to Hoover, 29 May 1930, Box 27, Davis to Cordell Hull, 2 Jan. 1929, Box 27, undated memo for late 1920s stating that businessmen were not in favor of high tariff walls, Box 31—all in Davis Papers; *Bankers Magazine* 122 (June 1931): 711–12 (Atterbury); 120 (June 1930): 763 (Youngman); 123 (Aug. 1931): 126–27 (Youngman); Owen D. Young, *High Courage* (New York, 1932), p. 16; Hoover, *Memoirs,* 2: 296 (cites opposition of Lamont, Wiggin, Sabin, Mitchell, Morgenthau, and Villard); *Tariff Review* 81 (Mar. 1930): 84 (Rowell); 81 (Apr. 1930): 115 (Ford); 81 (June 1930) 181, 184 (Ford and General Motors cited in opposition to the Hawley-Smoot Tariff); Oswald Garrison Villard, *The Tariff Scandal* (New York: League for Independent Political Action, 1930), pp. 1–13; Sabin to Hoover, 10 June 1930, and Villard to Hoover, 20 May 1930, TF, HHPPF; Newton D. Baker to George Foster Peabody, 28 Mar. 1931, 14 May 1932, Box 186, Baker Papers; Walter Sholes (American consul, Brussels) to State Dept., 29 Oct. 1931, File 666.003/2520, NA, RG 59.

[85] Letters to Hoover about 1930 tariff and letters to Reed Smoot and Willis Hawley about 1930 tariff, both in Richey File, and Jan.–Dec. 1930 letters to Tariff Commission—all in TF, HHPPF.

[86] Lee to Hoover, 27 May 1930, Fisher to Hoover, 2 June 1930, Davis to Hoover, 2 June 1930, TF, HHPPF. To all of his critics Hoover sent a standard reply: "It is certainly a difficult question [but] . . . whatever the merits or demerits of the Tariff Bill may be, it has been given a name much worse than it deserves and very little real analysis has been made."

[87] *Chicago Journal of Commerce,* 5 May 1930, p. 1; 6 May 1930, p. 14; Oswald Garrison Villard to Hoover, 20 May 1930, TF, HHPPF; Butler, "Partisan Positions," pp. 631, 635–36; Raymond F. Mikesell, *United States Economic Policy and International Relations,* pp. 62, 78; *Harper's* 161 (June 1930): 5.

[88] Romasco, *Poverty of Abundance,* pp. 214–15; *Cotton* 89 (Oct. 1925): 1224; 92 (June 1928): 808; *Wall Street Journal,* 10 Aug. 1925, p. 1; *ABA Journal* 15 (May 1923): 720. A noteworthy feature of the 1929–1930 tariff revision was that for the first time the two leading business organiza-

tions, the NAM and the U.S. Chamber of Commerce, sent representatives to testify at the congressional hearings. Neither group assumed a stand on specific duties, but both strongly supported Hoover's attempt to strengthen the 1922 flexible provisions. At the same time they opposed the attempt by a group of Republican Progressives and Democrats to repeal the 1922 flexible provisions.

[89] Hoover, *Memoirs*, 2: 292–94; 3: 290; *Nation's Business* 20 (Oct. 1932): 14; "Platform of American Industry for 1932," Box 192, Baker Papers; Norman H. Davis to Cordell Hull, 2 Jan. 1929, 7 Apr., 7 Nov. 1932, Box 27, Davis Papers; *American Industries* 29 (Apr. 1920): 6–8; 29 (May 1929): 4–7; 29 (June 1929): 3–5; 30 (Aug. 1929): 1–32; 30 (Jan. 1930): 3–5.

[90] In the final draft of the Hawley-Smoot bill only one of the three original flexible provisions of the 1922 act remained essentially unchanged. This was Section 315, which became Section 336 of the new act. Sections 316 and 317, became Sections 337 and 338, respectively, and increased the power of the president to take action against countries engaging in unfair trade practices or discriminating against American commerce. While Congress refused to make the cost formula of Section 315 less rigid, it did allow Hoover to appoint new members to the Tariff Commission. As a result of Hoover's influence, despite the continuing liability of the "equality of cost" principle, the efficiency of the reorganized body was increased to the degree that by March 1933 it considered 250 rate changes and made recommendations in 75 cases—half of which were for downward revision. See n. 62, this chapter, and Bidwell, *Invisible Tariff*, pp. 121–23; William Starr Myers and Walter H. Newton, *The Hoover Administration*, p. 441.

[91] Butler, "Partisan Positions," pp. 143–44, 235–36, 469.

[92] *Nation's Business* 12 (Sept. 1933): 13. In 1928 the Democratic platform made a significant concession to the principle of protectionism by calling for a tariff to take into consideration the "actual difference between cost of production at home and abroad." The traditional Democratic platform phrase "tariff for revenue only" was eliminated entirely. It was not simply the depression, therefore, which turned more Democrats in the direction of protection. It had been a gradual process over the entire decade. See Kirk Porter and Donald Bruce Johnson, *National Party Platforms, 1840–1960* (Urbana, Ill., 1961), p. 272; *Chicago Journal of Commerce*, 21 June 1932, p. 12.

[93] Hoover press release, 16 June 1930, and Hoover's suggestions to Walter H. Newton for defending the tariff, 3 Sept. 1930, TF-664, HHPPF; Hoover press release, 17 June 1930, TF, HHPP; *FRP, 1929*, 1: 993–98, 1003–4; Arndt, *Economic Lessons*, pp. 17, 32, 72, 229. What Hoover and his nationalist supporters did not see was that once the U.S. ceased to export capital as a result of the depression, the high American tariff became a major obstacle to the adjustment of payments between nations. It had been a symptom of, but not the major cause of, the international balance-of-payment problems until then.

[94] Hoover to John F. Kennedy, 3 Feb. 1962, Individual File, Herbert Hoover Post-Presidential Papers, Hoover Library, West Branch, Iowa; Hoover, *Memoirs,* 3: 296–97; Mikesell, *Economic Foreign Policy,* pp. 63–64. In 1933 Hoover repeatedly pointed out the negative effects of reciprocal tariffs, which he called "preferential agreements." Among other things he told one of his close friends they would result in flooding the U.S. with goods from countries with depreciated currencies, would "destroy many domestic industries," and possibly "embroil us with foreign nations." See Hoover to John Callan O'Laughlin, 10, 19 Apr., 26 June 1933, Box 43, John Callan O'Laughlin Papers, Library of Congress.

[95] Jones, *Tariff Retaliation,* p. 32.

[96] Auld, *Rebuilding Trade,* pp. 5–10; Richard N. Gardner, *Sterling-Dollar Diplomacy: Anglo-American Collaboration in the Reconstruction of Multilateral Trade* (Oxford, 1956), p. 21.

[97] Gardner, *Economic Aspects,* pp. 26, 40, 45; Mikesell, *Economic Foreign Policy,* pp. 66–67; Gardner, *Sterling-Dollar Diplomacy,* pp. 21–22; Richard N. Kottman, "The Canadian-American Trade Agreement of 1935," *JAH* 52 (Sept. 1965): 279, 281; Harry C. Hawkins and Janet L. Norwood, "The Legislative Basis of United States Commercial Policy," and John M. Leddy, "United States Commercial Policy and the Domestic Farm Program," both in *Studies in United States Commercial Policy,* ed. William B. Kelly, Jr., pp. 93–97, 176–83, 190–91; Kelly, "Antecedents," pp. 63–66; Bidwell, *Invisible Tariff,* pp. 133–37.

[98] Kelly, "Antecedents," pp. 66–67 (fn. 187); Percy W. Bidwell, *What the Tariff Means to American Industries* (New York, 1956), pp. 29 (fn. 19), 107 (fn. 17); Gabriel Kolko, *The Roots of American Foreign Policy* (Boston, 1969), pp. 62–63.

Chapter 4

[1] American Manufacturers Export Assoc. to Pacific Coast Steel Co., 23 Nov. 1922, and William Pigott to State Dept., 5 Dec. 1922, File 800.51/444, NA, RG 59.

[2] NAM, *Proceedings,* 1926, p. 104.

[3] Cleona Lewis, *America's Stake in International Investments,* pp. 194–97; Clyde William Phelps, *The Foreign Trade Expansion of American Banks,* p. 211. Phelps also notes that the decline was partially caused by "unduly rapid and unwarranted" expansion in the abnormal war years, by lack of experienced personnel in the new foreign branches, and by poor commercial and geographical locations (pp. 164–65). These reasons were not readily admitted by commercial bankers.

[4] Lewis, *America's Stake,* p. 197; *ABA Journal* 16 (Dec. 1923): 366–67; 16 (Jan. 1924): 463.

[5] Lewis, *America's Stake,* pp. 296–97, 368, 575–616, 599; Carl P. Parrini, *Heir to Empire,* pp. 101–2.

[6] Lewis, *America's Stake,* p. 605; *Business Week,* 19 Oct. 1929, p. 22.

⁷ Lester V. Chandler, *Benjamin Strong: Central Banker,* pp. 270–71; Lewis, *America's Stake,* p. 605.

⁸ William R. Braisted, "The United States and the American China Development Company," *Far Eastern Quarterly* 11 (Feb. 1952): 147–66; George W. Edwards, "Government Control of Foreign Investments," *American Economic Review* 18 (Dec. 1928): 691–92; Norman A. Graebner, ed., *An Uncertain Tradition,* pp. 62–78.

⁹ N. Gordon Levin, Jr., *Woodrow Wilson and World Politics,* pp. 19, 239; Noel Pugach, "Making the Open Door Work: Paul S. Reinsch in China, 1913–1919," *Pacific Historical Review* 38 (May 1969): 169–70; Parrini, *Heir to Empire,* pp. 172–84; *FRP, 1913,* pp. 170–71; *1918,* pp. 169–78.

¹⁰ Walter LaFeber, *The New Empire: An Interpretation of American Expansion, 1860–1898* (Ithaca, N.Y., 1963), pp. 210–83; Edwards, "Government Control," pp. 692–93; Benjamin H. Williams, *Economic Foreign Policy of the United States,* p. 86; Robert Freeman Smith, "The Formation and Development of the International Bankers Committee on Mexico," *Journal of Economic History* 23 (Dec. 1963): 574–85; Eugene P. Trani, "Harding Administration and Recognition of Mexico," *Ohio History* 75 (Spring-Summer 1966): 144–45; Thomas W. Lamont to Norman H. Davis, 27 July, 25, 28 Oct., 19 Nov. 1920, House of Morgan telegram to Denkstein (Mexico), 14 Dec. 1920—all in Box 33, Davis Papers.

¹¹ Trani, "Harding and Recognition of Mexico," pp. 139–47, and J. H. Wilson, "American Business and Recognition of the Soviet Union," *Social Science Quarterly* 52 (Sept. 1971), *passim.*

¹² Herbert Hoover, *Memoirs,* 2: 13–14. Domestic economic considerations as much as the need to reconstruct postwar Europe motivated Hoover's attempts at loan control. In particular he feared that higher foreign interest rates would attract too much American capital away from needed domestic development to wasteful foreign ventures.

¹³ Edwards, "Government Control," p. 693; Parrini, *Heir to Empire,* pp. 185–86; Joseph Brandes, *Herbert Hoover and Economic Diplomacy,* p. 153; Herbert Feis, *The Diplomacy of the Dollar,* pp. 7–8.

¹⁴ Brandes, *Hoover,* p. 153; Hoover to Warren Harding, 31 Dec. 1921, Personal File-Foreign Loans (hereafter cited as PF-Loans), HHCD; Hoover, *Memoirs,* 2: 85.

¹⁵ Edwards, "Government Control," pp. 694–95, 697; State Dept. press release, 3 Mar. 1922, PF-Loans, HHCD; Williams, *Economic Foreign Policy,* p. 88.

¹⁶ Grosvenor M. Jones memorandum to Hoover, 1 Apr. 1922, and Hoover, "Suggestions in Connection with Foreign Loans," 6 Apr. 1922, PF-Loans, HHCD.

¹⁷ Hoover, *Memoirs,* 2: 85–86, 89; Parrini, "American Empire," p. 201; Brandes, *Hoover,* p. 153; Hoover to Coolidge, 31 Dec. 1921, and Jones memoranda to Hoover, 1, 5 Apr. 1922, PF-Loans, HHCD.

¹⁸ Hoover to Willis K. Clark, 8 Mar. 1922, PF-Loans, HHCD. For details of the Queensland loan see Parrini, *Heir to Empire,* pp. 196–200.

[19] Parrini, *Heir to Empire,* pp. 194–95, 206–9; Brandes, *Hoover,* p. 4; Julius Klein memorandum to Hoover, 9 Dec. 1921, BFDC File, Hoover to Charles Evans Hughes, 29 Apr. 1922, PF-Loans, Hoover, "Summary of Achievements of the Dept. of Commerce," 25 July 1924, AF-1924 (1)—all in HHCD.

[20] Jones to Klein, 6 Apr. 1922, and Hoover to Hughes, 29 Apr. 1922, PF-Loans, HHCD; Brandes, *Hoover,* p. 218; Parrini, *Heir to Empire,* pp. 194–95, 200–201, 204–5. According to Parrini, Hoover apparently thought that if the loans were reproductive in character, equal bidding clauses would be a sufficient guarantee to American manufacturers. A minority of State Dept. officials, led by Stanley K. Hornbeck of the Western European Affairs Division agreed with Hoover, but they were unable to influence the official position of the State Dept.

[21] *New York Journal of Commerce Bulletin,* 13 Mar. 1922, p. 11; Philadelphia Board of Trade, *Proceedings,* 23 Jan. 1922, p. 34.

[22] Chandler, *Strong,* p. 265; Strong memorandum to Charles Evans Hughes, 14 Apr. 1922, PF-Loans, HHCD.

[23] Strong memorandum to Hughes, 14 Apr. 1922; Strong to Hughes, 9 June 1922, Foreign Loans File (hereafter cited as FLF), HHCD.

[24] Hoover to Hughes, 29 Apr. 1922, PF-Loans, HHCD; italics added.

[25] Betty Glad, *Charles Evans Hughes and the Illusions of Innocence,* pp. 311, 313–14, 317–19; Robert L. Heilbroner, "The Perils of American Economic Power," *Saturday Review,* 10 Aug. 1968, p. 24; Williams, *Economic Foreign Policy,* pp. 229–30; Parrini, *Heir to Empire,* p. 207 (fn. 89).

[26] Williams, *Economic Foreign Policy,* pp. 88–95; Brandes, *Hoover,* pp. 194–95, 201. It should be noted that bankers quite commonly attached restrictive clauses to their own foreign loans to insure their safety, but until the depression of 1929 these bankers and the State Dept. resisted the suggestion that loans "be earmarked for the purchase of goods in the United States." Not until 1934 with the creation of the Export-Import Bank did it become common to require that a portion of foreign loans be used to purchase American products. See: Ilse Mintz, *Deterioration in the Quality of Foreign Bonds Issued in the United States, 1920–1930,* pp. 74–75; Brandes, *Hoover,* p. 205; Barton J. Bernstein, ed., *Towards A New Past,* p. 247.

[27] Hoover, *Memoirs,* 2: 90; Davis, Polk, Wardwell, Gardiner, and Read to State Dept., 17 Mar. 1926, File 861.51/2010, NA, RG 59. For details of the coffee valorization problem, see my chapter 6.

[28] 124 (Feb. 1932): 121–22. For other criticisms of loan supervision see: *Wall Street Journal,* 18 Jan. 1928, p. 1; *Cotton* 92 (May 1928): 686; *Nation's Business* 20 (Feb. 1932): 13.

[29] *Wall Street Journal,* 22 Sept. 1923, p. 4; 3 Oct. 1925, p. 1; 15 July 1925, p. 15; *New York Journal of Commerce Bulletin,* 13 Mar. 1922, p. 11; Parrini, *Heir to Empire,* pp. 191–94; Williams, *Economic Foreign Policy,* pp. 237–38; Chandler, *Strong,* p. 266; *Nation's Business* 10 (5 June 1933): 23–24; twelfth meeting of the Council of the International Chamber of Commerce, report by Kent as chairman of the Committee on Economic Resto-

ration, 20–21 July 1923, File 600.00171/127, NA, RG 59; speech to ICC by Kent, Mar. 1923, and Kent to Hughes, 9 Feb. 1923, Kent Papers; Lamont, address to Bankers Convention in New York, 3 Oct. 1922, File 700.00/126, and Lamont to Joseph P. Cotton (State Dept.), 3 July 1929, File 600.00171/266, NA, RG 59.

[30] Hoover, addresses to U.S. Chamber of Commerce, 8 May 1923 and 7 May 1924, AF-1921–1923 and 1924 (1), HHCD.

[31] *Iron Age* 128 (6 Aug. 1931): 397; 131 (9 Feb. 1933): 245; *Nation's Business* 15 (Apr. 1927): 89–90; Speyer to Davis, 26 May 1932, Box 53, Davis Papers.

[32] Hoover, *Memoirs*, 2: 86, 88; 3: 9–11; Chandler, *Strong*, pp. 255, 414–15; Brandes, *Hoover*, pp. 153–54, 185, 205, 218; Feis, *Diplomacy of the Dollar*, pp. 9–10, 13, 29.

[33] Hoover, *Memoirs*, 2: 36–44; Brandes, *Hoover*, pp. 41–42, 50–51, 53–55. In 1920 the Dept. of Commerce employed 13,005 people and received an annual appropriation of approximately $24.5 million. By 1928 these figures had increased to 15,850 and $37.6 million, respectively. A year before the appearance of Lay's book, a presidential executive order "assigned to the Commerce Department's agents the prime responsibility in economic matters and provided for the cooperative exchange of information among all American agents abroad." The desire of Hoover and the business community to see the Commerce Dept. direct the economic foreign policy of the United States ultimately did not prevail. In 1939 Congress approved the transfer of the foreign activities and personnel of the Depts. of Agriculture and Commerce to the State Dept.

[34] Brandes, *Hoover*, p. 41; Hoover to Hughes, 16 Dec. 1921, and Hughes to Hoover, 16 Dec. 1921, HHPPF; Charles Evans Hughes, *The Pathway of Peace*, p. 257.

[35] Hughes, *Pathway of Peace*, pp. 265–66; Glad, *Hughes*, pp. 247, 306–9; Edwards, "Government Control," pp. 695–96; Brandes, *Hoover*, pp. 56, 201, 203, 205; U.S., Congress, Senate, Committee on Finance, *Hearings on S. R. 19: Authorizing the Financial Committee of the Senate to Investigate the Sale, Flotation, and Allocation by Banks, Banking Institutions, Corporations or Individuals of Foreign Bonds or Securities in the United States*, 72d Cong., 1st sess. (hereafter cited as U.S. Senate, *1931–1932 Loan Investigation*), 3, pt. 2: 725.

[36] Hoover to Hughes, 21 Nov. 1924, and Joseph C. Grew to Harold Phelps Stokes, 10 Sept. 1925, Frank B. Kellogg to Speyer and Co., 9 Oct. 1925, and Grosvenor Jones memoranda to Hoover, 21 Jan. 1926, 5 Nov. 1927—all in PF-Loans, HHCD; Feis, *Diplomacy of the Dollar*, pp. 43–44; Williams, *Economic Foreign Policy*, p. 95; Edwards, "Government Control," p. 699; *FRP, 1928*, 2: 898–903; *1930*, 3: 96–106.

[37] For details, see Brandes, *Hoover*, chapter 3.

[38] Hoover, *Memoirs*, 2: 90; Brandes, *Hoover*, pp. 135–36; Edwards, "Government Control," pp. 698–99; Williams, *Economic Foreign Policy*, pp. 94–95; Hoover, press release, 4 Jan. 1926, FLF, HHCD.

[39] Hoover, *Memoirs,* 2: 88–90; Hoover to Frank B. Kellogg, 17 May 1926, PF-Loans, HHCD; U.S. Senate, *1931–1932 Loan Investigation,* 3, pt. 2: 724–27, 745–48, 825–46, 1610–15.

[40] U.S., Congress, Senate, Subcommittee of the Committee on Foreign Relations, *Hearings on S. C. R. 22: Relative to Engaging the Responsibility of the Government in Financial Arrangements between Its Citizens and Sovereign Foreign Governments,* 68th Cong., 2d sess., 25–26 Feb. 1925 (hereafter cited as U.S. Senate, *1925 Loan Hearings*), p. 1; idem, *Hearings on S.C.R. 15: Relative to Engaging the Responsibility of the Government in Financial Agreements between Its Citizens and Sovereign Foreign Governments,* 69th Cong., 2d sess., Jan.–Feb. 1927 (hereafter cited as U.S. Senate, *1927 Loan Hearings*), p. 1.

[41] U.S. Senate, *1925 Loan Hearings,* pp. 2, 7, 20, 45; Mintz, *Deterioration in Foreign Bonds,* p. 6. Mintz's figures show that only 18 percent of the bonds issued between 1920 and 1924 defaulted in the 1930s, compared with 50 percent of the bonds issued in the last half of the decade.

[42] Some public criticism was evident before the 1925 and 1927 hearings. See Brandes, *Hoover,* pp. 201–2.

[43] Brandes, *Hoover,* pp. 47, 96–105, 199, 202; *Wall Street Journal,* 17 May 1922, p. 15; 5 Jan. 1928, p. 1; 16 Jan. 1928, p. 1; *Bankers Magazine* 114 (May 1927): 649; 115 (Dec. 1927): 779–80; 124 (Feb. 1932): 123–24; Hoover to Hughes, 29 Apr. 1922, PF-Loans, HHCD.

[44] Hoover, *Memoirs,* 3: 5–15; Lewis, *International Investments,* pp. 380–82; Mintz, *Deterioration in Foreign Bonds,* pp. 76–78; Mary Jane Matz, *The Many Lives of Otto Kahn,* p. 255; *Wall Street Journal,* 17 Apr. 1928, p. 1; *ABA Journal* 20 (Nov. 1927): 301–2; *Nation's Business* 15 (June 1927): 29. Also see testimony of major banking figures in U.S. Senate, *1931–1932 Loan Investigation.*

[45] *Cotton* 92 (May 1928): 686; Mintz, *Deterioration in Foreign Bonds,* p. 72.

[46] Edwards, "Government Control," p. 701; Williams, *Economic Foreign Policy,* pp. 95–98; *Wall Street Journal,* 1 Jan. 1926, p. 1; *FRP, 1930,* 3: 103.

[47] James W. Angell, *Financial Foreign Policy of the United States,* pp. 117–22; Harold G. Moulton and Leo Pasvolsky, *War Debts and World Prosperity* (Washington, 1932), p. 401; H. W. Arndt, *The Economic Lessons of the Nineteen-Thirties,* p. 13, 232–33.

Chapter Five

[1] Norman H. Davis to Bernard Baruch, 10 July 1920, Baruch to Davis, 12 July 1922, Ray Stannard Baker to Davis, 2, 15 Mar. 1922, Davis to Baker, 8 Mar. 1922, John Foster Dulles to Davis, 16 Mar. 1922, Box 3, Davis to William R. Castle (State Dept.), 20 July 1932, Box 8—all in Davis Papers; Davis to Cordell Hull, 3 Apr. 1933, File 550.S1/592, NA, RG 59; *Chicago Journal of Commerce,* 14 July 1932, p. 12; *ABA Journal* 21 (Nov. 1928):

445; 25 (Dec. 1932): 54; George L. Ridgeway, *Merchants of Peace,* pp. 129–30, 336–37, 350–63; Hoover to Frank B. Kellogg, 17 Mar. 1927, Conferences File-Economic, HHCD; Hoover memorandum, 4 Feb. 1923, Foreign Affairs File-Financial (hereafter cited as FA-Fin.), and draft of 5 Jan. 1933 letter to Senator Reed Smoot (with pencil corrections by Hoover), Debts File-Speech Drafts (hereafter cited as DF-Drafts), HHPP; Harold G. Moulton and Leo Pasvolsky, *War Debts and World Prosperity* (Washington, 1932), pp. 48–70.

[2] This Jan. 1920 memorandum was privately discouraged by the Dept. of the Treasury in a series of letters between Assistant Secretaries Norman H. Davis and Russell Leffingwell, and Paul Warburg, one of the leaders of the movement for an international business conference. It was also officially and publicly criticized by Treasury Secretary Carter Glass on 28 Jan. 1920 in a communication to Homer L. Ferguson, president of the U.S. Chamber of Commerce. See Box Aug. 1918–1931, Paul M. Warburg Papers; Paul P. Abrahams, "American Bankers and the Economic Tactics of Peace: 1919," *JAH* 56 (Dec. 1969): 580–82.

[3] Benjamin D. Rhodes, "Reassessing 'Uncle Shylock': The United States and the French War Debt, 1917–1929," *JAH* 55 (Mar. 1969): 787–89; J. M. Galloway, "The Public Life of Norman H. Davis," *Tennessee Historical Quarterly* 27 (Summer 1968): 144; Hoover, *Memoirs,* 2: 177–78; Hoover to Andrew W. Mellon, 6 Jan. 1923, PF, HHCD; Harvey O'Connor, *Mellon's Millions,* pp. 332–33; Robert K. Murray, *The Harding Era,* pp. 361–64; Carl P. Parrini, *Heir to Empire,* pp. 256–57.

[4] Moulton and Pasvolsky, *War Debts,* pp. 71–108; Benjamin H. Williams, *Economic Foreign Policy of the United States,* pp. 221–24. This percentage of cancellation appears perhaps overly generous if the loans to the Allies are viewed strictly as business transactions, which they were not. According to Williams the loans did not meet normal business standards because the credit of the Allies was not good and the purposes for which they were used could not always be justified in economic terms. The loans, Williams concludes, "were political in character as, indeed, are practically all loans from one government to another." He also notes that since prices in the 1920s were only two-thirds what they had been during the war, the Allies found themselves in the position of paying off their debts in currency which had a higher value than when the debts were incurred. To pay off the full amounts owed to the United States the Allies would have had to export to this country "fifty percent more goods than they received" (pp. 218–19, 225–26).

[5] Hoover memorandum, 4 Feb. 1923, FA-Fin., and draft of letter to Senator David Reed 5 Jan. 1933, DF-Drafts, HHPP; Hoover to Andrew W. Mellon, 6 Jan. 1923, PF, HHCD; Hoover to Adolph S. Ochs, 3 May 1926, HHPPF; Hoover, *Memoirs,* 2: 179, 345–46.

[6] Fragment of undated manuscript written between 1918 and 1922, Vanderlip Papers, beginning on p. 3 with words "Another momentous inheritance of the World War." Vanderlip, interview for *Giornale d'Italia,* 22 Apr. 1922,

Vanderlip Papers; Vanderlip, *What Next in Europe?* chapters 10, 16, 17; *ABA Journal* 104 (Apr. 1922): 733–36. In an undated, handwritten manuscript written in the first half of the 1920s (probably in 1922) Vanderlip outlined plans for what he called a United States of East Europe, which would have in time included Germany, Poland, and Russia, as well as the "succession states." (Vanderlip Papers.)

[7] *ABA Journal* 15 (Nov. 1922): 260–61, 267, 282–85, 289, 293, 378–79.

[8] Ibid., p. 379. McKenna was the sole exception because he represented English procancellation sentiment as opposed to American.

[9] Ibid., 16 (Oct. 1923): 222.

[10] Warburg to Norman H. Davis, 17 Nov. 1919, 26 Nov. 1919, Box Aug. 1918–1931, Paul M. Warburg Papers; *Wall Street Journal,* 26 Sept. 1923, p. 1; *Chicago Journal of Commerce,* 8 Dec. 1922, p. 1; 26 Dec. 1922, pp. 1–2; *ABA Journal* 15 (Feb. 1923): 537; *Coast Banker* 29 (Oct. 1922): 416; *Congressional Digest* 2 (Oct. 1922): 81–83; Bernard Baruch, *The Public Years,* p. 108; Lewis Corey, *The House of Morgan: A Social Biography of the Masters of Money* (New York, 1930), p. 431.

[11] Lester V. Chandler, *Benjamin Strong,* p. 273; *Coast Banker* 28 (Mar. 1922): 281; *Magazine of Wall Street* 30 (28 Oct. 1922): 978; *ABA Journal* 15 (Nov. 1922): 327; 15 (Dec. 1922): 420; Newton D. Baker to Judge John H. Clarke, 10 Mar. 1924, Box 59, Baker Papers; Arnold to Hoover, 4 May 1922, BFDC File, HHCD.

[12] *Bankers Magazine* 105 (Nov. 1922): 809; 114 (May 1927): 648–49; *ABA Journal* 19 (Nov. 1926): 279–80; 21 (Aug. 1928): 250–52; 24 (Sept. 1931): 145; 25 (May 1933): 20–21, 60–62; U.S. Chamber of Commerce, *Annual Report,* May 1926, p. 44; May 1933, p. 15.

[13] Chandler, *Strong,* pp. 273, 277, 280; James Speyer to Norman H. Davis, 24 June 1932, Speyer to Baron Koranyi, 23 June 1932, Box 53, Davis Papers; Fred I. Kent, address delivered 6 May 1924, p. 6, Kent Papers; *Chicago Journal of Commerce,* 26 Dec. 1922, p. 1; Ridgeway, *Merchants of Peace,* p. 130; *ABA Journal* 15 (Nov. 1922): 263, 327; 16 (Oct. 1923): 222; 25 (Oct. 1932): 20–21, 65; *Coast Banker,* 29 (Nov. 1922): 490; *Magazine of Wall Street* 30 (14 Oct. 1922): 896.

[14] Ridgeway, *Merchants of Peace,* p. 141; *Wall Street Journal,* 1 Dec. 1923, p. 5; *Nation's Business* 10 (Dec. 1922): 38–39; *ABA Journal* 24 (July 1931): 19; *Bankers Magazine* 104 (Apr. 1922): 632; *Coast Banker* 31 (Oct. 1923): 409; *Magazine of Wall Street* 30 (5 Aug. 1922): 488; *Pacific Banker,* 10 Nov. 1921, p. 6; 12 Jan. 1922, p. 1; 13 Apr. 1922, p. 1; 26 Oct. 1922, p. 1.

[15] *ABA Journal* 15 (Dec. 1922): 427–28; 16 (May 1924): 736, 756; 18 (Jan. 1925): 426, 474; 19 (Nov. 1926): 279–80; 19 (Jan. 1927): 501; 22 (July 1929): 22; 24 (July 1931): 19; 25 (July 1932): 30–31; 25 (Sept. 1932): 28; 25 (May 1933): 20–21, 60–62; 25 (June 1933): 21, 57–58; Davis to Newton D. Baker, 8 Sept. 1926, Box 252, Davis Papers; Young to Hoover, 5 Jan. 1926, HHPPF; Betty Glad, *Charles Evans Hughes and the*

Illusions of Innocence, p. 219; Paul M. Warburg to Norman Davis, 26 Nov. 1919, Box Aug. 1918–1931, Paul M. Warburg Papers.

[16] Included among the anticancellationist forces by 1930, aside from government officials, were the national leaders of the U.S. Chamber of Commerce, NAM, ABA, and NFTC. The *Pacific Banker, Bankers Magazine, Coast Banker, Wall Street Journal, Cotton,* and *Iron Age* were also in this camp, in addition to prominent business figures such as John Hays Hammond, Henry Ford, Norman H. Davis, Rudolph Spreckels, Elbert H. Gary, Julius H. Barnes, D. R. Forgan, Henry M. Robinson, and Vanderlip.

[17] See note 12, this chapter, for approval of debt settlements, plus: *Wall Street Journal,* 23 Dec. 1925, p. 11; 20 Jan. 1928, p. 1; *Bankers Magazine* 106 (June 1923): 974–75. For praise of the Dawes and Young plans see: Fred I. Kent, "Aspects of the International Financial Situation," pp. 1–6, and address before the NFTC, 6 June 1924, Kent Papers; *Bankers Magazine* 109 (Dec. 1924):1113, 1115, 1117, 1119–20; 110 (Jan. 1925): 57–59, 61, 62, 64; *Wall Street Journal,* 12 Apr. 1924, p. 1; 13 May 1924, p. 1; 5 Aug. 1924, p. 1; 12 Dec. 1924, p. 1; 27 Apr. 1928, p. 6; 17 June 1929, p. 1; 22 Jan. 1930, p. 1; *Cotton* 88 (May 1924): 660; *American Industries* 25 (Sept. 1924): 33; *Bradstreet's* 52 (19 Apr. 1924): 252; *ABA Journal* 18 (July 1925): 9–11; 22 (July 1929): 22; 22 (Nov. 1929): 462; 22 (May 1930): 1020–21, 1078–80; *Chicago Journal of Commerce,* 10 Apr. 1924, pp. 2, 14; 11 Apr. 1924, p. 2; *Coast Banker* 33 (Oct. 1924): 629; *Nation's Business* 12 (Oct. 1924): 38; 17 (July 1929): 11–12; David Loth, *Swope of G.E.,* p. 152.

[18] Ridgeway, *Merchants of Peace,* pp. 270–71; NFTC, *Proceedings,* 1924, p. v; 1925, p. viii; 1926, p. ix; 1928, pp. vii, 16, 23–24; 1931, p. 297.

[19] Davis to James T. Shotwell, 29 Dec. 1926, Box 53, Davis Papers; Herbert Feis, *1933: Characters in Crisis,* pp. 26, 49–51, 53, 102–3, 133.

[20] 87 (Feb. 1923): 273–74; 89 (July 1925): 891–92; 90 (Dec. 1925): 117; 90 (Mar. 1926): 422; 90 (June 1926): 746. These views are representative of the southern textile producers and the extreme pessimism reflects in part the depression which this industry experienced in 1924 and 1925. Cotton growers were generally more optimistic about the debt-funding agreements.

[21] 25 (July 1932): 30–31; 25 (Sept. 1932): 28.

[22] *Pacific Banker,* 10 Nov. 1921, p. 6; 10 Aug. 1922, p. 1; *Annalist* 20 (2 Oct. 1922): 315.

[23] *Coast Banker* 29 (July 1922): 107; *Pacific Banker,* 27 July 1922, p. 1.

[24] Easley to Newton D. Baker, 2 Sept. 1926, Box 252, Baker Papers.

[25] Harold Tiffany Butler, "Partisan Positions on Isolationism vs. Internationalism, 1918–1933" (D.S.S. dissertation, Syracuse Univ., 1963), pp. 165–66, 174–78, 264–65; Rudolph Spreckels to Franklin D. Roosevelt, 21 Dec. 1932, President's Personal File 3733, Franklin D. Roosevelt Papers, Franklin D. Roosevelt Library, Hyde Park, New York; J. Chal Vinson, "War Debts and Peace Legislation: The Johnson Act of 1934," *Mid-America* 50

(July 1968): 206–13; Richard Lowitt, "Progressive Farm Leaders and Hoover's Moratorium," *Mid-America* 50 (July 1968): 236–39; Robert James Maddox, *William E. Borah and American Foreign Policy*, pp. 126–35. A notable exception to the anticancellationist position of most farm spokesmen can be found, according to Lowitt, in a letter by Henry A. Wallace to George W. Norris in which Wallace endorses some form of cancellation "so as to avoid bringing [the debts] up at recurring intervals and thus disorganizing the international structure of trade."

[26] Butler, "Partisan Positions," pp. 157–59, 247–53, 651.

[27] Ibid., pp. 638–40. The remaining percentages of the total circulations for and against the debt-funding agreements came from independent newspapers.

[28] Ralph Easley to Newton D. Baker, 2 Sept. 1926, Box 252, Baker Papers.

[29] Ray Stannard Baker to Davis, 1 Mar. 1922, Box 3, and Davis to Shotwell, 29 Dec. 1926, Box 53, Davis Papers; Newton D. Baker to Judge John H. Clarke, 10 Sept. 1926, Box 59, and Davis to Baker, 8 Sept. 1926, Box 252, Baker Papers. Norman Davis had served as financial adviser to the Treasury in 1917 and in that capacity he approved the wartime loan policy of the U.S.; therefore, he was not as free to become an outright cancellationist as was Newton D. Baker, the former secretary of war under Wilson. As assistant secretary of the treasury in 1919, however, Davis did appear before the Ways and Means Committee with a plan for deferring interest payments on the war loans to foreign governments. See Galloway, "Public Life of Davis," pp. 143–44.

[30] Over half of Germany's foreign indebtedness by 1931 was in the form of short-term loans which were being rapidly recalled. Unfortunately German bankers had re-lent this money to domestic concerns on what amounted to long-term conditions, so the country faced a severe capital shortage which reached crisis proportions in 1931. See H. W. Arndt, *The Economic Lessons of the Nineteen-Thirties*, pp. 25–29.

[31] Hoover, Outline Diary of Events Leading to the Moratorium (hereafter cited as Diary), 6, 7 May 1931, Foreign Loans File (hereafter cited as FLF), HHPP; idem, *Memoirs*, 2: 346.

[32] Hoover, Diary, 11 May 1931; idem, *Memoirs*, 3: 67–68; Robert H. Ferrell, *American Diplomacy in the Great Depression*, pp. 33, 35–43; Norman A. Graebner, ed., *An Uncertain Tradition*, pp. 170–71, 177. Many temperamental differences existed between Hoover, Stimson, and Mellon. Hoover openly preferred to work with Under-Secretaries William R. Castle, Jr., and Ogden L. Mills, both of whom became acting secretaries of their respective departments when Stimson and Mellon were out of the country.

[33] Arndt, *Economic Lessons*, p. 29. The failure was precipitated by the French withdrawal of short-term credits and this in turn triggered a financial crisis throughout Central Europe.

[34] Hoover, Diary, 19 May 1931. Hoover delivered this address on 15 June, but eliminated the section on foreign debts because the situation had so de-

teriorated that he feared "any discussion without action might only make things worse." See William Starr Myers and Walter H. Newton, *The Hoover Administration*, p. 89.

[35] Hoover, Diary, 19, 20, 21, 22 May 1931; idem, *Memoirs* 3: 65; James W. Angell, *Financial Foreign Policy of the United States*, p. 119; Arndt, *Economic Lessons*, pp. 29–30, 180–83.

[36] Hoover, Diary, 5 June 1931. In his memoirs (3:68), Hoover says both Mills and Stimson supported him at this meeting, but his diary clearly indicates that Mills's opposition lasted until 18 June.

[37] Hoover, Diary, 5 June 1931. On this day Hoover wrote that the New York bankers had "apparently got wind of my discussion with different people on the question of reviewing the capacity to pay." This is the first indication in his diary of eastern banking interests trying to influence the president's action on the financial crisis in Central Europe.

[38] Hoover, Diary, 6 June 1931. The House of Morgan had been a leading participant in the Dawes and Young plan loans, but apparently had not extended large amounts of short-term credit, the type of indebtedness most threatened by the collapse in the German banking system.

[39] Hoover, Diary, 8, 9, 13, 14 June 1931.

[40] Ibid., 13, 14 June 1931; Hoover, *Memoirs*, 3: 68.

[41] List of pledged congressmen and senators, DF-Moratorium, HHPP. Hoover was unable to obtain the positive support of the Democratic leaders, Senator Joseph T. Robinson and Speaker John Nance Garner. Both agreed, however, not to oppose the moratorium publicly. See: Hoover, Diary, 20 June 1931; idem, *Memoirs*, 3: 69.

[42] Hoover, Diary, 20 June 1931; idem, *Memoirs*, 3: 70; Ferrell, *American Diplomacy*, p. 113. Apparently those nationalists in Congress who opposed the moratorium, especially the Progressives led by Hiram Johnson, resented the fact that Hoover had canvassed individual members of Congress instead of calling a special session to consider the question. See Vinson, "War Debts," p. 210.

[43] Ferrell, *American Diplomacy*, pp. 110, 113. For details of the French objections and the unsuccessful pressure brought to bear on Germany by the United States between 28 June and 4 July (in conjunction with England and France) to obtain a guarantee that the Germans would not use the moratorium to allocate more money for armaments, see Moulton and Pasvolsky, *War Debts*, pp. 191, 325–30; Robin M. Rudoff, "The Hoover Moratorium and German Naval Rearmament, 1931–1932: A Case of International Blackmail," paper presented to the Southwest Social Science Association meeting, Dallas, Texas, 27 Mar. 1970.

[44] The transatlantic telephone conversations over the moratorium and related economic issues mark the first time this means of communication was used as a diplomatic tool. Stimson told Hoover at the time that he found it "very unsatisfactory," but the president disagreed. See Hoover-Stimson conversation, 20 July 1931 (10 A.M.), Disarmament File, HHPP; Hoover, *Memoirs*, 3: 71.

[45] Hoover, Diary, 23 June, 4, 5, 6 July 1931; Ferrell, *American Diplomacy,* pp. 113–16; Arndt, *Economic Lessons,* pp. 235–36.

[46] Hoover-Stimson conversations, 17 July 1931 (11:30 A.M., 5:15 P.M.), 19 July 1931 (9 A.M.), DF-1931–1932, State Dept. press release, 21 July 1931, DF-Moratorium—all in HHPP; Hoover, *Memoirs,* 3: 73, 77; Arndt, *Economic Lessons,* pp. 9–13, 283–95.

[47] Hoover-Stimson conversations, 17 July 1931 (5:30 P.M.), 19 July 1931 (9 A.M.),·21 July 1931 (5:30 P.M.), DF-1931–1932, HHPP.

[48] Hoover-Stimson conversations, 19 July 1931 (9 A.M.), 21 July 1931 (5:30 P.M.), DF-1931–1932, HHPP; Hoover, Diary, 18 July 1931; idem, *Memoirs,* 3: 73.

[49] In this incident Stimson appears both more pro-French and more pro-German than Hoover and considerably less under the anti-German influence exerted by various members of the House of Morgan, such as S. Parker Gilbert, R. C. Leffingwell, and Thomas W. Lamont, than was Hoover. See: Moulton and Pasvolsky, *War Debts,* p. 304; Gilbert memorandum to Lamont, 19 May 1932, Lamont to Stimson, 23 May 1932, Lamont to J. P. Morgan, R. C. Leffingwell, and S. Parker Gilbert, 19 Apr. 1932—all in File 462.00 R 296 A1/154½, NA, RG 59.

[50] Hoover, Diary, 19 July 1931; State Dept. press release, 21 July 1931, DF-Moratorium, HHPP. Total American bank holdings for all of Central Europe were probably in excess of $1.7 billion.

[51] Hoover-Stimson conversations, 20 July 1931 (10 A.M., 4 P.M.), DF-1931–1932, HHPP; Hoover, *Memoirs,* 3: 73. In the long run, the precipitous reduction by the French of their German credits strengthened the position of the United States at this conference. Some Wall Street bankers attacked the stabilization plan on 22 July but under the influence of Dwight Morrow they were all persuaded to accept it. See: Myers and Newton, *Hoover Administration,* p. 104; Harold Nicolson, *Dwight Morrow,* pp. 395–96.

[52] Hoover, Diary, 18, 20, 21, 22 July 1931; Hoover-Stimson conversation, 21 July 1931 (5:30 P.M.), DF-1931–1932,.HHPP; Ferrell, *American Diplomacy,* pp. 116–17. See my chapter 8 for a discussion of the Stimson Doctrine.

[53] Hoover memorandum, 4 Feb. 1923, FA-Fin., HHPP; Hoover to Hughes, 6, 16 Dec. 1921, HHPPF. Although until the Young Plan there was no legal connection between reparations and debts, a few government figures in addition to Hoover admitted the relationship on occasion, as did some businessmen, but it never became official policy. See: Glad, *Hughes,* p. 221; Moulton and Pasvolsky, *War Debts,* pp. 193, 297, 321; Ferrell, *American Diplomacy,* p. 110; Merchants Assoc. of New York to Hughes, 25 Jan. 1924, Box 63, Hughes Papers.

[54] Howard H. Quint and Robert H. Ferrell, eds., *The Talkative President: The Off-the-Record Press Conferences of Calvin Coolidge* (Amherst, Mass., 1964), pp. 178–86, 198–200; Glad, *Hughes,* pp. 218–35; Herbert Feis, *The Diplomacy of the Dollar,* pp. 40–45; Hoover, *Memoirs,* 2: 181–82. For the details of both plans see Moulton and Pasvolsky, *War Debts,* pp. 161–233.

Secretary of State Hughes played the leading behind-the-scenes role in arranging the Dawes Commission, with Hoover and Mellon helping him select the American members.

[55] Glad, *Hughes,* pp. 229, 231; Graebner, *Uncertain Tradition,* p. 144.

[56] Robinson quoted in Glad, *Hughes,* p. 235; Norman H. Davis, "American Foreign Policy: A Democratic View," *Foreign Affairs* 3 (15 Sept. 1924): 27, 32.

[57] Moulton and Pasvolsky, *War Debts,* pp. 303–4, 420–21. This would not have meant a greater ideological use of force as Herbert Feis has suggested on the basis of his experience as an economic adviser to the State Department under Hoover and Roosevelt. As noted in chapter 1, what was required was probably impossible at the time. It was, to recapitulate, the recognition that international disequilibrium was being perpetuated, not ameliorated, by the postwar attempt of the United States to lead the world back to the gold standard, relying upon traditional market forces to effect the necessary economic adjustments between nations. A foreign policy based on such a recognition would have demanded even more domestic economic planning than Hoover and the Federal Reserve Board envisaged; more government responsibility in foreign affairs than even the Wilsonians thought necessary; more social and economic sacrifices than middle class Americans wanted in the midst of burgeoning consumerism; and in general a less conventional and ethnocentric view of international relations on the part of government and business leaders. See Feis, *Diplomacy of the Dollar,* p. 46; Arndt, *Economic Lessons,* pp. 221–42, 290, 294–302.

[58] *FRP, 1930,* 3: 103; James A. Thomas, "Business Principles in World Politics," *Asia* 25 (Feb. 1925): 99, 166; Arndt, *Economic Lessons,* pp. 110, 226, 292–93.

[59] Rexford G. Tugwell, et al., *Statement by Members of the Faculty of Political Science, Columbia University, on the War Debt Problem* (Carnegie Endowment for Peace, 1927); 1927 Advisory Council of the American Assoc. Favoring Reconsideration of the War Debts, Box 252, Newton D. Baker Papers; Frederic M. Sackett (ambassador to Germany) to Hoover, 15 Sept. 1931 (transmitting criticism of banker Frederick H. Allen), and Hoover to Sackett, 26 Sept. 1931, Foreign Affairs File-Diplomats (hereafter cited as FA-Diplomats), HHPP; Moulton and Pasvolsky, *War Debts,* pp. 415, 421–22; Feis, *1933: Characters in Crisis,* pp. 17–18, 21–23, 73–74.

[60] Hoover, *Memoirs,* 3: 171–72, 178; Thomas W. Lamont to J. Ridgely Carter, 4 May 1932, and Lamont to Stimson, 23 May 1932, File 462.00 R 296 A1/154½ NA, RG 59; James Speyer to Baron Koranyi, 23 June 1932, Box 53, Davis Papers.

[61] Merchants Association of New York to Hughes, 25 Jan. 1924, Box 63, Hughes Papers; Fred I. Kent, "Aspects of the International Financial Situation," pp. 6–7, Kent Papers; James Speyer to Norman Davis, 24 June 1932, and Speyer to Baron Koranyi, 23 June 1932, Box 53, Davis Papers; *Chicago Journal of Commerce,* 28 July 1932, p. 1; 24 June 1932, p. 12; 29 June 1932,

p. 12; *ABA Journal* 25 (Dec. 1932) : 13, 54; Ridgeway, *Merchants of Peace,* pp. 348–49.

[62] Walter E. Edge (ambassador to France) to Hoover, 18 July 1932, FA-Diplomats, HHPP; Hoover, *Memoirs,* 3: 171; William C. Bullitt to Louis Wehle, 3 Dec. 1932, PPF 693, Roosevelt Papers; Feis, *1933,* pp. 17–18.

[63] Edge to State Dept., 13 Dec. 1929 (transmitting S. Parker Gilbert letter), FA-Diplomats, HHPP; Lamont to J. P. Morgan, et al., 19 Apr. 1932, Lamont to J. Ridgely Carter, 4 May 1932, Lamont to Stimson, 23 May 1932, Lamont to Ramsay MacDonald, 13 May 1932—all in File 462.00 R 296 A1/ 154½, Carter to Lamont, 31 May 1932, and Lamont to Stimson, 22 July 1932 (transmitting J. Tsushima letter) File -/291½, NA, RG 59; Moulton and Pasvolsky, *War Debts,* pp. 354–66.

[64] Memoranda of Lamont and Stimson conversations, 17 Nov. (10:50 A.M.) and 28 Nov. (4:40 P.M.) 1932, File 800.51 W 89/588½, Lamont to Paris office of House of Morgan, 28 Nov. 1932, File -/598½, NA, RG 59; Hoover, *Memoirs,* 3:184.

[65] Hoover, *Memoirs,* 3: 178–83; Hoover to Roosevelt, 17 Dec. 1932, Roosevelt to Hoover, 19 Dec. 1932, PPF 820, Roosevelt Papers; Lloyd C. Gardner, *Economic Aspects of New Deal Diplomacy,* pp. 26–27; Feis, *1933,* pp. 36, 40, 76.

[66] Daniel R. Fusfeld, *The Economic Thought of Franklin D. Roosevelt and the Origins of the New Deal,* p. 291, fn. 7; Charles H. Strong to Roosevelt, 7 July 1932, PPF 7421, Roosevelt Papers; Newton D. Baker to Walter Lippmann, 15 July 1932, Box 149, Baker Papers.

[67] Hoover, *Memoirs,* 3: 183–91; Louis B. Wehle, *Hidden Threads of History: Wilson through Roosevelt* (New York, 1953), pp. 114–15, 120; Arthur M. Schlesinger, Jr., *The Coming of the New Deal* (Boston, 1959), pp. 203–10; Beatrice Farnsworth, *William C. Bullitt and the Soviet Union,* pp. 79–84; Moley background press conference, 27 Apr. 1933 (as described in a confidential memorandum by M. J. McDermott, chief, Division of Current Information, State Dept.), and Roosevelt press conference, 14 June 1933, Edgar B. Nixon, *Franklin D. Roosevelt and Foreign Affairs,* 1: 82–89, 228–35; Feis, *1933,* pp. 34–47, 68–73, 76.

[68] Hoover to John Callan O'Laughlin, 24 Oct., 13 Nov., 5 Dec. 1933, O'Laughlin Papers; Schlesinger, *Coming of the New Deal,* pp. 186–88, 196–98, 200–204, 206–7, 213–32, 247–48; Baker to Judge John H. Clarke, 22 June, 12 July 1933, Box 59, Baker Papers; Gardner, *Economic Aspects,* pp. 14, 29; Committee for the Nation to Roosevelt, 20 July 1933, Nixon, *FDR and Foreign Affairs,* 1: 321–22; Feis, *1933,* pp. 40, 51, 53, 71, 102–3, 251.

[69] Ridgeway, *Merchants of Peace,* p. 362; Gardner, *Economic Aspects,* pp. 20, 22; Williams, *Economic Foreign Policy,* pp. 229–35; *Chicago Journal of Commerce,* 22 June 1931, p. 14; Arndt, *Economic Lessons,* pp. 37–40, 71–72.

[70] Lamont to Ramsay MacDonald, 13 May 1932, File 462.00 R 296 A1/ 154½, NA, RG 59.

[71] This is generally the conclusion of public opinion analysts. See: Bernard R. Berelson, et al., *Voting: A Study of Opinion Formation in a Presidential Campaign* (Chicago, 1954), pp. 109–14; Elihu Katz and Paul F. Lazarsfeld, *Personal Influence: The Part Played by People in the Flow of Mass Communications* (Glencoe, Ill., 1955), pp. 32–33, 310–12, 325; Alfred O. Hero, *Opinion Leaders in American Communities* (Boston, 1959), pp. 10–16. For the *Reader's Guide* survey, see President's Research Committee on Social Trends, *Recent Social Trends in the United States* (New York, 1934), p. 439.

[72] *Recent Social Trends,* pp. 434–35. Representative examples of business approval of Hoover's moratorium include: *Nation's Business* 19 (Aug. 1931): 13; *Chicago Journal of Commerce,* 22 June 1931, p. 14. For Lamont's comments about general public opinion see Lamont to Stimson, 23 May 1932 (enclosing memorandum), File 462.00 R 296 A1/154½, and Lamont to Stimson, 10 June 1932, File -/291½, NA, RG 59. *Literary Digest* noted on 30 July 1932 that within the nation's press a minority were openly advocating debt cancellation while the majority favored drastic revisions as long as the term cancellation was not used.

[73] Neither Hoover nor Stimson was noted for using foreign policy as a medium for expressing popular opinion, and the key men of the original Brain Trust (Moley, Tugwell, and Berle) had formulated most of their economic views at Columbia Univ. before taking office. See: Graebner, *Uncertain Tradition,* p. 175; *Harper's* 161 (June 1930): 5; Fusfeld, *Economic Thought,* pp. 209–16.

[74] Selig Adler, *The Isolationist Impulse,* pp. 229–32; Vinson, "War Debts," pp. 206–22. The passage of the Johnson Act did mark the beginning, however, of greater nationalist influence over both economic and political foreign policy.

[75] Butler, "Partisan Positions," pp. 637–38.

[76] Young to Hoover, 5 Jan. 1926, HHPPF.

[77] Ernest R. May, "An American Tradition in Foreign Policy: The Role of Public Opinion," in William H. Nelson, ed., *Theory and Practice in American Politics,* pp. 103, 122.

Chapter Six

[1] J. W. Alexander (sec. of commerce) to D. F. Houston (sec. of the treasury), 24 Feb. 1920, File 640, NA, RG 151; W. S. Culbertson (ambassador to Chile) to Hoover, 22 June 1932, FA-Diplomats, HHPP; Charles Evans Hughes, *Our Relations to the Nations of the Western Hemisphere,* p. 83; Benjamin H. Williams, *Economic Foreign Policy of the United States,* pp. 28–36, 96, 100, 103, 110; James W. Angell, *Financial Foreign Policy of the United States,* pp. 35–38, 80–84, 90–99; NFTC, *Proceedings,* 1920, pp. 218–19, 522.

[2] Thomas W. Lamont to Norman H. Davis (under-sec. of state), 25 Oct.,

19 Nov. 1920, House of Morgan telegram to Denkstein (Mexico), 14 Dec. 1920, Box 33, Davis Papers; Grosvenor M. Jones (chief, Finance and Investment Division, BFDC) to J. Fiedheim, 15 Nov. 1923, and Jones to Hoover, 30 Aug. 1924, File 640, NA, RG 151; *ABA Journal* 14 (July 1921): 4–5; 15 (Apr. 1923): 659–64, 690–91; 16 (Jan. 1924): 417; 17 (June 1925): 774; 18 (Aug. 1925): 107; 19 (Sept. 1926): 158, 178; 21 (Jan. 1929): 636–37, 713; 21 (Feb. 1929): 766; 24 (Sept. 1931): 153–54, 173; NFTC, *Proceedings,* 1920, pp. 511, 687, 719, 726–28; 1921, pp. 344–45, 575; 1923, pp. 138–39, 142; 1926, pp. 49, 61, 417–18; *Southern California Business* 1 (Sept. 1922): 80, 98; Commerce Dept. press release, 11 Feb. 1933, found as appendix 18 in "Accomplishments in Major Policy in American Foreign Relations with the Countries of the Far East from March 4, 1929 to March 2, 1933," prepared by the Far Eastern Division of the State Dept. at Hoover's request, Executive Depts. File-State, HHPP (hereafter cited as State Dept., "Far Eastern Accomplishments").

[3] NFTC, *Proceedings,* 1920, pp. 209–19, 520–22, 687–88, 726; 1921, p. 351; 1922, pp. 354–57; 1923, pp. 258–59; 1926, p. 289; *Southern California Business* 1 (Oct. 1922): 23, 40–41; 1 (Nov. 1922): 7–8, 46–48; 2 (Apr. 1923): 20; 2 (May 1923): 17, 43; 3 (Aug. 1924): 20, 50; *American Industries* 25 (June 1925): 41–44; *Cotton* 91 (June 1927): 789–90; Grosvenor Jones to Hoover, 30 Aug. 1924, File 640, NA, RG 151; Akira Iriye, *After Imperialism,* pp. 278–79; State Dept., "Far Eastern Accomplishments," appendix 18.

[4] *ABA Journal* 19 (July 1926): 3; 21 (Sept. 1928): 242–43; 25 (May 1933): 56; NFTC, *Proceedings,* 1927, pp. 180, 233, 490, 496–97; Thomas W. Lamont to Charles Evans Hughes, 15 Jan., 9 Feb. 1924, Hughes Papers.

[5] James W. Angell, *Financial Foreign Policy of the United States,* pp. 79–80; Williams, *Economic Foreign Policy,* p. 183; Barton J. Bernstein, ed., *Towards a New Past,* pp. 240, 245, 250, 255–56; J.-J. Servan-Schreiber, *The American Challenge* (New York, 1968), passim; Paul A. Baran and Paul M. Sweezy, *Monopoly Capitalism,* p. 53; Culbertson to Hoover, 21 Nov. 1930, FA-Diplomats, HHPP. For a similar statement by another government official defending U.S. expansion into the Far East, see NFTC, *Proceedings,* 1920, p. 218.

[6] Hughes, 30 Oct. 1922 speech, Box 172, Hughes Papers; Charles Evans Hughes, *The Pathway of Peace,* pp. 98–101, 128, 133–34, 153–68; idem, *Our Relations,* pp. 3, 11, 14, 41, 45, 49, 51, 54, 58, 63–64, 112; Herbert Hoover, *Addresses Delivered during the Visit of Herbert Hoover to Central and South America, November–December, 1928* (hereafter cited as Hoover, *South American Addresses*), pp. 4, 12–13, 16, 22, 29–30, 36, 47, 51, 58–59; Alexander DeConde, *Herbert Hoover's Latin American Policy,* pp. 59, 63–65; Betty Glad, *Charles Evans Hughes and the Illusions of Innocence,* pp. 237–41, 254–56, 266–67; Bryce Wood, *The Making of the Good Neighbor Policy,* pp. 6, 126–27; Eugene P. Trani, "Harding Administration and Recognition of Mexico," *Ohio History* 75 (Spring-Summer 1966): 137–48.

[7] Hughes, *Pathway of Peace*, pp. 58–59, 169; idem, *Our Relations*, pp. 75–84; DeConde, *Hoover's Latin American Policy*, pp. 7, 59, 69; Hoover to O.K. Davis, 24 Oct. 1925, Inter-American High Commission File (hereafter cited as IAHC File), HHCD; Joseph S. Tulchin, *The Aftermath of War*, pp. 103–12, 235.

[8] Charles Evans Hughes, *Pan American Peace Plans*, pp. 7–23, 68; idem, *Our Relations*, pp. 85–86, 91, 100–103; Frederick B. Pike, *Chile and the United States, 1880–1962* (Notre Dame, Ind., 1963), pp. 214–31; Glad, *Hughes*, pp. 264–67; David D. Burks, "The United States and the Geneva Protocol of 1924: 'A New Holy Alliance'?" *AHR* 64 (July 1959): 891–93, 899–900.

[9] DeConde, *Hoover's Latin American Policy*, pp. 39–43; Cordell Hull, *Memoirs*, 1: 310–11; Hull to Roosevelt, 27 May 1933, in Edgar B. Nixon, *Franklin D. Roosevelt and Foreign Affairs*, 1: 182–83.

[10] Hughes, *Our Relations*, pp. 81–84; DeConde, *Hoover's Latin American Policy*, p. 60; Glad, *Hughes*, p. 243. It should be noted, however, that Hughes did negotiate the agreement for withdrawing American troops from the Dominican Republic in 1924.

[11] Christian A. Herter (Hoover's secretary) to Charles E. Herring of the BFDC, 11 Apr. 1921, Mellon to Warren Harding, 30 Nov. 1921, Commerce Dept. press release, 19 Dec. 1921, Hoover to Representative James W. Huster, 24 Apr. 1922, Hoover to the Brazilian president of the Inter-American High Commission—all in IAHC File, HHCD; Commerce Dept. memoranda on engineering standards, 3, 9 Aug. 1922, and Julius Klein to Hoover, 17 July 1922, BFDC File, HHCD; *ABA Journal* 21 (Feb. 1929): 756; 21 (Mar. 1929): 855; DeConde, *Hoover's Latin American Policy*, pp. 5–6; William Starr Myers, *The Foreign Policies of Herbert Hoover, 1929–1933* (New York, 1940), p. 41; Lloyd C. Gardner, *Economic Aspects of New Deal Diplomacy*, p. 62; Joseph Brandes, *Herbert Hoover and Economic Diplomacy*, pp. 197–98; Tulchin, *Aftermath of War*, pp. 115–16.

[12] Latin America is the area of the world in which the United States has most intensively tried to export what it considers to be its most valuable products—capitalism and democracy. In addition to recommending standard political and economic procedures followed in the United States, this country has found it possible to bypass bureaucratic red tap and institute new methods which in some instances were not yet in practice in the United States. This was the case with the cash accounting system set up by Charles Dawes for the Dominican Republic in 1929. Other ideas tested in Latin America in the 1920s with varying degrees of success or failure included various budget reforms, the entire concept of free elections accompanied by foreign electoral supervision, and a variety of recommendations from technical commissions. See: William Appleman Williams, "Latin America: Laboratory of American Foreign Policy in the Nineteen-twenties," *Inter-American Economic Affairs* 11 (Autumn 1957): 3–30; Charles G. Dawes, "Santo Domingo Notes," 2, 4, 20, 29 Apr. 1929, Charles G. Dawes Papers, Northwestern Univ. (hereafter

cited as Dawes Papers); Theodore Paul Wright, Jr., *American Support of Free Elections Abroad,* pp. 62, 87–89, 95, 144–49, and passim; Henry L. Stimson, *American Policy in Nicaragua,* pp. 59, 91, 98–99.

13 Hoover, *Memoirs,* 2: 210; Wood, *Good Neighbor Policy,* pp. 5–7, 52–58; DeConde, *Hoover's Latin American Policy,* pp. 59–65; Harold Nicolson, *Dwight Morrow,* p. 271; Stanley Robert Ross, "Dwight Morrow and the Mexican Revolution," *Hispanic American Historical Review* 38 (Nov. 1958): 509; Robert H. Ferrell, *Frank B. Kellogg and Henry L. Stimson,* pp. 27–63; Gardner, *Economic Aspects,* pp. 49–51.

14 Hoover, *South American Addresses,* pp. 3, 7, 29, 58; Hoover, *Memoirs,* 2: 211–15; DeConde, *Hoover's Latin American Policy,* pp. 51, 59, 79–89; Myers, *Foreign Policies of Hoover,* pp. 43, 50–53; Confidential Summary of Latin American Opinion by the International Pan American Committee, 17 July 1929, Executive Depts.-State (hereafter cited as ED-State), HHPP.

15 Hoover, *Memoirs,* 2: 333–34; DeConde, *Hoover's Latin American Policy,* pp. 60–63, 112–13; Wood, *Good Neighbor Policy,* pp. 41–47, 122–35; Robert H. Ferrell, *American Diplomacy in the Great Depression,* pp. 218–20; idem, "Repudiation of a Repudiation," *JAH* 51 (Mar. 1965): 669–73; Cordell Hull, *Memoirs,* 1: 308–41; Frank B. Kellogg to Hoover, 5 Mar. 1929, ED-State, HHPP; *FRP, 1930,* 1: 387–89; memorandum of Harry F. Guggenheim (ambassador to Cuba), 29 Mar. 1933, File 837.51/1558, NA, RG 59.

16 Williams, *Economic Foreign Policy,* pp. 175–216.

17 Marvin D. Bernstein, ed., *Foreign Investments in Latin America: Cases and Attitudes* (New York, 1966), pp. 43–46; Angell, *Financial Foreign Policy,* pp. 135–36; Raymond F. Mikesell, ed., *U.S. Private and Government Investment Abroad* (Eugene, Ore., 1962), pp. 52–55; Cleona Lewis, *America's Stake in International Investments,* pp. 606, 623–27; *ABA Journal* 19 (July 1926): 4; 21 (Feb. 1929): 756; 23 (Nov. 1930): 417; 24 (Aug. 1931): 75.

18 Grosvenor Jones to Carlton Jackson (acting commercial attaché, Bogotá), 6 June 1924, File 640, NA, RG 151; *ABA Journal* 24 (Aug. 1931): 75; Angell, *Financial Foreign Policy,* pp. 39, 80–81.

19 Gardner, *Economic Aspects,* pp. 47, 61; Wood, *Good Neighbor Policy,* pp. 129, 131. "Customary methods of diplomacy" included, according to Wood, "financial inducements, protests, discriminatory practices of an economic or ceremonial character, as well as various measures designed to create positive collaboration among the American states" (p. 159).

20 Bernstein, *Foreign Investments,* pp. 43, 45, 51; Gardner, *Economic Aspects,* pp. 52–61; Wood, *Good Neighbor Policy,* pp. 285–87, 311.

21 Wright, *Support of Free Elections,* pp. 134–35; Wood, *Good Neighbor Policy,* pp. 7–8, 159–63, 309–12, 329–30, 343–46, 349–50; Williams, *Economic Foreign Policy,* pp. 109–33; O. Edmund Smith, Jr., *Yankee Diplomacy,* pp. 24–25.

22 Alan K. Manchester, *British Preëminence in Brazil* (New York, 1964;

reprint of 1933 Univ. of North Carolina Press ed.), pp. 334–36, 340–41; William O. Scroggs, "The American Investment in Latin America," *Foreign Affairs* 10 (Apr. 1932): 503–4; State Dept. memorandum, 13 Mar. 1930, File 832.51/559, NA, RG 59. The 4 file boxes in PF-Loans, HHCD, indicate that for all of Hoover's attempts to establish loan controls, only one Latin American loan was opposed by his department as "economically unsound." This was a 1928 loan to Bolivia which the State Dept. refused to oppose. But the Commerce Dept. was generally more sceptical than the State Dept. of Chile's and Colombia's capacity to pay. Also see Grosvenor Jones to Robert Lamont (sec. of commerce), 21 Jan. 1932, File 640, NA, RG 151. For a detailed comparison of English and American investments in Brazil as of the depression, see Theodore M. Berson, " 'Dependência do Imperialismo': Foreign Investment in Brazil, 1935," *Business History Review* 43 (Summer 1969): 192–200. American investments did not begin to surpass those of England until just before World War II.

[23] Brandes, *Hoover,* pp. 130, 132; Louis Domeratsky (assist. director, BFDC) to Hoover, 9 Nov. 1925, Grosvenor Jones memoranda, 5 Apr. 1922, 18 Mar., 5, 30 Apr., 27 July 1925, Hoover memorandum, 25 Aug. 1925, Kellogg to Hoover, 4 Nov. 1925—all in PF-Loans, HHCD. Hoover only opposed price controls and commodity monopolies which he deemed—not in the interest of the United States. As food administrator during the war he had organized the International Sugar Committee which controlled the price of Cuban sugar to keep it from rising as a result of increased demand. See Robert F. Smith, *The United States and Cuba,* pp. 20–21.

[24] James Speyer to Hoover, 9 Dec. 1925, Grosvenor Jones to Hoover, 12 Nov. 1925, Hoover memorandum, 25 Aug. 1925, State Dept. to Speyer, 6 Nov. 1925, Hoover to Walter McCreery (commercial attaché, Rio de Janeiro), 5 Jan. 1926, Hoover to Kellogg, 8 Feb. 1926—all in PF-Loans, HHCD; *ABA Journal* 19 (July 1926): 3; 21 (Sept. 1928): 228.

[25] Hoover memorandum, 25 Aug. 1925, Box 378, HHCD. As middlemen, coffee importers and roasters could pass higher prices on to wholesale distributors and retailers without having to worry about consumer reaction. This example of business opposition to the government's attempt to control economic activity in Latin America was unusual. Ordinarily the Closed Door policy worked to the advantage of American businessmen. In this case it did not benefit all groups involved in the Brazilian coffee industry.

[26] Young and Griffin Coffee Co. to Hoover, 13 Mar. 1925, S. A. Schonbrunn and Co. to Hoover, 13 Mar. 1925, Dannelmiller Coffee Co. to Hoover, 14 Mar. 1925, Hoover to Sen. James Couzens, 15 Sept. 1925, Hoover to National Coffee Roasters Assoc., 12 Dec. 1925—all in PF-Loans, HHCD; Brandes, *Hoover,* pp. 132–36.

[27] Hoover, *South American Addresses,* p. 57; Lamont to Hoover, 24 Apr. 1930, George Milnor (Grain Stabilization Corp., Chicago) to Commerce Dept., 10 Apr. 1931, Hoover to George Zabrizkie, 3 Sept. 1931—all in Countries File-Brazil, HHPP; Herbert Feis (State Dept. economic adviser) to Henry S. Thompson, 4 Mar. 1932, File 832.51/664, NA, RG 59; *ABA*

Journal 22 (Jan. 1930): 662, 711–12; 24 (Sept. 1931): 144; DeConde, *Hoover's Latin American Policy,* pp. 74–75.

[28] State Dept., Review of Questions of Major Interest in the Relation of the U.S. with Latin American Countries, 1929–1933 (hereafter cited as State Dept., Review of Latin American Countries), pt. 1, and Kellogg to Hoover, 5 Mar. 1929, ED-State, Stimson to Hoover, 22 Oct. 1930, 2, 9 Mar. 1931, Countries File-Brazil, HHPP; Wright, *Support of Free Elections,* p. 142; DeConde, *Hoover's Latin American Policy,* pp. 52, 54–55, 58, 93–100; Ferrel', *American Diplomacy,* pp. 219–20; *FRP, 1928,* 1: 334–35; *1930,* 1: 387–89.

[29] Julius Klein (acting sec. of commerce) to Hoover, 22 Dec. 1932, FA-Disarmament, HHPP; State Dept., Review of Latin American Countries, pt. 1; Ferrell, *American Diplomacy,* pp. 223–30; Robert A. Divine, *The Illusion of Neutrality* (Chicago, 1962), pp. 32–41. Divine points out that the administration's original resolution was amended, limiting its application to the Western Hemisphere, out of the suspicion of some members of the House of Representatives that Stimson intended to use it against Japan in the Manchurian crisis.

[30] Wright, *Support of Free Elections,* pp. 1–2, 128–36, 152–57.

[31] State Dept. memorandum of conversation with Gen. Pierce, 24 Feb. 1930, File 835.51/634, Robert Woods Bliss (U.S. ambassador, Argentina) to Stimson, 30 June 1931, File -/688, Frederick Herbert Jackson to Hoover, 4 June 1931, File 832.51/606—all in NA, RG 59; William R. Castle to Hoover, 27 June 1931, Lawrence Richey (Hoover's corresponding secretary) to Frederick L. Long, 1 July 1931, Hoover to Ogden Mills (acting sec. of the treasury), 14, 25 Aug. 1931, Hoover to Gen. Pierce, 25 Aug. 1931—all in ED-State, HHPP; Klein (now assist. sec. of commerce) to C. B. Lastreto, 22 Apr., 13 May 1932, and Grosvenor Jones to Lastreto, 3 June 1932, File 640, NA, RG 151; *ABA Journal* 24 (Aug. 1931): 75; DeConde, *Hoover's Latin American Policy,* p. 70.

[32] Stimson to U.S. embassy, Brazil, 16, 18 June 1931, File 832.51/606A, and Stimson to U.S. embassy, Argentina, 18 July 1931, File -/606B, NA, RG 59; Lewis, *America's Stake,* pp. 399–400; Scroggs, "American Investment," p. 504.

[33] Francis M. Weld to Stimson, 2 Oct. 1931, File 832.51/626, U.S. embassy, London, to Stimson, 5 Oct. 1931, Stimson to Weld, 6 Oct. 1931, and Feis memorandum, 10 Oct. 1931, File -/627, Weld to Stimson, 7 Oct. 1931, File -/629, memoranda of conversations with Jesse Knight (attorney for White, Weld and Co.), 8 Oct., 7 Nov. 1931, Files -/632, 651, Office of Economic Adviser (OEA) memorandum, 5 Nov. 1931, and Harvey H. Bundy (assist. sec. of state) to White, Weld and Co., 9 Nov. 1931, File -/640—all in NA, RG 59.

[34] Lafferty to Castle, 2 Oct. 1931, and Castle to Lafferty, 21 Oct. 1931, File 832.51/642, Arthur T. Remick to presidential secretary, 20 Aug. 1932 (with attached OEA note), File -/721, NA, RG 59.

[35] Harrison to Bundy, 5 Jan. 1933, File 832.51/746, and memorandum of

conversation with Valentim Boucas (technical sec., Brazilian Finance Committee), 16 Feb. 1933, File -/752, NA, RG 59. Other plans were also turned down by the State Dept., such as the idea of setting aside a certain percentage of the dollars received from Brazilian exports to the United States to be used as collateral for a commercial loan from the RFC. See Fred I. Kent to Stimson, 26 May 1933, File 832.51/770A, NA, RG 59.

[36] W. R. Manning (Division of Latin American Affairs), note attached to House of Morgan telegram to State Dept., 10 Mar. 1933, File 832.5151/129, and William Phillips (under-sec. of state) to Roosevelt, 27 June 1933, File -/149A, Nevil Ford (vice-president, First National Old Colony Corp.) to Feis, 6 June 1933, File 832.51/774, Kent to Phillips, 28 June 1933, and Phillips to Kent, 28 June 1933, File -/780, Edwin C. Wilson (Division of Latin American Affairs) to Jefferson Caffery (assist. sec. of state), 30 Aug. 1933, File -/790—all in NA, RG 59. For the standard reply of the State Dept. to inquiries from individual bondholders about defaulted Brazilian bonds, see File 832.51/770–72, NA, RG 59.

[37] State Dept., Review of Latin American Countries, pt. 2; DeConde, *Hoover's Latin American Policy,* pp. 71–75. Government pressure was particularly evident in Argentina, where an attempt was made to get Brown Brothers to renew a $50 million loan; see Files 835.00/560, 635, and 835.51/692–711, NA, RG 59.

[38] Allan M. Pope (president, Investment Bankers Assoc.) to Theodore Joslin (Hoover's secretary), 14 Apr. 1932, File 800.51/710, and OEA memorandum, 18 Oct. 1933, File -/887, OEA to Wilson, 17 Nov. 1933, File 832.51/824, Phillips to U.S. Embassy, London, 22 Nov. 1933, File -/825A, Feis memorandum, 20 Nov. 1933, File -/829, Feis to Allen Dulles, 29 Dec. 1933, File -/846, Phillips to U. S. Embassy, London, 11 Jan. 1934, File -/849, Bondholders Protective Council to J. Reuben Clark, 2 Jan. 1934, File -/850, U.S. Embassy, London, to Phillips, 1 Feb. 1934, File -/867, memorandum of Division of Latin American Affairs, 23 Feb. 1934, File -/894, memorandum of Division of Latin American Affairs, 1 Nov. 1933, File 832.5151/194 —all in NA, RG 59; Grosvenor Jones to Lamont, 6 June 1932, File 640, NA, RG 151; Nixon, *Roosevelt and Foreign Affairs,* 1: 115–16, 152, 334–36, 338, 348–49, 377–82, 396–99, 408–9, 417–18, 462–64.

[39] Wood, *Good Neighbor Policy,* pp. 286–87, 311; Gardner, *Economic Aspects,* pp. 58–60; Bernstein, *Towards a New Past,* pp. 246–47. Sec. of State Hull opposed the philosophy behind the Johnson Act, which prohibited loans to countries which had defaulted on payments to the United States government, saying he thought it "furnished the last excuse the debtors needed for not paying anything more." He was able, however, to get Sen. Johnson to exclude the private loans to Latin America from his bill. See: Henry Morgenthau, Jr., diary, Franklin D. Roosevelt Library (hereafter cited as Morgenthau Diary), pp. 48–49; Hull, *Memoirs,* 1: 303, 382. This was perfectly in keeping with the Good Neighbor and Closed Door policies of the United States because it was ostensibly a friendly gesture toward Latin nations

while at the same time it preserved for American bankers the opportunity to begin loaning to Latin America when financial conditions improved. To forbid American loans in the area might have encouraged foreign bankers to try to enter the picture more actively as the depression dissipated.

Chapter Seven

[1] The vertically integrated companies produced, refined, and often transported and marketed their own oil. The best representative example of the large, vertically integrated oil corporation in the 1920s was Standard Oil of New Jersey. The opposition to Jersey Standard which had existed before World War I within the government and the oil industry as a result of the antitrust suit of 1911, diminished after the war. This was largely due to the fact that other large oil companies also assumed vertically integrated structures as they expanded their operations and in doing so found they had more in common with Jersey Standard than with the small, nonintegrated companies. Also, the war made the government acutely aware of the value of oil as a strategic raw material and Jersey Standard was in the best position to compete abroad for new oil fields. So the traditional prewar division within the oil industry which had pitted Jersey Standard against all the other companies was replaced after the war by one which represented basic organizational as well as dimensional differences. As one author has remarked, it became a question of "integrated versus non-integrated, rather than Standard versus independent." It should also be noted that Jersey Standard was the first major oil company to adapt its expanded, integrated operations to a modern, multidivisional, decentralized structure toward the end of the 1920s. See: Harold F. Williamson, et al., *The American Petroleum Industry,* 2: 307, 311, 329–30; Alfred D. Chandler, Jr., *Strategy and Structure,* pp. 200–277; Carl Eis, "The 1919–1930 Merger Movement in American Industry," *Journal of Law and Economics* 12 (Oct. 1969) : 275, 283.

[2] Williamson, *American Petroleum Industry,* 2: 300, 303, 311; George Sweet Gibb and Evelyn H. Knowlton, *History of Standard Oil,* 2: 288, 299; M. L. Requa, Review of "American Petroleum Supply and Demand," Aug. 1925, pp. 4–5, 16–17, and passim, Requa File, and address of Ralph Arnold, chairman of petroleum and gas section, American Institute of Mining and Metallurgical Engineers, Oil File (hereafter cited as OF), ннср; *Magazine of Wall Street* 26 (18 Sept. 1920): 700; *Cotton* 90 (Jan. 1926): 232; U.S. Federal Trade Commission, *Report on Foreign Ownership in the Petroleum Industry,* 12 Feb. 1923, p. 33. There exists some evidence, though far from conclusive, that the oil companies exploited the fear of an oil shortage in the postwar period so as not to have to convert to peacetime production and so as to obtain greater government support for their overseas ventures. See: Williams, *Economic Foreign Policy,* pp. 78–81; E. H. Davenport and Sidney Russell Cooke, *The Oil Trusts and Anglo-American Relations,* pp. 90–98.

[3] Requa was also a California politician and oilman. Before World War I

he had helped to organize the Independent Oil Producers Agency in California, which was originally intended to protect the independents against Southern Pacific and Standard Oil. As the years went by, however, Requa became more closely identified with the big producers in California. During the war he served as general director of the Oil Division, United States Fuel Administration, where his efforts to control prices of crude oil were criticized by the independent producers. At the same time he was an "advocate of quick development" at home and abroad to insure adequate war supplies for the United States. After the war, as vice-president of Sinclair Consolidated Oil Co., he became an "implacable foe" of the wasteful flush field production which resulted in declining and unstable prices for crude oil. Consequently he became more and more concerned with conserving domestic sources of oil by reducing the amount of competitive pumping. To the degree that both Requa and Hoover adhered to this philosophy, they were opposed by the small domestic independents. But at the same time they both endorsed measures which generally favored the small, nonintegrated companies in their struggle for survival against the integrated concerns. They did this by supporting high tariffs on imported crude oil, low rates for transporting oil within the United States, voluntary production controls to stabilize domestic prices, and state-supervised conservation programs. In these efforts they often found themselves opposed by the American Petroleum Institute, which was dominated by the large oil corporations and enjoyed the legal representation of Charles Evans Hughes. The big producers preferred to control production and prices by establishing oil pools exempt from antitrust laws. They became more receptive to Hoover's voluntary controls after 1929. See: J. Leonard Bates, *The Origins of Teapot Dome: Progressives, Parties and Petroleum, 1909–1921* (Urbana, Ill., 1963), pp. 103–7, 112, 141–45, 220, 225; Williamson, *American Petroleum Industry,* 2: 270, 287–89, 319, 327–29, 336–37; John R. Hadley to Hoover, 7 Apr. 1921, and Requa to Hoover, 1 June 1921, OF, HHCD; Requa to Hoover, 24 Aug., 8 Sept. 1925, 18 Mar. 1927, HHPPF.

[4] Requa to J. Howard Pew, 12 Oct. 1925, HHPPF; Hoover, *Memoirs,* 2: 69–70; Williamson, *American Petroleum Industry,* 2: 320–28; *ABA Journal* 24 (Jan. 1932): 442.

[5] In March 1929, eight days after he was inaugurated, Hoover terminated further leasing on the public domain and ordered a review of existing leases. He also appointed Requa chairman of a conference of all the major oil producing states to meet at Colorado Springs. From this and subsequent meetings came the Oil States Advisory Committee in 1931 and finally the Interstate Oil Compact Commission in 1935. This latter was backed with New Deal regulatory legislation. And so Hoover's long-sought cooperation between the states, the federal government, and the oil industry was imperfectly reached by the middle of the 1930s. It was not a completely voluntary system (which he favored), but neither was it one of rigid governmental control (which he opposed). The haste with which Hoover acted after becoming president can be explained by his growing impatience with the abuse

of the leasing system in the 1920s. It is also possible that in addition he
wanted to eradicate the last vestiges of Teapot Dome from his own and his
party's record. When that scandal originally was disclosed both Hoover and
Requa had defended Sec. of the Interior Albert Fall and opposed a full investigation even though the regional associations of the independent oil
producers called for one. See: Hoover, *Memoirs*, 2: 53–55, 69, 237–39;
William Starr Myers and Walter H. Newton, *The Hoover Administration*,
pp. 376, 391; Williamson, *American Petroleum Industry*, 2: 336, 545–51;
Burl Noggle, *Teapot Dome: Oil and Politics in the 1920's* (New York,
1962), pp. 209–10; Robert A. Waller, "Business and the Initiation of the
Teapot Dome Investigation," *Business History Review* 36 (Autumn 1962):
343–44, 349; Bates, *Origins of Teapot Dome*, p. 232; Christian Herter to
Klein, 17 Jan. 1923, BFDC File, HHCD; Donald C. Swain, *Federal Conservation
Policy, 1921–1933* (Berkeley, 1963), pp. 54–55, 63–65; David H. Stratton,
"Behind Teapot Dome: Some Personal Insights," *Business History Review*
31 (Winter 1957): 389, 399.

[6] Hoover to Raker, 21 Jan. 1924, Requa to Hoover, 2 May 1921, Com-
merce Dept. memorandum, 3 May 1921, American Petroleum Institute to
Hoover, 7 May 1921, Ira Jewell Williams to Requa, 12 May 1921, Requa,
"Review," p. 26—all in Requa File, HHCD.

[7] N. Gordon Levin, *Woodrow Wilson and World Politics*, pp. 245–46;
Federal Trade Commission, *Foreign Ownership*, p. 33; Davenport and
Cooke, *Oil Trusts*, pp. 159–60; U.S., Congress, Senate, Special Committee
Investigating Petroleum Resources, *Diplomatic Protection of American
Petroleum Interests in Mesopotamia, Netherlands East Indies, and Mexico*,
79th Cong., 1st sess., 25 Apr. 1945 (hereafter cited as U.S. Senate, *Diplo-
matic Protection*), pp. 3, 13–14; John A. DeNovo, "Movement for an
Aggressive American Oil Policy Abroad, 1918–1920," AHR 61 (July 1956):
854–76; Daniel M. Smith, *Aftermath of War*, pp. 47–50.

[8] John A. DeNovo, *American Interests and Policies in the Middle East,
1900–1939*, pp. 179, 182; U.S. Senate, *Diplomatic Protection*, p. 50.

[9] Editor of *Engineering and Mining Journal* to Hoover, 13 May 1921,
Ralph Arnold to Hughes, 23 Apr. 1921, Hughes to Hoover, 23 Apr. 1921,
Commerce Dept. list of "thoroughly American" oil companies invited to
May Conference, 6 May 1921, memorandum of the Foreign Relations Com-
mittee of the American Petroleum Institute, 23 Apr. 1921, Hoover to A. C.
Bedford (chairman of board, Jersey Standard), 9 May 1921, Bedford to
Hoover, 10 May 1921—all in OF, HHCD; Benjamin Shwadran, *The Middle
East, Oil and the Great Powers* (New York, 1955), pp. 209, 215; DeNovo,
American Interests, pp. 186–87.

[10] The Standard Oil official quoted was Everit J. Sadler in a letter to
Walter C. Teagle on 27 Sept. 1921. The seven companies originally partici-
pating in the American group were Jersey Standard, New York Standard,
Texas Co., Sinclair Consolidated Oil Co., Pan-American Petroleum and
Transport Co., Atlantic Refining Co., and Gulf Oil Corp. The offer for a

share in the Turkish Petroleum Co. was made in December 1921 by Sir John Cadman, technical advisor of Anglo-Persian. The offer was contingent upon Jersey Standard's sharing its northern Persian concession with Cadman's company. This deal has been described as the "decisive step in the adjustment of Anglo-American differences over oil fields." It should also be noted that it came during the Washington Disarmament Conference, when the United States and England were settling other outstanding differences, and was a prelude to new negotiations with the British over German reparations and their war debt. See: Gibb and Knowlton, *History of Standard Oil,* 2: 292–93; Sister Gertrude Mary Gray, "Oil in Anglo-American Diplomatic Relations, 1920–1928," (Ph.D. dissertation, Univ. of California, Berkeley, 1950) (hereafter cited as Gray, "Oil"), pp. 194–95; Carl P. Parrini, *Heir to Empire,* pp. 255–56.

[11] Smith, *Aftermath of War,* pp. 47–48; U.S. Senate, *Diplomatic Protection,* pp. 14–19.

[12] For details of these conferences see Gray, "Oil," pp. 157–87, 205–32, 249–63.

[13] U.S. Senate, *Diplomatic Protection,* pp. 20–21; DeNovo, *American Interests,* pp. 187–88.

[14] Gray, "Oil," p. 149; Hughes to Hoover, 17 Aug. 1922, Hoover to Hughes, 19 Aug. 1922, Hughes to Teagle, 22 Aug. 1922, HHPPF. Possibly Hughes's association with Jersey Standard and the American Petroleum Institute as legal counselor made him more wary than Hoover of appearing to use his government position to help his former clients obtain an oil monopoly.

[15] Admiral Chester had originally been sent by Theodore Roosevelt to obtain concessions from Turkey for American businessmen. Not until 1910 was a contract actually negotiated, but it failed to pass the Turkish Parliament in 1911. Intervening wars prevented further negotiation until 1920, when Chester brought his case to the State Dept. for support. Although Washington officials endorsed a policy of impartiality with regard to the activities of Jersey Standard and Chester's Ottoman-American Development Co. in Mesopotamia, the treatment accorded the competing firms was not equal. For one thing, Secretary Hughes did not make himself as available to representatives of the Chester concession as to those of the American group. In addition, the State Dept. insisted on setting specific standards for the Ottoman-American Development Co. which it did not require of the Turkish Petroleum Co., namely, that 51 percent of the stock "be put in a voting trust controlled by Americans." Finally, Hughes refused to give Otto Kahn, representing Kuhn, Loeb and Co., any encouragement about the possibility of floating a loan to support the Chester concession. Under the circumstances the odds for obtaining a concession in Mesopotamia were all on the side of the American group, whose efforts had the official sanction of the government and whose leadership was in the experienced hands of Jersey Standard. See: Commerce Dept. memorandum, 28 May 1923, OF, HHCD;

FRP, 1922, 2: 966–83; Shwadran, *Middle East,* pp. 197–99, 220–23; Hughes, memorandum of conversation with Otto Kahn, 2 May 1923, Memoranda of Charles Evans Hughes, NA, RG 59.

¹⁶ DeNovo, *American Interests,* pp. 192–94; Gray, "Oil," pp. 246–48, 260–62, 270.

¹⁷ Hornbeck memorandum, 26 Apr. 1923, File F.W. 890g.6363 T84/92, NA, RG 59; Morris to Christian Herter, 23 Nov. 1923, and Hughes to Hoover, 8, 17 Nov. 1923, OF, HHCD; Hoover to Hughes, 3 Aug. 1923, HHPPF.

¹⁸ DeNovo, *American Interests,* pp. 199–200; Gibb and Knowlton, *History of Standard Oil,* 2: 297–308; Williams, *Economic Foreign Policy,* p. 68.

¹⁹ No American firms had been involved in Russian oil production on a large scale before the war, although Standard Oil of New York and the Vacuum Oil Co. had minor holdings and Jersey Standard had a small interest in the Nobel Brothers Petroleum Corp. The Nobel company was the largest foreign petroleum company operating in prewar Russia. The potential of the oil fields in the Caucasus and the disturbed conditions there following the Bolshevik revolution tempted the board of directors of Jersey Standard to conclude that the time was ripe for a speculative investment in that part of the world. So the company bought half interest in the Nobel holdings in July 1920 *after the property had already been nationalized.* Convinced that the collapse of the Soviet regime was imminent, Jersey Standard took a calculated gamble which never paid off, and then spent much time and effort in the 1920s trying to punish the Soviets for thwarting what might have been "among the most brilliant [transactions] ever consummated in the petroleum industry."

Jersey Standard's anti-Soviet campaign received the backing of the government and began in the same year that the ill-fated Jersey-Nobel alliance was made. The company turned down a Soviet offer of a fifty-year concession because it preferred to try to obtain direct compensation for what it deemed to be its confiscated property. When the Soviets then made the same offer to Standard Oil's major world competitor, Royal Dutch-Shell, the American efforts to prevent foreign domination of the rich Baku oil fields in the Caucasus led to the behind-the-scenes oil machinations at the Genoa and Hague conferences in 1922. Throughout the 1920s, Jersey Standard and Royal Dutch-Shell vacillated between condemning the Soviets for stealing property and trying to negotiate lucrative oil contracts with them. New York Standard and Vacuum never publicly took the same hard line about compensation as did Jersey Standard and Royal Dutch-Shell. See: Gibb and Knowlton, *History of Standard Oil,* 2: 330–35, 354; E. Dana Durand (chief, Eastern European Division, BFDC) to Hoover, 20 June 1922, Russia File, HHCD; State Dept. memorandum of conversation with Bedford, 31 Jan. 1922, File 861.6363/78, NA, RG 59.

²⁰ Gray, "Oil," pp. 178, 186; Louis A. Sussdorff, Jr. (chargé d'affaires, The Hague) to State Dept. 27 July 1922, File 861.6363/88, 19 Sept. 1922,

File -/104, NA, RG 59; Gibb and Knowlton, *History of Standard Oil,* 2: 338–41. Jersey Standard assented to but did not sign the September agreement.

[21] Hughes memoranda, 8 May, 6 June 1923, Memoranda of Charles Evans Hughes, NA, RG 59.

[22] Vacuum Oil Co. to Frank B. Kellogg, 14 Mar. 1928, File 861.6363/240, NA, RG 59.

[23] Harry Curran Wilbur to Kellogg, 5 Apr. 1928, File 861.6363 Standard Oil/1, NA, RG 59; Gibb and Knowlton, *History of Standard Oil,* 2: 345–52; Frank A. Southard, Jr., *American Industry in Europe* (Boston, 1931), pp. 67–68; Peter G. Filene, *Americans and the Soviet Experiment, 1917–1933,* p. 118.

[24] Robert F. Kelley (chief, Eastern European Division) memorandum, 8 Feb. 1927, File 861.6363/222, F. W. B. Coleman (U.S. Legation, Riga) to State Dept., 8 Feb. 1927, File -/223, Ray Atherton (U.S. Embassy, London) to State Dept., 4 Mar. 1929, File -/263; Jacob Gould Schurman (U.S. Embassy, Berlin) to State Dept., 1 May 1928, File 861.6363 Standard Oil/2, Richard M. Tobin (U.S. Legation, The Hague) to State Dept., 18 June 1928, File -/4—all in NA, RG 59; Gibb and Knowlton, *History of Standard Oil,* 2: 353–58; Williamson, *American Petroleum,* 2: 528–30.

[25] U.S. Senate, *Diplomatic Protection,* pp. 45–48; Gibb and Knowlton, *History of Standard Oil,* 2: 391–94; Peter Mellish Reed, "Standard Oil in Indonesia, 1898–1928," *Business History Review* 32 (Autumn 1958): 329–37. The change in Dutch policy resulted from a change in the minister of colonies in 1925 and growing fear of Japanese economic expansion into Indonesia.

[26] Sinclair had been encouraged by Hoover to negotiate a concession in Persia, but a former economic adviser in the State Dept., Arthur C. Millspaugh, became director of Persian finances in 1922 and he wanted the concession to go to Jersey Standard. With both firms competing for its favor, the State Dept. first announced that it would not support any American concession in northern Persia "which might create bad relations with the British Government," and later said it had no preference and would support any American company which received a concession. Since Jersey Standard arranged with Anglo-Persian to share a concession in northern Persia (in return for entrance of the American group into the Turkish Petroleum Co.) and had the backing of the House of Morgan for a $10 million loan to the Persian government, the policy of impartiality obviously was of little aid to the Sinclair interests, who justly complained about the inequities of the situation. In this case, however, neither company received a concession. The Persian government so resented Jersey Standard's alliance with the British company that it withdrew from negotiations. The Sinclair concession signed on 20 Dec. 1923 fell through in 1924 after Sinclair's credit had been damaged by the Teapot Dome scandal and the Soviet Union had canceled his

transit rights for Persian oil through its territory. In that same year the Soviets also canceled a concession Sinclair had received for the northern half of the island of Sakhalin. This was another Sinclair oil venture which suffered from lack of direct government support and the diminished stature of Henry Sinclair in Washington after the Teapot Dome investigation. Sinclair had apparently promised to obtain recognition for the USSR in return for the transit rights and the Sakhalin concession. Prior to 1924, however, the State Dept. had decided it was not worth disturbing American-Japanese relations by backing the Sinclair concession when the Japanese were still occupying northern Sakhalin. See: DeNovo, *American Interests,* pp. 281–86; Gibb and Knowlton, *History of Standard Oil,* 2: 308–17; Gray, "Oil," pp. 192–200; Hughes memorandum of telephone conversation with Thomas W. Lamont, 24 Mar. 1923, Memoranda of Charles Evans Hughes, NA, RG 59; Feis memorandum, 9 Nov. 1923, OF, HHCD; Evan E. Young (chief, Eastern European Division) and J. V. A. MacMurray (chief, Far Eastern Division) memorandum, 24 Feb. 1924, File 861.6363/180, NA, RG 59; *FRP, 1923,* 2: 798–812.

[27] U.S. Senate, *Diplomatic Protection,* pp. 61–73; Williamson, *American Petroleum Industry,* pp. 509, 521; Gibb and Knowlton, *History of Standard Oil,* 2: 359–91; Gray, "Oil," pp. 88–93; Federal Trade Commission, *Foreign Ownership,* p. 58; Bernstein, *Foreign Investments,* pp. 129–44; Joseph S. Tulchin, *The Aftermath of War,* pp. 134–54.

[28] Raymond A. Esthus, "The Changing Concept of the Open Door, 1899–1910," *MVHR* 46 (Dec. 1959): 435–53; Paul A. Varg, "The Myth of the China Market, 1890–1914," *AHR* 78 (Feb. 1968): 742–58; Gerald E. Wheeler, *Prelude to Pearl Harbor,* pp. 6, 28; Noel Pugach, "Making the Open Door Work: Paul S. Reinsch in China, 1913–1919," *Pacific Historical Review* 38 (May 1969): 157–76.

[29] William Appleman Williams, "China and Japan: A Challenge and a Choice of the Nineteen-twenties," *Pacific Historical Review* 26 (Aug. 1957): 261; C. F. Remer, *Foreign Investments in China,* pp. 328–30; *FRP, 1920,* 1: 497–559. The compromise worked out with Japan was known as the Lamont-Kajiwara agreement, whereby Japan was promised that certain railway projects in southern Manchuria and eastern Inner Mongolia were to be excluded from the scope of the consortium. Japan later gave up these special loan privileges at the Washington Conference.

[30] Lansing to William C. Redfield (sec. of commerce), 11 Jan. 1918, File 76338, NA, RG 40; American Group, "The Chinese Consortium: Its Organization and Aims," 2 Dec. 1921, and Hughes to Hoover, 27 Sept. 1921, China File, HHCD; Williams, "China and Japan," pp. 260–61; Lamont to Norman H. Davis, 14 June 1920, Box 33, Davis Papers; Levin, *Wilson and World Politics,* pp. 115, 239.

[31] NFTC, *Proceedings,* 1927, p. 493; Stanley K. Hornbeck (chief, Far Eastern Division) memorandum, 8 Aug. 1933, File 895.51/5808, NA, RG 59;

Hughes to Lamont, 13 Apr. 1922, Morgan and Co. to other members of the American Group, 24 Apr. 1922, *FRP, 1922,* 1: 765–67; Frederick V. Field, *American Participation in the China Consortiums,* pp. 173–85.

[32] Hughes memoranda of conversations with Japanese Ambassador Baron Shidehara, 15 Aug., 9 Nov. 1922, 24 May 1923, Box 176, Hughes Papers; Mahlon F. Perkins (U.S. Legation, Peiping) to Stimson, 8 May 1930, File 895.51/5252, and 24 June 1930, File -/5296, Stimson to Perkins, 24 June 1930, File -/5296, and 25 June 1930, File -/5299, Division of Far Eastern Affairs memorandum, 21 June 1930, File -/5312—all in NA, RG 59; Akira Iriye, *After Imperialism,* pp. 280–83.

[33] Klein to Arnold, 23 Aug., 10 Oct. 1921, and extract from *Far Eastern Review,* Jan. 1923, File 640-China Consortium, F. R. Eldridge (chief, Far Eastern Division, BFDC) to N. W. Sample, 22 Aug. 1922, File 640-Chinese Government Loans—both in NA, RG 151; Eldridge memorandum, 24 June 1921, Hughes to Hoover, 29 June 1921, Hoover to Charles Denby, 22 July 1921, China File, Grosvenor Jones to Hoover, 4 Nov. 1926, PF-Loans—all in HHCD.

[34] C. C. Batchelder (acting commercial attaché, Peking) to Klein, 8 Jan. 1920, H. G. Brock (acting director, BFDC) to Batchelder, 27 Apr. 1920, File 492.1-Japanese-Chinese Situation, 1920–1931, Arnold to Klein, 24 May 1921, File 640-China Consortium—all in NA, RG 151; Batchelder (now acting chief, Far Eastern Division, BFDC) to Christian Herter, 9 Dec. 1921, China File, HHCD. Both consortiums had been created on the tacit assumption that their purpose (and therefore scope) would be limited to general loans to the Chinese government for such national projects as currency reform and specific loans for national internal improvement programs, such as railroad building, in order to prevent any one nation from monopolizing these important financial transactions, as Japan had attempted to do.

[35] R. P. Schwerin (president, Federal Telegraph Co.) to Batchelder, 30 Nov. 1921, Batchelder to Klein, 6 Dec. 1921, China File, HHCD; Harry W. Kirwin, "The Federal Telegraph Company: A Testing of the Open Door," *Pacific Historical Review* 22 (Aug. 1953): 271–86; Hughes memoranda of conversations with Japanese ambassador, 8 Mar., 10 May, 15 June 1923, Box 176, Hughes Papers.

[36] Davis to Lamont, 23 Feb. 1921, Box 33, Davis Papers; Hughes memorandum, 23 May 1921, Box 174, Hughes Papers.

[37] Frank Rhea (trade commissioner, Peking) to Arnold, 6 Jan. 1921, Frederick Sites (representative of U.S. Steel Products Corp.) to Arnold, 11 May 1921, Arnold to Klein, 24 May 1921, Klein to Arnold, 23 Aug. 1921, Batchelder to Arnold, 10 Oct. 1921, Arnold to Stevens, 9 Jan. 1922, File 640-China Consortium, NA, RG 151; Paul Whitham (trade commissioner, Peking) to James A. Farrell, 23 May 1921, Whitham to Stevens, 19 May 1921, Schwerin to Batchelder, 30 Nov. 1921, China File, HHCD.

[38] Batchelder to Klein, 9 Feb. 1922, File 640-China Consortium, Batchelder to Arnold, 10 Jan. 1922, File 620-China Investments—both in NA, RG 151;

Klein answered this criticism by saying that bankers were generally not "concerned with the trade or manufacturing phases of our economic life." Arnold also seemed more indifferent than his banking critics to the changing political regimes in China until the Nationalist Revolution. See Arnold to Klein, 10 June 1922, 29 Nov. 1924, China File, HHCD.

[39] Joseph Brandes, *Herbert Hoover and Economic Diplomacy,* pp. 57–58; Whitham to BFDC, 6 Dec. 1918, Denby to Paul S. Reinsch (U.S. minister, Peking), 7 Nov. 1918, Arnold to BFDC, 9 Nov. 1920, File 620-China Investments, Whitham to Merle Thorpe (editor, *Nation's Business*), 6 Jan. 1919, File 492-Far East Trade Promotion, Eldridge to Lansing W. Hoyt (trade commissioner, Shanghai), 2 Dec. 1922, File 640-China Loans, Arnold to Klein, 4 Dec. 1926, File 492-China—all in NA, RG 151.

[40] Remer, *Foreign Investments in China,* pp. 316–28, 335; Eldridge to Klein, 23 Aug. 1921, File 640-China Consortium, NA, RG 151.

[41] Dyer to Hoover, 21, 25 Apr. 1921, 26 July 1921, Hoover to Representative Andrew J. Volstead, 14 Apr. 1921, Hoover to Dyer, 27 Apr. 1921, Hoover to Harding, 22, 26 Apr. 1921 (drafts), Hoover to Representative Bertrand H. Snell, 29 Nov. 1924—all in China File, HHCD. Dyer's interest in the bill stemmed from the trade his constituents in the St. Louis area conducted with the Orient.

[42] NFTC, *Proceedings,* 1920, pp. 385–98; 1921, pp. 509–18; *Southern California Business* 3 (Aug. 1924): 20, 50; U.S. Chamber of Commerce endorsement of China Trade Act, 5 Feb. 1921, Portland Chamber of Commerce to Hoover, 26 May 1921, Hoover to Portland Chamber of Commerce, 28 May 1921, China File HHCD. This file also contains numerous letters of support for the act.

[43] Mellon to Dyer, 17 May 1921, Mellon to Hoover, 18 June 1921, Hoover to Mellon, 23 June 1921, China File HHCD; Remer, *Foreign Investments in China,* pp. 319–20.

[44] Hoover, undated press release for 1922, Hoover to Sen. Albert B. Cummins, 15 Feb. 1923, Hughes to Hoover, 9 Oct., 8 Nov. 1922, Hoover to Hughes, 12 Oct. 1922, Klein to Hughes, 22 Nov. 1922, Hoover to Hughes, 5 Mar. 1924, Hoover to Mellon, 1 May 1924, McKinzie Moss (assist. sec. of the treasury) to Hoover, 11 Mar. 1924—all in China File, HHCD; Mellon to Representative George S. Graham, 15 Mar. 1924, in U.S., Congress, House, Committee on the Judiciary, *To Amend the China Trade Act of 1922,* House Report No. 321, 68th Cong., 1st sess., 18 Mar. 1924, p. 11; U.S., Congress, House, Committee on the Judiciary, *Hearing on H.J.R. 149: To Amend the China Trade Act of 1922 and the Revenue Act of 1921,* 68th Cong., 1st sess., 30–31 Jan. 1924, pp. 33–34.

[45] Remer, *Foreign Investments in China,* pp. 323–24; Lawrence Richey (Hoover's corresponding secretary) to Robert Lamont (sec. of commerce), 16 July 1932, Countries File-China (hereafter cited as CF-China), HHPP; memoranda from the Office of Solicitor General, Dec. 1927, Jan. 1928, China File HHCD.

[46] Remer, *Foreign Investments in China,* pp. 274–85, 324–28; State Dept., Far Eastern Accomplishments, appendix 18.

[47] Wheeler, *Prelude to Pearl Harbor,* pp. 28–29; Iriye, *After Imperialism,* pp. 26, 279; Remer, *Foreign Investments in China,* pp. 76, 85, 98–102, 333–34, 338, 553. Remer's figures indicate that U.S. portion of China's total trade rose from 9.5 percent in 1899 to 16.5 percent in 1930, compared to a rise from 11.5 to 24.7 percent for Japan. In terms of China's total shipping the percentages were 0.7 to 6.8 percent for the United States and 7.2 to 29.3 percent for Japan. The American share of the total foreign investment in China increased from 2.5 to 6.1 percent, while Japan's went from 0.1 to 35.1.

[48] Iriye, *After Imperialism,* pp. 185, 279; Wheeler, *Prelude to Pearl Harbor,* pp. 28–29; State Dept., "Far Eastern Accomplishments," pp. 17–19, 33, appendixes 18, 37, 39; Dept. of Commerce press release, 5 Feb. 1924, and Eldridge to Harold F. Stokes (Hoover's personal assistant) 15 Jan. 1926, Japan File (hereafter cited as JF), HHCD. Although the depression caused a general decline in American foreign trade, in 1931 the volume of trade with both China and Japan temporarily increased only to fall again in 1932. Nonetheless, in 1932 the Far East still offered an outlet for 20 percent of the total exports of the United States, which led the State Dept. to conclude that "our policy and action in the Far East are matters of great practical importance to the present and future welfare of the United States." The depression also narrowed the American trade deficit with both countries.

[49] Remer, *Foreign Investments in China,* pp. 74–80; Lewis, *America's Stake,* p. 627; State Dept., "Far Eastern Accomplishments," appendixes 18, 37; NFTC, *Proceedings,* 1925, p. 87; *ABA Journal* 21 (Jan. 1929): 636. By 1930 the United States had actually invested between $41 and $45 million in Chinese government securities and obligations of the Chinese government (in addition to direct business investments) but most of this represented loans floated before 1920, almost all of which were in default during the 1920s. For details see Remer, pp. 295–301, 308.

[50] Lamont to Norman H. Davis, 14 June 1920, Box 33, Davis Papers; Parrini, *Heir to Empire,* pp. 202, 264; Stimson (London) to State Dept., 29 Mar. 1930, File 500.A 15A 13/802, NA, RG 59. Stimson was specifically thinking of the fact that in January 1931 Japan would want a 240,000,000-yen loan refunded in the United States and he thought bankers would be reluctant to advance the money if Japan continued with her naval expansion. The loan was actually refunded in 1930 with government approval after the London Conference succeeded in negotiating a treaty. See Morgan and Co. to Joseph P. Cotton (under-sec. of state), 8 May 1930, File 894.51/296, NA, RG 59.

[51] Leland Harrison (assist. sec. of state) to Riggs National Bank, 23 May 1923, *FRP, 1923,* 2: 508.

[52] *FRP, 1923,* 2: 503–8; Hughes, memorandum of conversation with representatives of National City Co., 3 Jan. 1923, Memoranda of Charles Evans Hughes, NA, RG 59; Herbert Feis, *The Diplomacy of the Dollar,*

pp. 33–37; Brandes, *Hoover,* pp. 203–4; Iriye, *After Imperialism,* pp. 185–90; Wheeler, *Prelude to Pearl Harbor,* pp. 38–43.

[53] *ABA Journal* 21 (Jan. 1929): 636–37; NFTC, *Proceedings,* 1925, pp. 83–84; Feis, *Diplomacy of the Dollar,* pp. 35–36; *FRP, 1923,* 2: 504–6. The only time bankers voluntarily promoted the idea of American purchases was when they anticipated reluctance on the part of the State and Commerce departments to approve a foreign loan. The argument was unsuccessfully used, for example, with respect to the proposed South Manchurian Railway loan of 1923.

[54] Lamont to Hughes, 4, 7 Feb. 1924, Hughes to Lamont, 5 Feb. 1924, Box 62, Hughes Papers; Lamont to Hoover, 8 Feb. 1924 (including suggestions for press release), Commerce Dept. press release, 8 Feb. 1924, PF-Loans, HHCD. The business community, largely due to the contributions of large eastern firms, contributed over 50 percent of the $11.6 million collected by the American Red Cross for earthquake relief in 1923 and 1924. While this total sum is indicative of the genuine friendliness businessmen and many Americans felt for Japan, it came at the very time when the movement to exclude Japanese immigrants was reaching its climax. See Merle Curti, *American Philanthropy Abroad* (New Brunswick, N.J., 1963), pp. 339–46.

[55] Halleck A. Butts (acting commercial attaché, Tokyo) to Klein, 4 Sept. 1924, File 640-Japanese Loans, Eldridge to Arnold, 19 Sept. 1923, File 602.2-Oriental Development Co., NA, RG 151; Eldridge to Hoover, 15 May 1923, Box 55, R. O. Hall (acting chief, Finance and Investment Division) to District Offices, 22 Apr. 1927, JF, HHCD; Lamont to Korekiyo Takahashi (Japanese financial minister), 31 Mar. 1932, File 739.94/4954, NA, RG 59; Iriye, *After Imperialism,* p. 32.

[56] Grosvenor Jones to Hoover, 9 Apr. 1925, PF-Loans, HHCD; Feis, *Diplomacy of the Dollar,* p. 38; Iriye, *After Imperialism,* p. 191.

[57] Dorothy Borg, *American Policy and the Chinese Revolution, 1925–1928,* pp. vii–ix. MacMurray was chief of the Far Eastern Division from 1919 to 1925 and then minister to China from 1925 to 1929. Nelson was chief of the Far Eastern Division from 1925 to 1929 and minister to China from 1929 to 1933. Both men devised interpretations of the Washington Conference based on a combination of independent and collective actions which were often pursued simultaneously. This was particularly evident in Johnson's case on the question of extraterritoriality. See Russell D. Buhite, *Nelson T. Johnson and American Policy toward China, 1925–1941,* pp. 41, 49.

[58] Borg, *American Policy,* pp. xi–xii, 425–26; Russell D. Buhite, "Nelson Johnson and American Policy toward China, 1925–1928," *Pacific Historical Review* 35 (Nov. 1966): 465.

[59] Betty Glad, *Charles Evans Hughes and the Illusions of Innocence,* p. 292; Wheeler, *Prelude to Pearl Harbor,* p. 9; William R. Braisted, "China, the United States Navy, and the Bethlehem Steel Company, 1909–1929," *Business History Review* 42 (Spring 1968): 62–66; Hughes memoranda, 7 June 1923, 27 May, 9 Oct 1924, Box 174, Hughes Papers.

[60] Hoover to Hughes, 25 June 1924, Hughes to Hoover, 11 July 1924, American Assoc. of China to Hoover, 18 March 1924, Max Shoop to Hoover, 22 Sept. 1924, Pressed Steel Car Co. to Hoover, 18 Nov. 1924, China File, HHCD; Eldridge to Arnold, 1 Sept. 1922, M. H. Bletz (chief, Foreign Construction Division, BFDC) to Frederick Feiker (director, BFDC), 3 Sept. 1931, W. H. Rastall (chief, Industrial Machinery Division) to Whitin Machine Works, 10 Aug. 1932—all in File 640-Boxer Indemnity, NA, RG 151; U.S., Congress, House, Committee on Foreign Affairs, *Hearings on H.J.R. 201: To Provide for the Remission of Further Payments of the Annual Installments of the Chinese Indemnity,* 68th Cong., 1st sess., 31 Mar., 1–2 Apr. 1924, pp. 62–69, 76–87.

[61] Iriye, *After Imperialism,* pp. 55–58, 107–8; Borg *American Policy and the Chinese Revolution,* pp. viii–ix, 271–83, 414–15, 418–31; Williams, "China and Japan," pp. 272–75; Buhite, "Nelson Johnson," pp. 451–65; idem, *Johnson and American Policy toward China,* pp. 24–35, 38–52.

[62] NFTC, *Proceedings,* 1927, pp. 178–80, 489–97; Hoover to Thomas F. Millard, 25 Nov. 1924, Hugh White to Hoover, 1 May 1924, 30 Jan. 1925, Nelson to Hoover, 3 Feb. 1925, Hoover to White, 4 Feb. 1925, U.S. Chamber of Commerce to Hoover, 2, 13 June 1927—all in China File, HHCD; A. Bland Calder (trade commissioner, Shanghai) to Klein, 31 Aug. 1927 (with enclosed clipping from *China Courier*), C. P. Hopkins (acting director, BFDC) to Arnold, 20 Sept. 1929, File 492-Far East, Arnold to William L. Cooper (Director, BFDC), 25 Dec. 1930, Cooper to Robert W. Lamont (sec. of commerce) 8 Jan. 1931, File 640-China Loans—all in NA, RG 151; Borg, *American Policy,* pp. 318–65 (for general discussion of press, business, and missionary reaction to the Nationalist Revolution); Iriye, *After Imperialism,* pp. 282–83; Fred L. Israel, "The Fulfillment of Bryan's Dream: Key Pittman and Silver Politics, 1918–1933," *Pacific Historical Review* 30 (Nov. 1961): 366–71; Buhite, *Johnson and the American Policy toward China,* pp. 112–13.

[63] Calder to BFDC, 12 Oct. 1929, File 492-Far East, NA, RG 151; State Dept. memorandum of conversation with representatives of Morgan and Co., 31 Jan. 1931, File 895.51/5494, NA, RG 59; Red Cross report on China, 25 Sept. 1929, Countries File-China, HHPP.

Chapter Eight

[1] Hoover, *Memoirs,* 1: 35–72; 2: 180–81; Hughes to Hoover, 25 June 1924, China File, HHCD; Ray Lyman Wilbur (sec. of interior) to Hoover, 26 Jan. 1933, Foreign Affairs File-Far East (hereafter cited as FA-Far East), HHPP. Other references to Hoover's Chinese expertise can be found in CF-China, HHPP.

[2] Betty Glad, *Charles Evans Hughes and the Illusions of Innocence,* p. 320; Requa to Hoover, 6, 26 Apr. 1924, HHPPF; Hoover to Requa, 21 Apr. 1924, Japan File, and Hoover to Representative John E. Raker, 19 Feb. 1924,

Immigration File, HHCD. This Immigration File and Personal File-Japanese Immigration, HHCD contain numerous letters from lumber companies, exporters, and land companies in opposition to exclusion. Most of them Hoover referred to the Dept. of Labor, saying that immigration legislation was not under his jurisdiction. Representative samples of business criticism of the government's immigration policy (usually on the grounds that restrictions should be based on quality, not quantity) include: *American Industries* 19 (Feb. 1919): 7; 20 (June 1920): 11; 24 (Apr. 1924): 27–32; 24 (May 1924): 27; *Iron Age* 104 (11 Sept. 1919): 730; 111 (18 Jan. 1923): 235; 111 (26 Apr. 1923): 1186; 111 (31 May 1923): 1573; *Magazine of Wall Street* 25 (1 May 1920): 957–59; 30 (2 Sept. 1922): 653; Philadelphia Board of Trade, *Proceedings,* 23 Jan. 1922, p. 22; *Bankers Magazine* 108 (June 1924): 853–54; *ABA Journal* 16 (Oct. 1923): 200. There was a tendency for large and small businessmen to divide on this issue, with the former being more critical of immigration restrictions than the latter.

[3] Dorothy Borg, *American Policy and the Chinese Revolution,* p. xii; William Appleman Williams, "China and Japan: A Challenge and a Choice of the Nineteen-twenties." *Pacific Historical Review* 26 (Aug. 1957): 275–77; Akira Iriye, *After Imperialism,* pp. 258–59, 300–301.

[4] John F. Carter (Division of Western European Affairs) memoranda, 17, 19, 20 Dec. 1929, and Carter to Alexander Gumberg, 19 Dec. 1929, File 711.61/79, NA, RG 59. In particular, Litvinov, Gumberg, and Borah believed the Hoover administration was scheming to neutralize the CERR through the creation of an international railway consortium.

[5] Castle to Hoover, 27 Jan. 1930, FA-Diplomats, HHPP (CF-China contains the extensive correspondence concerning the wheat negotiations, and FA-Far East contains early business reactions to the Manchurian crisis); *Bankers Magazine* 123 (Aug. 1931): 229–30; State Dept., "Far Eastern Accomplishments," p. 30; documents on RFC loan, File 893.48/706–8, American Group to State Dept., 16 June 1933, File -/750, NA, RG 59.

[6] F. R. Eldridge to Hoover, 12 Apr. 1923, and C. K. Moser (chief, Far Eastern Division, BFDC) to Hoover, 25 May 1928, China File, HHCD; *ABA Journal* 25 (May 1933): 56. As early as 1923 even the rabid Sinophile Julean Arnold did not object to American money entering Manchuria in the form of loans to Japanese agencies. And by 1925 some American businessmen with Far Eastern interests were beginning to think that only an unofficial international economic conference (modeled after the Dawes Commission) could settle the Chinese financial situation. See: Arnold to Klein, 7 Aug. 1923, File 602.2-Oriental Development Company, NA, RG 151; and James A. Thomas, "Business Principles in World Politics," *Asia* 25 (Feb. 1925): 100–103.

[7] C. F. Remer, *Foreign Investments in China,* pp. 97, 265, 270–71, 282, 334–35; State Dept. "Far Eastern Accomplishments," appendix 18; Hornbeck memorandum, 30 Sept. 1931, File 811.7693/2136, NA, RG 151; Herbert Feis, "The International Trade of Manchuria," *International Con-*

ciliation, no. 269 (Apr. 1931), pp. 232–33, 262; Wallace M. Alexander, "The U.S. View of Trade Relations with Japan," *International Conciliation,* no. 281 (June 1932), pp. 296–97.

[8] Radio Corp. of America to Stimson, 25 Sept. 1931, State Dept. to Radio Corp., 1 Oct. 1931, File 811.7693/11, State Dept. memorandum of conversation with Katsuji Dubuchi (Japanese ambassador), 1 Oct. 1931, File 793.94/2143, NA, RG 59.

[9] State Dept. memorandum of conversation with industrialist Count Kabayama, File 793.94/3477, and Myrl S. Myers to State Dept., 18 Apr. 1932, File 893.00 P. R. Mukden/54, NA, RG 59; Armin Rappaport, *Henry L. Stimson and Japan, 1931–1933,* pp. 107–9. The large firms do not appear to have harbored any strong anti-Japanese sentiments after making their adjustments. Small firms, however, such as Frazer Federal, were usually unable to make satisfactory settlements.

[10] *ABA Journal* 14 (July 1921): 4–5; *Chicago Journal of Commerce,* 2 Jan. 1932, p. 14; *Business Week,* 30 Sept. 1931, p. 37; 27 Jan. 1932, pp. 24–25; Stanley Washburn to Elihu Root, 9 Nov. 1931, and Washburn to Elon H. Hooker, 10 Nov. 1931, Box 4, Stanley Washburn Papers, Library of Congress; Washburn to Hoover, 19 Nov. 1931, FA-Far East, HHPP; Newton D. Baker to Judge John H. Clarke, 22 Feb. 1932, Box 59, Baker Papers; Rappaport, *Stimson and Japan,* p. 66.

[11] The strongest criticism of Stimson's doctrine came from Dr. Abbott Lawrence Lowell, a few Wilsonian internationalists, and former pro-Japanese officials such as John V. A. MacMurray. See: Lowell, "Manchuria, the League and the United States," *Foreign Affairs* 10 (Apr. 1932): 366–68; MacMurray, "Manchurian Diplomacy as an Asiatic Problem," *Yale Review* 23 (Sept. 1933): 336–77; Eleanor Tupper and George E. McReynolds, *Japan in American Public Opinion,* pp. 313–14. The fact that England did not initially accept the Stimson doctrine did not appreciably increase criticism of it in this country, according to Robert A. Hecht, "Great Britain and the Stimson Note of January 7, 1932," *Pacific Historical Review* 38 (May 1969): 177–92.

[12] *Literary Digest* 111 (24 Oct. 1931): 5–6; 111 (19 Dec. 1931): 14; Tupper and McReynolds, *Japan in American Public Opinion,* pp. 292–93, 312–44; Rappaport, *Stimson and Japan,* p. 138; State Dept. memorandum, 17 Apr. 1932, File 793.94/5257, NA, RG 59; signed statement of support for Stimson's policy, 12 Nov. 1931, Box 100, Baker Papers.

[13] *Literary Digest* 111 (5 Dec. 1931): 3–4; 112 (5 Mar. 1932): 7; Tupper and McReynolds, *Japan in American Public Opinion,* p. 337; Jerome D. Greene, "The Situation in the Far East," *International Conciliation,* no. 281 (June 1932): 283; Rappaport, *Stimson and Japan,* pp. 89, 149.

[14] *Literary Digest* 112 (5 Mar. 1932): 7; 112 (19 Mar. 1932): 21; Rappaport, *Stimson and Japan,* pp. 122–23, 147–48; Richard N. Current, *Secretary Stimson,* pp. 119–21; Gerald E. Wheeler, "Republican Philippine Policy, 1921–1933," *Pacific Historical Review* 28 (Nov. 1959): 387–90.

Included among the prominent individuals in favor of sanctions were John Foster Dulles; Jane Addams; Edward N. Hurley, former chairman of the Federal Trade Commission; Reinhold Niebuhr; Raymond L. Buell; James D. Mooney, vice-president of General Motors; Silas Strawn, president of the United States Chamber of Commerce; and the following organizations: the Foreign Policy Assoc., the American Academy of Political and Social Science, the American Friends Service Committee, the World Peace Commission of the Methodist Episcopal Church, the League of Nations Association, the Women's International League for Peace and Freedom, and the League for Independent Political Action.

[15] Rappaport, *Stimson and Japan*, pp. 89–90, 139; Hornbeck memorandum on economic boycott, 6 Dec. 1931, File 793.94/4314, NA, RG 59; Charles G. Dawes, *Journal As Ambassador to Great Britain*, pp. 416–27; Russell D. Buhite, *Nelson T. Johnson and American Policy toward China*, pp. 67–68; Henry L. Stimson and McGeorge Bundy, *On Active Service in Peace and War*, p. 233.

[16] In the early stages of the Japanese invasion of Manchuria, neither Hoover nor Stimson publicly appeared to favor either side, and the secretary of state had previously made it clear in the Sino-Soviet dispute of 1929 that the United States did not intend to intervene militarily in such crises. Given the pro-Japanese sentiments of Hoover's closest personal adviser on the Far East, William Castle, and Hoover's own admiration for the economic achievements of Japan, it is not surprising to find him hypothesizing about the reasons behind Japanese action at a cabinet meeting in the middle of Oct. 1931. He viewed the increasing lack of order in China and Bolshevik infiltration as reasonable justification from the standpoint of the Japanese for violating the Nine Power Treaty. He also outlined at this meeting three major aspects of the problem: 1) it was primarily a controversy between China and Japan; 2) it was not an issue which required the United States to go to war, regardless of this country's commitments to China; 3) it was a situation in which the United States was required to use all moral pressures, including co-operation with the League of Nations, but to exclude any economic or military sanctions because they "are the roads to war." Before the end of the year Stimson had acquiesced on all three points although he was to change his mind on the third one. It should also be noted that Hoover had not always opposed economic sanctions. When speaking in favor of the League in 1920 he had said that an economic boycott was "a more potent weapon for good than any threat of military aggression" and should be used against nations which "disregard the decisions of international tribunals and start ventures that could involve the world in war." Hoover's memoirs do not indicate this change of heart. See: Hoover, *Memoirs*, 2: 366–70; Hoover, statement in *Chicago Daily News*, 15 Sept. 1920, Speeches and Addresses, Hoover Papers, Stanford University; Current, *Stimson*, pp. 71–83; Stimson to Elihu Root, 14 Dec. 1931, Box 147, Root Papers; Paul H. Clyde, "The Diplomacy of 'Playing No Favorites': Secretary Stimson and Manchuria,

1931," *MVHR* 25 (Sept. 1948): 187–202; Henry L. Stimson, *The Far Eastern Crisis,* pp. 76–77; *FRP, 1929,* 1: 64.

[17] Hoover, *Memoirs,* 2: 366–67; Current, *Stimson,* pp. 95, 97, 100, 102; Hornbeck memorandum, 12 Jan. 1932, File 793.94/3610⅗, NA, RG 59; Stimson quoted in Stimson and Bundy, *On Active Service,* p. 245. Stimson explicitly told Ambassador Dawes on 19 Nov. 1931 that the United States did "not intend to get into a war with Japan." See Clyde, "No Favorites," p. 200.

[18] Hoover, *Memoirs,* 2: 370, 375–76; Current, *Stimson,* pp. 106–7; Stimson to Lippmann, 19 May 1932, Box 149, Baker Papers; Rappaport, *Stimson and Japan,* pp. 139–40; Stimson and Bundy, *On Active Service,* pp. 261–62.

[19] Hecht, "Great Britain and the Stimson Note," pp. 184–91; Hoover, *Memoirs,* 2: 376–78 (fns. 7–8); Hoover to secretaries of war and interior, 13 Jan. 1933, Hoover to Stimson, 24 Feb. 1933, FA-Far East, HHPP; Stimson, "The Pact of Paris: Three Years of Development," *Foreign Affairs* 11 (Oct. 1932): ix; Current, *Stimson,* p. 113.

[20] Hornbeck memorandum, 4 Feb. 1932, File 793.94/4059, NA, RG 59; Tupper and McReynolds, *Japan in American Public Opinion,* pp. 364–65; Gabriel Kolko, "American Business and Germany, 1930–1941," *Western Political Science Quarterly* 15 (Dec. 1962): 713–14. Kolko notes that businessmen continued to deal with Hitler's Germany while these same men and the business press publicly opposed fascism and nazism. The same was true in this case. Most business journals and individual businessmen deplored the tactics of the Japanese in Manchuria, but not to the point of endorsing a general boycott or in any way disrupting normal economic relations with Japan. See *Chicago Journal of Commerce,* 27 Jan., 2, 4, 26 Feb. 1932, all on p. 14.

[21] Davis to Stimson, 13 Oct. 1931, File 793.94/209⅓, and Davis to Sir John Simon (British foreign sec.), 14 Dec. 1932, File 795.94 Commission/921, NA, RG 59; Baker to Judge John H. Clarke, 22 Feb., 3 Mar., 12 Aug. 1932, Box 59, Baker to Arthur A. Craven, 27 Feb. 1932, Box 79, Baker to Walter Lippmann, 26 May 1932, 13 Jan. 1933, Box 149, Baker to James T. Shotwell, 14 Jan. 1933, Box 208—all in Baker Papers; Hoover, *Memoirs,* 2: 370; Tupper and McReynolds, *Japan in American Public Opinion,* p. 333.

[22] Walter Lippmann to Stimson, 16 May 1932, Box 146, Baker Papers; Lamont to Stimson, 11 Mar. 1932, File 793.94/4803⅓, NA, RG 59; Kent to Yuki, 2 Feb., 3 May 1932, Kent Papers.

[23] Kent to Yuki, 16 Nov. 1931, 19 Jan. 1932, Kent Papers; Lamont to Philip C. Nash (director, League of Nations Assoc.), 4 Oct. 1932, Lamont to Stimson, 4 Oct. 1932, File 795.94 Commission/449½, NA, RG 59.

[24] Report of Thomas C. Cranford, Jr. (assist. military attaché, Tokyo), 17 Nov. 1931, File 793.94/316, Hornbeck memoranda, 21 Nov., 6 Dec. 1931, File -/2888, 4314, R. C. Miller (Division of Far Eastern Affairs) to Hornbeck, 19 Nov. 1931, File -/3164, Perkins to Stimson, 12 Dec. 1931,

File -/3176, Cameron W. Forbes (U.S. ambassador, Tokyo) to Stimson, 16 Feb. 1932, File -/4233, NA, RG 59; Buhite, *Johnson and American Policy toward China,* p. 68.

[25] Hornbeck memorandum, 19 Jan. 1932 (with Stimson's initialed approval), File 793.94/3607, Feis memorandum, 21 Jan. 1932, File 893.77/2823, memorandum of conversation between Lamont and Castle, 29 Jan. 1932, File 894.51/325, memorandum of telephone conversation between Lamont and Castle, 1 Feb. 1932, File 811.43 Japan-America Society/1—all in NA, RG 59. Apparently only Ambassador Forbes disagreed with the unofficial loan ban. See Forbes to Stimson, 27 Feb. 1932, File 793.94/5019, NA, RG 59.

[26] Stimson to McFadden, 10 Feb. 1932, File 894.51/327, Castle to Stimson (Geneva), 19 Apr. 1932, File -/348, Stimson to State Dept., 6 May 1932, File -/356, Castle memorandum, 22 Nov. 1932, File -/390, NA, RG 59.

[27] Lamont to Stimson, 18 Mar. 1932, File 894.51/331¾, OEA memorandum, 14 Jan. 1932, File -/332, Feis memorandum, 19 Mar. 1932, File -/339, NA, RG 59.

[28] Lamont to Takahashi, 10, 31 Mar. 1932, File 793.94/4953–54, NA, RG 59; Shigeji Tajima to Kent, 12 Dec. 1931, 12 Mar. 1932, Yuki to Kent, 30 Dec. 1931, 11 Mar. 1932, Eigo Fukai to Kent, 9 Mar. 1932—all in Kent Papers.

[29] Current, *Stimson,* pp. 107–9; Stimson and Bundy, *On Active Service,* pp. 259–60; Rappaport, *Stimson and Japan,* pp. 165–69; Stimson, "Pact of Paris," pp. i–ix; *FRP, 1929,* 1: 61–64; 2: 243; *1930,* 3: 92–93.

[30] Rappaport, *Stimson and Japan,* pp. 170–77, 202–3; Hornbeck memorandum, 12 Jan. 1932, File 793.94/3610⅗, NA, RG 59.

[31] Borah to Stimson, 25 Aug. 1932, reprinted in *Pacific Historical Review,* 22 (Nov. 1953): 392; Hornbeck memorandum, 11 July 1932, File 861.01/1785, and Stimson to Borah, 8 Sept. 1932, File -/1786, NA, RG 59; Rappaport, *Stimson and Japan,* pp. 183–88.

[32] Hornbeck memorandum, 25 Jan. 1933, File 711.94/769½, and Stimson to Hornbeck, 28 Jan., 1 Feb. 1933, File -/770, NA, RG 59.

[33] *Literary Digest* 115 (28 Jan. 1933): 7; 115 (17 June, 1933): 12; Roosevelt press release, 17 Jan. 1933, Hornbeck memoranda, 2 Feb., 9 May 1933, Hornbeck to William Phillips (acting sec. of state), 2 Jan. 1934, Hornbeck to Hull, 26 Feb. 1934—all in Edgar B. Nixon, *FDR and Foreign Affairs,* 1: 4, 34, 103–7, 567–70, 658–61; Cordell Hull, *Memoirs,* 1: 270–74; Gerald E. Wheeler, "Isolated Japan: Anglo-American Diplomatic Co-operation, 1927–1936," *Pacific Historical Review* 30 (May 1961): 165–78. For a concise discussion of the evolution of Roosevelt's thinking about Japan see William L. Neumann, "Franklin D. Roosevelt and Japan, 1913–1933," *Pacific Historical Review* 22 (May 1953): 143–53. Raymond Moley and Rexford Tugwell both opposed Roosevelt's acceptance of Stimson's policy in 1933, saying that it "invited a major war in the Far East." See Current, *Stimson,* p. 122; Bernard Sternsher, "The Stimson Doctrine: FDR *versus*

Moley and Tugwell," *Pacific Historical Review* 31 (Aug. 1962): 281–89.

[34] Hornbeck memorandum, 13 Apr. 1935, Box 8, Moore Papers; Gerald E. Wheeler, *Prelude to Pearl Harbor,* p. 11; Stimson, *Far Eastern Crisis,* pp. 233–37; Hull, *Memoirs,* 1: 290–91, 888–916; Stimson and Bundy, *On Active Service,* pp. 255–56.

[35] Stimsonianism has been defined by Arthur M. Schlesinger, Jr., as "the view that an orderly world requires a single durable structure of world security, which must everywhere be protected against aggression: if aggression were permitted to go unpunished in one place, this by infection would lead to a general destruction of the system of world order." See Richard M. Pfeffer, *No More Vietnams? The War and the Future of American Foreign Policy* (New York, 1968), p. 7.

[36] Hoover's enunciation of these ideas after World War II can be found in: Hoover, *40 Key Questions about Our Foreign Policy Answered by Herbert Hoover* (Scarsdale, 1952), and in the series of volumes by Hoover entitled: *Addresses upon the American Road, 1945–48* (Princeton, 1948), *1948–50* and *1950–55* (Palo Alto, 1950, 1955), *1955–1960* (Caldwell, Ida., 1960).

Selected Bibliography

The major primary sources used in this study were the private papers of individual political and business leaders, supplemented by their published memoirs and speeches; congressional hearings and reports; the records of the State and Commerce departments at the National Archives; and finally business journals, newspapers, and proceedings of commercial organizations. Most of the manuscripts of businessmen yielded only a smattering of information on foreign policy issues. Among the most valuable, however, were the Hoover Papers at West Branch, Iowa, the Newton D. Baker and Norman H. Davis Papers at the Library of Congress, the Fred I. Kent Papers at Princeton University, and the Frank A. Vanderlip Papers at Columbia University. The congressional hearings and reports combined with documents from the Departments of State and Commerce constituted a very important source because they provided evidence of the cooperation, or lack thereof, between government officials and various segments of the business community.

The remaining primary material consisted of approximately seventy-five national, state, and local business publications only thirty of which contained enough relevant information on foreign affairs to warrant listing here. While business opinion about diplomacy was obtained from these publications, they were the least valuable of the major sources in the sense that they seldom revealed the attempts being made by the business community to influence government policy.

Unpublished Documents

Anderson, Chandler P. Papers. Manuscript Division, Library of Congress. Washington, D.C.

Baker, Newton D. Papers. Manuscript Division, Library of Congress. Washington, D.C.

Borah, William E. Papers. Manuscript Division, Library of Congress. Washington, D.C.

Davis, Norman H. Papers. Manuscript Division, Library of Congress. Washington, D.C.

Dawes, Charles G. Papers. Northwestern University. Evanston, Ill.

Fischer, Irving. Papers. Princeton University Library. Princeton, N.Y.

Hammond, John Hays. Papers. Yale University Library. New Haven, Conn.

Hoover, Herbert. Papers. Herbert Hoover Presidential Library. West Branch, Iowa.

————. Hoover-Woodrow Wilson Correspondence, 1914–1919. The Hoover Institution on War, Revolution, and Peace. Stanford University. Palo Alto, Calif.

Hughes, Charles Evans. Papers. Manuscript Division, Library of Congress. Washington, D.C.

————. Memoranda of Conversations of the Secretary of State, 1921–1923. U.S. Department of State. Record Group 59. National Archives. Washington, D.C.

Kent, Fred I. Papers. Princeton University Library. Princeton, N.J.

Loeb, Jacob M. Papers. American Jewish Archives. Cincinnati, Ohio.

McCormick, Vance. Papers. Yale University Library. New Haven, Conn.

Marshall, Louis. Papers. American Jewish Archives. Cincinnati, Ohio.

Moore, R. Walton. Papers. Franklin D. Roosevelt Library. Hyde Park, N.Y.

Morgenthau, Henry, Jr. Diary. Franklin D. Roosevelt Library. Hyde Park, N.Y.

Morgenthau, Henry, Sr. Papers. Manuscript Division, Library of Congress. Washington, D.C.

Peabody, George Foster. Papers. Manuscript Division, Library of Congress. Washington, D.C.

Perkins, George W. Papers. Butler Library, Columbia University. New York, N.Y.

Roosevelt, Franklin D. Papers. Franklin D. Roosevelt Library. Hyde Park, N.Y.

Root, Elihu. Papers. Manuscript Division, Library of Congress. Washington, D.C.

Rosenwald, Julius. Papers. American Jewish Archives. Cincinnati, Ohio.

Schiff, Jacob H. Papers. American Jewish Archives. Cincinnati, Ohio.

Straus, Oscar S. Papers. Manuscript Division, Library of Congress. Washington, D.C.

U.S., Department of Commerce. General Records of the Department of Commerce, 1918–1933. Record Group 40. National Archives. Washington, D.C.

————: Records of the Bureau of Foreign and Domestic Commerce, 1918–1933. Record Group 151. National Archives. Washington, D.C.

U.S., Department of State. General Records of the State Department, 1918–1933. Record Group 59. National Archives. Washington, D.C.

Vanderlip, Frank A. Papers. Butler Library, Columbia University. New York, N.Y.

Warburg, Felix. Papers. American Jewish Archives. Cincinnati, Ohio.

Warburg, Paul M. Papers. Yale University Library. New Haven, Conn.

Washburn, Stanley. Papers. Manuscript Division, Library of Congress. Washington, D.C.

Published Documents

Conference on Unemployment. *Recent Economic Changes in the United States: Report of the Committee on Recent Economic Changes of the President's Conference on Unemployment.* Washington, D.C., 1929.

Richardson, James D., ed. *A Compilation of the Messages and Papers of the Presidents.* Vol. 18. New York, 1922.

U.S., Congress, House, Committee on Foreign Affairs.
Disarmament Hearing on H.J.R. 424. 66th Cong., 3d sess., 14, 15 Jan. 1921.
Hearings on H.J.R. 201: To Provide for the Remission of Further Payments of the Annual Installments of the Chinese Indemnity. 68th Cong., 1st sess., 31 Mar., 1–2 Apr. 1924.

U.S., Congress, House, Committee on the Judiciary.
Hearing on H.J.R. 149: To Amend the China Trade Act of 1922 and the Revenue Act of 1921. 68th Cong., 1st sess., 30–31 Jan. 1924.
To Amend the China Trade Act of 1922. House Report no. 321. 68th Cong., 1st sess., 18 Mar. 1924.

U.S., Congress, House, Committee on Military Affairs. *World Disarmament Hearing.* 66th Cong., 3d sess., 11 Jan. 1921.

U.S., Congress, House, Committee on Naval Affairs. *Hearings on Disarmament: Its Relation to the Naval Policy and the Naval Building Program of the U.S.* 66th Cong., 3d sess., Jan.–Feb. 1921. (Cited in the notes as U.S. House, *Hearings on Disarmament.*)

U.S., Congress, House, Committee on Ways and Means. *Hearings on H.R. 15597, H.R. 15927, H.R. 16517.* 71st Cong., 3d sess., 27–28 Jan. 1931. (Cited in the notes as U.S. House, *1931 Embargo Hearings.*)

U.S., Congress, House. *Tariff Act of 1922.* Document no. 393. 67th Cong., 2d sess.

U.S., Congress, Senate, Committee on Finance.

Hearing on H.R. 15275: An Act Imposing Temporary Duties upon Certain Agricultural Products to Meet Present Emergencies, to Provide Revenue, and for Other Purposes. 66th Cong., 3d sess., 6–8, 10–11, 13 Jan. 1921. (Cited in the notes as U.S. Senate, *Emergency Tariff Hearing,* Jan. 1921.)

Hearing on H.R. 2435: An Act Imposing Temporary Duties upon Certain Agricultural Products to Meet Present Emergencies, to Provide Revenue, and for Other Purposes. 67th Cong., 1st sess., 18–19, 21–23, 26 Apr. 1921. (Cited in the notes as U.S. Senate, *Emergency Tariff Hearing,* Apr. 1921.)

Hearings on H.R. 7456: To Provide Revenue, to Regulate Commerce with Foreign Countries, to Encourage the Industries of the United States and for Other Purposes. 67th Cong., 1st sess. [Cited in the notes as U.S. Senate, *Hearings on H.R. 7456 (Fordney).*]

Minority Report to Accompany H.R. 7456. Senate Report 595. 67th Cong., 2d sess., 20 Apr. 1922.

Hearings on S.R. 19: Authorizing the Financial Committee of the Senate to Investigate the Sale, Flotation, and Allocation by Banks, Banking Institutions, Corporations or Individuals of Foreign Bonds or Securities in the United States. Pts. 1–2. 72d Cong., 1st sess., Dec. 1931–Jan. 1932. (Cited in the notes as U.S. Senate, *1931–1932 Loan Investigation.*)

Hearing on H. J. R. 147: To Authorize the Postponement of Amounts Payable to the U.S. from Foreign Governments during the Fiscal Year 1932, and Their Repayment over a Ten-Year Period Beginning July 1, 1933. 72d Cong., 1st sess., 26 Dec. 1931.

U.S., Congress, Senate, Special Committee. *Hearings on S.R. 206: A Resolution to Make Certain Investigations Concerning the Manufacture and Sale of Arms and Other War Munitions.* 73d–74th Cong., Sept. 1934–Feb. 1936. (Cited in the notes as U.S. Senate, *Munitions Industry Hearing.*)

U.S., Congress, Senate, Special Committee Investigating Petroleum Resources. *Diplomatic Protection of American Petroleum Interests in Mesopotamia, Netherlands East Indies, and Mexico.* 79th Cong., 1st sess., 25 Apr. 1945. (Cited in the notes as U.S. Senate, *Diplomatic Protection.*)

U.S., Congress, Senate, Subcommittee of the Committee on Finance. *Hearings on H.R. 2667: An Act to Provide Revenue, to Regulate Commerce with Foreign Countries, to Encourage the Industries of the United States, to Protect American Labor and for Other Purposes.* 71st Cong., 1st sess.

U.S., Congress, Senate, Subcommittee of the Committee on Foreign Relations.

> *Hearings on S.C.R. 22: Relative to Engaging the Responsibility of the Government in Financial Arrangements between Its Citizens and Sovereign Foreign Governments.* 68th Cong., 2d sess., 25–26 Feb. 1925. (Cited in the notes as U.S. Senate, *1925 Loan Hearings.*)

> *Hearings on S.C.R. 15: Relative to Engaging the Responsibility of the Government in Financial Arrangements between Its Citizens and Sovereign Foreign Governments.* 69th Cong., 2d sess., Jan.–Feb. 1927. (Cited in the notes as U.S. Senate, *1927 Loan Hearings.*)

U.S., Department of Commerce, Bureau of Foreign and Domestic Commerce.

> *Commercial and Industrial Organizations of the United States.* Revised ed.

> *The Future of Our Foreign Trade.* By Herbert Hoover.

U.S., Department of State. *Papers Relating to the Foreign Relations of the United States.* 1918–1933. (Cited in the notes as *FRP.*)

U.S., Federal Trade Commission. *Report on Foreign Ownership in the Petroleum Industry.* 12 Feb. 1923.

U.S., Tariff Commission.

> *Annual Report.* 1918–1930.

> *Colonial Tariff Policies.* Washington, D.C., 1922.

> *Reciprocity and Commercial Treaties.* Washington, D.C., 1919.

Autobiographies, Memoirs, Correspondence, and Speeches

Adler, Cyrus. *Jacob H. Schiff: His Life and Letters.* 2 vols. London, 1929.

Baker, Ray Stannard. *Woodrow Wilson: Life and Letters.* Vol. 6. New York, 1937.

Barron, Clarence Walker. *More They Told Barron: Conversations and Revelations of an American Pepys in Wall Street.* New York, 1931.

Baruch, Bernard. *The Public Years*. New York, 1960.

Costigan, Edward P. *Public Ownership of Government: Collected Papers of Edward P. Costigan*. New York, 1940.

Dawes, Charles G. *Journal As Ambassador to Great Britain*. New York, 1939.

————. *Notes As Vice President, 1928–1929*. Boston, 1935.

Ford, Henry. *My Life and Work*. New York, 1922.

————. *My Philosophy of Industry*. New York, 1929.

————. *Today and Tomorrow*. New York, 1926.

Hammond, John Hays. *The Autobiography of John Hays Hammond*. 2 vols. New York, 1935.

Hoover, Herbert. *Address Delivered during the Visit of Herbert Hoover to Central and South America, November-December 1928*. Washington, D.C., 1929. (Cited in the notes as Hoover, *South American Addresses*.)

————. *American Individualism*. New York, 1923.

————. *Memoirs*. 3 vols. New York, 1952.

————. *The New Day: Campaign Speeches of Herbert Hoover*. Stanford. 1928.

Hughes, Charles Evans. *Our Relations to the Nations of the Western Hemisphere*. Princeton, 1928.

————. *Pan American Peace Plans*. New Haven, 1929.

————. *The Pathway of Peace: Representative Addresses Delivered during His Term as Secretary of State, 1921–1925*. New York, 1925.

Hull, Cordell. *Memoirs*. 2 vols. New York, 1948.

Kahn, Otto. *Of Many Things: Being Reflections and Impressions on International Affairs, Domestic Topics and the Arts*. New York, 1926.

————. *Our Economic and Other Problems: A Financier's Point of View*. New York, 1920.

Kennan, George F. *Memoirs, 1925–1950*. Boston, 1967.

Lamont, Thomas W. *Across World Frontiers*. New York, 1951.

Lansing, Robert. *War Memoirs*. Indianapolis, 1935.

Nagel, Charles. *Speeches and Writings, 1900–1928*. 2 vols. New York, 1931.

Rockefeller, John D., Jr. *The Personal Relation in Industry*. New York, 1923.

Shotwell, James T. *The Autobiography of James T. Shotwell*. New York, 1961.

Sloan, Alfred P., Jr. *My Years with General Motors*. Edited by John McDonald and Catherine Stevens. New York, 1964.

————. *Adventures of a White Collar Man*. New York, 1941.

Sorensen, Charles E. *My Forty Years with Ford.* New York, 1956.

Stimson, Henry L. *American Policy in Nicaragua.* New York, 1927.

———. *The Far Eastern Crisis: Recollections and Observations.* New York, 1936.

——— and Bundy, McGeorge. *On Active Service in Peace and War.* New York, 1947.

Vanderlip, Frank A. *From Farm Boy to Financier.* New York, 1935.

———. *What Happened to Europe?* New York, 1920.

———. *What Next in Europe?* New York, 1922.

White, William Allen. *The Autobiography of William Allen White.* New York, 1946.

Newspapers, Periodicals, and Proceedings of Commercial Organizations

American Economist. Published bimonthly in New York by the American Protective Tariff League. Superseded in 1926 by the monthly publication *Tariff Review.*

American Industries: The Manufacturers' Magazine. Published monthly in New York by the National Manufacturing Co. for the National Association of Manufacturers. During the years 1926–1928, it appeared under the title *Pocket Bulletin.*

The Annalist: A Magazine of Finance, Commerce and Economics. Published weekly in New York by the New York Times Co.

Arizona Bankers Association. *Proceedings* (of annual meetings).

Baltimore. Published monthly by the Merchants and Manufacturers Association of Baltimore.

The Bankers Magazine. Published monthly in New York by the Bankers Publishing Co.

Bradstreet's: A Journal of Trade, Finance and Public Economy. Published weekly in New York by the Bradstreet Co.

Business Week. Published weekly in New York. Superseded the *Magazine of Business* in 1929.

Chicago Journal of Commerce and Daily Financial Times. A daily newspaper.

Cleveland Chamber of Commerce. *Annual* (proceedings of annual meetings and board of directors' reports).

Coast Banker (and California Banker). Published monthly in San Francisco. Absorbed *Western Banker and Financier* in 1922 and by 1924 was the official organ of the state banking associations of Utah, Arizona, and Nevada, carrying banking and financial information about 11 western states.

The Commercial and Financial Chronicle. Published weekly in New York.

Cotton. Published monthly in Atlanta, Georgia, by the W. R. C. Smith Publishing Co.

Iron Age. Published weekly in New York by the Iron Age Publishing Co.

Journal of the American Bankers Association. Published monthly in New York.

Los Angeles Chamber of Commerce. *Members' Annual* (proceedings of annual meetings).

The Magazine of Wall Street. Published bimonthly in New York by the Ticker Publishing Co.

Manufacturers Record: Blue Book of Southern Progress. Published weekly in Baltimore by the Manufacturers Record Publishing Co.

Merchants Exchange of St. Louis. *Annual Statement* (of trade and commerce for St. Louis, including annual reports by board of directors).

Minneapolis Civic and Commercial Association. *Members Bulletin.* Published weekly.

National Association of Manufacturers. *Proceedings* (of annual conventions).

National Foreign Trade Council. *Proceedings* (of annual National Foreign Trade Conventions).

Nation's Business: A Magazine for Businessmen. Published monthly in Washington, D.C., by the U.S. Chamber of Commerce.

Oregon Business. Published monthly in Portland by the state Chamber of Commerce.

Pacific Banker. Published weekly in Portland.

Philadelphia Board of Trade. *Proceedings* (of annual meetings).

Protectionist. Published monthly in Boston by the Home Market Club.

Southern California Business. Published monthly by the Los Angeles Chamber of Commerce.

United States Chamber of Commerce. *Annual Report* (of the board of directors).

Wall Street Journal. A daily newspaper.

Secondary Books

Adams, James Truslow. *Our Business Civilization: Some Aspects of American Culture.* New York, 1929.

Adler, Selig. *The Isolationist Impulse: Its Twentieth Century Reaction.* New York, 1957.

Angell, James W. *Financial Foreign Policy of the United States: A Report to the Second International Studies Conference on the State and Economic Life, London, May 29 to June 2, 1933*. Reprint. New York, 1963.

Arndt, H. W. *The Economic Lessons of the Nineteen-Thirties*. New York, 1965. (Reprint of 1944 Royal Institute of International Affairs edition.)

Baran, Paul A., and Sweezy, Paul M. *Monopoly Capitalism: An Essay on the American Economic and Social Order*. New York, 1966.

Bauer, Raymond; Pool, Ithiel de Sola; and Dexter, Lewis Anthony. *American Business and Public Policy: The Politics of Foreign Trade*, New York, 1963.

Bernstein, Barton J., ed. *Towards a New Past: Dissenting Essays in American History*. New York, 1968.

Bidwell, Percy W. *The Invisible Tariff: A Study of the Control of Imports into the United States*. New York, 1939.

Blum, John Morton. *From the Morgenthau Diaries: Years of Crisis, 1928–1938*. Boston, 1959.

Borg, Dorothy. *American Policy and the Chinese Revolution, 1925–1928*. New York, 1968. (Reprint of the 1947 American Institute of Pacific Relations edition.)

Braeman, John; Bremner, Robert H.; and Brody, David; eds. *Change and Continuity in Twentieth Century America: The 1920's*. Columbus, Ohio, 1968.

Brandes, Joseph. *Herbert Hoover and Economic Diplomacy: Department of Commerce Policy, 1921–1928*. Pittsburgh, 1962.

Buhite, Russell D. *Nelson T. Johnson and American Policy toward China, 1925–1941*. East Lansing, Mich., 1969.

Chandler, Alfred D., Jr. *Strategy and Structure: Chapters in the History of American Industrial Enterprise*. Cambridge, Mass., 1962.

Chandler, Lester V. *Benjamin Strong: Central Banker*. Washington, D.C., 1958.

Cohen, Bernard S. *The Influence of Non-Governmental Groups on Foreign Policy-Making*. Boston, 1959.

Coit, Margaret L. *Mr. Baruch*. Cambridge, Mass., 1957.

Current, Richard N. *Secretary Stimson: A Study in State Craft*. New Brunswick, N.J., 1954.

Davenport, E. H., and Cooke, Sidney Russell. *The Oil Trusts and Anglo-American Relations*. New York, 1924.

DeConde, Alexander. *Herbert Hoover's Latin American Policy*. Stanford, 1951.

DeNovo, John A. *American Interests and Policies in the Middle East: 1900–1939*. Minneapolis, 1963.

Donald, W. J. *Trade Associations*. New York, 1933.

Dorfman, Joseph. *The Economic Mind in American Civilization*. Vols. 3–5. New York, 1959.

Dunn, Robert W. *American Foreign Investments*. New York, 1926.

Ellis, Ethan L. *Frank B. Kellogg and American Foreign Relations, 1925–1929*. New Brunswick, N.J., 1961.

Farnsworth, Beatrice. *William C. Bullitt and the Soviet Union*. Bloomington, Ind., 1967.

Fay, Charles Norman. *Business in Politics: Considerations for Business Leaders*. Cambridge, Mass., 1926.

Feis, Herbert. *The Diplomacy of the Dollar: First Era, 1919–1932*. Baltimore, 1950.

———. *1933: Characters in Crisis*. Boston, 1966.

Ferrell, Robert H. *American Diplomacy in the Great Depression: Hoover-Stimson Foreign Policy, 1929–1933*. New Haven, 1957.

———. *Frank B. Kellogg and Henry L. Stimson*. Vol. 11 in *The American Secretaries of State and Their Diplomacy*, edited by Ferrell. New York, 1963.

Field, Frederick V. *American Participation in the China Consortiums*. Chicago, 1931.

Fischer, Louis. *Oil Imperialism: The International Struggle for Petroleum*. New York, 1926.

Forbes, B. C. *America's Fifty Foremost Business Leaders*. New York, 1948.

Fusfeld, Daniel R. *The Economic Thought of Franklin D. Roosevelt and the Origins of the New Deal*. New York, 1956.

Gardner, Lloyd C. *Economic Aspects of New Deal Diplomacy*. Madison, Wis., 1964.

Garraty, John A. *Right-Hand Man: The Life of George W. Perkins*. New York, 1957.

Gersting, J. Marshall. *The Flexible Provisions in the United States' Tariff, 1922–1930*. Philadelphia, 1932.

Gibb, George Sweet, and Knowlton, Evelyn H. *History of Standard Oil*. Vol. 2, *The Resurgent Years, 1911–1927*. New York, 1956.

Glad, Betty. *Charles Evans Hughes and the Illusions of Innocence: A Study in American Diplomacy*. Urbana, Ill., 1966.

Graebner, Norman A., ed. *An Uncertain Tradition: American Secretaries of State in the Twentieth Century*. New York, 1961.

Grassmuck, George L. *Sectional Biases in Congress on Foreign Policy*.

The Johns Hopkins University Studies in Historical and Political Science. Baltimore, 1951.

Hero, Alfred O. *Opinion Leaders in American Communities*. Boston, 1959.

Hoag, C. Leonard. *Preface to Preparedness: The Washington Disarmament Conference and Public Opinion*. Washington, D.C., 1941.

Homan, Paul T. *Contemporary Economic Thought*. New York, 1928.

Hornbeck, Stanley K. *The United States and the Far East*. Boston, 1942.

Iriye, Akira. *After Imperialism: The Search for a New Order in the Far East, 1921–1931*. Cambridge, Mass., 1965.

Jones, Joseph M., Jr. *Tariff Retaliation: Repercussions of the Hawley-Smoot Bill*. Philadelphia, 1934.

Kaplan, A. D. H. *Big Enterprise in a Competitive System*. Revised ed. Washington, D.C., 1964.

Kelly, Alfred H. *A History of the Illinois Manufacturers' Association*. Chicago, 1948.

Kelly, William B., Jr., ed. *Studies in United States Commercial Policy*. Chapel Hill, N.C., 1963.

Kolko, Gabriel. *The Triumph of Conservatism: A Reinterpretation of American History, 1900–1916*. New York, 1963.

Levin, N. Gordon, Jr. *Woodrow Wilson and World Politics: America's Response to War and Revolution*. New York, 1968.

Lewis, Cleona. *America's Stake in International Investments*. Washington, D.C., 1938.

————. *The United States and Foreign Investment Problems*. Washington, D.C., 1948.

Loth, David. *Swope of G.E.: The Story of Gerard Swope and General Electric in American Business*. New York, 1958.

Maddox, Robert James. *William E. Borah and American Foreign Policy*. Baton Rouge, La., 1969.

McClure, Wallace. *A New American Commercial Policy*. New York, 1924.

McKenna, Marian C. *Borah*. Ann Arbor, Mich., 1961.

Matz, Mary Jane. *The Many Lives of Otto Kahn*. New York, 1963.

Mikesell, Raymond F. *United States Economic Policy and International Relations*. New York, 1952.

Mintz, Ilse. *Deterioration in the Quality of Foreign Bonds Issued in the United States, 1920–1930*. New York, 1951.

Mooney, James D. *The New Capitalism*. New York, 1934.

Morison, Elting E. *Turmoil and Tradition: A Study of the Life and Times of Henry L. Stimson*. New York, 1960.

Moulton, Harold G., and Pasvolsky, Leo. *War Debts and World Prosperity*. Washington, D.C., 1932.

Murray, Robert K. *The Harding Era: Warren G. Harding and His Administration*. Minneapolis, 1969.

Myers, William Starr, and Newton, Walter H. *The Hoover Administration: A Documented Narrative*. New York, 1936.

Nelson, William H., ed. *Theory and Practice in American Politics*. Chicago, 1964.

Nevins, Allan, and Hill, Frank Ernest. *Ford*. Vol. 2, *Expansion and Challenge, 1915–1933*. New York, 1957.

Nicolson, Harold. *Dwight Morrow*. New York, 1935.

Nixon, Edgar B. *Franklin D. Roosevelt and Foreign Affairs*. Vol. 1, *January 1933–February 1934*. Cambridge, Mass., 1969.

O'Connor, Harvey. *Mellon's Millions: The Life and Times of Andrew W. Mellon*. New York, 1933.

O'Connor, Raymond G. *Perilous Equilibrium: The United States and the London Naval Conference of 1930*. Lawrence, Kan., 1962.

Osgood, Robert E. *Ideals and Self-Interest in America's Foreign Relations*. Chicago, 1953.

Parrini, Carl P. *Heir to Empire: United States Economic Diplomacy, 1916–1923*. Pittsburgh, 1969.

Phelps, Clyde William. *The Foreign Trade Expansion of American Banks*. New York, 1927.

Prothro, James Warren. *The Dollar Decade: Business Ideals in the 1920's*. Baton Rouge, La., 1954.

Pusey, Merlo J. *Charles Evans Hughes*. 2 vols. New York, 1951.

Rappaport, Armin. *Henry L. Stimson and Japan, 1931–1933*. Detroit, 1962.

Remer, C. F. *Foreign Investments in China*. New York, 1933.

Ridgeway, George L. *Merchants of Peace: Twenty Years of Business Diplomacy through the International Chamber of Commerce, 1919–1938*. New York, 1938.

Roads to Peace: A Handbook to the Washington Conference. New Republic Pamphlets, no. 2. New York, 1921.

Rosenau, James N., ed. *Domestic Sources of Foreign Policy*. New York, 1967.

Schattschneider, E. E. *Politics, Pressures and the Tariff: A Study of Free Enterprise in Pressure Politics, As Shown in the 1929–1930 Revision of the Tariff*. New York, 1935.

Schneider, Wilbert M. *The American Bankers Association: Its Past and Present*. Washington, D.C., 1956.

Simonds, Frank H. *American Foreign Policy in the Post-War Years.* Baltimore, 1935.

Smith, Arthur D. Howden. *Men Who Run America: A Study of the Capitalist System and Its Trends Based on Thirty Case Histories.* New York, 1935.

Smith, Daniel M. *Aftermath of War: Bainbridge Colby and Wilsonian Diplomacy, 1920–1921.* Philadelphia, 1970.

Smith, O. Edmund. *Yankee Diplomacy: United States Intervention in Argentina.* Dallas, 1953.

Smith, Robert F. *The United States and Cuba: Business and Diplomacy, 1917–1960.* New York, 1960.

Southard, Frank A. *American Industry in Europe.* Boston, 1931.

Sprout, Harold, and Sprout, Margaret. *Toward a New Order of Sea Power: American Naval Policy and the World Scene, 1918–1922.* Princeton, 1940.

Steigerwalt, Albert K. *The National Association of Manufacturers, 1895–1914: A Study in Business Leadership.* Grand Rapids, Iowa, 1964. (Cited in the notes as Steigerwalt, *NAM.*)

Stein, Herbert. *The Fiscal Revolution in America.* Chicago, 1969.

Stimson, Henry L., and Bundy, McGeorge. *On Active Service in Peace and War.* New York, 1947.

Studenski, Paul, and Krooss, Herman E. *Financial History of the United States.* New York, 1952.

Sutton, Francis X., and others. *The American Business Creed.* Cambridge, Mass., 1956.

Timmons, Bascom N. *Portrait of an American: Charles G. Dawes.* New York, 1953.

Tompkins, Pauline. *American-Russian Relations in the Far East.* New York, 1949.

Tulchin, Joseph S. *The Aftermath of War: World War I and U.S. Policy toward Latin America.* New York, 1971.

Tupper, Eleanor, and McReynolds, George E. *Japan in American Public Opinion.* New York, 1937.

Vinson, John Chalmers. *The Parchment Peace: The United States and the Washington Conference, 1921–1922.* Athens, Ga., 1955.

Ware, Louise. *George Foster Peabody: Banker, Philanthropist, Publicist.* Athens, Ga., 1951.

Weinstein, James. *The Corporate Ideal in the Liberal State, 1900–1918.* Boston, 1968.

Wheeler, Gerald E. *Prelude to Pearl Harbor: The United States Navy and the Far East, 1921–1931.* Columbia, Mo., 1963.

Wiebe, Robert H. *Businessmen and Reform: A Study of the Progressive Movement.* Cambridge, Mass., 1962.

————. *The Search for Order, 1877–1920.* New York, 1967.

Wike, J. Roffe. *The Pennsylvania Manufacturers' Association.* Philadelphia, 1960.

Williams, Benjamin H. *Economic Foreign Policy of the United States.* New York, 1929.

Williams, William Appleman. *The Contours of American History.* Chicago, 1966. (Quadrangle reprint of the original 1961 World Publishing Co. edition.)

————. *The Tragedy of American Diplomacy.* New York, 1962. (Revised and enlarged Delta edition of the original 1959 World Publishing Co. edition.)

Williamson, Harold F., and others. *The American Petroleum Industry.* Vol. 2, *The Age of Energy, 1899–1959.* Evanston, Ill., 1963.

Wood, Bryce. *The Making of the Good Neighbor Policy.* New York, 1961.

Wright, Theodore Paul, Jr. *American Support of Free Elections Abroad.* Washington, D.C., 1964.

Articles

Abrahams, Paul P. "American Bankers and the Economic Tactics of Peace: 1919." *Journal of American History* 46 (December 1969): 572–83.

Braisted, William R. "China, the United States Navy, and the Bethlehem Steel Company, 1909–1929." *Business History Review* 42 (Spring 1968): 50–66.

Brune, Lester H. "Foreign Policy and the Air Power Dispute, 1919–1932." *The Historian* 23 (August 1961): 449–64.

Buhite, Russell D. "Nelson Johnson and American Policy toward China, 1925–1928." *Pacific Historical Review* 35 (November 1966): 451–65.

Burks, David D. "The United States and the Geneva Protocol of 1924: 'A New Holy Alliance'?" *American Historical Review* 64 (July 1959): 891–905.

Burns, Richard Dean. "Inspection of the Mandates, 1919–1941." *Pacific Historical Review* 37 (November 1968): 445–62.

Carlton, David. "Great Britain and the Coolidge Naval Disarmament Conference of 1927." *Political Science Quarterly* 83 (December 1968): 573–98.

Clyde, Paul H. "The Diplomacy of 'Playing No Favorites': Secretary Stimson and Manchuria, 1931." *Mississippi Valley Historical Review* 25 (September 1948): 187–202.

Current, Richard N. "The Stimson Doctrine and the Hoover Doctrine." *American Historical Review* 59 (April 1954): 513–42.

Davis, Norman H. "American Foreign Policy: A Democratic View." *Foreign Affairs* 3 (September 1924): 22–34.

DeNovo, T. A. "Movement for an Aggressive American Oil Policy Abroad, 1918–1920." *American Historical Review* 61 (July 1956): 854–76.

Edwards, George W. "Government Control of Foreign Investments." *American Economic Review* 18 (December 1928): 684–701.

Eis, Carl. "The 1919–1930 Merger Movement in American Industry." *Journal of Law and Economics* 12 (October 1969): 267–98.

Fifield, Russell H. "Secretary Hughes and the Shantung Question." *Pacific Historical Review* 23 (November 1954): 373–85.

Galloway, J. M. "The Public Life of Norman H. Davis." *Tennessee Historical Quarterly* 27 (Summer 1968): 142–56.

Heald, Morrell. "Business Thought in the Twenties: Social Responsibility." *American Quarterly* 13 (Summer 1961): 126–40.

———. "Management's Responsibility to Society: The Growth of an Idea." *Business History Review* 31 (Winter 1957): 375–84.

Hecht, Robert A. "Great Britain and the Stimson Note of January 7, 1932." *Pacific Historical Review* 38 (May 1969): 177–91.

Kirwin, Harry W. "The Federal Telegraph Company: A Testing of the Open Door." *Pacific Historical Review* 22 (August 1953): 271–86.

Koistinen, Paul A. C. "The 'Industrial-Military Complex' in Historical Perspective: World War I." *Business History Review* 41 (Winter 1967): 378–403.

———. "The 'Industrial-Military Complex' in Historical Perspective: The InterWar Years." *Journal of American History* 46 (March 1970): 819–39.

Lowell, Abbott Lawrence. "Manchuria, The League and the United States." *Foreign Affairs* 10 (April 1932): 351–68.

Maddox, Robert James. "William E. Borah and the Crusade to Outlaw War." *The Historian* 29 (February 1967): 200–220.

———. "Keeping Cool with Coolidge." *Journal of American History* 53 (March 1967): 772–80.

Neumann, William L. "Franklin D. Roosevelt and Japan, 1913–1933." *Pacific Historical Review* 22 (May 1953): 143–53.

O'Connor, Raymond G. "The 'Yardstick' and Naval Disarmament in the

1920's." *Mississippi Valley Historical Review* 45 (December 1958): 441–63.

Pontecorvo, Giulio. "Investment Banking and Speculation in the Late 1920's." *Business History Review* 32 (Summer 1958): 166–91.

Reed, Peter Mellish. "Standard Oil in Indonesia, 1898–1928." *Business History Review* 32 (Autumn 1958): 329–37.

Rhodes, Benjamin D. "Reassessing 'Uncle Shylock': The United States and the French War Debt, 1917–1929." *Journal of American History* 55 (March 1969): 787–803.

Ross, Stanley Robert. "Dwight Morrow and the Mexican Revolution." *Hispanic American Historical Review* 38 (November 1958): 506–28.

Stein, Herbert. "Pre-revolutionary Fiscal Policy of Herbert Hoover." *Journal of Law and Economics* 9 (October 1966): 189–223.

Sternsher, Bernard. "The Stimson Doctrine: FDR *versus* Moley and Tugwell." *Pacific Historical Review* 31 (August 1962): 281–89.

Stratton, David H. "Behind Teapot Dome: Some Personal Insights." *Business History Review* 31 (Winter 1957): 385–402.

Snyder, J. Richard. "Coolidge, Costigan and the Tariff Commission." *Mid-America* 50 (April 1968): 131–48.

"Tariff Problems of the United States." *American Academy of Political and Social Science* 141 (January 1929): 1–264.

Taussig, F. W. "The Tariff Controversy with France." *Foreign Affairs* 6 (January 1928): 177–90.

Thomas, James A. "Business Principles in World Politics." *Asia* 25 (February 1925): 99–103, 165–66.

Trani, Eugene F. "Harding Administration and Recognition of Mexico." *Ohio History* 75 (Spring–Summer 1966): 137–48.

Vinson, J. Chal. "The Annulment of the Lansing-Ishii Agreement." *Pacific Historical Review* 27 (February 1958): 57–69.

———. "The Imperial Conference of 1921 and the Anglo-Japanese Alliance." *Pacific Historical Review* 31 (August 1962): 257–67.

———. "War Debts and Peace Legislation: The Johnson Act of 1934." *Mid-America* 50 (July 1968): 206–22.

Waller, Robert A. "Business and the Initiation of the Teapot Dome Investigation." *Business History Review* 36 (Autumn 1962): 334–53.

Wheeler, Gerald E. "Republican Philippine Policy, 1921–1933." *Pacific Historical Review* 28 (November 1959): 377–90.

———. "Isolated Japan: Anglo-American Diplomatic Cooperation, 1927–1936." *Pacific Historical Review* 30 (May 1961): 165–78.

Wicker, Elmus R. "Federal Reserve Monetary Policy, 1922–1933: A

Reinterpretation." *Journal of Political Economics* 73 (August 1956): 325–43.

Williams, William Appleman. "China and Japan: A Challenge and a Choice of the Nineteen-twenties." *Pacific Historical Review* 26 (August 1957): 259–79.

———. "Latin America: Laboratory of American Foreign Policy in the Nineteen-twenties." *Inter-American Economic Affairs* 11 (Autumn 1957): 3–30.

———. "The Legend of Isolationism in the 1920's." *Science and Society* 18 (Winter 1954): 1–20.

Wilson, J. H. "American Business and the Recognition of the Soviet Union." *Social Science Quarterly* 52 (September 1971).

Winkler, Fred H. "The War Department and Disarmament, 1926–1935." *The Historian* 28 (May 1966): 426–46.

Unpublished Studies

Abrahams, Paul P. "The Foreign Expansion of American Finance and Its Relationship to the Foreign Economic Policies of the United States, 1907–1921." Ph.D. dissertation, University of Wisconsin, 1967.

Butler, Harold Tiffany. "Partisan Positions on Isolationism vs. Internationalism, 1918–1933." D.S.S. dissertation, Syracuse University, 1963.

Diggins, John P. "Mussolini's Italy: The View from America, 1922–1941." Ph.D. dissertation, University of Southern California, 1964.

Gray, Sister Gertrude Mary. "Oil in Anglo-American Diplomatic Relations, 1920–1928." Ph.D. dissertation, University of California, Berkeley, 1950. (Cited in the notes as Gray, "Oil.")

Lower, Richard Coke. "Hiram Johnson and the Progressive Denouement." Ph.D. dissertation, University of California, Berkeley, 1969.

Parrini, Carl Philip. "American Empire and Creating a Community of Interest: Economic Diplomacy, 1916–1922." Ph.D. dissertation, University of Wisconsin, 1963.

Stalker, John Nellis, Jr. "The National Association of Manufacturers: A Study in Ideology." Ph.D. dissertation, University of Wisconsin, 1950. (Cited in the notes as Stalker, "NAM.")

Index